D0481298

It's All News to Me

Books by BOB CONSIDINE

MacARTHUR THE MAGNIFICENT

THIRTY SECONDS OVER TOKYO (with Capt. Ted W. Lawson)

WHERE'S SAMMY? (with Sammy Schulman)

INNOCENTS AT HOME

GENERAL WAINWRIGHT'S STORY (with Jonathan M. Wainwright)

THE BABE RUTH STORY (with Babe Ruth)

DEMPSEY (with Bill Slocum)

RAPE OF POLAND (with Stanislaw Mikolajczyk)

RED PLOT AGAINST AMERICA (with Robert E. Stripling)

THE MARYKNOLL STORY

KHRUSHCHEV (with W. R. Hearst, Jr., and Frank Conniff)

THE MEN WHO ROBBED BRINK'S (with Specs O'Keefe)

IT'S THE IRISH

PANAMA CANAL

IT'S ALL NEWS TO ME

It's All News to Me

A Reporter's Deposition

by
BOB CONSIDINE

A Duell, Sloan and Pearce Book
MEREDITH PRESS
New York

Copyright © 1967 by Robert B. Considine

All rights reserved. No part of this book in excess of five hundred words may be reproduced in any form without permission in writing from the publisher.

Second printing, May 1967

Library of Congress Catalog Card Number: 67-12635

MANUFACTURED IN THE UNITED STATES OF AMERICA FOR MEREDITH PRESS

VAN REES PRESS • NEW YORK

For Mil

who wouldn't marry a Government clerk

675085

Pride Goeth Before ...

It takes a roaring amount of conceit to practice daily journalism, particularly if it assumes the form of a column. The deep-domed cosmic thinker who either rattles or soothes the President of the United States is of the same species as the gassy advice columnist who counsels "Puzzled" to stop sprinkling her corn flakes with powdered LSD.

Each plays God.

The straight newswriters, who operate more often than not without the dazzling shield of a by-line, are not immune to the contagion of earthbound divinity. They dream of a day when their names, too, will be "on the trucks"—breathtaking lithographs plastered to the sides of delivery vans careening through the streets of great cities: "READ JOE DOAKES, EXCLUSIVELY IN THE. . . ."

The Almighty, apparently concerned, has arranged that certain little setbacks, comeuppances, shake the pretenders to the throne firmly enough to remind them they must remain mortal—for a time, at least.

I speak with the accent of experience. Somebody always pulls a rug.

My column, features, and news stories were appearing in perhaps three hundred papers here and abroad at the precise period when a child of ours named Dennis chose to jump out a window of an abandoned inn in Allenhurst, New Jersey, where we were summering. He was intent not upon suicide, but was a dutiful participant in a game of follow the leader. The leader, an Irish-Catholic kamikaze, jumped first, as befits authority, and better, too. Dennis plunged into a large bush which seemed to offer a good landing place.

Alas. The bush was in fact a new burgeoning of an old tree, flourishing from the original stump. Dennis' right leg, ill-protected by a very short pair of shorts, hit the spear of the broken stump. It turned out to be as bad a wound as if it had been inflicted by a bazooka.

The boy was on the operating table at Fitkin Memorial Hospital in Neptune, New Jersey, an excruciatingly long time. Then a woman who seemed to have emerged from Surgery walked down the long hall toward the waiting room where Millie and I sat, silently reciting the Rosary. The woman advanced resolutely toward where we sat; the closer she came, the more ominous she loomed. At last she was in the waiting room.

"I understand there's a newspaperman here," she said. Our hearts stopped. She, clearly, was the bearer of terrible news.

"I am," I said huskily.

"Oh, fine," she said brightly. "I'll buy one."

Then there was the exclusive interview with Frank Hague, perennial mayor of Jersey City. Hague held the key to whether racing would return to Jersey after years in hibernation. A mutual friend approached me one day at Belmont and said that Hague was in his box on the mezzanine and was in the mood to give me the scoop of the ages: Racing would indeed resume in Jersey.

"He wants to break the news in a big syndicated column like yours," the bloke said. [I was either flattered or fulfilled.]

So we trooped to Hague's box. He had apparently just blown a big bet and was glaring straight ahead, black derby rammed down close to his nose. Ten feet short of the box, the pal who had professed to be closer to Hague than his wallet took off his own hat, held it on his chest as if he had picked up the distant strains of the national anthem, coughed, and whimpered, "Mr. Mayor, sir, I want you should meet Bob Considine, one of the greatest sportswriters in New York."

It must have taken Hague's head a full minute to turn to the point where he could survey me with his glacial eyes.

"No," Hague said.

I was doing nicely in the papers with my column on the night Millie showed up forty minutes late for a sit-down dinner at the apartment of our friends, the Walter Shirleys. The host was not amused.

"Millie, dear," Walter said gently but firmly, "Bob's column isn't that good."

I was indeed "on the trucks" but not on the wagon one night, late, when I asked a cabdriver to take me for a spin through the old Swamppoodle section of Washington, near the Union Station. It was un-dilutedly Freudian, of course.

The driver remembered he had picked me up in front of the Washington *Herald*. I was then its sports editor.

"Know anybody on that paper where I picked you up?" he asked as we tooled down Second Street, N.E., where I had lived as a child.

"Sure."

"Know that fellow Considine?"

"Yeah," I said uneasily.

The driver chuckled.

"I knew that bum when he didn't have shoes," he said.

I once had the privilege of introducing Harry S. Truman to a dinner gathering at the Overseas Press Club. In searching for something meatier than "Ladies and gentlemen, the former President of the United States," I hit upon and delivered the following:

"President Truman will be remembered by the future historian as the Chief Executive who had more difficult decisions to make than most of the others combined. He faced and overcame with courageous decisions more crises than confronted Washington or Lincoln, Wilson or FDR. Six come readily to mind.

"He had to make the agonizing decision to drop the atomic bombs on Hiroshima and Nagasaki, which killed tens of thousands and opened the Atomic Age.

"He set in motion, with a firm decision, the wheels of the greatest humanitarian effort in history, the Marshall Plan.

"He proposed and implemented the Point IV program that re-vitalized the industrial complexes and economic security of friend and foe.

"He drew the line in Greece and Turkey and told the Communists on that side of the world that they must not cross it.

"He stopped Communist aggression on the other side of the world by making a stand in Korea.

"And he re-established civilian control over the military by firing the most popular military figure in modern history, Douglas Mac-Arthur."

Throughout the introduction I could hear Truman clucking agreement and whispering to Margaret Truman Daniel, who sat next to him, "By golly, that fellow's right." Or "Yessırree." Or "He can say that again!"

Then with a great hambone gesture I said, "And now, ladies and gentlemen, here he is—President Harry S. Truman!"

He jumped up, plainly pleased, and said, "Thank you, Eric Sevareid!"

It was, I believe, the loudest laugh ever recorded at the club. Mr. Truman looked baffled. Margaret tugged at his coat tail, and he bent over to hear what she was trying to tell him.

"His name is Considine, not Sevareid," she whispered.

Mr. Truman straightened up and shrugged.

"I made a natural mistake," he said. "I got two fat reporters mixed up."

Playing God can be a taxing role.

Contents

Illustrations

A Newspaperman's Prayer

by Bob Considine

(Distributed by King Features Syndicate)

Dear God, may I be fair. Circumstances and dumb luck have placed in my thumby paws a degree of authority which I may not fully comprehend. Let me not profane it.

Give me the drive that will make me check and countercheck the facts. Guide me when, lost for want of a rudder or a lead, I stumble through the jungle of speculation. Grant me, as the poet sang:

> The courage to change
> The things I can change;
> The serenity to accept
> Those I cannot change, and
> The wisdom to know the difference.

The twenty-six sharp-edged tools we call our alphabet can do what other tools do; build or destroy. Let me build. But let me know clearly, also, what should be destroyed, what darkness, what bigotry, what evil, what curse, what ignorance.

Never let me slip into writing *down,* in fatuous fear that readers will not understand. Let me write from the shoulder, and always with the assumption that those who read know more than I.

Such news as I find or comes my way, let me tell it quickly and accurately and simply, with an eye to my responsibilities. For news is precious. Few could live without it. When it is stopped or thwarted or twisted, something goes out of the hearts of men it might have nourished. Confront a starving man with his choice of a succulent meal or the promise to reveal instantly news of great importance, and he will first take the news. *Think* pieces, as we say in the trade to identify articles and columns contrived out of airy nothingness, or from a prone position, can never replace the meat and potatoes of news.

Let me champion just causes, avoid expediency, never lose the stimulation engendered by printer's ink. Remind me to be kind to copyboys, for I'll meet them on the way back down—when they are editors. Protect the innocent from me when, with deadlines pressing, my aim grows fuzzy.

Make me use my legs and eyes, the better to track down and see the truth. Deafen me to the Lorelei song of rootless hearsay, rumor, and the gossip of town loafers. If word that could cause great harm comes to me, even from sources far above reproach, let me have the dexterity and decency to pick up a phone and ask the subject about it.

When the customers write in to accuse me of being a bum, let me consider carefully the possibility or probability that I am . . . and try to do better. Let me work harder, try harder, and recall with proper humility that history produced some notably abler reporters, including four journeymen named Matthew, Mark, Luke, and John.

Let my stomach rebel at plucking meat from publicity handouts and let me not be miffed when someone says, "You had a pretty good piece last week but I can't remember what it was."

As long as our men fight, sweat, freeze, and die in actual or cold war, sacrifices which at times should make our food stick in our throats and our luxuries a torment, let me never cheaply use the words "courage" or "guts" to describe the means by which a pitcher wins a ball game, a gridman bucks a line, a golfer sinks a putt, or a fellow makes a speech.

And above all, let me recall repeatedly what the great teachers of the past . . . Moses and Socrates and Christ . . . would have done if by some alchemy they had been given the breathtaking break of swift and farflung communications.

It's All News to Me

1. *Caveat Emptor*

For me, this blessed peonage of newspaper work began under the warped scepter of Edward R. McLean during his last and not always lucid years as owner of the Washington *Post*. That was September, 1930, and it would seem to me neat and proper to clean one's desk of his memories at least every third of a century.

I had been poking gingerly at sportswriting since discovering shortly after the middle of the 1920's that Considine was a hard name for the sports department of the Washington *Herald* to spell. By that time I had begun to reach the third and sometimes even the fourth round of local tennis tournaments and was consequently injured one morning, while still suffused in the blush of a previous day's victory, to read in the *Herald* that the match had been won by Robert Constantine. I repaired to the desk of the paper's sports editor, William Henry Coyle, who silently accepted the correct spelling of a name he had seen only in the agate type beneath "Other results."

Then Coyle said that there was little interest in tennis in Washington and none whatsoever among members of his staff. "If you want to see any tennis news in this paper, you'll have to write it yourself," he said resignedly.

Not long after that I was approached by Orrel Mitchell, a crack young athlete and scholar who lived two doors from our house in the Swamppoodle section of the city, hard by the railroad tracks leading into Union Station. Orrel was working part-time on the Washington *Post*. He explained unhappily that he had been stuck with the task of writing a review of the tennis season just past. Would I write it for him? There was two dollars in it for me if I did.

It was in all probability the fastest-concluded business transaction in the entire Hoover administration. The following Sunday my affront

3

on basic English appeared in one of the obscurer reaches of the *Post*'s sports section. I was pink with pride, a color which matched that of the page on which this delible piece was printed. (When the *Post*'s ebbing fortunes prompted replacement of the pink stock by regular white newsprint, a reader complained bitterly that this compromised his habit of reaching thumb and forefinger into the edge of his *Post,* pinching off the edges of the sports section, "and shaking the rest of the paper on the floor.")

The *Post*'s résumé of that long-interred tennis season was by-lined "By Orrel Mitchell," of course. But I treasured it as if it were a page from the Book of Kells. "By Bill Henry" was another by-line that raised goosebumps all over me and nurtured the blooming-ham factor without which no writer, however unsung, can exist. I became Bill Henry the hard way. I was at that time playing in and had reached one of the late rounds of the Maryland indoor singles championship at the Fifth Regiment Armory in Baltimore. William Henry Coyle called me in with an odd proposition. Was I going to *win* the tournament? I nodded as if I knew what I was nodding about. He then said that such a win would enable him to give the story an unusual (for tennis) amount of space, "because," he added, "you're a Washington boy and it figures to be a dull Monday paper anyway."

He ordered me to go home, fetch my tennis clothes and a racquet, and report back to the paper's photo studio.

The three-column cut was made hours before the final round of the tournament began. Dutifully, I won the tournament, wrote a glowing story about the conquest—comparing it roughly to the triumph of Judas Maccabeus over the Hellenized Assyrians—and wired it to the *Herald.* It appeared Monday morning, wrapped around my picture, under the "By Bill Henry" credit. It was the greatest notice I've had so far.

Coyle said, as he handed me a voucher for ten dollars the next day, that he used his first two names as the by-line to spare me possible prosecution by the U.S. Lawn Tennis Association, whose rules forbade an amateur's writing about a tournament in which he was a participant. Coyle was as ignorant as I about the existence of an authentic and thriving Bill Henry on the other side of the country—Bill Henry of the Los Angeles *Times.*

The evening of that Monday the story appeared I just happened to have the clipping in my pocket when I slid into my seat in Prof.

Douglas Bement's Creative Writing course at George Washington University. Several members of the class read it, after slight prodding, and muttered congratulations. But a middle-aged lady who, like myself, was a Government clerk taking night classes at the University, had a question unrelated to the triumph. She said, "The fellow who wrote this story, this Bill Henry, says here that you lost the first set because you were 'too caustic.' What do you suppose he meant by that?"

"I meant . . . I mean *he* meant, or I guess he meant, that I should have taken more chances in the first set," I stammered, blushing.

She eyed me steadily, a gaze that was depressingly omniscient.

"I think you meant to write 'too *cautious,*'" she said, and left the impostor for dead.

The experience should have made me grateful for and content with my job as a clerk in the State Department's Division of Communications and Records. The job paid a good steady $1,680 a year. If I worked at it long enough I would be eligible for consular work without having to take the consular corps examination. All that Secretary of State Frank Billings Kellogg appeared to demand of me, aside from facelessness, was that I appear each morning no later than 9 A.M. and keep in alphabetical, numerical, and geographical order certain department files. These included the Kellogg-Briand Pact which condemned "recourse to war for the solution of international controversies." It was signed by fifteen peace-loving nations, including Germany, Japan, and Italy.

The dream of a permanent by-line of my own remained a troubling burr on the backside of this otherwise secure existence. And so one fine day in 1929 the obstructing curtains parted and there, ahead, stretched the way. I would write a weekly column of tennis news, gossip, playing hints, history, fact, fancy, call it "Speaking of Tennis," sign it with my own name, properly spelled, and see it emblazoned on the sports pages of the Washington *Star!* After all, the *Star* was the only paper our house subscribed to. It thumped against our paint-peeling door each evening and every Sunday morning and was thoroughly devoured by my mother, beginning with the obituary page. The *Star* was the fattest and most respected paper in Washington and thus, I felt, best fixed financially to sustain the additional burden of paying me for "Speaking of Tennis."

I wrote and rewrote that first column until I could have recited it backwards in Urdu. Then I walked it down Pennsylvania Avenue from the State Department to the *Star*. The *Star*'s meticulous sports editor, Denman Thompson, read the long piece in unnerving silence, instinctively correcting it with a blunt pencil as he proceeded. When he finished, he handed it back to me with the suggestion of a shudder.

"Sorry," Denman said. "We take Tilden's weekly column."

The totally uphill path back to the State Department led past the *Post*. I climbed to its rickety sports department and by extraordinary coincidence its young sports editor, Shirley Povich, was at his desk. I believe he had slept on it the night before. Anyway, Shirley was the only person around the premises at that time of day. He read the piece, and said he'd let me know. I went back to clerking in the State Department, properly deflated.

"Speaking of Tennis" appeared, every inconsequential word of it, by God, the following Sunday in the *Post*. Shirley paid me five dollars and ordered one for each Sunday thereafter. I took my best girl, Millie Anderson, to dinner. It seemed like found money.

It still does . . . most of the time.

In the late summer of 1930 Bill Dismer, the regular reporter of high-school sports for the *Post,* told Povich that he intended to retire to, or advance to, his family's hardware business. There were several applications for his job, mine among them. I was hesitant to ask Shirley outright to hire me. Instead, I communed with Walter Haight, Shirley's rotund assistant. Walter said he thought he could fix it.

Shirley was notoriously argumentative at that period in his life. If someone pressed a point of view upon him, Shirley would move to the other side, take up a position, and argue the opposite side. He had not gone to Georgetown Law for naught. Haight bided his time, and one day the trap was sprung.

"I'm thinking of hiring Considine to take Dismer's place," Shirley told him.

"Don't do it," Walter said. "He's a tennis player."

Shirley was immediately offended. "What's wrong with tennis players?" he demanded.

Walter shrugged. "They're either Filipinos or finks," he said, airily.

That did it, as Walter guessed it would.

"Well, I'll show you!" Shirley said heatedly, in what may have been a defense of both categories.

He offered me the job, and after a decent interval of soul-searching and compulsion, I took it. The soul-searching had to do with security.

The Government offered it; the staggering *Post* did not. The compulsion was provided by Millie.

"Take it," she said. "If you flop, well, I'm working. Whatever, I have no intention of ever marrying a Government clerk."

Have been winning bread for kith and kin through newspaper work since that dire ultimatum.

Thanks to (1) Millie and (2) God, who surely won't mind the billing.

It was a wonderful change of pace for me. Suddenly, it was not necessary that I report to work at 9 A.M. On the *Post,* even if one showed up at 3 P.M., he might find the dilapidated sports department totally deserted. I therefore was able to sleep the sleep of a laborer who dreams tormentedly of being late for work, awakens in a dismal sweat, and then discovers to his utter bliss that it is Sunday. Beyond that homely creature comfort there was an additional joy to this new work. Meager and obscure as the job and I were, I had a feeling of massive fulfillment. I had acquired a "local habitation and a name." I was no longer a State Department clerk subject to slights (unquestionably deserved but nonetheless painful) imposed by superiors I considered outrageously rude. For example, I had experienced difficulty forming a State Department tennis team to play in the Government League, though I was the singles champion of the city's public courts and the Department had some reasonably good players among its younger career diplomats. John Farr Simmons, later of ambassadorial rank and still later President Truman's Protocol Officer, finally made that State Department team possible. He explained to others in the Department that it was not a bad idea even though the suggestion had come from a noncareerist. At the *Post,* too, there would be no chance that I would ever again be upbraided by John Carter, a State Department career man who dabbled in journalism under the by-line of "Jay Franklin." He once ordered me to wrap some article of his clothing and send it to an address in Chevy Chase, presumably his home. It seemed hardly a task to impose on one busily engaged at the time in misfiling the documents of the London Naval Conference. By happy inadvertency, I dispatched the laundry to a wrong address. Mr. Carter was not amused.

Now, thanks to Shirley Povich, I ventured forth each day with credentials that proclaimed I represented the majesty of the Washington *Post*.

We were a shabby outfit, soon after plunged into receivership when McLean's physical, mental, and financial troubles transported him to a sanitarium at Towson, Maryland. Like certain beach crabs which continue to observe the rise and fall of tides, even though transported in tanks far from the beach, our salaries submerged with McLean's decline. My substantial $25 a week, plus $10 additional for "Speaking of Tennis," was reduced to a total of $31.50.

I had dreamed for years of moving to New York and finding fame and fortune there. Now, in January, 1931, with better newsmen than I selling apples on freezing street corners, I had the ignorance and the nerve to ask Shirley to help me conquer New York. Patiently, he sat down and wrote letters of recommendation to eight New York sportswriters he knew. I gambled an entire week's salary on the expedition.

And blew it. It was a disaster. The then plentiful New York papers were firing, not hiring. I could not even get inside the sports departments of five of the eight names on my list. The three men who sent word out to the guard at the door that it was safe to pass me were Joe Williams of the *Telegram,* Richards Vidmer of the *Herald Tribune,* and Bill Hennigan of the *Mirror.* I had lied at each of their reception desks when asked to fill out a form stating why I wanted in. I swore that my purpose was not to seek work but to offer startling news: Emmett Pare, an amateur tennis player of some skill, was about to turn *pro!*

Williams, one of the most trenchant sportswriters of my time, explained wearily that I was a fool to look for a job in New York when I had one in Washington. But as I left his office, he stopped me at the door.

"I'll read the clippings you brought with you," he said.

For some inscrutable reason, I was offended.

"I don't carry clippings with me," I said, and plunged out into the Labradorian weather in a steamy huff.

It was a long ride back to Washington.

The debacle made me more grateful than ever for the job on the *Post.* The pure joy and privilege of working in that sports department transcended the need for more money to pay the rent and buy the groceries. None of those exploited around our shop, in the pre-Newspaper Guild days, gave a damn how many hours we worked. The paramount ambition was to get the paper on the street more or less on time and write something for it worth reading.

Even at its nadir, the *Post* rewarded industry above and beyond the call of duty. Aubrey Taylor and Don Reed, who were running the paper in those early thirties under the beady eye of some fiscal wraith we knew only as "The Receiver," agreed to pay me an additional five dollars a week for a Sunday piece by-lined "The Drifter." (Walter Haight suggested that we liven it up a bit and call it "The Grifter.") It was a different sort of Washington column and an extraordinarily dull one to boot. Each week's effort was expended on exploring a Washington thoroughfare from its source to its mouth, or delta. I'd walk its length, note its features (equestrian figures, flophouses, etc.), study its origin—which in some cases reached back to the majestic genius of Pierre Charles L'Enfant, the French-born American soldier, engineer, and architect who was assigned by President Washington to draw plans for a capital city, driven to distraction by Thomas Jefferson, and dismissed after rejecting five hundred guineas and a patch of muddy Washington real estate for his timeless designs.

Slowly, surely, Shirley rounded out my lopsided sports knowledge. Once, in preparing for the composing room a routine AP story about a ball game played by the Brooklyn team, I wrote a head that read: "EAGLES WIN, 7-5."

Shirley looked at it and sighed.

"They are better known as the Dodgers," he said witheringly, plainly wondering what he had bought in the way of boobs.

Another time I complained in my "Speaking of Tennis" column: "Didn't see a line in the newspapers about the recent meeting of the Middle-Atlantic Tennis Association." Shirley read copy on the piece. When I glanced at it the following Sunday I was struck by a small but ever-so-crisp prefix. The edited sentence read: "Due to my reportorial shortcomings, I didn't see a line in the newspapers about the recent meeting of the Middle-Atlantic Tennis Association."

In 1932, when Jack Espey left the *Post* to handle publicity for George Washington University, Shirley upgraded me from high school sports to college games. And because the *Post* was always shorthanded in those days, the city side let me work a bit on the story of the Bonus Marchers and their humane, but still terrible, rout from Washington by troops commanded by Gen. Douglas MacArthur, Army Chief of Staff. On the ultimate day of the exodus, the splendid World War I hero, then a stylish fifty-two, rode down Pennsylvania Avenue on his white horse, followed by a handful of men, machines, and horses from

Fort Myer, Virginia. With him that day was his public relations aide, a forty-two-year-old major called Ike, whose quick, radiant grin and easy manner with reporters helped cushion the shock of seeing U.S. troops with bayonets bared, and a primitive tank or two, push ragged and bemedaled World War I veterans and their families out of their nation's capital. Tear gas was used to stir the more determined squatters.

My chief memory of that dismal day was experiencing the heat from a blazing encampment in Anacostia which had been set afire by the troops after the siege and defeat of the bonus-seekers. My sadness and muddled indignation were tempered by a feeling of relief that my main beat, my niche in the news business, was sports . . . wherein all was clean and noble and inspiring. I never expected to see General MacArthur or Major Eisenhower, his aide, again.

In January, 1933, halfway through the hiatus between the election and inauguration of Franklin D. Roosevelt, a considerably less historic event occurred. One bleak day during that period Shirley decided to replace a fine older man named Frank Young as the *Post*'s baseball writer. It broke Frank's heart and loosened his tears, for he loved the game in general and the Senators (or Nats, as they were then more frequently called) in particular. What was even more depressing for Frank, understandably, was that Povich—with the consent of managing editor Don Reed—chose me for the job. I couldn't carry Frank's typewriter, so far as knowledge of the game was concerned.

Once again, Shirley took me by the hand. This time the path led first to the office of Clark Griffith, the remarkable old fellow who meant as much to baseball, the so-called national pastime, as did Connie Mack, John McGraw, Ban Johnson, Charles Comiskey, or any other founding father. Griff originated the slick gimmick of having the President of the United States toss out the first ball of the season. For years, the Washington club's opener was scheduled a day ahead of any other, the better to frame this bold exploitation of the Chief Executive.

As time and administrations passed, a President would no more think of missing the opportunity to lend his presence on opening day than he would think of denouncing the sound dollar and motherhood. Many years after President William Howard Taft became the first patsy of this dodge, President Eisenhower said to hell with it: he had a golf date in Augusta, Georgia, that particular day. His decision struck consternation on all sides, not one side of which would have blamed him for neglecting to throw out the first football of the Washington Redskins season or the first two-year-old at Laurel race track, to name two other profit-making sports promotions in the area.

Griff sized me up that day, through the filter of his shaggy gray eyebrows, and didn't much like what he saw. Frank Young had never caused him any trouble, but how could he be sure of a tennis player?

Turned out that his misgivings were fairly well-founded. As suzerain of his tight little organization, surrounded by his doting wife, "Aunt Addie," five adoring nephews and nieces, and reverent retainers, Griff was distressed or angered by a number of pieces I later wrote. He had been a radical in his days as a player and later as a manager. He had helped raid the established National League for a cadre of stars around which the American League had been formed. But by the time I darkened his doorstep, or so he believed, he was somewhat more conservative than Louis XIV and just as sensitive to criticism.

What burned Griff especially was to be reminded in print that he was a delightfully inconsistent cuss.

One night at his ballpark while we watched a feebly lighted local charity game involving local celebrities who were expected to ride out their base hits mounted on donkeys, I asked Griff if he thought big league baseball would ever be played under the lights. His answer was an explosive *"Never!"* and I duly recorded it. A few years later he was night baseball's most wanton entrepreneur—so much so that Shirley wrote that Griff had applied to the baseball commissioner's office to play seven *day* games during the upcoming season. I bugged him along the same lines, suggesting that his keen sense of commerce had overcome righteous principle.

He threatened to denounce me to the other Washington papers as a fraud when I arranged a meeting between him and George Preston Marshall, who was eager to move his Boston Redskins to Washington, and then wrote that they had discussed the possible shift. This was technically true, but barely so. Griff had been an outspoken enemy of pro football ever since two local semi-pro teams of some years before, the Mohawks and the Apaches, had failed to pay him for the use of his park. He and Marshall had talked mostly about baseball, but I featured the fleeting mention of the Redskins move.

I watched the other papers for a day or two, fearing the worst. Nothing appeared. Then, not too many weeks later, a grand announcement appeared. The Boston Redskins would become the Washington Redskins and present, at Griffith Stadium, a star-studded team that had a fair little backfield manned by Ernie Pinckert, Riley Smith, Cliff Battles, and Sammy Baugh. It won the National Football League championship, and Griff made enough from the rent he charged and the food and program concessions he demanded to pay his entire baseball-team roster—and then some.

From the first day I met him, Griff assured me, as he did all others within earshot, that he was the sworn enemy of "those rich fellows" who threw their bankrolls around and were arrogant enough to think they could "buy" a pennant. Real baseball men, like himself, won their pennants by shrewd horsetrading and the purchase of promising youngsters. He proved his point dramatically that season of 1933 when he assembled, via trade, a team that had Goose Goslin, Earl Whitehill, Luke Sewell, Heinie Manush, Joe Kuhel, Al Crowder, Monte Weaver, and other solid senders, and appointed young Joe Cronin their manager.

The club won the American League pennant, but fell apart the following year. Griff sold Cronin, by then married to Griff's fine niece and adopted daughter, to Tom Yawkey of the Boston Red Sox, the richest of "those rich fellows." The price, $250,000 plus an able-bodied shortstop replacement named Lynn Lary.

I don't want to imply that Griff was generally sore about what I wrote about this ball club, such as "Buddy Myer's eighth-inning home run upped the team's output for the season to 32, only 14 behind Lou Gehrig." Or, just before Christmas, 1934, a year of disaster which saw the team finish deep in the second division, "Old Griff, mellowed by the approaching Yuletide, made a magnanimous gesture of good will today. He conceded the 1934 pennant to the Detroit Tigers."

I liked Griff and his family very much. In a fit of admiration, as one of his seemingly endless birthdays approached, I took up a collection from Jack Keller and Francis Stan of the *Star,* Buck O'Neill and Kirk Miller of the *Times,* Dick McCann of the *News,* and Shirley, of course, to buy him a present. Keller made discreet inquiry of Aunt Addie as to what Griff might need.

"Get Clark a suitcase with his named spelled out all the way in great big letters," the formidable matriarch of the clan decreed. "Some dirty rat stole the one that only had his initials on it."

Keller and I brought the bag to Griff's office in the midst of his birthday party, which was limited to the family, the staff, and Arch McDonald, the team's marvelous radio broadcaster.

Griff was touched and asked us to thank "my boys." So was Aunt Addie. As Keller and I prepared to leave the family affair, after a swift gulp of red wine out of a Dixie cup, Aunt Addie touched my sleeve.

"You know something, Mr. Constantine," she said warmly, "I've never believed all those terrible things they say about you."

Shirley sent me to Biloxi, Mississippi, with the ball club in the Spring of 1933. It was a hardship trek. There was not enough money available at the *Post* to buy me a train ticket. Millie and I, who had been married in the summer of 1931, rode down in the car of Louie Jordan, then a *Post* photographer. He had a Ford coupe, and it was one hell of a long, cramped trip.

But it changed my life. Some pieces I wrote during the days and weeks at Biloxi appealed to Mike Flynn, managing editor of the rival Washington *Herald*. He delegated his sports editor, Bryan Morse, to offer me a job at the end of the Biloxi stay and just before the season opened. It was a heady offer: $38.50 a week, seven dollars more than I was making on the *Post*. It was tempting. Millie was making $35 a week in the State Department, to my $31.50, and there was already talk that I had married her for her money. I wanted to shoot past her like a rocket, so I told Bryan I wanted at least $45. He was understandably shaken and said he would have to check with Mike Flynn.

When I told Shirley what had happened, he tried to get me $45 from the *Post*'s "receiver." The man said no.

By a curious coincidence, I knew another receiver, or representative of a receiver. He was George Allen, at that time administering mouth-to-mouth resuscitation to stately old (and half-filled) Wardman Park Hotel. George, an "I'm Just a Country Boy from Booneville, Mississippi" type from way back, had a strong streak of Mississippi in him, true. Mississippi riverboat. He was to move from his hotel baby-sitting job to Commissioner of the District of Columbia, confidant of Presidents Roosevelt, Truman, and Eisenhower (he wrote the best-selling *Presidents Who Have Known Me*), head of the Reconstruction Finance Corporation, treasurer of the Democratic National Congressional Committee, and a place on the boards of more

U.S. corporations than Nicholas Murray Butler had degrees. But when I approached him, the money involved was insignificant—to all but myself.

"Ask the *Herald* for sixty bucks a week and a year's contract," George advised fearlessly.

I did, all set to join in the laughter that followed.

But I got it, just in time to cover the opening game. Millie—no fool, she—promptly quit working.

A few weeks after I joined the *Herald,* Bryan Morse took drunk. This offended Mike Flynn, who had won a stirring battle with the jug not too long before. Mike fired Bryan and to the astonishment of all, in that obscure pocket of American letters, named me sports editor. I knew nothing about makeup, handling a staff, giving assignments, getting proper (free, if possible) seats for advertisers, and a host of other details alien to a person content merely to write.

My first act of office as sports editor was vainglorious. I assigned myself the task of writing a daily column, indented with a 6-pica cut of my bar mitzvah picture. What to name the column was a problem. (It was a big thing in those days, a catchy name.) All the good stock heads seemed taken. Arthur Brisbane, who appeared daily in the *Herald,* wrote under a simple and arresting roof: "Today." Damon Runyon, long a fixture on the *Herald's* sports pages, had chosen "Both Barrels." Shirley, with an envious sense of immediacy, had copyrighted "This Morning." Grantland Rice had a lock on "Sportlight," Bill McGeehan owned "Down the Field," Westbrook Pegler "Fair or Foul."

There wasn't much time to make up my mind. I had gotten the assignment from myself about four o'clock in the afternoon and the paper was going to press at six. After dining lightly on my fingernails, I rolled a sheet of copy paper in the typewriter and wrote: "ON THE LINE."

Then, under it, I typed: "By Bob Considine."

Something was wrong. I x'd it out and made it read:

"ON THE LINE
With Considine"

It moved no earth, not even under its creator, but it was a handy enough stock head in that it covered considerable latitude. It would apply to all sports that need boundary markings on their playing fields, including dice. It suggested that I might be calling a reader personally to impart some toothsome morsel of news. It hinted of straightforwardness, as in "I'm laying it on the line, see?"

Moreover, it might help readers learn to pronounce Considine properly, for it rhymes with line. But that turned out to be a forlorn hope. I've been called Consideen more often than Considine ever since.

Having firmed up a stock head, there was the little matter of what to write under it. But that, too, came. Ring Lardner had died that day, and if that could not bring forth words there was scant chance they'd ever come. During four slipshod years of night classes at George Washington I had figuratively and sometimes literally sat at the feet of Douglas Bement, who conducted a class in creative writing. He was married to an exciting-looking woman, for a professor's wife, either French or Spanish or both. He sometimes sauntered into class in plus-fours, puffing a slender pipe. He was Ronald Colman, playing a quietly gay dean. He introduced me to Lardner, not the man, alas, but his product . . . Champion . . . Haircut . . . The Golden Honeymoon . . . Liberty Hall . . . and the sports coverage.

I wrote my first "On the Line" column about Lardner as if I had lost a dear friend—and in a sense I had.

"Pretty good piece," Mike Flynn said the next day. "Runyon's the big shot today, but Lardner's the one they'll be reading twenty-five or fifty years from now. His stuff will live."

It is a grand feeling to have a column in a metropolitan daily, replete with a carefully selected (and somewhat retouched) photo betokening manliness, courage, strength—but also hinting of good nature, kindliness to dogs and cats, and other rare qualities. But from the start there was a cloud over me. I was a fifth-rate sports editor. Simple as that.

I had neither the stomach nor will to fire anybody, even when ordered, as I was in the case of a great old cartoonist, Bud Counihan. When one of the staff got drunk for a few days it seemed best to phone his wife and ask her to keep him away from the office and I'd write his pieces until the fogs dispersed.

But this was not my trouble. My failing, mainly, was that I considered the symmetrical makeup of the *New York Times* sports page, the first page, that is, and Shirley's first page at the *Post* constituted the ideal way to present the news. I became symmetry-happy, balancing heads, boxes, and story lengths to such a fine degree that the first page of *my* sports section could have walked a tightrope across Niagara Falls without recourse to a parasol. Also, I kept all cuts to discreet sizes and considered it unwarranted to splash a headline across the top of the page each day, willy-nilly. Worse, I stubbornly resisted the pleas of our circulation manager, Happy Robinson, to pour on a lot of early Fall football stories and features about Georgetown, George Washington, Catholic University, Maryland, Navy, and other resident or adjacent teams. Instead, I gave by far the biggest play to Griff's baseball club, which was hammering toward its first pennant since 1925 (and the last it was to cop for decades, by the way).

I was out of my depth. Without the sure touch of George Garner on the copy desk, the *Herald* would have hit the streets now and then without a sports section. George and I had attended St. Aloysius grammar school together, and Gonzaga High until I became a dropout after two years. He had gone on to Georgetown and preceded me to the *Herald.*

Now, as if we were back in the sixth grade again, under the watchful eye of Sister Bernard, George helped me with my lessons. He kept our holey craft afloat, particularly when I was on the road with the ball club, competing against the man who had brought me into the business and directing my first faltering steps. Shirley and I were now equals, in grade at least: each was a sports editor, sports columnist, and baseball writer covering the Senators. Rivals!

"Anything I can do to help you, let me know," he said the day Mike Flynn had made the announcement.

Without thinking how ridiculous it must have sounded to him, I made the same offer. The difference in the twin offers, of course, was that I had nothing in the bank.

Just before the World Series of 1933, in which the New York Giants beat Washington four games to one, I began feeling hot breaths on my neck. Bryan Morse had been editing our sports pages by remote control. Whenever he spotted an error, though it be ostensibly a typographical fluff, he would circle it with a red pencil and mail the page to Mike Flynn. To boot, Ray Helgeson, our mercurial City Editor who had worked on the New York *Mirror* and the Chicago *Examiner,* burst into the sports department one night and said to me, "Get me twenty more tickets to the Series." I told him that the *Herald* had been given its full quota, the same as Griff allotted to the other Washington papers.

Ray looked at me with surprised disgust.

"What the hell kind of sports editor are you?" he asked. He didn't wait for an answer. It was just as well, for I didn't really know.

I was soon told.

The *Herald* was on lease from the Hearst chain, but many pipe lines were kept open between New York and Washington. Through one of them one day came Ed Frayne, sports editor of the New York *American*. He was a quiet-spoken man with heavy lenses, impersonally friendly and, to me, vaguely ominous. His sports pages were colorfully explosive compared to mine. And that's why he was in Washington, I began to comprehend.

Shortly after he returned to New York, I was leaving the *Herald* building late one night, so punchy from work that I was trying to remember where I had parked my car. I stopped by the lobby counter to pick up a fresh copy of the paper. The old fellow who manned the counter looked at me.

"You know you're out as sports editor, don't you?" he asked.

It was my introduction to one of the peculiarities of my craft: Everybody knows the verdict before the condemned man is told.

Bernie Harter, a decent, industrious man who had been Frayne's work-horse assistant on the *American* replaced me and granted me a last request. He hired Vincent X. Flaherty, who had been doing some piecework for me, as a regular member of the staff. Vinny and I grew up in generally the same area of Washington. He became a rolling-stone college football player, an end, in a day when it was comparatively easy to touch down at several campuses in quick succession without awakening sleeping eligibility dogs. Somewhere along the athletic scholarship road—not known for the finer things of life—Vinny picked up not only a voracious appetite to write but also the gift of fulfilling the desire.

He had something else that made him a natural for a sports section. He was an instinctive promoter.

In the years that stretched from there, Flaherty, overriding a speech impediment that would blast most men's careers, was responsible for some pretty profound sports developments. He wangled a berth on the College All Stars for a comparatively obscure George Washington University halfback named Tuffy Leemans, Tuffy's steppingstone to the New York Football Giants and a place in the pro-game's history. After World War II, in which he served as a correspondent, Vinny arranged two fund-raising TV telethons, featuring Bob Hope and Bing Crosby, that raised several million dollars for U.S. Olympic teams. After he moved his typewriter to the Los Angeles *Examiner* as its sports columnist, he began a campaign—mainly at his own expense— to bring big league baseball to California. More than any other individual, he must be given credit for inducing the Dodgers to move from Brooklyn to L.A. and the Giants to find their way to San Francisco. Vincent Xavier Flaherty, who was once paid fifteen dollars a week by a grateful Washington *Herald,* made the national pastime national, brought millions to Walter O'Malley and Horace Stoneham . . . and had difficulty persuading the Dodgers' management to sell him two good seats to the 1966 World Series at Chavez Ravine.

The reason for that is he no longer writes a column.

A similar fate faced me when I went to spring training camp with the Washington ball club in 1934. I had flopped as sports editor and seemed to be more or less on probation as sports columnist and baseball writer. My precious sixty-dollar-a-week, one-year contract, only one of its kind in Washington, was a guttering flame. There was no word from the office about its renewal. So I called George Allen, by that time District of Columbia Commissioner (in charge of making F.D.R. chuckle).

"What's your problem?" George asked cheerfully.

It took twenty minutes to tell him, even in the *Reader's Digest* version. My lament ended with, "What do you think I should do?"

"Demand one hundred twenty a week and a two-year contract," George snapped and hung up. He was busy.

Taking a firm stand on the quicksand of my predicament, I did just that. A week passed, an inch at a time. Then a telegram from Mike Flynn. I had to read it twice to believe it. It read, "OKAY FOR $120 A WEEK. TWO-YEAR CONTRACT MAILED YOU TODAY FOR SIGNING."

I learned later that when my demand first arrived at the office it evoked derisive laughter. Several days after its arrival, someone at the *Herald* called Ed Frayne in New York to tell him about the preposterous attitude.

"If you don't want to give him what he wants, we'll take him on the *American*," Ed said.

This remarkable bid was brought to the attention of Mrs. Eleanor Patterson, absolute ruler of our domain in her roles as publisher, editor, and executive in charge of paying for the paper's million-dollar-a-year deficit. She had never shown the remotest interest in me or the sports department in general. But now that someone else was interested . . . well, by God, nobody was going to steal "one of my boys," Mrs. Patterson cried out.

That's why my terms (George Allen's terms, really) were met.

Moreover, that's how I was transported into the cast of characters who supported her, the star in a daily newspaper soap opera which could have been called "Life With Cissy."

Cissy. That's what everybody called her, except to her face.

2. *Cissy*

T HIS was Cissy. . . .

There could never have been anyone quite like her before and little
likelihood of a duplication in the future. She spun through the thick
atmosphere of American journalism like a maverick meteor, then
flamed out. No person who witnessed that incandescent passage can
forget her, any more than the elderly astronomers forget Halley's
Comet. No reporter she touched was precisely the same thereafter.

Eleanor Medill Patterson Gizycka Schlesinger was a female buc-
caneer, her transient son-in-law, Drew Pearson, decided. She could
weep over a sick kitten and call the crippled President of the United
States, Franklin D. Roosevelt, a slacker. She was the most extraordinarily generous publisher in newspaper history, and she was also
a niggardly bitch.

I loved her.

Cissy was an arresting-looking woman, tall, with good movement,
equally at home in rough-riding togs as in something by Dior. She was
no chick when she came around to the newspaper business. But more
than one of the younger bucks who worked for her mused over what
it might be like to work with her on a different plane. She had the
kind of hair that used to be portrayed in the shampoo ads, a cascade
of darker Titian that fell to her hips, and strange dark eyes that could
be as merry as Mrs. Santa Claus's and malevolent as Mrs. Medici's.
No man really *knew* Cissy, but God knows a lot of them tried.

Some tried too hard; that could be fatal.

Cissy stood on the edge of the business for years, watching her
mercurial brother Joseph Medill Patterson and her difficult cousin
Robert Rutherford McCormick carve and sometimes hack their
niches. She beheld and benefited from the harvest when Joe and

20

Bertie together converted their grandfather's Chicago *Tribune,* always a substantial winner, into the most successful newspaper in the publishing world. She watched with interest, and perhaps envy, when Joe moved along to New York to found the tabloid *Daily News,* which swiftly won and held the nation's circulation peak.

Cissy bided her time, but hardly in purdah.

She had two debuts, the additional one in Washington, which did not happen to every gangly rich girl from Chicago. When at nineteen she married Josef Gizycka, a high-octane Polish count with a low-calorie bank rating, the feature writers of those early 1900's hinted as bluntly as the libel laws permitted that this was yet another sorry example of a fine young American girl having her pretty head turned by a fortune-hunting cad with a waxed mustache. Whatever the justification for this sort of scandal-mongering, Cissy and her swain gave them something *really* to relish. After three years of generally jarring life with Gizycka, Cissy fled his mortgaged castle, baby Felicia in her arms, and made good her escape to London. Gizycka countered by kidnapping the child and taking her back to Poland. The *Tribune* and just about every other U.S. newspaper thundered. The State Department fumed; President William Howard Taft wrote pointed letters to Czar Nicholas; Pope (later Saint) Pius X expressed concern. Cissy got Felicia back in 1908 and came back to America. Including what amounted to ransom, the adventure of getting back her child cost Cissy about half a million dollars.

It would have been worth it, if they had ever become warm friends.

But Cissy and her vibrant daughter fissioned as the daughter grew, and in the end Felicia, hardly felicitously, charged that her mother must have been lunatic when she signed the will that left her only certain real estate, household effects, and $25,000 a year for life.

How much of that split could be traced to Cissy's busy but generally unproductive life during Felicia's maturing years is not measurable. But it was the life of a gadabout. She traveled restlessly at times, secreted herself on a ranch near Jackson Hole, Wyoming, at other times, knew the rollicking social life of Washington during Warren Harding's earlier days in the White House, and wrote two novels. One of them, *Glass Houses,* filled with thinly veiled or completely exposed well-known habitués—and sons of habitués—of Washington's top-drawer social set, was a kind of blueprint of the intemperance and intolerance she would later show as an editor and publisher. The other, *Fall Flight,* concerned a betrayed American heiress.

Washington was evolving as her home. Felicia fell in love and married up-and-coming Drew Pearson whose activities in those precolumn days in the early 1920's included such posts as director of the American Friends Service Committee in Serbia, Montenegro, and Albania; instructor in industrial geography at the University of Pennsylvania; lecturer; and occasional contributor to newspaper syndicates: "Europe's 12 Greatest Men," etc. Cissy gave her blessing, packed them off in style, and the following month in 1925 married her old friend Elmer Schlesinger, a New York attorney who had served as a dollar-a-year man in Washington with the Shipping Board.

Schlesinger's death in 1929 is a date totally unnoticed in the story of American journalism. But it is a significant milestone. Cissy was deeply attached to him; had great respect for him, she once told me. There is some good chance, therefore, that had he lived, she would have been content to share his life in the law and high finance.

But now she was alone, more alone than she had ever been before or would ever be again. The dynamos began to spin faster. She needed something to sink her teeth into, to occupy her restless mind. She tried writing again, factually this time. And she decided that she must have a writing name: thereafter, she was Eleanor Patterson. Period.

She needed something to write *on,* and that was provided, too. When she approached her friend William Randolph Hearst, Sr., and asked him to sell her his feeble Washington *Herald,* a pale competitor of the Washington *Post* in the capital's morning field, the laird of San Simeon laughed and asked her why she would want to add to her troubles.

The *Herald* had been a money-burning furnace for years. It had reached one of its drearier depressions while controlled, oddly enough, by one of its most well-heeled patrons: Herbert Hoover. Little is known of the late President's dip into daily journalism. But he had the *Herald* for a period after World War I and used it to promote the political fortunes of good friends in government and espouse the blessings of Prohibition. In those pre-Guild days, several members of the City Room staff worked for nothing, including future Pulitzer Prize winner Eddie Folliard. Desks were so scarce that Folliard and other lesser staffers sometimes were forced to use two huge rolls of newsprint as office equipment, one roll to plant a typewriter on, the other to sit on while working. Work was interrupted or demolished when either roll had to be trundled to the press room and fed into the hungry maw of the roaring machinery. It is not known why Mr. Hoover lost interest in the publishing business, but a possible clue lingered in the folklore of Washington journalism for years after he moved on to more rewarding fields, including the Presidency. Seems that Barney Hughes, a distinguished old copyboy, lost his balance one day while taking a refreshing drink of Ed Pinaud's Hair Tonic, tumbled down a flight of steps, and crashed through a dozen clouded glass doors stacked at the foot of the steps, awaiting installation.

Whatever was the case, or loss, Mr. Hoover surrendered, and it was from the National Savings and Trust Co. of Washington that Mr. Hearst bought the dubious "good will, etc." of the *Herald* on November 16, 1922, for $100,000. He made it a corporate part of his Washington *Times* Company, which had cost him more dearly. Hearst editor-columnist Arthur Brisbane (ostensibly acting on his own) bought the *Times* from Frank Munsey in 1917 for $500,000. In 1919, Mr. Hearst assumed the purchase contract from his employee for $325,000 and picked up unpaid notes to the amount of another $250,000.

Now, in 1930, with Cissy breathing heavily on his neck, Mr. Hearst had two, not one, losing properties in Washington. The feebler was the *Herald* whose circulation was 60,000. Cissy asked her friend to sell it to her. Mr. Hearst was not selling anything in those days, whatever the drain. But he shrewdly reckoned that she might be just the right transfusion the paper needed. He appointed her its editor at $15,000 a year. She accepted instantly, despite the protests of her brother and cousin, Joe and Bertie, that there was something nutty about working for $300 a week for a rival publisher while deriving a million-dollar-a-year income from her share of the Chicago *Tribune* and New York *Daily News*.

Cissy could not have cared less about the improbability of her position. She had a new baby in her lap, a new toy, a pulpit, a power, all rolled into one. It was enough to make her sensitive nostrils flare. And it did, on the front page of her *Herald* on July 26, 1930, just four days after she took over. The cause of the flaring was a report that Alice Longworth, still an impressive figure in the political and social life of Washington, would campaign for Ruth Hanna McCormick, then a candidate for the U.S. Senate from Illinois.

"INTERESTING, BUT NOT TRUE" read the startling box on Page 1 of the normally dull *Herald*. "The news is that Mrs. Alice Longworth will not only be a confidential adviser to Mrs. Ruth Hanna Mc-Cormick, but that she will campaign publicly for her lifelong friend.

"Interesting, but not true. Mrs. McCormick takes no advice, political or otherwise, from Mrs. Longworth. Mrs. Longworth gives no interviews to the press. Mrs. Longworth cannot utter in public. Her assistance will, therefore, resolve itself, as usual, into posing for photographs.—ELEANOR PATTERSON"

The *Herald* was never the same after that. Nor was Washington.

Cissy gave every outward appearance of being a dilettante stray in the newspaper game. The first person she hired after becoming editor was an interior decorator to fortify her Spartan office with chintz. The lengthening bread lines and increasing number of apple vendors in Washington made a sorry background for her arrival at the office each day in her chauffeured sixteen-cylinder Cadillac or the Duesenberg landaulet. She was often accompanied by her flock of big playful French poodles, all of them apparently descended from a dour dog she called affectionately the Old Bitch. Sometimes at night she would sweep into the office in an evening gown—in sharp contrast to her frequent daytime appearances in riding habit—en route to the theater or perhaps a White House party.

But as a matter of fact, Cissy worked exceedingly hard at her job. She was in many regards as keen as any cub reporter, and as eager to learn the trade.

"What can I do to get closer to our readers?" she asked managing editor Mike Flynn.

Mike was a real pro—a good, tough Irishman who had won an exhausting marathon against the bottle and now found himself burdened not only by a weak paper but a Hearst-blessed appendage who dressed and talked a bit like Rosalind Russell. His Humphrey Bogart brow furrowed in thought.

"Get out and meet them," he answered. "All you know is Society people and they don't buy the *Herald*."

Out of this exchange emerged "Maude Martin, jobless maid." In this disguise, Cissy haunted Washington's relief agencies collecting material for the series that was to launch her as a woman-of-the-people. It was a genuine hardship for her, but she was game right up to the incident that turned out to be her breaking point. It occurred during her brief stay at the Gospel Mission, a grubby haven for derelicts in Washington's Skid Row, not far from the glittering Capitol.

The adventure was notable in several ways. Cissy was the first person ever to arrive at the Mission in a Duesenberg, and the first claimant of a cot there ever to have journeyed from No. 15 Dupont Circle, her superb town house designed years before by Stanford White. She was certainly not the first waif ever granted asylum in the Mission who arrived with alcohol in the veins, but probably the first who ever brought aboard a load induced by vintage Mumm's. Cissy liked good champagne, and this seemed as good a night as any to fortify herself with it. It also seemed a good idea to take along some proper sheets and pillow cases, night gown, dressing robe, slippers, toiletry case, and that paragon of able-bodied chauffeurs, LaForte.

"Wait," she commanded LaForte as she sailed into the Mission. She was escorted to her freshly deloused room, ordered in advance by the *Herald,* and prepared herself for sleep. In the morning, there would be some sample bums to talk to, for her story.

Cissy never got to meet them, as it turned out. Dressed like a silken model for Harper's Bazaar caught anachronistically in a Barbary Coast bawdy house, Cissy reclined on her pillow, tucked her familiar sheets around her chin, and tried to forget the unshielded light overhead. She had coldly resisted the suggestion that most Mission residents, when able, turn out their lights at night.

Cissy's eyes were not very strong. She suffered from occasional attacks of conjunctivitis, or "pinkeye" as she called it, which occasionally caused associates to believe she was less than cold sober. "Mother, you're drunk!" Felicia accused her once at an otherwise pleasant party at Dupont Circle. It was a case of pinkeye, not pink champagne, Cissy tried vainly to explain.

But now as she lay in the Gospel Mission there was no question in Cissy's mind about her eyesight. The creature walking across the garish ceiling was a cockroach. She found the sight completely demoralizing. She let loose a cry that must have startled her fellow inmates, threw her mink over her nightgown, put on her slippers, and quit the premises.

LaForte had the motor running.

The series was bound to be an attention-grabber. The *Herald*'s promotion department, eager to bask in her good graces, composed full-page panegyrics heralding the coming series.

There was reason to believe that Cissy herself believed her notices. At least, there must have been considerable pride of authorship involved because of her violent reaction to a sorry snafu that struck the first article of the series. By a freak of fate and bad composition, the first edition of that fated night's run came off the presses with her story wildly garbled.

The by-line was there all right, bigger than life, but the story started out with some bewildering paragraph that belonged far down in the pillars of type. Somewhere else in the typographical Babel reposed the misplaced lead.

Even in those early stages of her editorial career there were *Herald* employees bucking to be mentioned in her will, apparently. One of these seized the first few papers off the press that sorry night and sped off for Dupont Circle, where Cissy paced impatiently. He never read below her impressive by-line.

But Cissy did, and her yell of rage shook the mansion. LaForte was summoned and the primed Duesenberg shot to the *Herald,* bearing in its back seat an author whose emotions ranged from helpless tears to mule-skinning profanity.

All was quiet in the *Herald*'s City Room when Cissy swept in like an unannounced cyclone. The early edition had been swiftly replated when the error was caught and was by now running smoothly; most of the staff were out for "lunch," as dinner time was always called on morning papers.

Her stentorian *"Who is responsible for this!"* would have scared a dog out of a boneyard. Heads swung in shock, and the City Room went into what might be called Condition B—for buck-passing. The instinct for survival, highly developed in newspaper people, impelled those present at the time to point toward the Copy Desk.

Cissy closed in on it. What followed might have been the most magnificent firing act of her life. But, as noted before, it was "lunch" time. The disorderly half-moon table which had been pointed out to her as guilty was manned at the moment only by a graying lush who had dropped in to bum a quarter and was awaiting the return of a copyreading benefactor.

"You are fired!" Cissy thundered, pointing like Brünnhilde ordering a war.

The bum laughed at her, which did not help matters. It was the first time he had ever been fired from the *Herald* while not employed.

When Cissy arrived at the office the next day, she looked into the City Room and noticed a graying man busy at a desk not far from the Copy Desk. She sailed resolutely into Mike Flynn's nearby office.

"I fired that man last night; get him out of here," she said, livid.

Mike looked in the direction she was pointing, took off his glasses, and shook his head.

"That's Bob McClellan, our Day City Editor, Mrs. Patterson."

"I don't care who he is," Cissy said. "Get him out of here."

It was useless, Flynn discovered, to explain that (1) she was wrong, (2) Bob had only recently battled his way up to the position after being canned for drinking too enthusiastically at the wrong times; and (3) a cruel blow like this would knock him off the wagon again. But Cissy was running the paper now, as any phone call to San Simeon would confirm. Mike fired McClellan, whose first act of outrage was to prove Mike's third point.

The remarkable aspect of Cissy's inhuman conduct in McClellan's case was that she did not almost immediately rehire him and appoint him Pope. Cissy could blow hotter and colder than the surface of the moon. She made a special point of saving sway-backed old work-horses ticketed for the LePage's plant. Her disparagers swore this dated from an impetuous chapter in her life as a horsewoman. They assured all who would listen that Cissy extracted a dramatic price from a favorite hunter who threw her and trotted back to the barn at Dower House, Cissy's place in the Maryland hunt country which had once belonged to Lord Baltimore. Cissy is suppose to have walked home in her fashionable jodhpurs, fetched a pistol, and killed the animal.

Whether true or false, Cissy was a big woman. She always had room for remorse. McClellan in time went back to work for her and married one of her prettier reporters.

The desire to catch her eye, join her shifting court, became one of the major preoccupations of the *Herald* staff. Reporters got hair-cuts more frequently than in the past and admired her dogs. Composi-tors began wearing neckties. Pressmen replaced their ink-stained paper birettas with fresh ones. Bill Shelton and his business office people became, if possible, ever more unctuous. Eddie Bratburg, who might have carried a spear in *The Front Page,* devised a signal system with the front counter to alert him whenever Cissy entered the build-ing. He was an assistant city editor and had every intention of bettering his position. Whenever Cissy would enter the City Room en route to her office, the phones on Eddie's desk and those adjoining it would be ringing urgently and he would be reaching for them and barking hosts of orders. Cissy was pleased by such industry until she learned about the hoax, probably from a rival for her uncertain smile.

Then one day there was a new man at Eddie's desk: handsome, rakish, pencil-thin Ray Helgeson, fresh from Hearst's Chicago *Examiner* and the hard school of knocks whose dean was Walter Howey. He was but one of a stream of men and women Mr. Hearst was happy to send to her aid in Washington from his enormous pool of executives, editors, specialists, and ordinary working stiffs.

"He sincerely admired her journalistic enterprise," W. A. Swanberg was to write years later in *Citizen Hearst*. And he added, "When Mrs. Patterson, who rode in her own private railroad car, arrived at San Simeon for a visit, he invariably had the other guests out on the terrace to meet her with armfuls of flowers, and hired a band to furnish a musical welcome."

Cissy was making her mark in the Hearst complex. "Publisher" was added to her title. The *Herald* was beginning to be talked about and bought. Local and national advertisers who had been avoiding the paper like a plague for years began showing an interest. The *Herald* was still operating in the red, but a deal was made whereby Cissy was given a percentage of all new advertising revenue. Cissy responded magnanimously by giving up her $15,000-a-year pin money. She remained a director of the Chicago *Tribune,* which was in bitter competition with Hearst's *Examiner,* and of the New York *Daily News,* then engaged in lethal conflict with Hearst's two New York morning papers, the *American* and the *Mirror.*

Cissy revered the man who had entrusted his sick *Herald* to her doting care. She saw eye to eye with him on every subject from politics to vivisection. They shared a lively interest in the former and deplored the latter in fulminating editorials. Mr. Hearst played an important role in gaining the Democratic nomination for Franklin D. Roosevelt in 1932. Cissy echoed the confidence. "He is a real American," she wrote of the candidate. "There is surely a special radiance about this man." She and Washington's other renowned Eleanor—Mrs. Roosevelt—became close friends.

Hearst talent wore a path to Cissy's *Herald* in the early days of the New Deal. Courtly, competent Tom White, Hearst's general manager, began dividing his valuable time between Hearst's over-all problems, which involved tens of millions of dollars, and Cissy's infinitely smaller-scaled fiscal aches and growing pains. She got her share of Hearst's efficiency experts, too, but more often than not ignored their recommendations—another trait she shared with W.R.

A particularly aggressive one named Bart Guild, who struck dismay wherever he roamed in search of heads to lop off the payrolls, struck no terror in Cissy. One night during his Washington stay, in the heady after-dinner dialogues at Dupont Circle, Guild held forth at some length about the number of Hearst people he had fired over the years. He concluded the grisly tale by announcing, ". . . but if I had my choice in this business I wouldn't be in this end of it all. I'd like nothing more than to be a simple newsboy selling papers on the corner."

He must have noted my look of disbelief, for he wheeled and roughly demanded, "And what would *you* like to be?"

I would mainly have liked to be someplace else at the moment, but the silence of the room—particularly of the hostess—required an answer.

"I'd like to be a newsboy, too," I said, "and have the corner opposite your corner."

"I'd run you off it," the hatchet man said angrily.

"Like hell you would," I said, bravely defending my nonexistent territory.

"Good for you," Cissy cut in, giving Guild a look that indicated he was not to stay very long in Washington.

Others came to help her make good.

Down from Boston, to be followed next day by the wife and children, came a lean redhead billed as just the picture-page editor Cissy needed. His arrival on the job coincided with a banquet given that night at the Willard Hotel for *Herald* newsboys. The paper had sandbagged local dignitaries into attending, and for these Cissy gave a special reception in a private dining room before the group joined the apple-cheeked youngsters for the dinner. Drinks were served. Among the many pictures taken was one which caught Cissy gesturing with her highball glass as if she was proposing a toast to the camera's lens.

With that infallible skill which picture-page editors have for selecting the worst of a choice of available shots, the eager-beaver from Boston chose the shot of Cissy confronting the camera with her drink.

She was again suffering from pinkeye at the time and thus looked plastered. The relative positions of her well-groomed body and the outstretched glass gave the drink the distorted size of a Jeroboam. To compound the felony of drinking at a newsboys' dinner, as his caption indicated, the benighted Bostonian ordered the picture set four columns and featured it in the center of a layout of potential advertisers, Y.M.C.A. types, and selected cherubs among the newsboys.

After the first edition came up, the man from Boston had misgivings. He ordered the drink air-brushed—erased—from the picture and a new cut made. In the next edition, which Cissy saw, she appeared with extended claw, apparently bent on garroting any newsboy who came within reach. The man from Boston was fired by phone. There was later a legend around the *Herald* that in his resultant state of shock he forgot to tell his wife he was returning to Boston and that the poor woman and the children caught a glimpse of him—a ghostly face in a window—as their trains shot past each other the next day.

Cissy inherited Hearst star Adela Rogers St. John for a spell, too, and they hit it off as only two women of the world could. An incurable matchmaker, Cissy tried to marry Adela off to Helgeson, but there were complications. Like other mates. Adela gave the girl reporters of the City Room and the chaste ladies of the Women's Page and Society a vicarious taste of what it was like to be in combat on big national stories. She had covered them all.

Adela astounded one and all by her facility. One day she spent a couple of hours with a Government stenographer and in short order produced a series of articles about Government Girls which, if produced today as a TV series for afternoon consumption, would clobber all competition. *Herald* people stood in awe of the prolific whirlwind from the big time. One day she tripped and dropped her purse as she entered the City Room. The purse opened and its disemboweled contents littered the floor.

"What a novel that'll make!" one of the *Herald* rewrite men gasped.

Pat Frank, who was to write the best-selling *Mr. Adam,* and a lot of other winners before he died, was brought in by Helgeson to nail down the kind of tough stories Ray wanted to break—and did. Pat hid in the broom closet of a grand jury room on one occasion, and the *Herald* broke the story of its deliberations. He nearly went to jail for his scoop. Cissy, exercised over the case, would willingly have gone to jail with him.

Nobody awed Cissy. The stimulation of battle over real or imagined wrongs to herself brought a flush to her cheeks and a glint to her swimming eyes. She was properly outraged when Eugene Meyer, who had bought the rundown Washington *Post* in 1933 and began to pump impressive sums into its rebirth, made Hearst an attractive offer for the *Herald* without so much as consulting Cissy. Hearst ignored the offer, but from then on Cissy regarded Meyer and his *Post* as her worst enemies. She delighted in luring *Post* people into her pasture. When the papers became embroiled in a court fight over "Dick Tracy," the adventure strip which was in effect owned by her brother Joe and cousin Bertie, and Meyer won the case, Cissy sent him a pound of raw meat with her card, on which she scrawled, "Have your pound of flesh!"

Another who chose to square off against Cissy was George Preston Marshall, then owner of the highly profitable Palace Laundry chain in Washington, bon vivant, sportsman, friend of Broadway and Hollywood folk and, on orders from San Simeon, publisher of Hearst's Washington *Times*. That afternoon paper used the building, presses, and some of the clichés left over from the morning *Herald*. George and Cissy, both headstrong and colorfully independent, had been friends for years. But in 1934, after Marshall was deputized as publisher of the *Times,* in the hope that he might inject as much zing into it as Cissy had into the *Herald,* there was a noticeable cooling off on Cissy's part. She came to regard him, quite correctly, as a rival for the major share of the dollar which advertisers earmarked for space in Hearst papers in Washington.

Their ultimate collision was characteristic of Cissy's sensitized explosion point, unlike anything known in nature until the isolation, some years later, of Uranium-235. One day Marshall ordered *his* side of the third floor hall painted a bluish-purple, the hereditary hue of the family laundry. Worse, he chose to have the work done during one of Cissy's trips out of the city. When she returned, she took one look at the *Times* side of the hall wall and ordered *her* side painted a clashing green. Both claimed victory to their now separate coteries of friends, but neither could arouse much enthusiasm among those, particularly those with hangovers, who had to walk through the hall each day.

Cissy won that one. Her impact at San Simeon was understandably greater than that of Marshall. He was thanked and returned to his mangles.

It was Cissy's building after that, and she shaped it and its inmates into the image and likeness of her steel-clad whims.

One of her surest innovations was pure Cissy. All the creature comforts she had known since birth—good food, proper wines, gracious service, travel, and chi-chi rampant—found expression on her expanded pages for women. Martha Blair, who was to marry Arthur Krock, introduced *Herald* readers to life behind the closed doors of the 1925 F Street Club. Igor Cassini, dashing son of an old friend, in time became her provocative society editor-columnist, and on one occasion provoked a group of blue-blooded ruffians from the Virginia horse country into tarring and feathering him.

Cissy was a stickler for good style. One night she dropped by the office on the way to a party dressed in a stunning gold lamé gown, with train held delicately across her left wrist as she moved to her office, dusting ashes from a cigarette held in a quill-tipped holder. She approved the first-edition pages spread before her, then floated regally back to the elevator. It held a motley group: respectful or ogling reporters, printers, publicity people, a souse or two, and up front and ready-get-set, a Western Union boy. When the door slammed open, the boy shot out across the lobby, bent on his errand. Cissy picked up her tight dress and sprinted after him, a frightening sight to the lad when he looked over his shoulder. She seized the terrified youngster by the collar, marched him back through the crowd that was still leaving the elevator, waited until it was empty, pushed him inside, stepped in after him, adjusted her train over her wrist again, and walked out ahead of him.

"Ladies first, young man," Cissy cooed.

Reporters found they could take advantage of Cissy up to a point. The trouble was the task of locating the point. Like the night of Betty Hynes's farewell party for Ray Helgeson. Ray had taken two major steps. He had fallen in love with a beautiful young girl reporter, and he had decided to return to Chicago. Cissy was certain to be offended on both points.

So Betty, who worshiped Cissy but never became a part of her innermost court (as did among a few others Evie Robert, personality-flashing wife of Roosevelt's Under Secretary of the Treasury), did not invite Cissy to the Helgeson bash. But if Cissy was out of sight that night, as we sat around the little apartment's chairs and floor drinking the fresh squeezings of Repeal, she was not out of mind. About 2:30 A.M. the *Herald*'s top crime reporter, Laz Sommers, who had come to George Washington University as a gifted athlete and had moved on to greater things as a speakeasy impresario, put in a call to Dupont Circle. It roused a butler and, in time, Cissy.

"Hello, you old bag," Laz said. "Get on your feet and come over to Betty Hynes's joint. We're having a hell of a party for Helgeson."

Then Laz, my friend, handed the phone to me. Cissy was asking a question. It was an ominous-sounding question.

"Who *is* this?" she was asking.

I told her it was me . . . I. Surprisingly, she was not the least bit angry.

"It sounds very gay," she said sleepily. "I'm sorry I can't come over, but I'll tell you what: Why don't you bring your little party over here to the house, and we'll have a nightcap and a bite to eat?"

There were thirty of us. Thirty-one, actually. Maybelle Jennings, the dear movie critic, was missing for a time after the alarming rabble arrived in the driveway of the splendid mansion. A search party quickly discovered her. Upon alighting from one of the cars and taxis that transported the well-oiled mob from Betty's to Cissy's, Maybelle had collapsed and fallen through a high hedge and was flat on her back in the formal garden on the other side of it, feet in the air. We were all accounted for now and filed into the stately foyer, chastened suddenly by the outrageous intrusion of our leader's domain. At least, we felt chastened until Sommers relieved the tension.

He goosed Cissy's butler, who was bowing us in with understandable disdain. The man must have leaped a yard in the air in the course of surely the most extraordinary experience of his life.

Cissy was a radiant hostess. She appeared in a lovely dressing gown, again with a train, and ordered out the kind of good whiskey and champagne we would have been drinking earlier if we had been able to afford it. She danced with some of us, and very well, too, laughed when one exuberant drunken employee tried to hitch a ride across the slick ballroom floor on her train, and found it not unamusing when the husband of one of her embarrassed girl reporters passed out. Cissy had seen lots of friends pass out before, but never one as dramatically as this. The man was seated in the middle of a divan facing a coffee table. He was stoned but upright. Then a butler came in and put down in front of him a silver tray filled with a huge mound of scrambled eggs, garnished with bacon and decorated with parsley twigs. It proved too much for the man to bear. He keeled over face first into the mountain of eggs and with such force that his head was almost completely submerged. Fast work prevented his becoming the first known American to die in scrambled eggs.

There was a touch of dawn when the party dissolved. George Waters, one of the *Herald*'s best police reporters, sought out Cissy and found her in the spacious kitchen, still serene.

"Thanks very much, Mrs. Patterson," George said. "You're a great sport to put up with a thing like this. Can I help with the dishes?"

Cissy looked at him glacially.

"I have sufficient help to do my dishes," she said. "You're fired."

Cissy was the utter mistress of the bold gesture. There was that pilgrimage to Edgar Allan Poe's room. . . .

One day she appeared in the doorway looking into our scabrous sports department, searched the room uncertainly, recognized me, and beckoned.

"We're going to the University of Virginia at Charlottesville," she said. "I've never seen Poe's room there. Be at Union Station at five."

"I've got to cover the doubleheader today," I said. "Washington's playing the Yankees. Its the biggest. . . ."

"Who's interested in baseball?" Cissy said impatiently. "Be at the station at five. Just ask the station master where the Ranger is."

The Ranger was her private car, a handsome gift from the late Schlesinger. It had a shiny brass-railed observation deck, a paneled drawing room fit for the queen who owned it, four bedrooms equipped with comfortable poster beds, not berths (and showers and hand basins whose spigots were marked 18 k.), a handsome dining room with a fine oval table and glittering ware, and beyond that a spotless galley and quarters for the two-man crew. No. 1 boy's Ranger insignia on the cap that topped his special uniform was spelled out in gold; No. 2 boy's in silver.

"They're fags, but cute," Cissy would say when conducting a tour of the fabled Pullman. It cost $5,000 a year just to park the Ranger in the station yard at Washington, and twenty-eight round-trip first-class fares every time she ordered it hitched to a train headed some place she wished to visit—even if she rode alone, as she sometimes did.

We had a nice ride south that night, just Cissy, Maybelle Jennings, and the fellow who was supposed to have covered a doubleheader that day at Griffith Stadium. Our drinks were elegantly served on the observation deck as the sun set. There was a leisurely dinner whose main course was the tender hearts of lamb chops, after-dinner coffee and liqueurs in the car's living room, and a good night's sleep. We awakened in the morning to find the Ranger parked on a siding at the foot of the hill leading up to the University campus.

LaForte was parked in the mud-splattered Duesenberg a few feet from the steps of the Ranger. He had driven through the night over Virginia roads, just to be there. We breakfasted, stepped into the car, purred up the hill, were led to Poe's room, and looked in. A stuffed raven peered down glassily from a beam.

"Nice," Cissy said. She turned and we followed her back to the car and rode down the hill in the early morning sunshine. That's right, she told the university's man, that's all she wanted to see.

At the little station at the foot of the hill Cissy said, pleased as a child with a ginger of an idea, "Let's go to Williamsburg now and see the Rockefeller restorations." Maybelle said she could not dream of anything nicer to do. I could not think. It was the earliest I had been up since I was an altar boy.

The overwhelmed station manager was delighted with the new plan.

"A wonderful coincidence, Mrs. Patterson," he beamed, bowing and tipping his little hat. "There's only one train down there and back each day and it'll be along in, let me see"—he flipped the lid of his big watch—"just two hours, by cracky. We'll hitch your Ranger on, and down you'll go." He seemed about to go into a joyful jig.

"I don't want to wait two hours," Cissie said, evenly. "Bring around an engine."

I waited for the man to fall over dead. But he survived.

"I don't think you understood me, Mrs. Patterson," he said. "I said the regular train—the only train today—is coming through soon and—"

"And I said bring around an engine," Cissie interrupted firmly. "You're in that business, aren't you?"

"But the *cost* to you, Mrs. Patterson. . . ." the poor man mewed.

He looked at her and swallowed noisily. "There *is* a spare freight engine here, but. . . ."

It took an hour to fire up the steamy monster and attach the Ranger to it. Cissy and Maybelle retired to their staterooms for a morning nap as we moved down the tracks in solitary grandeur, pulled by an engine that could have dragged two hundred freight cars. I fixed one of those much-too-early-in-the-morning Scotches and repaired to a chair on the observation deck to contemplate (1) my navel, and (2) the occasional sight of the smoke of the regular train following not too far behind.

Cissy wrote a piece for *Editor and Publisher* once upon a time which began:

> Arthur Brisbane once said that the only two men in the world he knew who never do anything they don't want to do are W. R. Hearst and Joe Patterson. It would be truer to say that neither of these men pays the slightest attention to nonessentials.

Like Cissy . . .

Exhausted from her assorted labors, feuds, fads, and crusades, Cissy took off for Miami Beach in the Ranger with her dogs, trunks, and trappings one bleak Washington morning, bound for a full month's vacation in the sun at the Flamingo Hotel. She had reserved the better part of an entire floor in its tower at stiff seasonal prices and looked forward eagerly to the respite from work and worry. Happy Robinson would join her there in a couple of days.

Happy, straight from the Hearst stable and a crackerjack, was her circulation director. He bowed to no man in the shop when it came to expressing and displaying undying loyalty to Cissy. Happy was a survivor of the mob-ridden circulation wars between Cousin Bertie's *Tribune* and Hearst's *Examiner*. He wore his scars with pride, as he did a .38 slug which had been shot into him and which he had never gotten around to having mined.

Happy's trip to Miami was to be a little reward, a bonus. The *Herald* was by now streaming into front doors in Washington, too. Circulation was mounting toward the 100,000 mark, and it was noised about that Eugene Meyer had made another futile effort to buy the property from Hearst, this time for a million dollars.

Happy breezed into the lobby of the Flamingo like a song and dance man coming on stage at the old Palace. "It's Happy, Chief, I'll be right up," he sang into the house phone. He did a kind of clog over to the elevator, beckoning to the bellhop to bring along his bags.

Then a man with striped trousers and a white carnation in his lapel tapped him on the shoulder.

"Sorry, sir," the man said. "You're not permitted above the ground floor."

Happy could be tough.

"Listen, buddy, I'm the guest of Mrs. Eleanor Patterson."

The man sighed.

"This," he said, "is a restricted hotel, sir."

Happy had eaten tougher men for less. But now he walked quietly back to the house phone, called Cissy and said, "Chief, they won't let me come upstairs because I'm a Jew."

There was an imperceptible pause on the other end of the line, then Cissy said airily, "Well, Happy, if that's the case I'll come down and see you."

"I'm gettin' out of this goddam joint, Chief."

"Now you stop," Cissy chided. "I'll be down."

Happy clumped to the nearest chair and glared at the imperturbable manager. After ten minutes he could no longer bear it. He snatched the house phone again, got Cissy, and shouted that he was leaving immediately.

"Happy," she said, "I *told* you I'll be right down."

And in a few minutes there appeared an explosive scene at the elevators. The doors flung open and out spilled Cissy, her boisterous French poodles, trunks, bags, gowns streaming from hangers—and a stricken manager trying to kiss her hand and implore her to change her mind.

Cissy had had enough of Meyer's overtures to Hearst. On April 18, 1937, she leased the *Herald* for five years. It was a complicated deal: $350,000 a year for the first year and thereafter for each year the paper lost money, minus 50 per cent of the amount the losses in the previous year were reduced below $700,000. If there should be a profit, the rental would be 50 per cent of the net. Three months later Cissy wrote out a check for a million dollars, which in effect gave her both the *Herald* and the *Times*. On January 1, 1939, the purchase of the papers was formalized. In the end they cost Cissy $1,557,500.

They were losing $1,750,000 a year.

Now came the full flowering of her colorful, courageous, even reckless skills. She combined the two failures into the whopping success that became the Washington *Times-Herald,* an around-the-clock no-holds-barred daily bombshell. No target was too big to tackle, including That Man in the White House, and in time two of the columnists who had helped so greatly in bolstering circulation, Walter Winchell and Drew Pearson.

Cissy told me once that the whole thing between Roosevelt and herself was smashed forever when the President, having consented to see her brother Joe, who wished to offer his services to the Army immediately after Pearl Harbor, "let Joe stand there like an office boy and then turned him down."

Actually, there had been a cooling off over a period of years. Cissy accompanied Hearst, Brisbane, and publisher Paul Block when the titans trained to Topeka in the summer of 1936 to look over (and enthusiastically approve of) Gov. Alf M. Landon as Presidential timber. But she remained friendly with Mrs. Roosevelt through the late thirties and with the more personable men around Roosevelt—notably Joseph P. Kennedy, Harold Ickes, and Harry Hopkins.

In time, she was to belt them all, sometimes in a manner that shocked even the most case-hardened of her editors. Ash DeWitt, probably the most capable executive who ever worked for her, walked out when—over his bitter protests—Cissy insisted on running a full page of dead U.S. Marines, killed on the beach of Tarawa. At a slant across the whole page she had ordered written Roosevelt's prewar pledge: "AGAIN AND AGAIN AND AGAIN I SAY, AMERICAN BOYS WILL NOT FIGHT ON FOREIGN BATTLEFIELDS. . . ."

In July, 1944, FDR rejected an appeal to allow draft deferments for premedical students under twenty-six. Cissy filled another picture page, this time with twenty State Department career men—ages twenty-four to thirty-seven—"who do not choose to fight."

Her accompanying editorial "hissed"—as *Time* magazine put it—"If the Army really needs *all* the able-bodied young men it can get, it can find in Secretary Hull's fold an assortment of rich, able-bodied and unmarried boys of no particular use to anyone. . . . There are plenty of intelligent girls available to more than adequately fill the jobs of these young men." *Time*'s account continued:

> "It would really be good for 'the panty-waist brigade' (and isn't *that* vulgar?)," snapped Cissie, to have a taste of war. Even Bill Bullitt "might have lost his insatiable appetite for intrigue before the present disaster" if he had "risked *his* young blood and guts and tears in the last World War instead of cutting dramatic capers at the Versailles Peace Conference."

And just while she was on the subject, "the President himself has no firsthand knowledge of war either, we might add. Like his little boy friends, Pearson and Winchell, he stayed far away from the battlefield of the first World War. Although at that time a young man, and in perfect physical condition, he did 'his bit' as Assistant Secretary of the Navy—right here in Washington."

Cordell Hull raged at his next press conference. He produced the deferment record, age, and marital status of every career man whose picture Cissie had printed. All but four were overseas, he said, many in jobs directly related to the military. Nobody in his department under twenty-six was draft deferred, he said. Cissy's attack, he said, was "violent and unfair, grossly unfair."

Cissy died one night; there probably was nothing more interesting to do at the time. She was in bed at Dower House reading a book when her time came. A maid named Eva Barowik tapped on her door and came in—that morning of July 24, 1948—with a message that the office was on the phone; she found Cissy. Her eyeglasses were on the pillow beside her head; her book was on her chest. The reading light was on. She was sixty-three.

Her sealed coffin was centered in the ballroom of the Dupont Circle home she had known so long. Dr. Dudley E. Stark of St. Chrysostom's Episcopal Church, Chicago, who did not know her very well, said some kind words. Daughter Felicia and granddaughter Ellen were there. Happy Robinson shed honest tears. The body was taken to Chicago by train and buried there.

Drew Pearson wrote the best obit. He and Felicia had managed to stay married three years. Ellen was a year old when they broke up in 1928. For a long time he and Cissy remained firm friends, but when they broke up her vilification was total. Still, on her death, Pearson wrote with grace and affection:

> A great lady died the other day—a lady who had caused me much happiness, and much pain. She was my ex-mother-in-law, Eleanor Patterson, who used to write about me in such scathing terms that even the very frank *Time* magazine had to interpret them with dots and dashes. And, though I never answered her, I want to write about her now because she represented a great newspaper cycle which may be coming to an end.
>
> Cissy Patterson's one ambition was to be as great a newspaper-man as her brother Joe, and though she may not have realized

it, she was. She and Joe had grown up together, and she worshiped him. That was how Cissy got her nickname; for Joe, as a little boy, could not pronounce "Eleanor."

Both inherited part of the Chicago *Tribune*—wealthiest newspaper property in the world. But neither was satisfied merely to be a cog in the *Tribune* machine, and their genius built up two great newspapers in other cities, the New York *Daily News* and the Washington *Times-Herald*.

Cissy Patterson always reminded me of the house on Dupont Circle in which she lived. Her mother, bored with Chicago, had moved there. The house was designed by Stanford White. Cissy's home was the scene of luxurious parties, hatched conspiracies to kill the League of Nations, official residence of frugal Calvin Coolidge, who moved in with 30 pairs of shoes, half a dozen pairs of hip boots, an array of flannel nightgowns and 100 woolen socks. It still stands, a monument to the past.

Her method of running a newspaper was brilliant, sometimes vitriolic, always personal. It was her paper, and she ran it as such. There was not a night she did not pass on its banner headlines and Page 1 makeup. Even when in Florida, she checked by phone.

Sometimes Page 1 featured headlines about "The Headache Boy"—Cissy's description of her ex-son-in-law. Not only did she play up every speech attacking me on the Senate floor, but she kept a file and I know helped Senators write those speeches.

Today, Senator Brewster of Maine has his offices stacked high with 75,000 reprints of a speech largely taken from Cissy's diatribes against me, which he is mailing to constituents at the taxpayers' expense.

People used to ask me why I didn't answer Cissy or sue her for libel. Well, she and I had been through a lot together and I concluded the public is the best judge of such things and will eventually decide that.

But I shall miss the personal journalism of my ex-mother-in-law, though I do not agree with it. I shall even miss her excoriating me. . . . And so the house on Dupont Circle now goes to the Red Cross and a great lady, representing a great age of journalism, will be troubled by such headaches as me no more.

Cissy's will, filed the day after her Chicago funeral, made instant millionaires of seven "loyal employees," to whom she bequeathed the *Times-Herald* and all that went with it. They were William C. Shelton, general manager; Frank C. Waldrop, editor-in-chief; Edmund P.

Jewell, advertising director; Mike Flynn, supervising managing editor; Happy Robinson, circulation; Irving Belt, mechanical superintendent, and Mason Peters, night managing editor. Federal taxes on their windfall were paid out of an estate which was valued tentatively at $16,-586,571, a conservative estimate.

Nothing approximating such a gesture had ever been made before in the newspaper business.

It was Cissy's hope, forlorn as it turned out, that the men to whom she willed her newspaper would cherish it until death did them part. But, ever the realist, she inserted a clause in her testament calculated to dampen defection. Heirs to the paper were expressly forbidden to sell "without the consent of all the beneficiaries."

They cashed in their chips at the first good invitation to become ex-newspapermen. Rejecting an offer from the Hearst organization that would have continued to utilize all their skills, they sold out to Bertie McCormick for good safe *Tribune* stock and cash, indifferent to the memory of Cissy's repeated differences with him. McCormick made a botch of the paper in attempting to make it an eastern Chicago *Tribune.* He, in turn, despite last-minute efforts by favorite niece Bazie Tankersley to salvage the paper, abruptly sold it to Eugene Meyer of the Washington *Post,* the man and institution Cissy abhorred. The *Post* soon devoured all of its flavor.

Cissy would have come to hate her newspaper heirs. Indeed, she was in the process of changing her will, as if she sensed what they would do, when her light went out. Several weeks before her death, Cissy decided that the person best fitted to carry on with the *Times-Herald* was her niece, Alicia Patterson Guggenheim, Joe's daughter and the wife of Harry F. Guggenheim, multimillionaire head of the foundation bearing his father's name, patron of many of the pioneers of the aerospace age, Navy captain in World War II and co-founder, with Alicia, of the nation's most successful post-war daily, *Newsday,* of Nassau County, New York. All of Cissy's love of her brother had been transferred to Alicia upon Joe's death.

So minded, Cissy wrote out a new will that dumped the loyal editors and company officials and named Alicia her sole heir to that thriving property, which by that time was grossing well over a million dollars a year profit. She knew Joe would have approved, but Joe was gone. She turned to Cousin Bertie, mailed him the draft of the proposed new will, and in due time received a reply from him.

Cousin Bertie, difficult as ever, wrote her a note criticizing the *syntax* of the new will. Cissy was furious. She shot back a singeing reply (in the course of some other differences of opinion they were having over how the New York *Daily News* should be operated).

The two were in the midst of this exchange when death put an end to it. Cissy had never gotten around to having the new will legalized. The oversight cost Mrs. Guggenheim, who died in 1963, a ten-million-dollar property which today—had it maintained the kind of drive Cissy had gaited it to—would be worth several times that sum. Less enchanted newspapers in New Orleans and Omaha have sold for about forty million dollars in recent years.

Cissy's will left Felicia the estates in Sands Point, Long Island, and the shooting lodge in North Dakota, the bulk of her jewelry, paintings, and furniture, and $25,000 a year for life. The granddaughter was provided for before Cissy died. Josephine Patterson Reeve Albright, another niece, was given the ranch at Jackson Hole, Wyoming. A Maryland neighbor, Ann Bowie Smith, was willed the magnificent Dower House with all its lands and accoutrements, including a huge hothouse wherein Cissy had raised prize orchids. Evie Robert, who had given Cissy so many laughs in life, became owner of her fabled black pearls, a sable scarf, and a half-a-million-dollar slice of Connecticut Avenue. Rhoda Christmas, who wrote about horses and dogs for the *Times-Herald,* wound up with Cissy's horses and dogs and was admonished in the will not to sell any of them and to "put them to death painlessly" when she felt their times had come. Margaret Barney, the diminutive personal secretary who had been at Cissy's side for years, was awarded a diminutive $10,000.

On successive days in September of the same year, Felicia contested the will on the grounds that her mother was demented when she drew it, Betty Hynes died beside a row of emptied sleeping pill bottles, and Charles B. Porter, Cissy's former treasurer at the paper, dived to his death through a screened window of his room in a cheap Clarksburg, West Virginia, hotel. (Later, big and handsome Joe Brooks, a trustee of Cissy's estate and one-time husband of Alicia Patterson, committed suicide.)

Felicia's petition charged that her mother was "not of sound mind" when the will was drawn two years before her death, and that "undue influence, duress, and coercion" had been brought to bear, by persons unnamed, to cause Cissy to sign the document. She asked for a jury trial of the unnamed Svengalis. After some weeks of dreary charges and countercharges the heirs to the *Times-Herald* silenced her with a lump sum of $400,000.

Friends of Betty Hynes had found her ill and distressed after publication of the will showed that she—who had worked so hard for Cissy—had been forgotten. She believed, and had reason to believe, that Cissy planned to help her pay the mortgage on a home she had purchased in Georgetown, in which she died.

Porter's death was harder to fathom. It remains something of a mystery. Drew Pearson, among others, contested the suicide conclusion reached by the Clarksburg police.

"Apparently some people believed Porter knew too much," he wrote darkly. "The circumstances surrounding Porter's death are strange indeed, including the fact that he jumped or was pushed through a window screen. This is not an ordinary act of suicide."

Like so many others, Porter had been in and out of Cissy's favor since their association began. Precisely where he stood with her at the time of her death has never been clarified. On the day the will was printed in the *Times-Herald,* Porter dispatched a long letter to a young friend named Roland De Corneille, a divinity student. It read, in part:

> E.P. was out to destroy me. That is certain. Dr. [deleted] predicted that I would be called back to the *Times-Herald* for more slaughter. Always there were indications that it would be so.
>
> Her death stopped it. [The doctor] said: "You had better discuss with me here and now what you will do in such an eventuality." I told him I would never go back. He said, "Wise indeed, because the next time you would be destroyed."
>
> Today's *Times-Herald* prints the will *in extenso.* The name "C. B. Porter" is shown all along the line being eliminated. That would give E.P. strange delight. Perhaps there are others too who will enjoy it. A last attempt to carry over after death one's hates.
>
> I am relieved because E.P. would have hounded me through her life as long as I remained here in Washington. She was forever asking why I did not get out of the country. . . . Please keep this letter. I might want to end it some day in the future.

Actually, Porter saw Cissy just before her death, and it was agreed that he would return to the fold—but not in his former role as one of her trustees—after he took a short trip back to Scotland. He was a product of Edinburgh University, held a degree in criminology and in law. He joined the business office of the *Herald* in 1933, interested Cissy, and rapidly rose to the posts of treasurer, trustee, and loosely defined overseer of her personal fortune. He was a bachelor and— though he worked for a 110 per cent patriot—never yielded his British passport.

According to De Corneille, an Amherst Phi Beta Kappa whose college training had been underwritten by Porter, Porter came under heavy pressure from "a person highly connected with the *Times-Herald*" after Cissy's death when it became known he had in his possession many documents related to Cissy's fiscal affairs. He was also believed to be writing a book about her.

Porter's last movements and last testament appeared to contradict the image of a man at baleful odds with the Patterson Establishment.

According to Washington cabdriver Henry Shepherd, who drove Porter 140 miles from Washington to Keyser, West Virginia, a week before he died, the cab had been hired for the trip by Mrs. Sibilla Campbell, Cissy's housekeeper.

Porter's will, penned but not validated four days before his plunge, named Mrs. Campbell as his executrix. When informed of this, Mrs. Campbell at first expressed surprise. She told County Coroner Dr. Kenna Jackson that she and the dead man had never been close friends. When Dr. Jackson described over the phone the three packed bags found in Porter's room, Mrs. Campbell told him that the small black one belonged to her. She would send someone to Clarksburg to claim the broken corpse and the man's property, she promised. This was attended to the following day by Stanley Epstein and John T. Barger, *Times-Herald* men bearing a notarized note, on plain stationery, signed "Sibilla Campbell, executrix in the will of Charles Bell Porter." Still later, Mrs. Campbell's lawyer, Charles F. R. Ogilby of Washington, was court-appointed to administer Porter's estate, the will having been ruled invalid for lack of witness.

Wholly forgotten because of these dire aftermaths were Cissy's large bequests to "needy children, especially homeless and orphaned children, in order that they may have some measure of advantages enjoyed by children more fortunately situated."

Somewhat to the chagrin of *Times-Herald* newsmen and women and faithful executives who were given the back of Cissy's perfumed hand, in the will, the favored heirs fared well despite the burden of millionaire status. There were lurid reports at one point that Mason Peters, youngest and gayest of the lot, had been lost at sea while sailing the yacht he had acquired with his bonanza. Untrue. Mason came up dry and solvent. Then it was whispered, with many a "Didn't I tell you?" nod, that the bookies had picked Happy Robinson clean. Untrue. They dented him, but not deep enough to draw blood. Mike Flynn, everybody's favorite millionaire, lived out his remaining years in happy retirement, moving between Washington and Florida whenever the sun did.

All but inevitably, Frank Waldrop and Bill Shelton used their windfalls to build more substantial fortunes.

It was only natural that all who passed through Cissy's hands wondered whether at any time she ever toyed with the thought of including them in her unprecedented will. Terrible legends took shape after her death, as to why this or that one was ignored. The worst of these folk stories concerned Charles Duffy, Cissy's colorful and competent city editor during the paper's best days. Duffy was commissioned in the Navy at the time of Pearl Harbor and Cissy gave him a loving farewell. He emerged a full commander, was given a hero's reception when he returned to the city room, took an independent Irishman's discerning look at the obsequiousness of his troops whenever Cissy hove into view, said to hell with that, and went back into the Navy. He became a four-striper.

Then (the legend went) came the day he and his loving Irish wife were instructed by Cissy's executors to appear for the reading of the will. "You're mentioned in it," he is said to have been told. Then the reading: Cissy had left the paper to *eight* loyal employees, including Charles Duffy! The Duffys sat there immersed in tears of gratitude, their years of labor finally miraculously rewarded.

But the lawyer was still reading. And in time he is said to have come to a codicil which read, in effect, that this was the way Cissy wanted all things done with one exception: "Wherever the name Charles Duffy appears it shall be stricken."

There were less substantial legends. Cissy at one time had been attracted to Eugene Warner, the handsomest of her reportorial staff. One day she invited my wife and me to bring him along on a date we had with her at her Sands Point place. When we arrived, Cissy was seated next to her pool, brushing her magnificent hair. Her poodles were galloping about.

She waved us a pleasant welcome as we approached and called out to my wife, "Guess what the Old Bitch did today?"

Before my wife could inquire about Cissy's favorite poodle, Gene spoke up.

"That's easy, I see you've been swimming," he volunteered.

Turned out to be a somewhat chilly day. But if Warner ever wondered why he did not make the will, despite his understandable mixup on which bitch was which, it did not crush him. He later became vice president of McGraw-Hill.

Other and closer associates of Cissy who were excluded—men who meant as much to her success as DeWitt, Helgeson, sports columnist Vincent X. Flaherty, editorial assistant Dick Hollander, etc.—had one serious flaw in Cissy's curious mind: They left her for better jobs.

I speak with a measure of authority.

One day early in December, 1936, I received a wire from W. R. Hearst, Sr., asking me to come to New York the following day and meet with him at his suite in the Ritz-Tower. ". . . with a view to working with the New York *American*." The reaction around the *Herald* was a warmhearted one. "A wire like that is like money in the bank," Mike Flynn said when he read it. "Ask him for at least three-fifty a week, to start. Salary doesn't mean anything to Hearst, if he wants you." I was making $140 at the *Herald*.

Cissy seemed delighted. "Another one of my boys has made the big time," she said. I must come by Dupont Circle that evening when she called Hearst in New York.

I did. The champagne was nicely iced in a bucket near her favorite divan. We sipped as she put in the call to New York, and after a bit I could hear Mr. Hearst's surprisingly little voice spilling out of the receiver. Cissy said some very flattering things about me, urging "Pay him well, W.R., he's a poor boy," and concluded with an astonishing statement.

"One more thing about him, W.R.," Cissy said into the phone, "he's my illegitimate son by Calvin Coolidge."

I went to New York the next morning, met and was deeply impressed by Mr. Hearst (who flustered me by repeatedly calling me *Mr.* Considine), and was directed to go to the office of one of the empire's top nabobs, J. D. Gortatowsky, where the contract was awaiting signature.

It called for $140 a week.

I thanked Mr. Gortatowsky, asked him to thank Mr. Hearst for me, and told him I was returning home to my job in Washington. On the train en route I wrote a sports column from some notes I had taken during an interview with a stern-looking little Japanese diplomat a few days before. The gist of the column was that the Japanese game of judo is not so much a sport as it is a demonstration that a fast and determined man, striking without telegraphing his attack, can defeat a much bigger and less alert man.

I took a cab from the station to the *Herald* and tossed my column on the desk of Bernie Harter, the sports editor, and told him I had turned down the New York *American* offer. Bernie was getting red in the face by now, and making voice-clearing sounds.

"Bob, I can't print this," he said, nodding at the column. "Mrs. Patterson sent me a memo today saying that you are off the payroll and nothing more of yours can ever be printed in the *Herald.*"

I was out of work. All efforts made to reach her, even by phone, were fruitless. But finally Miss Barney, the secretary, gave me the Word.

"She's mad at you because you *wanted* to leave the Herald," she said.

And that's how I happened to go to work in New York. For $140 a week.

I never expected or especially wanted to see Cissy again. But some months later she called me from Washington as if she were still my illegitimate mother.

"Did you see what that [censored] brother of mine, Joe, wrote in his editorial in the *News* today?" she asked indignantly. I had. It was a piece which called the elder Mr. Hearst a faker.

"Well!" Cissy said, in her best "they can't do that to me" manner. "That [deleted] Joe Patterson forgets that I've got a newspaper, too, and that I'm not going to stand by and see anybody—including my brother—say anything bad about that dear W.R. I'm going to devote an entire page to him. I've written the eight-column streamer already: 'A Tribute to a Great American—W. R. Hearst.' I've sent Jackie Martin out to San Simeon for a new picture. It's going to be wonderful. I'll show that [unprintable] brother of mine!"

I asked her what this had to do with me.

"Silly, I want you to write all the nice words on the page," Cissy
said, as if I should have known all along.

I worked for a month on the assignment, in addition to my regular
work in New York as a sports columnist and feature writer. The research involved a lot of reading and talks with a number of Mr.
Hearst's old associates, including the legendary S. S. Carvalho, about
the first associate he had when he stormed New York late in the nineteenth century. My article ran twenty typewritten pages, and it was
with a feeling of mingled relief and pride that I sent it off to Cissy in
Washington, airmail, special delivery, registered.

Three silent weeks passed. Then I called her. Had she received it?
Yes. Well, what did she think? There was a pained pause.

"Bob, I'm so sorry," Cissy said. "I lost it before I could read it.
Would you possibly have made a carbon copy of it?"

I had, and rushed it to Washington.

Three even more silent weeks went by. Again I called. Had she
received it? Yes! Had she read it? Yes!

"Not only read it, Bob," she said, making my head swim, "but it's
simply great! I've never read anything about W.R. quite like it. You
looked into that great man's soul."

There was time for a sigh of happiness before I asked her when she
was going to run the big tribute.

It seemed a lifetime before she answered.

"Bob," she said, "I'm not going to run it."

I couldn't believe her. But why? *Why?*

Cissy cleared her throat.

"I made up with Joe," she said.

She was saying something else and I was not listening attentively.

"What was that?" I asked, a trifle numbly.

"I was saying that I know how hard you worked on this and that
I want to pay you for all your pains," she said. "How much do you
want?"

I answered somewhat haughtily that I did not want anything. I
would charge it off to experience.

"Well, I know how we can do it," Cissy said. "Let's think of it as
you'd think of a magazine piece. What did you make from your last
article in *Cosmopolitan?*"

I said, "Mrs. Patterson, I made seven hundred and fifty for my last article in *Cosmopolitan,* but that has nothing to do with a piece about Hearst that you don't need. Please skip it. Forget it. Good-bye."

Several days later I received a letter from her. Enclosed was a check for $500. There was a note attached. It read:

"Dear Bob:
  I *called* Cosmo.
        Affectionately,
            Cissy."

3. *New York*

I HAD LONGED for New York for years, had dreamed of riding into it triumphantly, wanted, heralded, able to dictate the terms of its surrender. But Cissy's petulant rug-pulling deprived me of leverage, upended me. Reversing a classic humiliation, I was ridden *into* town on a rail.

New York, the newcomer soon learns, never adjusts itself to him; he adjusts himself to it.

Some are driven mad by its breathtaking bigness. On my first assignment to cover a fight at Madison Square Garden, I found myself seated in the press section next to a shabby-looking little guy. I introduced myself.

"Yeah, I heard about you," he said. "New, huh? Well, boy, you've got a lot to learn about New York. But it's a great feeling when you finally learn the ropes. I get over here from Staten Island, that's where my paper is, at least four or five times a year. Coming across, I always stand up in the front of the ferry. I look at the skyline, all lighted up. Then I shake my fist at it and I say to myself, 'I licked that!' "

I never saw him again, and that was 1937.

The adjustment process can take ludicrous turns. It is quite hard to learn to walk faster than the gait you have chosen as the speed at which you prefer to march through life. Until I picked up the pace, I had the uneasy feeling that New Yorkers walking behind me, and always gaining, were of a mind to walk right up my back, jump off my shoulders, and continue on their way without breaking stride. I was a slowly tumbling stone gathering moss in a churning millrace.

The speedy New Yorker is not necessarily going any place. He has simply been wound up to maintain a velocity in consonance with that of his fellow New Yorkers and maintains it to the death.

There were adjustments to be made in the matter of dress. I didn't know until I met Mark Hanna, the pin-neat agent for Quentin Reynolds and other well-known figures like Leo Durocher, that it was gauche to wear a blue shirt after sundown. Some years later, after Mark's funeral services at Campbell's, several of the members of the funeral party walked briskly to the nearest bar. It is in the Stanhope Hotel on Fifth Avenue, and the only time it loses its built-in decorum, as sterile as that of the neighboring funeral parlor, is when it is visited by mourners.

"How about that creep who did the eulogy, calling Hanna 'Mr. New York'?" Toots Shor grumbled, stirring his brandy and soda with a stout forefinger.

"Yeah," said Jack O'Connell, then editor of *Cosmopolitan,* "and all the business about the great things he did for his clients." He looked at me. "What did he ever do for you?" Jack asked.

What I said made them laugh, but I meant it from the heart.

"Mark taught me not to wear white shoes in New York," I said.

The atmosphere of working in New York was so different. On the *Herald* one thought of himself as an inhabitant of an atoll at the extreme end of the Hearst archipelago. We were under a benevolent trusteeship, seldom involved with central authority. The *American* was at the heart of the Establishment.

That courtly disciplinarian, Ed Frayne, placed strange store on his staff's reporting to work each day at 3 P.M., if the staff member was not on specific assignment in or out of the city. He frowned through his heavy lenses if the lesser members of his stable called him and said, for example, "I'm uptown, Ed. Is it okay if I drop by Jimmy Johnston's office at the Garden and see what I can pick up?"

No, I soon learned, that was not the way to do it. One came down to the *American* by three o'clock. It was a chore at any time of day or night, if the price of a cab ride was prohibitive. Arthur Brisbane had urged the selection of a site on South Street, downwind from the Fulton Fish Market, and we accepted as Gospel the malicious whisper that he also had an interest in the construction firm that won the bid from the incredibly patient Mr. Hearst. We believed, too, the story that Mr. Hearst had paid only one visit to his multimillion dollar eyesore. That solitary visit ended, it was said, several feet inside the cramped little lobby. At that point, the legend went, Mr. Hearst made an abrupt 180 degree turn, walked to his limousine, and was never seen again around the premises.

Whatever, Ed Frayne must have liked it, because he was so determined that we share it with him by no later than 3 P.M. each day. There would be a short round of pleasantries and story suggestions. Then, and only then, would Ed approve any "Is it okay if I drop by Jimmy Johnston's . . . ?" proposals. And you'd head uptown again via the rattly *American* shuttle bus to City Hall, a walk over to Chambers Street for the Eighth Avenue subway, express to Forty-second, and local to Fiftieth. Sometimes Jimmy would have had his traditional afternoon tea and departed. But, at least, the three o'clock crisis had been faced and resolved.

My first good assignment was the fight between Joe Louis and Bob Pastor at Madison Square Garden. Pastor put up a surprising resistance to the great young Negro who was soon—the following June—to win the heavyweight title from Jim Braddock (under circumstances that imperiled my job, by the way).

Pastor set out to last the full ten rounds of the Garden fight and succeeded. He was in reverse gear through much of the fight, but switched and charged now and then and bloodied Louis' nose. The packed house bellowed, scenting an extraordinary upset. Louis was given the decision after ten rounds, which was proper, but there was no question that Pastor had infuriated and embarrassed him. Only a strong finish had sufficed.

Typewriters on all sides of me began to be belabored by more experienced sportswriters the moment the decision was announced by Harry Balogh. But my fingers became becalmed after typing my byline. Here was my big chance, and I had come up empty. I stared at the barren page through distressed exhalations of cigarette smoke. The sound of the surehanded industry around me grew alarming. My Western Union operator sat there vamping with his key and trying not to look at me.

Miserably, I plagiarized myself. I fell back on a lead I had written a year or two before to describe an obscure fight in a dismal former brewery named Portner's Arena, in Alexandria, Virginia. In its original form, the tired little lead read: "Brushing away the crimson cloud that steamed from his battered nose, Joe Blow made Herman Bananas pay dearly for his indiscretions last night at Portner's Arena."

The story did not attract so much as a postcard, nor any verbal comment.

But that was not the case with the lead I wrote that night at the Garden: "Brushing away the crimson cloud that steamed from his battered nose, Joe Louis made Bob Pastor pay dearly for his indiscretions last night at Madison Square Garden."

Frayne was delighted. Damon Runyon, who had moved over to writing a general column, but kept his hand in the sports department, so long his preserve, wrote a report or letter to the great old Hearst editor, Edmond D. "Cobbie" Coblentz, Hearst's liaison with his publishers and other editors, about the new crop of Hearst sportswriters. Excerpt: "One of them, a chap we've already got—Considine. I think he will be a corker when he gets his sights adjusted. He is terrifically ambitious and a hard worker."

I got some mail, too, about the Louis-Pastor story. But as heady as it was, for a newcomer, it was clear that genius had not spurred this response. What had spurred it was New York . . . Madison Square Garden . . . instantly recognizable gladiators.

The experience came back to me when, shortly after that, Frayne handed me the annual Westminster Kennel Club dog show at the Garden. In Washington I had covered a much lesser mutt meet and had caused something of a ripple, at least in church circles, by getting away with a story that began: "Ch. Beauregard van Updyke of Terwilliger, a son of a bitch named Ch. Imogene Brockstine Agincourt, took Best-of-Breed in the Yorkshire class last night at the Auditorium."

With names and locale stepped up to the big leagues, my name would soon be on every New Yorker's lips. I thanked Ed for the assignment and prepared to depart from South Street to the yip-laced Garden.

"One last thing," Ed said, stopping me at the door. "Don't knock Kerry Blues."

To my astonishment, he was serious.

"I don't think I ever knocked a Kerry Blue in my life," I swore.

"Well, don't start tonight," Ed said.

It was not too much to ask.

"Why?"

Ed gazed at me solemnly.

"Mrs. Hearst, senior, has a Kerry Blue," he said.

Doomed, so far as a replay on the son-of-a-bitch theme was concerned, I went to work.

It was a vaguely troubled time, those cold winter months in early 1937. Millie and I missed Washington. We had acquaintances now, and though they were better known than our friends in Washington and nice to us when we occasionally met, we missed the older and truer ties. There wasn't enough money to take care of living costs in New York. We now had our infant son, Michael Riley (named, respectively, for Monsignor—later Bishop—Michael Ready and the baby's godfather, George Riley). We also had a wonderful nurse-cook named Veronica, and an apartment off Central Park West, after a cramped sojourn at the Hotel New Yorker.

It was that same winter that I managed to offend the undisputed star of our organization, Runyon. That was not particularly difficult. The creator of all those tough-tender Broadway characters was as thin-skinned as an aging Met soprano. He had everything his less distinguished colleagues might have wished for: prestige in the newspaper business, in magazines, and in Hollywood. He dressed expensively and well. (Hype Igoe, the New York *Journal*'s pixie boxing writer, broke in Runyon's custom-made shoes for him.) He was fussed over by owners and headwaiters at Lindy's, to which he gave great if passing fame as the Mindy's of his Broadway stories, the Stork Club, and wherever else he chose to patronize. He knew and was respected by a huge cross section of the citizenry, ranging from President Roosevelt to Al Capone, with whom he had a closer affinity. He was married to a still-beautiful ex-showgirl, his second wife, maintained a fine apartment at the Parc Vendome in Manhattan, and owned a white plaster jewel box of a home on one of the better islands in Biscayne Bay.

My troubles with him emerged, preposterously enough, from a small get-together Millie and I had at our apartment for a few equally impoverished yet hopeful friends in sportswriting, among them our friends from Washington, Dick and Mary McCann. Mary was Damon's daughter by his first wife. My wife and I had reason to believe that he treated his daughter, son-in-law, and Damon, Jr., with something considerably less than paternal affection. He just didn't give a damn, but we stood steadfastly in awe of the summits he had scaled by his drive and talent.

"I'd sure like to be able to cover a range like that," I said in the course of many tributes to him uttered during our party. There were fervent amens from all sides. A few weeks later, Mary, who hadn't been feeling too well, was at our apartment again.

"I told Daddy about what you said about him," Mary said.

"Oh? Was he pleased?"

"No, he didn't like it one little bit," Mary said.

I was suddenly alarmed.

"What did you tell him?" I asked.

"What you said," Mary said. "That you're out after his job."

There was nothing to say to her or to her father. So we had another Manhattan. We drank them, even after dinner, in those days.

Next, there was a piece I felt compelled to write for the "Home Magazine," a supplement in each Saturday edition of the New York *Journal* and the Chicago *Herald-American*. There was civil war in the boxing business at the time. The Garden, with Johnston as its current matchmaker, had ruled the game at its highest level since Tex Rickard's day as promoter of Jack Dempsey's early fights and his two memorable ten-rounders against Gene Tunney. After Tunney's retirement, the game began to disintegrate under the combined assaults of the Depression and less entrancing champions and contenders. Max Schmeling won the title in the finals of a loose elimination tournament when Jack Sharkey may or may not have fouled him in the fourth round of their fight. Brisbane's shouts of "Foul!" from ringside may have had as much to do with the referee's and the commission doctor's decision as Max's dented aluminum "cup" that protected his privates from blows below the belt line. Sharkey later won from Schmeling in fifteen rounds and lost to Primo Carnera under suspicious circumstances. Carnera was toppled by Max Baer in a kind of rehash of a movie they both played in called *The Prize Fighter and the Lady,* and Baer then lost to a solid underdog, Jim Braddock.

In the latter portion of that sequence, Joe Louis appeared, a product of a Golden Gloves tournament in Detroit. For reasons best known to the two suave Negroes who controlled him—John Roxborough of Detroit and Julian Black of Chicago—Louis cast his lot with the Twentieth Century Sporting Club. The ostensible head of the club was Mike Jacobs, who had been Rickard's trusted ticket scalper. His silent partners, it was eventually revealed in an explosive revelation by Harry Grayson, of the Scripps-Howard chain, were Runyon, Frayne, and the rollicking, hard-living Bill Farnsworth of the New

675085

York *Journal*. Each owned 25 per cent of Twentieth Century's stock. Louis was the company's goldmine, but the Garden controlled the heavyweight title's succession. The title belonged to Braddock, a poor drawing card. His obvious challenger was former champion Schmeling, who had catapulted back into prominence (to the joy of the Nazi Party) by giving Louis the worst beating of his life and knocking him out in the twelfth round of their 1936 fight.

Now, a year later, the Garden matched Braddock and Schmeling. From the start it was a forlorn gesture. I wrote a piece for the "Home Magazine" predicting that Schmeling would somehow be gypped out of his chance to become the first man ever to regain the heavyweight title. It turned out that way. Braddock obtained a Philadelphia court decision—the ruling was handed down by a Judge Fake—to fight Louis instead of Schmeling. Either would beat Jim for the title, but Louis was the more desirable conqueror. In the first place, "it would keep the title in America" instead of seeing it packed off to Hitler's Germany. In the second place, Louis was willing to give Braddock 10 percent of his ring earnings for the next ten years in payment for being granted the opportunity to flatten Jim.

The New York State Athletic Commission would not permit the Braddock-Louis fight to be held in the state, but Chicago gladly accepted it. The Garden went through with the pathetic pretense of a Braddock-Schmeling fight, even to the point of printing tickets for it. It was somehow fitting that the printer also gaffed. He spelled it "Schmelling."

As expected, Louis beat Braddock. There were moments of concern, however. Jim courageously decked the younger, stronger man for a two or three count in the first round. For the next six rounds Louis chopped him like a lumberjack would strip a great old oak of its limbs, one by one. In the eighth Joe hit him with a right hand that would have broken a moose's jaw. Jim crashed with a thud that shook the ring. It was a great night for all concerned: the new champion, his managers who cut him 50 percent, Mike Jacobs and his partners, and the loser—shorn of his title but now heir to 10 percent of Louis' purses for what looked like ten years of boom.

Runyon was angered and Frayne upset by the "Home Magazine" piece. They considered it "unloyal," and both stopped speaking to me. Farnsworth didn't give a damn. He liked to shock young sportswriters (and distress his associates) by boasting about a Cadillac he had bought in the immediate wake of a fight he had helped to promote for the benefit of Mrs. Hearst's Free Milk for Babies charity. Jacobs, too, remained friendly to me. He was as proud of the publicity my piece had given his iniquity as he was when he told me later, in the course of an interview for a magazine piece, that he had soaked Boo Boo Hoff, the Philadelphia mobster, $25,000 for twenty-five last-minute ringside seats for the first Dempsey-Tunney fight. (Boo Boo paid in thousand-dollar bills and was walking away with the tickets when Mike said to him, "Just a minute. The twenty-five grand was for getting the tickets for you. They're fifty bucks apiece." Boo Boo paid.)

Between the time the offending "Home Magazine" article appeared and the Braddock-Louis fight there were several reports that my days on the *American* were numbered; that Damon was going to have me fired. The charges were always vague, but depressing. As it turned out, it was the *American*'s days which were numbered. It succumbed to assorted ailments, man-made and banker-dictated, in June, 1937, a day or two after the Chicago title fight. As far as its sports section was concerned, the *American* went down with its flags flapping valiantly. It covered the Louis-Braddock fight with its varsity team: Runyon, Frayne, Sid Mercer, Jimmy Cannon, Bugs Baer, Bill Slocum, Sr., Lewis Burton, and me. In the tense minutes after the knockout, with all our typewriters going full tilt, Mercer's Western Union wire to New York broke down. Precious minutes passed while the operator worked fruitlessly to bring it back to life.

"Dammit, get that wire fixed or I'll miss an edition," Mercer snapped, writing against our deadline.

Cannon had a wry extension of that remark. Jimmy said, "Get that wire fixed or he'll miss a newspaper."

The afternoon *Journal,* which immediately became the *Journal-American,* got custody of most of the *American*'s best. I was shifted over to Hearst's morning *Mirror,* a hell-raising slapdash tabloid packed to its perpetually leaking seams with some of the worst and best journalism in New York. Its payroll was studded with the likes of Walter Winchell, Mark Hellinger, Jack Lait, Lee Mortimer, John McNulty, Jim Bishop, Jim Whittaker, Tex McCrary, who had been Brisbane's son-in-law, and good editors: Glenn Neville, George McDonald, Charlie Barth, Selig Adler, Mort Ehrman, Eddie Markell, and Hinson Styles.

The *Mirror*'s sports department was one of the most-admired and best-read (except by the proofreaders) of any in the land. It had the city's best horse handicapper, Fred Keats, an astral seer who had not set foot in the building for years, Murray Lewin, who had done some fighting and knew everybody in that bitter-sweet business, and talented baseball writers Ben Epstein (Yankees), Ken Smith (Giants), and Gus Steiger (Dodgers). Our rod and gun man, Jim Hurley, was considered the best of the lot. There was a covey of bright young men struggling up from copyboy status, Harold Weissman, John Hennigan, Leonard Lewin, Frank Blauschild, and Arthur Richman, a remarkable lad who chose to spend his vacations traveling with the acknowledged worst team in the majors, if not the world, the St. Louis Browns.

Holding the immediate reins on the staff were veteran toy department men, Bill Hennigan, Frank Kearns and Bill Carver, and over them sat the *Mirror*'s crowning anachronism, Clarence Cassin, head of the desk. He was a saintly soul put down by Providence into the profane bustle of tabloid journalism. No one in our department said even "Damn" more than once in his presence, for it upset him so much. It is questionable whether he ever even looked at some of the leg art which Manny Elkins and other fanciers among the picture editors assembled for each edition. Clarence set an example of diligence for all of us which few could or would emulate. Not for him the soothing dram after a long night's work; not for him the word that purged.

Not long after Braddock retired, after winning a surprising ten-rounder against Tommy Farr at the Garden, there was a report that he would try a comeback and even aim at a second fight against silent-partner Joe Louis. I asked Jim if it were true.

"Hell's bells, I'm not going to let them make a football outta my head," Jim said.

I used that quote as the lead on my story, turned it in to Clarence, and went my way. Clarence made only one change. He made it read: " 'Heck's bells, I'm not going to let them make a football outta my head,' Jim Braddock said yesterday."

Thus did piety persevere in one small corner of a babbling blat whose front page that very day may have proclaimed: "SEX FIEND SLAYS TOT."

Our proofreaders were sometimes less than abstemious. When Don McNeill, a handsome young man with flaxen hair, won the National

Indoor tennis championship, my lead sent from the Armory began: "Tow-headed Don McNeill blazed his way to victory yesterday . . ." It ran through all editions as: "Two-headed Don McNeill . . ."

The most astonishing coincidence of my life in newspaper work happened while on the *Mirror.* I wrote a lead about the victory the greatest U.S. polo team (led by Tommy Hitchcock and all ten-goalers) scored over a crack British team at Westbury, Long Island. It went: "Yankee Doodle went to town here today, a-ridin' on a polo pony."

At the other end of the press box, perhaps sixty yards away, the New York *Herald Tribune*'s Harry Cross simultaneously was writing: "Yankee Doodle went to town here today, a-ridin' on a polo pony."

It may have been the first reporting by ESP. Walter Winchell, no mean phrase maker himself, liked the lead. A few days later in his column in the *Mirror,* under a paragraph he called "Literary Lace," he warmly congratulated Harry Cross of the rival *Tribune* on his unique lead. It was never compulsory for *Mirror* writers to read other *Mirror* writers.

An air of the risqué and the rogue hung over the City Room. Jack Lait had engaged in countless larks and rumbles on Hearst's Chicago papers and never ran out of stories late at night, as long as the Cutty Sark, which he took neat, held out. Then there was Lee Mortimer, with whom Jack collaborated in several "Confidential"-type books that sold furiously and attracted some equally furious libel suits and threats of mayhem on sight. Indeed, Frank Sinatra did slug Mortimer. The *Mirror* wreaked a stern revenge. Frank's name was dropped from the agate-type "Birthday Greetings" which always concluded the daily prose and poetry turned out by the paper's poet laureate and radio columnist, Nick Kenny.

Both Hinson Stylcs and a good, hard-working, hard-drinking general assignments man named Walter Marshall were members of the Henry the Eighth club, a loosely knit, if not loosely living organization made up of men-about-town who had been married at least five times.

The *Mirror*'s most loyal readers were followers of Keats's race tips, and those dispensed by Ken Kling in his "Joe and Asbestos" strip. Through some unspelled-out alliance, beyond the control of the sports department, we also were the official record for the day's "number," at a time when countless millions of dollars were being wagered in dribs and drabs in the city's policy racket. We even carried tips on numbers concealed, more or less, in a delightful little single-column cartoon drawn by dapper Fred Weatherly, who kept his mustache waxed as if momentarily awaiting inspection by the colonel of the Coldstream Guards.

It is hard to believe, looking back, that the *Mirror* had a Society Editor. He was Howard Shelley. He came from quality folks and wrote under the name of Barclay Beekman. Almost every event he attended appeared to call for white tie and tails and decorations. The Horse Show at the Garden was hardly held to be constitutional unless Barclay was in his box, silk hat in place, Tiffany pencil and pad on his chubby little lap. He was a magnificent snob and possibly the most near-sighted of them all. At the opening of the Metropolitan's season he always took along a *Mirror* photographer, usually the hand-some and well-groomed Tony Sarno, and was more selective about the pictures he ordered than, say, his contemporary from the *New York Times*. As this or that superbly gowned lady emerged from her limousine, followed by a chivalrous escort, Barclay would bustle forward, search their faces from a range of a foot or two, then wheel and tell Sarno whether or not to waste a flashbulb.

"They're nobody!" Barclay would shout more often than not, thus saving money for Mr. Hearst, who was somewhat strapped financially at that stage of the Depression and that stage of his relationship with the Roosevelt Administration.

(We could never understand FDR's antipathy toward WRH. After all, Mr. Hearst had been largely instrumental in winning the 1932 nomination for him, by swinging California, and just about wholly instrumental in having him opposed four years later by Alf M. Landon. Very late on Election Night, 1936, Bill Hearst, Jr., and his brother John came into Jack White's Club 18 on Fifty-second Street while the floor show was blasting away. White rapped his cane on the floor, stopped the music and dancing, and announced, "Quiet, please! Here comes Maine and Vermont.")

For all his boorishness, Barclay Beekman was a sensitive soul. Late one night as I toiled, soiled, over some forgotten story, he loomed over my desk like the fairy godfather he was—resplendent in his working clothes. He didn't know my name, or maybe he thought I was the sterling young righthander for the Cleveland Indians.

"Feller," he said, crisply, and a bit lispingly, "did you ever know the Dowager Mrs. Cornelius Vanderbilt?"

Silently cursing my forebears for never having stolen a railroad, I muttered an apologetic No.

"Of course, you wouldn't," Barclay said, starting back to his desk. I tried to make amends.

"But I've met the Dowager Mrs. Chick Wergeles," I said to him, referring, of course, to the dear wife of one of the best fight-publicity men on Jacobs Beach.

Barclay Beekman, who looked a great deal like Queen Victoria, was not amused. He was hurt. Nor did he join in the hearty laughter when a 10 by 12 glossy print of him in his best white tie and tails was tacked on the City Room's bulletin board. Elkins' retouch artist had inked an ambassadorial ribbon across Barclay's starched chest. It read: "EAT AT JAKE'S."

He wouldn't return to work until he received an apology.

Our drama critic, Robert Coleman, came from a fine old Southern family, wrote pithy and nondrawling reviews, had the longest haircut in the world of the theater, and between his dandruff and the ashes that cascaded from the cigarette he always kept in his mouth, he sometimes resembled a snow-topped Alp on tour.

For all we knew, Coleman may have inspired one of Nick Kenny's most enduring bursts of blank verse:

> Snow fell from Heaven
> Like dandruff from God's shoulders.

George Clark, our Night Club Editor, was a sophisticated cynic who went in for king-sized cigarettes, an oddity at that time, and for light-hearted contempt. One day a Broadway impresario offered him a job as a press agent, at more money than the *Mirror* was paying him. George turned it down. It would mean leaving the *Mirror*.

"I've lived in a ho'house half my life, why should I now become a streetwalker?" George asked.

Every newspaper draws odd visitors, but the *Mirror* magnetized more than its just quota. One evening a disheveled man with a glazed look walked into the City Room. That in itself was not extraordinary. He might have been a rewrite man. But this one was different. He had a big ugly revolver in his paw and his finger was on the trigger. The only man in the room whose eyes were not riveted on the nut was

Charlie Barth. Charlie's head was bent over his makeup pad. He spent a lot of time each day deciding where each gem would be placed in the paper.

The man with the gun stood over Charlie, and in back of him. The gun seemed aimed directly at the back of Charlie's skull, like the crowning phase of a coup de grace.

"Which one is Jim Hurley?" the man with the gun asked.

Charlie never looked up. He waved idly in the direction of the sports department at the other end of the large room.

The man started across the room. All hands hit the deck and tried to squeeze under desks and tables.

Finally, in the hush of the ordinarily noisy room he bent down and poked his gun under a desk. It was Jim's desk and Jim was under it.

"Jim Hurley?"

"Don't shoot me," Jim said. "I have quite a family."

"Shoot *you*, Jim?" the man said, hurt. "You're my favorite writer. I just shot my wife and I come right here to give you the story."

Larry MacPhail, the mercurial man who was running the Brooklyn Dodgers at that stage in his life, dropped by the *Mirror* one night to see me. He wanted to shoot me for a story I had written about a bum deal he gave his first baseman, Dolph Camilli. I wasn't there.

"Sorry, he isn't in," Larry was told, very politely.

"Oh," he said, and went back to Brooklyn, consoled in all probability by the philosophy on which baseball is built: "Well, you can't win 'em all."

Along with countless thousands of others, I read the *Mirror* because of one man, Dan Parker.

He was the last and in my estimation the greatest of a breed of sports columnists who was prepared to back up anything he wrote, not with a lawyer but with his bulk, heart, and, on occasion, fists. He was in the tradition of Bat Masterson, Sheriff Bill McGeehan, Boze Bulger, Dave Egan (who editorially asked for contributions to a fund for a Boston cabdriver who ran over Casey Stengel), and Tommy Laird (who didn't like something a San Francisco Seals player shouted at him, tore out of the press box, picked up a bat, and chased the terrified player the length of the field and out the center field gate).

Incorruptible Dan Parker wore no man's collar. Let the business office clutter his sports pages with the ads of the horse-touting services and Dan would continue blasting them in his column. Let Jimmy

Johnston threaten him with multimillion dollar suits or physical harm (which was ludicrous in view of Dan's 6-feet-5 altitude and 230-pound tonnage) and Dan would continue to refer to the bantam-sized promoter as the Boy Bandit.

Everybody wrote that Primo Carnera was controlled by The Mob, but Dan named the mobsters. One of them who came under Dan's withering scorn sent a platoon of goons to Times Square one night to buy up and tear up all copies of the *Mirror* delivered to the area's newsstands. Dan called Carnera a tottering tower of Gorgonzola whose opponents were bribed or terrorized into taking dives. Then one tense night the two men met on stage at a New York Boxing Writers banquet. Dan was the only sportswriter in the land big enough to look Primo straight in the eye. For a moment the two stood facing one another in the suddenly quiet place. Primo then assumed a fighting stance. Dan promptly extended his hands, like a kid about to plunge into a swimming pool, and dived onto the stage, which all but brought down the house, literally. It was the perfect pantomime of any of Primo's fixed fights.

Dan could use his hands in earnest, too. Somewhere in the course of his hammer-and-tongs writings he sideswiped the New York *Enquirer's* Marcus Griffin, a biographer of Jimmy Johnston. After a period of wrangle in print and over the phone, Dan sent him a note saying that the next time their paths crossed, he, Dan, would take great pleasure in flattening him. Their paths crossed in the crowded press rows at Mike Jacobs' Tournament of Champions, a unique boxing show featuring four title fights. Dan and I were seated side by side. The action in the ring was fast and furious, the noise was great, but Dan heard his name being mentioned roughly.

He turned his head. Marcus Griffin was the one using his name. Dan stood up, knocked Marcus down with a single right-hand punch to the jaw, sat back down, and continued writing. He had hardly missed a sentence of the action in the ring. He continued working subsequently when the loser of the short-lived fight returned with a cop and demanded Dan's arrest on the spot. The cop was delighted to meet Dan in person. He was such a fan that for a moment it appeared that he might arrest Marcus for momentarily disturbing Dan's train of thought.

But virility was only one of Parker's gifts. He had the most delightful sense of humor of anybody in his field and possibly the truest ear for the language—the many languages of sports people, for that matter—since Lardner. Dan framed classic, imaginary dialogues between announcer Harry Balogh (who once introduced thirty-three-year-old Gus Lesnevich: "And now—a man who, like old wine, goes on forever. . . .") and fight publicist Mushky Jackson ("George Washington slept right here in Pompton Lakes. . . . You know Washington, dontcha? He freed the slaves.") He interviewed at hilarious length a hypothetical Greek dialectician whose hero was Jimmy (Dan spelled it Dzimmy) Londos.

Dan heard, and presented to the American language, fight manager Joe Jacobs' shuddering remark during a terribly cold World Series game in Detroit: "I shoulda stood in bed!" He heard the guy yell from the top gallery at the Garden at two fighters who had failed to throw a single punch halfway through the first round: "Hit him now, y'bum, y'got the wind witcha!" He duly noted for posterity Charley Dressen's elegy, "The Giants is dead."

Dan knocked out many a critic with a single written punch, too. A particularly obnoxious radio sportscaster named Bert somebody wired him, "Listen to my program tonight. I'm going to knock your brains out." Dan printed the telegram and commented, "Why should I double his Hooper rating?" He printed other abusive letters, if they were signed, and would add, "I returned the gentleman's letter with a suggestion as to where on his person he might best deposit it."

The *Mirror,* in which many a fish was wrapped and many a subway car littered, became a collector's item whenever Dan's muse moved him to verse. The presence of a Jewish bronco buster from the Bronx at the Garden's Rodeo caused Dan to pen a rhymed saga that began:

> I'm an old cow hand
> From the Concourse Grand.

It ended, many marvelous lines later, with:

> Yipee, ei ei—oy oy!

*Mirror*s were hard to find every March 17 because, as any fool knew, that would be the day Dan's St. Patrick's Day Parade poem would be printed. The scholarship of his effort that day was worthy of Padraic Colum and was as saucy as G. B. Shaw. Dan knew the prides, prejudices, failings, and foibles of every county whose colors were marched past the Cardinal.

But he reserved his best for boxing. As if in gratitude for his genius, boxing gave Dan the one, the only, Tony Galento. Dan wrote volumes about that incredible fat, hairy gladiator-bartender from Orange, New Jersey. The one sample picked by W. C. Heinz in his masterful *Fireside Book of Boxing* concerned Tony's fight against a harmless setup named Charley Massera. Dan sang:

> Oh, Tony Galento, he trains on pimento
> And gargles the ale when it's cool.
> My pronunciamento concerning Galento
> Is: "Switch to that pasta fazoole!"
> They say a left hook
> To the chops closed the book
> Of the prize fighter Charley Massera.
> Though it may not have landed
> It left Charley stranded.
> (And how is your dear old Aunt Sarah?)

It was Dan's kind of fight, and Tony's, for that matter:

> Outside the Orange Armory thousands lingered, hoping to hear the thud. Everyone knew Massera was going out like an empty beer barrel, the only element of doubt being "when?"

> Tony's belly rolled like jelly
> And Massera's fist
> Bounced into it—almost through it—
> Right up to the wrist.

As a boxer, Tony uses the Ely Culbertson, or approach system. He approaches an opponent wide open, as if inviting a liver massage. After getting what he wants, he switches to the Irish attack, better known as "The back of me fisht to you!" Next, he tries "The Shoemaker's Revenge," or "Giving It the Heel." Two rounds of this and Tony decided the customers had had enough. Did I say Tony? I meant Charley. One of Tony's left hooks landed somewhere—no one is quite sure—and Charley landed on his haunches. He's up. He's down. He's out. It all happened in 45 seconds. Yussel Jacobs, in Tony's corner, summed it up succinctly when he warbled: "He certainly stood down the second time when you left him have that left."

Some of the boys said Charley almost choked on his mouthpiece after he had been counted out. If he did, it was from laughing.

Tony was back behind the bar in his white apron, with most of the grease wiped off him, in about ten minutes, and from then until dawn his cash register burned out six bearings handling the biggest night's trade in the history of the jernt.

I was immensely proud of being on the same sports section with Dan Parker. He was great to work for, kind, considerate, and helpful when his advice was sought. Then one day, about a year after I went to work for the *Mirror,* Dan stopped speaking to me. For a day or two I supposed his ulcer was acting up again and that he was sore at the world in general. When it became abundantly clear that he was angry with only one guy in that world, me, I went into his office.

"What's up?"

"I'd rather not talk about it," Dan said, concentrating on a column he was writing.

"I've got to know, Dan," I said.

He paused for a long time, then turned in his chair and looked at me.

"I don't like what you've been saying around town," he said.

I asked him what I had been saying around town.

"That you're going to get my job," Dan said evenly.

The emotion that immersed me was not anger. It was disappointment.

When I could speak, I said, "Do you believe that, Dan? If you do, I don't want to work for you. You know damned well that I couldn't carry your jock strap."

Dan sighed. "I don't know what to believe . . ." He turned back to his typewriter.

"I can't leave it hanging like that, Dan. I've got to know who gave you that story. I have a right to know."

Dan must have thought so, too.

"Damon Runyon," he said.

I just didn't know what to say to him, so I walked out and went back to work. The frost stayed on the pumpkin as the date of the second Louis-Schmeling fight approached. I wanted to be there at ringside when it happened, having covered most of Joe's fights either for the Washington *Herald* or the New York *American.* But such was the spell that Runyon could exert, even over an honest sports editor like Dan Parker, that it was questionable up to a late hour whether there would be any need for me at the fight. Dan, of course, would do the lead story. That was proper and the best thing that could happen for the paper. Murray Lewin would do the expert story, and the dressing rooms would be adequately covered.

Dan did me a favor, unexpectedly. I could cover the fight for the *Mirror* with a feature. I sat behind him at what turned out to be Louis' finest hour or, rather, his finest two minutes and four seconds. When it was finished, and the ecstasy of the stadium had swept over and inoculated the reporters at ringside, Dan turned to me and shook my hand warmly. It was like a reprieve from the Governor. I sat back down and wrote a feature. It went like this:

> Listen to this, buddy, for it comes from a guy whose palms are still wet, whose throat is still dry, and whose jaw is still agape from the utter shock of watching Joe Louis knock out Max Schmeling.
>
> It was, indeed, a shocking thing, that knockout—short, sharp, merciless, complete. Louis was like this:
>
> He was a big lean copper spring, tightened and retightened through weeks of training until he was one pregnant package of coiled venom.
>
> Schmeling hit that spring. He hit it with a whistling right-hand punch in the first minute of the fight—and the spring, tormented with tension, suddenly burst with one brazen spang of activity. Hard brown arms, propelling two unerring fists, blurred beneath the hot white candelabra of the ring lights. And Schmeling was in the path of them, a man caught and mangled in the whirring claws of a mad and feverish machine.
>
> The mob, biggest and most prosperous ever to see a fight in a ball yard, knew that here was the end before the thing had really started. It knew, so it stood up and howled one long shriek. People who had paid as much as $100 for their chairs didn't use them—except perhaps to stand on, the better to let the sight burn forever in their memories.
>
> There were four steps to Schmeling's knockout. A few seconds after he landed his only real punch of the fight, Louis caught him with a lethal little left hook that drove him into the ropes so hard that his right arm hooked over the top strand, like a drunk hanging on to a fence. Louis swarmed over him and hit Max with everything he had—until Referee Donovan pushed him away and counted one.

Schmeling staggered away from the ropes at that, dazed and sick. He looked drunkenly toward his corner, and before he had turned his head back Louis was on him again, first with a left and then with an awe-provoking right that made a crunching sound when it hit the German's jaw. Max fell down, hurt and giddy, for a count of three.

He clawed his way up as if the night air were as thick as black water, and Louis—his nostrils like the mouth of a double-barreled shotgun—took a quiet bead and let him have both barrels.

Max fell almost lightly, bereft of his senses, his fingers touching the canvas like a comical stewbum doing his morning exercises, knees bent and tongue lolling in his head.

He got up long enough to be knocked down again, this time with his dark unshaven face pushed in the sharp gravel of the resin.

Louis jumped away lightly, a bright and pleased look in his eyes, and as he did the white towel of surrender which Louis' handlers had refused to use two years ago tonight [when Max beat Joe so badly] came sailing into the ring in a soggy mess. It was thrown by Max Machon, oblivious to the fact that fights can no longer end this way in New York.

The referee snatched it off the floor and flung it backwards. It hit the ropes and hung there, limp as Schmeling. Donovan counted up to five over Max, sensed the futility of it all, and stopped the fight.

The big crowd began to rustle restlessly toward the exits, many only now accepting Louis as champion of the world. There were no eyes for Schmeling, sprawled on his stool in his corner.

He got up eventually, his dirty gray and black robe over his shoulders, and wormed through the happy little crowd that hovered around Louis. And he put his arm around the Negro and smiled. They both smiled and could afford to—for Louis had made around $200,000 for two minutes and four seconds and Schmeling $100,000.

But once he crawled down in the belly of the big stadium, Schmeling realized the implications of his defeat. He, who won the title on a partly phony foul, and beat Louis two years ago with the aid of a crushing punch after the bell had sounded ending a critical round, now said Louis had fouled him. That would read better in Germany, whence earlier in the day had come a cable from Hitler, calling on him to win.

It made a couple of anthologies, including *A Treasury of Great Reporting,* assembled for Simon and Schuster by Columbia's Prof. Richard B. Morris and CCNY's Louis L. Snyder, and another by Frank Luther Mott, dean of Missouri's School of Journalism. But it never would have been written if Parker had not given me the opportunity.

The sports beat was an entrancing one in the last days of peace leading up to World War II. Paul Gallico's thesis in his memorable *Farewell to Sports,* to the effect that the Golden Age of Sports had turned to dross, found itself under attack in every field. We had no Ruth, Gehrig, or Grove, but we had DiMaggio, Williams, and Feller. We had no Dempsey, Tunney, or Greb, but we had Louis, Henry Armstrong, and Ray Robinson. Bobby Jones and Walter Hagen were gone, but in their stead stood Sam Snead, Byron Nelson, and a struggling young pro named Ben Hogan. Red Grange, Jim Thorpe, and Bronco Nagurski had vanished, but Sammy Baugh, Sid Luckman, and Don Hutson somehow sufficed. Big Bill Tilden and Little Bill Johnston had left the center court, replaced by pulverizing Ellsworth Vines, Don Budge and Jack Kramer. Helen Wills, Suzanne Lenglen, and Joyce Wethered had called it a day, and now we turned handsprings over Alice Marble, Pauline Betz, and Babe Didrikson. We had no Earl Sande, but there was a boy around who showed great promise named Eddie Arcaro. Man o' War was down on the farm in Lexington, but the youngest of his countless sons, War Admiral, was doing him proud—and then a beast named Whirlaway came along who could run faster (and wider) than both of them.

We had carry-over and developing sportswriters to tell the world about this transition from what Paul Gallico called the Golden Age and Westbrook Pegler, "The Era of Wonderful Nonsense."

All Gaul may have been divided into three parts, but Pegler's Law ruled that sportswriting could be divided into but two: the Gee Whiz group and the Aw Nuts clan. Unchallenged head of the former classification was Grantland Rice. He was the dearest, most gentle, and most successful man in the craft. He was extraordinarily kind and helpful to young and uncertain newcomers. He would spot a yearning younker on the edge of the crowd that always assembled around him during bull-session time and with an easy sweep of his arm bring him into the conversation, somehow remember his name. "What do *you* think about what we've been talking about, Bob (Joe, Bill, Ralph, Homer . . .)?

Bill Corum was much the same kind of openhearted, good-talking, good-drinking man, ready to pick up his battered portable and go anywhere in the land where the action was fast. And where the horses were fast. Bill could write warmly about every sport and all the people in each sport. But his heart belonged to racing. In his final year of covering the Kentucky Derby he picked the first four to finish in perfect order: Ponder, Capot, Palestinian, and Rockport. Ponder paid $34 to win, $11.60 to place, and $6.20 to show; Capot, $9.60 and $5.80; and Palestinian, $4.80. The favorite of the crowd of 100,000, Olympia, with Eddie Arcaro up, went off at 4 to 5 and finished far up the track. The mathematics department of Bill's alma mater, Columbia, asked by *Journal-American* sports editor Max Kase to calculate the odds against such an astonishing feat, threw up its hands in defeat. Bill never covered another Derby. He couldn't, because Churchill Downs made him president of the track.

John Kieran, whose authorship of the *New York Times*'s sports column spanned the transitional years, was the intellectual the fraternity always pointed to when we needed evidence to prove that mentally we were a cut above the status of arrested development. The New Yorkese flavor of his speech contrasted his immense scholarship. Patronizingly introduced by the stuffy headmaster of a fashionable prep school, John unconcernedly addressed the boys in Latin. He was as sweet-tempered and unassuming as Rice. One day, seated next to him at a noisy World Series game in Yankee Stadium, I noticed that between innings he'd put his nose into an antique book whose leather flaked on touch. I asked him what he was reading. "It's *Curiosities of Literature,*" John said. Hearing no response, he added helpfully, "By Isaac D'Israeli." John still wanted to help. "You know," he said, as if I were feigning ignorance, "Disraeli's father."

There were so many of these good men still around in those days, each with a helping hand outstretched, each more interested in boosting than knocking.

I think now of Frank Graham, who never wished to offend a player he was interviewing by pulling a pad and pencil, but who could later write everything the man had said and without a flaw. Frank, too, was one with Rice. So were other old-timers around the town and country: Harry Salsinger and Sam Greene in Detroit, George Cairns and

Austen Lake in Boston, Ed Danforth and O. B. Keeler in Atlanta, Fred Russell in Nashville, Sec Taylor in Des Moines, George Barton in Minneapolis, Curley Grieve in San Francisco, Jimmy Burns in Miami, Jimmy Isiminger and Red Smith in Philadelphia, John Carmichael and T-Bone Otto in Chicago, Gordon Cobbledick in Cleveland, Havey Boyle and Chet Smith in Pittsburgh, Red McQueen in Hawaii, Buck O'Neill in Washington, Roy Stockton and Jim Gould in St. Louis, Royal Brougham in Seattle, and in New York men of the caliber of Tommy Holmes, Stanley Woodward, the Bill Slocums, Sr. and Jr., Arthur Daley, Al Laney, Allison Danzig, Burris Jenkins, Willard Mullin, Tom Meany, Clem McCarthy, Al Buck, and Walter Stewart, Jack Singer, Richards Vidmer, Alan Gould, Ted Husing, Scotty Reston, Drew Middleton, Caswell Adams, Jack Mahon, Stu Cameron, and the best-rounded sportswriter of them all, Sid Mercer.

We had great cudgelers during that period, too, willing and able to pick up where Pegler left off when he took his look-of-eagles and his blackjack into the sphere he liked to call "cosmic thinking." Peg considered calling his new column "Sweetness and Light."

We had Dave Egan in a perpetual tantrum in Boston, Joe Williams and Davis J. Walsh jabbing superbly in New York, Prescott Sullivan and Tom Laird fulminating in San Francisco, Jack Miley and Jimmy Cannon ready to tackle anything or anybody around the big town, and Bill Cunningham trumpeting defiance from his Boston redoubt.

We had pixies galore. Let us consider just three of them.

Hype Igoe had been as close to Jim Corbett as he was to Jim Braddock, as much of a confidant of Joe Gans as of Barney Ross, as trusted by Stanley Ketchell as by Billy Conn. He was a ruddy, jolly little man who worked hard and lived harder. He was immune to the erosion of time.

Hype was drinking beer very late one night in Mickey Walker's saloon across the street from the Garden. Hype was worried. His companion Jack Miley, another impressive consumer of the suds, was assigned by the *Daily News* to cover the Army-Navy football game in Philadelphia some hours later that day. Hype implored his friend to leave the saloon and get to Philadelphia.

He said later that he must have dozed a bit. He remembered opening his eyes, seeing Miley sitting opposite him, as usual, and he ordered two more beers.

"For the last time, Jack, get to Philadelphia and cover that game," Hype said crossly. "Do you want to blow your job?"

Jack seemed surprised.

"I've been to Philadelphia, Hype," he said. "I covered the game. I took a slow train back, just dropped in here for a beer, and found you sitting in the same spot where I left you last night."

Hype got "rolled" in a strange town once, and showed up at the press gate of the fight arena minus his ticket and any sort of identification, and was turned away. He was feeling very bad anyway and this frustration made him sicker. He found his way to a public rest room nearby, for he was too fastidious a man to be sick in front of fans crowding into the arena.

As he was leaving his place of woe, Hype noticed with interest the enamel button which, when pushed, flushed the water closet he had been using. It bore a neat legend: "PRESS."

Hype unscrewed the button, attached it to his lapel, and sailed through the press gate unimpeded.

Hype was a devoted father for a man whose job and nature militated against his getting home much more often than Halley's Comet squirts past Earth. Whenever he did drop by, Hype liked to bring presents for the children. Detained late one night at the *Journal,* he despaired of finding anything suitable to take home with him. Then he was struck with a fine idea. He went up to the roof of the building, picked up a wire-mesh box of homing pigeons, and took them home to the kids. The *Journal* used pigeons for swift transit of undeveloped film and captions and notes from the baseball and football fields, remote disaster stories, shipboard interviews, and others events.

The Igoe children loved the birds, made pets of them, fattened them up, and happiness abounded until the search for the culprit who had made off with them, under cloak of night, narrowed down to Hype. He confessed after considerable grilling. The *Journal* sent its aviary keeper to Hype's house and he repossessed the birds, to the wails and laments of the children.

Hype was forgiven, but not for long. The same birds were pressed into service shortly thereafter. Some great dignitary was arriving from Europe and would submit to pictures and interviews on the ship as it reached Quarantine. Film and the story of the arrival, plus the interview, scribbled in "takes" on oiled paper, were stuffed in the little capsules the pigeons carried, and off they shot—straight to Hype's house instead of to the *Journal.* It was badly scooped by the *World-Telegram,* the *Sun,* and the *Post,* none of whose pigeons suffered from split personalities, or divided loyalties.

The pixie in Henry McLemore was so pronounced it tended to overshadow the fact that he was the nimblest sportswriter of that happy period. His impish manner and unpredictability combined to make him unique. He was to serve in the Army through all of World War II, but in the period leading up to the bombing of Pearl Harbor, he could not have cared less about its meaning: At a party given at Grossinger's resort in the Catskills, where Barney Ross was training for a fight, Henry seized the microphone during a floor show and suggested that the audience—predominantly Jewish—join him in singing the "Horst Wessel" song. He lived.

Introducing saintly Granny Rice at a distinguished dinner given in Rice's honor by members of the Detroit Athletic Club, Henry said fondly, "Over the years, Granny has taken more punishment than the mothballs in a public urinal." The first time Henry saw our daughter Debbie, who was then two, she was happily tubbing herself at our apartment, her hair pinned up prettily out of the way of the large bar of bath soap she was wielding.

"You're the most beautiful girl I've ever seen," Henry said, standing at the side of the tub. Then he joined her in the tub, fully dressed and they had a fine sloshing time together.

Henry was a rarity in other respects. Although he worked for the United Press, he could write well. He could write funny, write sad, and as must all wire-service slaves, write fast. There was no end to his imagination, in a pinch.

En route to a World Series in St. Louis, Henry got snarled in a card game and blew the entire $250 his office had pressed upon him to cover his expenses during the long trip. Later that day, burdened by not only the financial disaster but a ringing hangover, Henry stared unhappily at the sheet of paper he had rolled into his typewriter in the cramped confines of the press box at Sportsman's Park. I had drawn the seat directly behind him and slightly higher and thus commanded an unintended but uninterrupted view of Henry's typewriter and the tempests that afflicted him. He was on his deadline, suffering the unanaesthetized birthpangs of a lead. He looked up, as a hurt fighter does, and his eye riveted on a fat Goodyear blimp floating idly over the ballpark. Henry's typing fingers instantly sprang to action. I couldn't resist looking over his shoulder as he wrote: "By Henry McLemore. Aboard Goodyear Blimp over Sportsman's Park, St. Louis, Oct. 6.—The Cardinals, spilling out of their dugout, resemble a swiftly blooming and burgeoning flower, as I look down on the field far below me."

It went on and on, a virtuoso performance. But there was more to his mad flight of fancy. At the end of the story, Henry attached a memo to UP's New York office. It read: "P.S. Blimp hire cost $250. Rush."

Got it, too.

Harry Grayson, sports editor of Newspaper Enterprise Association, the mail-sheet department of the Scripps-Howard chain, trod the sports world of that era with the confidence of a man who was to the manner born and a law unto himself. He liked Runyon, Farnsworth, and Frayne personally, but saw that as no reason to prevent his documented report on their financial involvement in Mike Jacobs' Twentieth Century Sporting Club. Harry liked Mike, too, and Mike showered him with kindnesses. But one day as Harry looked down on Forty-ninth Street from the window of his room high in the Forrest Hotel and saw Mike sunning himself in a chair outside the Jacobs Ticket Office, he found no good reason to resist the temptation to lob a filled water pitcher out the window. It hit the pavement with a splintering crash just a few feet from where Mike dozed. If it had hit him on the head it would have driven him into the sidewalk like a croquet pole.

Harry smoked cigars that always appeared to be sputtering down the last half inch to the explosion. In fact, Harry himself always seemed on the point of detonation. Almost everything he said was delivered with gusto and finger-jabbing. He preferred to stand very close to the person he was addressing or arguing with. Harry had many fine traits, including love of his son and worship of his nephew, the Stanford All America Bobby Grayson. But attentiveness was not one of his strengths.

One night in the crowded confines of the Theatrical Grill in Cleveland, where Cleveland's night life began and ended, he stood up to illustrate how a fighter he liked had cranked up a right-hand punch. In the course of the backswing, Harry's fist hit a souse at the next table. The guy tipped over backwards in his chair and his drink went flying through the smoky air. Harry looked down briefly on the chaotic scene, said "Oh," turned back to us, and resumed his story.

Harry hated Cleveland with all his heart, but that's where Scripps-Howard headquartered its NEA in a dismal building not far from the Stadium and the lake front. One ghastly winter morning before dawn Harry, unable to find a cab, leaned miserably against the sleet and snowstorm sweeping off the lake as he trudged to work. A car pulled over to the curb near him, and the motorist rolled down a window and shouted above the horrid storm, "Hey, Mac, how do you get out of Cleveland?"

Harry lunged at him and would have probably choked him to death if the window had been lowered sufficiently. Instead, all he could do was roar at the startled man, "You dumb son of a bitch, do you think I'd be in Cleveland if I knew how to get out?"

Harry was a real swinger and often had to prove it. His idea of a lively night, perhaps dating back to his days as a Marine in World War I, was to go into the toughest bar in town for a few beers. There was always an excellent chance that he would overhear a patron—usually the big tough guy down at the other end of the bar—say something Harry didn't agree with. He would drop everything to try to set the guy straight. Sometimes the guy didn't want to be set straight, didn't want to be interrupted by the gray-haired, blue-eyed stranger who stood inches from his face and blew cigar sparks and smoke. It was interesting to make the rounds with Harry when the moon was full, but not especially healthy.

I flew around the world with Harry near the end of the war, courtesy of the Air Transport Command. It may have been the junket that killed all junkets. A montage of that voyage remains vividly clear, each vignette in living color:

Harry, taking the occasion of a spit-and-polish dinner at the Officers' Club at Gander to deliver a stinging denunciation of their commander-in-chief, F.D.R.

Harry, in Casablanca's Old Medina, beset by two screaming Arab prostitutes when all he wanted was to see the sights.

Harry, shaking his head and muttering "This goddam Egypt!" as we looked down from the balcony of our room in a *Calcutta* hotel while buzzards wheeled over a cholera victim.

Harry, viewing with distaste a dirt-covered holy man lying in a prayer trance near a burning ghat in New Delhi, "Hey, get up, you filthy old faker!"

Harry, shaking hands with Chiang Kai-shek in Chungking (Chiang had a nervous habit of smiling and repeating "Hao ... hao ... hao") and saying to me, too loud, "This bum's in a rut!"

Harry, being threatened with eviction from the China Burma India theater for poking Gen. Albert C. Wedemeyer in his beribboned chest to stress a point.

Harry, still on probation while we were being entertained at Lord Louis Mountbatten's digs in Colombo, being hit a resounding whack on the back by Supremo—who was jolly pleased with some ribald story Harry had told him.

Harry, looking around Jerusalem and mulling over what I had just told him: that here in 70 A.D. more than fifty thousand Jews had been killed by Titus. "Thank Christ we got inoculated against *that*," Harry said fervently.

But the prime feature of our global trip was Harry's meeting with Pope Pius XII and their wholly improbable togetherness.

The episode began on a low note. I woke up Harry at the crack of noon that warm Sunday in Rome. We had had a rough Saturday night in a wine cellar owned, if memory serves, by a family named Borgia. We suffered from the wrath of grapes.

"Get up, Harry, we're going to see the Pope."

Harry, sleeping in his shorts in the curtainless room in the war-stained Excelsior, stirred just enough to say, "To hell with the Pope."

The only course left to me as a defender of the faith was to get him up, see that he shaved and put his war correspondent's uniform on frontward. We reported to the bus on time and joined the other correspondents who had been granted an audience with the Pontiff.

"I'm only doing this for you because you're Catholic or something," Harry said unhappily as we marched into the papal palace. "But get this straight: I'm not going to kiss that guy's ring."

Feeling a bit faint, and fingering the rosary in my pocket, I led Harry along the glorious hallways, wondering if, after their having weathered the sin of purchased indulgences, they might now collapse on a former altar boy at St. Aloysius' in Washington, D. C., and on his militantly agnostic pal.

"Nobody wants you to kiss His Holiness' ring," I hissed at him.

But Harry wasn't listening. He had spotted the first Swiss guard he had ever seen. Naturally, he stopped.

"Are you kidding?" he said to the stiff and proper man, bedecked in the uniform that Michelangelo designed as a gag, only to have the Pope who gave him the demeaning assignment applaud his sketches and order the uniforms. "What are you, some kind of a nut?" The Swiss Guard never blinked, never got around to piercing Harry with his halberd.

And so it went until we reached the vicinity of the magenta silk-covered door that led into Pius XII's office. There at its threshold more bad news awaited. Franklin Gowen, a State Department career officer who served as the strong right arm of the White House's representative at the Vatican, Myron Taylor, took me aside. He said he had selected me as the member of the party who would introduce the others to the Pope. I can hardly remember my wife's name, much less casual acquaintances.

"No."

"Oh, yes, you will," Mr. Gowen said. "What's more, you must put His Holiness at his ease at the start with some compliment or discreet pleasantry, then explain the mission of your group and get along with the introductions."

"I've had very little experience putting Popes at their ease," I said lamely. Just then, to make things less bearable, two things happened. A papal household monsignor prematurely opened the door to the Holy Father's office and we beheld the spectacle of the Vicar of Christ busily engaged in the task of personally arranging the chairs we were to sit on during his proposed talk to us. The other happening concerned Harry.

"Remember, I'm not kissing that guy's ring, see?" he said.

It was just too much, with a hangover. But one manages to survive, somehow. Upon signal, we all trooped in and found His Holiness, a vision in white silk, standing serenely near his desk, on which there rested, among other objects, a white portable typewriter. As if in a dream I heard Mr. Gowen introduce me. I genuflected and kissed the ring on Pius XII's delicate, long-fingered, almost translucent right hand. (I was to kiss both those hands—described as "fluttering white doves"—under different conditions years later.)

"Your Holiness," I said on this occasion, voice cracking. "We are a group of American news correspondents on tour of the various theaters of war. We have only one thing in common with you as a group. We're all touch-typists together."

It was a demented opening. But Eugenio Pacelli smiled, as if he had been put at ease. Gowen nodded to me to begin the introductions. I don't remember the first ten in line. I kept worrying about No. 11, Harry. He was getting ever closer. And then at last there they stood, face to face, the spiritual leader of 400,000,000 Catholics and, well, let's face it, Harry.

"Hi'ya," Harry said, taking the Pope's hand and pumping it. "Harry Grayson of NEA."

Taking a long chance that the Pope had never heard of NEA, I said "Your Holiness, Mr. Grayson writes for a well-known news service named Newspaper Enterprise Association in our country. Its main office is in a state we call Ohio. The city where it is located is called Cleveland."

"Cleveland?" the Pope repeated. He looked at Harry with fresh interest. "I know Cleveland. I spent a most enjoyable time in Cleveland when I visited your country in 1935. Would you by any chance know my friend Bishop Ready in Cleveland?"

It was just too much. Grayson knew him. Now the two of them, perhaps the least likely acquaintances in Christendom, talked animatedly about their mutual friend. It was with some difficulty that I got the line moving again.

When we were all introduced and seated, the Pope sat down at his desk and gave us a little talk on our obligations as newsmen. Then he distributed rosaries and papal medals and it was time to bid him farewell. As we filed out, the Pope stopped only one of us. Harry.

"Our blessing on you and your family, Mr. Grayson," Pius XII said to Harry, the only one whose name he could recall. He made a gentle little Sign of the Cross over Harry's gray mane.

Suddenly, incredibly, Harry dropped to one knee, seized the Pope's hand, and kissed his ring. I turned away, not wishing to be a witness to what had to be a trying time for my friend. To have stared in wonderment would have been a rude and perhaps sacrilegious invasion of privacy.

Harry and I walked out together in silence unbroken except for Harry's occasional obscene references to Swiss Guards stationed here and there along the route. Once outside, Harry bit the end off a cigar and squirted the bitten part at the base of a Bernini column. He

puffed on the cigar as he applied the match, got it going to his satisfaction, and cocked his head in the direction of the Pope's palace.

"That guy's okay," Harry said.

I felt that the papacy had seldom had a finer or less expected tribute
paid it.

I sometimes miss sportswriting. There is within its narrow confines
a blithe togetherness seldom apparent in other reaches of the news
business. There will always be jealousies among men who write as
competitors. But at day's end, it is easier for sportswriters to get
together for a meal or a drink than for, let us say, editorial writers,
financial editors, publishers, and even police reporters. The friendships
I formed in sportswriting are more lasting and rewarding than any
formed in the other fields I bumbled into. I don't subscribe for a minute to the old wives' tale that most of the best writing in today's newspapers appears on their sports pages. It is popular to repeat that a
lot of prominent columnists, correspondents, and literary figures
started out in sports: Brisbane (who covered the John L. Sullivan-
Charley Mitchell fight at Chantilly in 1888 as part of an audience of
forty spectators), Heywood Broun, Westbrook Pegler, Paul Gallico,
Quentin Reynolds, James Reston, Frank Conniff, Stanley Frank, Drew
Middleton, etc. But as many or more beat a path to fame without the
stimuli of the crack of a bat, thump of a punch, thunder of hooves, and
the encouragingly loose reins of the sports department's Copy Desk.

Still, there is always something special about a good sportswriter
that the best in the other departments seldom attain. He attracts more
and tenacious readers and holds them longer than the other featured
stars. Nobody proved this more in life or death than Runyon. He had
been out of daily sports journalism for ten years when he died of
cancer in December, 1946. But it was as a sportswriter (rather than
as a short-story writer, trial reporter, Hollywood scenarist, and man-
about-town chronicler) that he was remembered. He was mourned by
millions, this lonely and often irascible man. It is inconceivable that
any outstanding pundit of Walter Lippmann's stature, or even an
Ernie Pyle or Ernest Hemingway, could have served after death as
the rallying point of the remarkable cancer research fund that bears
Runyon's name. With Walter Winchell quietly footing the administra-
tive costs for fourteen years, and Dan Parker, John Daly, Arthur God-
frey, Leonard Lyons, Ray Robinson, and others pitching in, some

$30,000,000 had been raised twenty years after Winchell started the ball rolling with a $5,000 check and a pitch on the air.

It was rewarding, being a part of the world of sports. It was a nice feeling to have a seat in the press row at every big event that came along. But the War pulled back a vast curtain and gave me my first view of the world, its wonders, and its peoples. Luckily, there was a handy steppingstone into that broader life.

It was called International News Service.

4 *INS—(R.I.P.)*

At noon, EDT, May 24, 1958, the teletypes of the United Press and International News Service paused briefly all over the nation and beyond some of the seas. The machines sounded their separate and intensely competitive bells to indicate that news of "bulletin" importance was about to move on their wires. And then the two old foes gave forth with the following: "The United Press Associations and International News Service joined forces today around the world in the creation of a single news agency named United Press International."

There were curses, consternation, and tears in the INS newsroom. Guildsmen had been assured a day or two before by general manager Joe Kingsbury Smith that all rumors that INS would be sold to UP were completely without foundation. He was correct in his notice to employees, Joe said subsequently. The Guild's inquiry had asked if it were true that INS was about to be *sold* to UP. Actually, Joe explained, it was *merged*.

A better verb would have been *swallowed*. The new organization, UPI, kept most of the old UP personnel. It picked up only a handful of INS men, several of whom soon quit. They could not endure the transition from their wild and wonderful news service to an atmosphere which, by comparison, was about as challenging as a Western Union branch.

Even as the keys of the teletypes clacked the doom of INS, two strangers entered the shocked newsroom. They strolled over to Milton Kaplan, then manning the news desk. One of the men introduced himself as a UP. Milt, who doesn't look unlike Michelangelo's Christ in the Pietà, graciously shook hands.

"I'll be working around here the rest of the day," UP said. "I guess you read the wire."

"Yes, I did," said one of the hardest-working and most dedicated INS men of all. "May I get you a desk . . . typewriter . . . phone?"

"Yes, thank you," UP said.

Milt turned to the other man, who looked as if he intended to buy a derby at the earliest opportunity.

"And may I do the same for you?" Milt assumed he, too, was UP.

"Naw," the mugg said. "I'm from Pinkerton. I'm here to see you guys don't steal nothing, see?"

We died with vinegar in our wounds.

A lot of us kidded INS. Unlike Avis Rent A Car, we could not claim to be only second best. We were, at most, third best among the wire services. Today, with the rise of the *New York Times* wire, and Los Angeles *Times*-Washington *Post,* Chicago *Daily News,* and other wires, we might have pushed down to sixth or seventh place among the most respected dispensers of spot news and features.

But for a long time, as we trailed behind UP and the Associated Press, scorned and often bad-mouthed by both, we were some of the proudest people in the news business. Proud and often deeply moved by events which the reading public never noticed, or considered trite: the big "play" an INS story might get in a paper that subscribed also to AP and UP. If the paper ignored us when we felt we had covered a big story better than the AP and UP and printed their accounts rather than our INS copy, we would be inclined to dismiss the paper's telegraph editor as a drunk or some old doddering teetotaler who had worked for either of our sworn enemies for years and had been hopelessly brainwashed against all things Hearst-owned.

There was astonishing opposition to us. When Clark Lee, the great AP correspondent resigned after Bataan and Corregidor to accept a much more remunerative job with INS, he dropped by AP's New York office to say good-bye to associates he had been close to for years. Kent Cooper, the top AP man at the time, would not see him; he was "busy." A day or two before actually starting writing for INS, Clark visited AP again. There was a bustle and hustle as he entered. Kent Cooper wanted to see him immediately.

Cooper greeted him with the deceptive smile of winter sunshine and congratulated him on risking his life so many times for AP—for a stipend, by the way, that would have caused the New York Yankees batboy to hold out. As a fruit of this noble service to the cause, Cooper went on, he was going to send Clark to South America to head up one of AP's bureaus.

"I didn't know what to say to him," Clark told me one night, as we leaned on the rail of the *Appalachian* on the way to the A-bomb tests at Bikini in 1946. "I knew he knew I had resigned. It had been in the papers and some of the AP guys had given me farewell parties. But I had to say it all over again for him. And I did. He said, and he acted very mad, 'INS! You can't do that, Clark. You *can't* resign. Your *father* worked all his life for AP. INS is *Hearst!*'

"I told him what he already knew, that I had signed a contract and was ready to go to work for INS," Clark said quietly, as we looked into the phosphorescent water. "Then I started for the door. I said good-bye and thanks for all the wonderful things that had happened to me at AP. But he wouldn't let me go. He said, 'Lee,'—he had called me Clark all those years—'a funny thing happened to me today at the meeting of the Pulitzer Prize selection group. I forgot to bring up your name.' "

We at INS were never sore at Mr. Hearst, senior, or his son and namesake, who took the folding of the wire service quite hard. They and their corporation underwrote our adventures, our fun, and our games to the extent of several million dollars a year during the last down-grade. That lost fortune provided a unique stage in the theater of news-gathering, filled to its proscenium with an arresting cast of characters.

I caught the last fifteen years of the act which had been opened in 1909 when the elder Hearst magnificently ordered the creation of a special news service to supply his own newspapers exclusively. He wished it to be as impartial as AP and UP, and maintained a most commendable hands-off policy toward it through the next forty-two years until his death in 1951. His editorials, policy direction, and often subtly couched "suggestions" moved to his papers along a separate wire service, Universal. INS went its own way as a separate entity, either impervious to, or ignorant of, what was known as "Hearst policy." It began to attract clients from the outside world, which threw it into direct competition with the much larger AP and UP.

So far as manpower was concerned, the odds against INS men were prohibitive in most of their jousts with the other two. We had one man—Jim Brown—covering India during most of World War II. He'd get an occasionally tart "bullet" from our foreign editor Jack

Oestreicher if he found himself in Lahore when the action was taking place in Trivandrum, 1,700 impassable miles to the south. No computer could calculate the number of times Jimmy Kilgallen, Dave Walsh, Inez Robb, Charlie Einstein, Lawton Carver, and other willing round-the-clock reporters were thrown into the fray alone, and expected to outproduce the rivals or, that failing, outwrite them.

I lost track of the number of times I was the loner from INS, but I remember that when Eisenhower went to Abilene, Kansas, in 1952 to announce his candidacy, INS convered that event with one man (me), UP with seven, and AP with twelve.

There were other times when we overcovered a story, surrounded it, permeated every cell of it. It would be like a four-alarm fire that had brought every piece of a town's equipment to the scene of the blaze. In the confusion, we'd sometimes squirt our hoses on each other, when we weren't squirting them on the opposition.

There was that sunny Sunday in Monaco when Father Francis Tucker, the ecclesiastic Cupid in the story-book romance of dashing Rainier III and beautiful Grace Kelly, mounted the pulpit to make a few final observations about the impending wedding. Monagasques found the news largely filled with newsmen and photographers. There were 1,700 of us assigned to that story from all parts of the world, as opposed to only 2,200 actual Monagasques.

Halfway through his sermon in which he showered blessings down on the betrothed the priest paused and branched off into spot news.

"It will never break up," the priest said as if tearfully denying some unprinted report. "I believe Rainier will keep his oath. As for Grace Kelly, she will keep her oath, or she won't be a Catholic. I can bear witness that this man [Rainier] is being faithful to his pledge to his country. Two years ago he broke off a sentimental friendship for your sake. . . ." It was another way of stating that the groom was finished for keeps with French actress Gisèle Pascal.

There was a scuffling in the front of the church. UP's Bob Musel was bolting out a side door. AP, in the person of Eddy Gilmore, was making a more discreet but still determined march up the middle aisle toward the main doors. I felt trapped, ground between Church and that portion of State called INS. This was the last Mass of the day, and my religion requires that I attend Mass each Sunday. On the other hand, there went UP and AP, headed for telephones, each bearing the story of Tucker's bad taste.

A fast decision had to be made, and it was. I decided that it would be easier to face my confessor than Barry Faris, my leader at INS headquarters in New York. So I rushed out, found a phone, called the INS agency which had been set up in a water closet and bidet shop in Monte Carlo, and dictated the story. Later that day I ran into a young colleague, Olga Curtis, a beautiful and talented girl who felt eclipsed by the presence on our team of our strikingly efficient and confident Dorothy Kilgallen. Olga had been crying, her eyes said. I asked her to have a drink. She shook her head.

"Why did you write the story about Father Tucker?" she wailed. "I was assigned to cover the Mass . . . the first good assignment I've had since I've been here in this damned place. I worked hard on my story, took it to the office, and that man on the desk said that your story had moved on the wire a long time before." I thought she would cry again, and I don't think she was listening when I told her that nobody had told me that she was assigned.

So now I had accumulated two sins for the day: leaving Mass early for commercial reasons (thus emulating the originator of that practice, Judas Iscariot), and inadvertently hurting a fellow INS'er. (Olga recovered to become women's editor of the *Denver Post.*)

But on big stories of that nature, we had an incomparable *esprit de corps* and sometimes even teamwork. It was a heady experience to field as many or more troops than either AP or UP chose to commit. But the rare occasions of our numerical superiority had its penalties. We must be perfect in order to justify the terrible expense. Perfect was subject to different interpretations.

The trial of Dr. Hermann Sander in Manchester, New Hampshire, was a case in point.

The day the waspish doctor took the stand to deny the prosecution's charge that he had practiced euthanasia on an elderly woman patient with a terminal case of cancer, INS had the finest day's file I'd ever seen. It started before that wintry daybreak with Fanny Hurst's vivid feature about the women queued up in the snowy streets, waiting and hoping to be admitted to the ugly courthouse where a man that most of them seemed to know would face his worst moment of truth. The popular novelist had been retained for the duration of the trial, a familiar and generally rewarding INS ploy. Her feature drew a brilliant parallel between those waiting women and the crones of Place Concorde, knitting and waiting for the arrival of wailing tumbrels.

It was followed on the wire by an extraordinarily sensitive piece done by John O'Hara, another INS special. It was a reminiscence of his father's hard times as a small-town doctor. Dr. Patrick Henry O'Hara of Pottsville, Pa., led the same overworked life that had brought Dr. Sander to this spent and drained hour. It was pure *New Yorker,* but only INS had it.

Our *Q* and *A* during the doctor's long stay on the stand was handled by, in my opinion, the finest virtuosos of that black art of recording precisely what was asked and answered no matter how swift the give-and-take: Inez Robb and Jimmy Kilgallen. Their notebook pages hit me like a heavy snowfall as I sat at the end of our press table in the courtroom. With each highlight, I'd scoop up their work and run down to an evil little cubbyhole in the cellar, colder than a Deepfreeze, where sat Phil Reed, our editor in charge. I'd bang out a new lead, Phil would grab it from the typewriter in short takes, read it like lightning, and our teletype operators thrust it into the trunkline that reached newspaper, radio, and TV clients across the U.S.

It was one of those glorious days when all thought of food and drink is driven from one's system; when nothing mattered except to show those dull bastards from AP and UP that—given the manpower—we could leave 'em for dead every time we met. We actually shouted like schoolchildren when wires of congratulation came in from such clients as the Yankee Network (". . . INS averaging six to eight minutes ahead of opposition.")

By 9 P.M. we had run out of story and steam. Inez had found strength enough to do her regular column in addition to her long hours of exacting additional reporting. Kilgallen had written an overnight. INS'ers from the Boston bureau had come up with half a dozen fine local stories. I had done my "On the Line" column; Phil had finished editing it, and pretty soon the teletypes choked to a stop. We all just sat there in our own chosen attitudes of collapse, wondering how we'd make it to the hotel in the storm.

Phil picked up the phone and called Barry Faris in New York. It was a good connection, and the acoustics in our refrigerator were excellent, alas.

"Now, about tomorrow," we could hear Barry say, and even thought we heard the rustle of his assignment sheets.

"Tomorrow!" Phil cried out in anguish. "What have you got to say about *today!*"

There was a dreadful pause, and we all hung on breathlessly.

"Long," Barry said. "Now, about tomorrow . . ."

Barry was our beadle. He kept order in the house—at least when he was physically present or watching things by telephone and cable—from the time he joined INS in 1915 until he went down with the sinking ship nearly half a century later.

He was a seasoned newsman for a decade before he joined INS: priceless experience lapped up hungrily while working for the St. Joseph (Missouri) *Gazette,* St. Louis *Globe-Democrat,* Fort Worth *Record,* Kansas City *Post,* San Francisco *Call,* Los Angeles *Tribune,* Denver *Post,* Indianapolis *Sun* and UP, an organization on which he was to declare a total war that lasted longer than the War of the Roses.

For years he ran a one-man show in a way that won grudging admiration from the competition. He was head of news and of personnel and handled both with a gruff exterior that camouflaged his infatuation with the former and his sentimental regard for the latter.

In his best years his faith in the integrity and efficiency of his troops could not be shaken in any emergency. He ignored Roy Howard's false Armistice exclusive that ended World War I—on the UP wire, at least—a week early. On the night the AP sent out its wrong verdict in the Hauptmann case and frantic and angry phone calls from INS clients demanded to know why INS had not confirmed the verdict, Faris stood in the New York newsroom next to the silent Western Union key manned by the veteran operator Tom Walsh. Jimmy Kilgallen was in the courtroom at Flemington, New Jersey. That was enough for Faris. He just stood there, quietly smoking. To hell with panicky clients.

After five taut minutes Jimmy sent a short lead: "A premature verdict of life imprisonment for Bruno Richard Hauptmann for the kidnap-murder of Charles A. Lindbergh, Jr., emanated from the courtroom at 10:21 P.M. The jury had not as yet entered the courtroom. . . ."

Someone shouted to Barry that more INS clients were on the wire, angry.

"Tell 'em to use the goddam AP!" he shouted back.

Many editors needed no such invitation. Their presses were rolling with extra papers. The New York *American* in a most unbrotherly disregard for not only Kilgallen but its own treasured Damon Runyon, who was posted in the half-empty courtroom, ran off 55,000 copies carrying the AP story. The Washington *Post* and countless other papers placed their trust in AP, caring not a whit that INS was saying "premature" and UP was saying nothing.

AP and INS shared a room just outside the courtroom, after much earlier wrangling for separate bureaus.

"Naturally, we weren't speaking," Kilgallen recalled a long time later. "Well, that night of the verdict we're hanging around, waiting for the jury to make up its mind. You know how it is. You wander in and out of the courtroom, in and out of the bureau. It came up 10:30, and no action. The judge was still at his home, four blocks down the street.

"Then 10:31 and suddenly the red light comes up on the AP teletype, and it starts chugging. It's a bad feeling. I felt so helpless. I couldn't just walk over there and see what the opposition was saying. I couldn't have gotten near the machine, with those AP guys. But I got a break. A few days before, by mutual consent, we had agreed to let Bill Chaplin share our room. Bill worked for one of the radio networks which subscribed to *both* our wires. He was my friend from a long way back. He took a look at AP's wire, sent a bulletin to his network, then told me. That's when I sent my short lead."

For the next sixteen terrible minutes, Faris stood his ground, refusing to query Kilgallen. During all that time, at the rate of sixty words a minute, the AP ground out its story—one of several alternates providing for as many types and gradations of verdict.

Then a sudden and horrible silence.

Kilgallen's flash had hit the world: "HAUPTMANN GETS ELECTRIC CHAIR."

"Barry had great gobs of common sense," Jim said of his old boss, in comparing him with some of the more famous editors of his time. "All the others were merely geniuses."

Faris' common sense filtered down to some of the hands he employed.

Quentin Reynolds used to say that if he never worked for Faris he probably never would have sent a cable from Paris in 1940 during his early days as a *Collier's* war correspondent. He handed the cable to a stubborn French official and demanded that it be sent to the White House. It read: "DEAR UNCLE FRANKLIN: I AM HAVING DIFFICULTY GETTING ACCREDITED TO THE FRENCH ARMY. TIME IS IMPORTANT. WOULD YOU PHONE OR CABLE PREMIER REYNAUD AND ASK HIM TO

HURRY THINGS UP? IT WAS GRAND OF YOU TO PHONE ME LAST NIGHT. PLEASE GIVE MY LOVE TO AUNT ELEANOR. QUENT."

It worked.

There was a Faris flair in Kilgallen's scoop on the release of Tokyo Rose from a remote West Virginia prison, long after she had been tracked down in Japan by Clark Lee. The only phone in the vicinity of the prison was in the kitchen of a neighboring farmhouse. UP had resourcefully tied it up by renting the only available bedroom in the house. Nothing daunted, Kilgallen rented the kitchen. Naturally, he refused to let UP use his phone when the story broke.

Faris had an uncanny rapport with his men bordering on ESP. Pierre Huss, INS's Berlin bureau chief in the early days of World War II, before the bombing of Pearl Harbor, was covering Hitler's panzers in Silesia in June, 1941, when he dispatched three expense accounts to INS-New York, care of the business office.

A harried accountant brought them into Faris' office.

"Your man Huss has lost his mind," he said. "Look at these."

Faris looked. All three slips had been dated ahead to June 21. One was a voucher for expenses incurred in Russian-held Poland. The second was from Minsk. The third was from Kiev.

"My God!" Faris cried out. "The Germans are going to invade Russia!"

The arrival of Seymour Berkson on the INS scene had an unsettling influence on Faris. Bit by bit, Berkson diminished Faris' authority. It was obvious from the day he was transferred from the Rome bureau to New York that Seymour had taken dead aim on Barry's title and chair. Moreover, he had the skills and everlasting drive needed—over and above the fact that the Hearst hierarchy admired him—to unseat the unseatable. Seymour was one of the most dynamic creatures I've ever met in the news business, an exasperating lint-picker, demanding, deflating, and the hardest-working man in the shop.

When I proposed after the war that my "On the Line" column be resumed as a general news and feature column, instead of sports, Seymour asked for six samples. I wrote them and, after a week or two, was sorry the matter had come up. He went over them word by word and had a question for every sentence. He was University of Chicago, linguist, author of a comprehensive study on the erosion of royal families, handsome, and stylish and—after hours—a most congenial host. But at INS he was frequently a terror and often impossible to communicate with. There were astonishing gaps in his fund of knowledge. Questioning a story of mine to the effect that the New York Yankees had signed the Georgia football star Frank Sinkwich to play both baseball and pro football, Seymour demanded to know how this could be possible.

"Why not?" I asked him.

"How can he be both a pro and an amateur?" Seymour demanded.

I told him I didn't understand him.

"If he's going to be a professional football player, how could he also play for the Yankees?"

"Why not?"

"The Yankees are amateurs, aren't they?"

In the course of his constant fine-tooth combing of my sample "On the Line" columns he came across a reference to St. Joseph. He wanted to know the saint's exact relationship with the Blessed Virgin and with Jesus, and demanded supporting evidence of his foster fatherhood.

I spent several hours with him in his office on Thanksgiving Day, 1946, going over the now thoroughly odious sample columns. Finally, I told him I had to get home. Millie had invited half a dozen of what she calls her "homeless" friends—childless couples and stray bachelors and spinsters. I was to mix the drinks and carve the turkey. Halfway through the carving job, the phone rang. It was Seymour. He had more questions to ask, and they were the least consequential or erratic that he had yet asked. After a few minutes on the phone, I began to hear peals of rage and shouts of hunger from the dining room. Two of our children, unfed, began to weep. It was too much.

"Goddam you, Seymour, you're ruining our Thanksgiving dinner," I said to him.

There was a pause.

"And goddam you, you're ruining mine," Seymour said.

He was still at the office.

When Seymour had reached a point where he began to exert at least as much authority as Barry, Faris went to Joseph V. Connolly, the debonair Hearst executive who had overall charge of both INS and profit-making King Features Syndicate and laid his predicament before that old friend.

"Stop worrying, Barry," Connolly told him. "You'll be managing editor of INS as long as I'm alive."

Whereupon, Joe went home—which was something of a novelty—and died.

Seymour's ascendancy produced a general edginess around INS. It introduced an era of "Who's responsible for this?" Sub-editors who once could clear up matters with an exchange of a few words now found themselves sending memos back and forth. Faris' iron-clad faith in his forces seemed now to waver on occasion, and peevishness sometimes replaced his lordliness. At one of the A-bomb tests at Yucca Flat, Nevada, the communications truck the Army had assigned to INS went on the blink. Instead of transmitting my story back to Las Vegas as I had written it, it sent only a long string of Z's. Jack Hanley, our San Francisco bureau chief, had moved over to Las Vegas to handle my story and was, of course, appalled when I seemed to have gone stark raving mad in the desert and forgotten the other twenty-five letters of the alphabet. With the aid of radio broadcasts of the big event, he patched together a story, put my by-line on it, and sent it out on the INS wire. It was about fifteen minutes behind AP's and UP's stories. Their communication trucks had worked perfectly.

Faris was soon on the phone to Jack. Jack explained.

"Don't give me that crap," Barry said angrily. "You know as well as I do that we were booby-trapped."

"But how?" Jack asked wonderingly.

"How!" Barry shouted across the country. "They cut our wires!"

"Who cut our wires?"

"The AP and the UP. Who the hell else would cut them!"

"But Barry," Jack said helplessly, "there weren't any wires to cut. Considine's story came down from Yucca Flat by wireless."

Faris was not a man to accept any such lunatic alibi.

"Wireless or not, they found some way to cut the wires—so watch it," he said and hung up.

Faris worshiped General MacArthur. He dispatched the whole varsity team of INS to San Francisco for MacArthur's Second Coming, his return after President Truman had fired him so unceremoniously. We soon ran out of things to write about. There are just so many ways of phrasing "Gen. Douglas MacArthur will come home next Thursday." But the words had to be turned out willy-nilly. Hanley vetoed my suggestion that he deploy one of our staff at the water's edge, to be on hand in case MacArthur walked in atop the Pacific. But a similarly ridiculous column of mine, scraping the bottom of the subject matter, easily passed muster and was sent out on the wire. In it I wrote that MacArthur was about to have one of the biggest letdowns of his life. I said that when he left Haneda Airport, Tokyo, Emperor Hirohito himself would be there to shake his hand. When he arrived at Honolulu he would find the outstretched hand of that renowned old salt, Adm. Arthur W. Radford. When he landed in San Francisco, there at the bottom of the steps, hand outstretched, would be his old comrade, Gen. Albert C. Wedemeyer.

"And when he reaches his destination, Washington, D. C., there to greet him—as President Truman's representative—will be none other save Gen. Harry Vaughan," I wrote meanly.

I was awakened the following morning before eight o'clock by a call from Faris.

"You've gotten us in one hell of a jam," he began. "That column of yours is absolutely libelous. The lawyers say that Vaughan can sue us right down to the bone. I want the name of the deskman who passed that column."

I told him I couldn't remember the name.

"Well, you haven't heard the last of this one," he said. "I'll be calling you back."

Jack Hanley called me a few minutes later.

"I'm quitting," he said. "I've taken a lot of abuse in my day, but what Faris just said to me is too much. He blames *me* for what you wrote, and I never even saw it before it went out. I'm quitting."

I asked him not to quit . . . at least not until Faris called back.

Barry never called back, and it was not until I reached New York a week later that I learned why he had not. As reconstructed by staffers, it went like this:

As was his custom, the first thing Faris did after reporting for work that frantic morning was to read the flimsies, the stack of yellow tissue carbon copies of all the golden words that had been expressed along our wire the night before. In time he came to and, with unconcealed delight, read my column. He came out of his fishbowl office into the newsroom, bearing the flimsies of my piece, slapped the pages on the news desk, and said to its editor, "By God, that's the way a piece should be written. This is the greatest column Considine ever wrote. By God, he really told 'em!"

Then he went back into his office, and all was quiet for about an hour. Then a roar of indignation sounded out of Berkson's office.

Presently, Seymour was seen rounding a corner at high speed, his fist clutching *his* flimsies of my column. He burst into Faris' office, and the startled desk men saw him thumping his fist (and my column) against the edge of Barry's desk. Then he slammed out of Barry's office, his face dark with rage, and slammed into his own.

All eyes were on Faris. After a bit he got up from his desk, picked up the crumpled remains of my column, strode out to the desk, and roared, "Who's responsible for letting this villainous attack on General Vaughan get on our wire!"

The phone calls to San Francisco followed, after our libel lawyer, Carl Helm, had been roused and alerted to the infamous attack.

"But why didn't he call back?" I asked those who were giving me the fill-in.

"The first edition of the *Journal-American* reached Berkson's office during the height of the storm," one of them said. "Your column was spread eight columns across the top of Page One. That's the kind of play Berkson has been hoping we'd get for a long time."

So it was a nutty shop at times, too.

"It was wild and wonderful," Einstein wrote when I asked him for his memory of the place he graced. Charles memoed:

> Bugs Baer called it the Unintentional News Service and changed our slogan from "Get it first—but first get it right" to "Get it first—correct it later." Seymour was not amused.
>
> A copyboy in the Chicago bureau thought he was working for the SIN and thus caroled the initials when he answered the phone; and it may not be wholly without symbolism that when the Mickey Mouse Club wanted to show a newsroom on television, it unerringly chose INS headquarters in New York.
>
> What remained clear, on the day of our doom, was that the magic and money-losing world of INS would be no more. The unpainted, plaster-cracked newsroom in New York, on the eleventh floor of the *Daily Mirror* building—where once an elevator slipped its cable and fell, only to find INS scooped on the story because an unresponsible elevator in their building did not strike staffers as being news—was gone to gather dust. So was the Chicago bureau, where the overnight shift staged cockroach races for enormous stakes; Philadelphia, where the bureau was behind a barber shop; the basement quarters in Columbus, the cubbyholes in St. Louis, Los Angeles, Detroit, and Boston. In Phoenix, the termination of the INS consisted of unplugging a teletype

machine, which was the entire bureau, occupying as it did four square feet of space in the newsroom of a local radio station.

No one can be so sentimentally nostalgic as a newspaperman, nor more instantly so, but surely the INS merits a niche apart even in a business where reminiscence sets in at the age of nineteen. In the newspaper trade, the phrase has it, you meet such interesting people, and all of them at one time or another worked for INS, including a Latin American cables man believed to be the only person in history with a medical discharge from the French Foreign Legion and a one-armed copyboy who inevitably, when harassed, would cry out, "For Christ's sake, I've only got two hands." In New York at one time there was another copyboy who planned a career as a prizefighter and who trained late at night in the newsroom, skipping rope while clad solely in a jock strap. On the staff also was Les Conklin, who used to report to work with a paper carton of martinis and who claimed to be one of the few persons ever to get thrown out of Bickford's— the beanery down the street.

Conklin, who was writing the INS baseball roundup at the time, gained revenge against the restaurant chain in time. Vern Bickford, then with the Boston Braves, pitched a one-hitter. "Bickford," Conklin's roundup began, "is still serving up the smallest portions."

On a less esoteric level, the INS personnel included Ferdinand Goodfellow, who once vomited into the lap of a teletype operator for the purpose of exploring, he said, the iron-clad rule that no operator can leave his machine while on duty. One unforgettable scene occurred in the New York headquarters the night the Germans overran Holland in the initial stages of World War II. The U.S. still was at peace in those days, and the staff of the bureau clearly indicated it. It included a German, a Briton, and a Japanese, whose tasks comprised the preparation of news reports for client papers in their respective homelands. An argument arose between the Englishman and the German as one inflammatory bulletin after another hit the news desk, and finally they came to blows in the middle of the newsroom.

Meanwhile, a mechanical worker in the traffic department, a little the worse for whiskey, stepped up to the Japanese. "You'll be next, you little son of a bitch," he declared with uncanny foreboding, and laid his fingers to the Oriental's throat, forcing him back toward a window. It was at this juncture that sports editor Lawton Carver, who had a cousin by marriage who was a singer, decided to call up the minstrel-in-law and hum a few bars of a song he recently had heard. Back at the foreign desk, the incoming war news was such that the cable department had sent out a hurry call for reinforcement. One newsman was located, off duty and experiencing no pain, in the Ink Well, a tavern on Third Avenue. He returned to the office but maneuvered only so far as the financial desk, where he fell to the floor, comatose. Another editor was reached at a formal-dress function at the Waldorf. He rushed back to the office dressed—spectacularly—as he was.

It was at this instant that Ed Kiely, who later reconstructed the tableau for a succession of awe-struck listeners, came to work. Kiely, who understandingly left INS to become an official of the Pittsburgh Steelers of the National Football League, then was a night rewrite man in sports. "I opened the door," he recollected, "and here were two guys beating the hell out of each other in the middle of the room. Over here somebody was trying to push a Jap out a window. Another guy was singing at the top of his lungs into a telephone. There was a man lying on his face on the floor. And the guy tearing off the carbon paper was wearing a tuxedo and a top hat. It was the damndest sight I ever saw."

But we also had Joe Smith's exclusive cable interview with Stalin, a forty-minute beat on the arrest of Hauptmann, Washington bureau manager Bill Hutchinson's remarkable scoops on the death sentences imposed on the six Nazi saboteurs who landed here by submarine, and his prediction that Hirohito would be retained as Emperor. Possibly the most important beat the news service ever chalked up, however, was one not of hours or even minutes, but of approximately fifty seconds. The ringing of four bells on the INS teletypes signaled the shortest flash in history: "F.D.R. DEAD."

My most valued keepsake is an autographed picture from Faris to me. I was in New York after INS folded and bumped into Barry at the restaurant Carver had opened. He began regaling witnesses as to how he discovered me in the bullrushes and transformed me into the Jewish George R. Holmes. Nothing would do but that we wind up at his apartment, which was then only a block away. We wound up crying over INS. He selected his all-time favorite photo of himself and inscribed it for me.

Just before I went to bed in my hotel, I looked at it closely, fondly. He had misspelled my name. In the morning I looked at it again and found out something else. He had misspelled his own name, too.

INS was a make-do wire service. We happened to have nobody in New Delhi on January 30, 1948, to cover the big prayer and pacification meeting led by Mahatma Gandhi. A Hindu who blamed the saint for the partition of India shot and killed him. Reuter's, of course, was well-staffed for this stupendous news event. In a matter of a minute or two its printers in papers all over the world were flashing the news of the assassination. One of those clients, happily, was INS-London. It quickly broke the news to INS-New York, which appropriated some additional material from AP and UP—by way of the *Mirror,* which subscribed to both. Hearst blood was thicker than water. With the vital statistics and purloined facts now in hand, all we needed was a by-line to prove that the sun never set on INS.

John Martin, who had successfully made the difficult leap from the AP's foreign desk to ours, reached for our slim deck of index cards containing the names and addresses of our overseas correspondents and stringers—a stringer being a locally employed reporter, expatriate, or beachcomber, sometimes reachable for special assignments. At AP the index was so voluminous, it was said, that among its Palestinian stringers was one listed as Christ, J. But now Martin's eye latched on to the yellowing card of an Indian stringer named J. B. Sahne. Nothing had been heard from him nor had his services been sought for many years. But in short order and shorter "takes," INS's wires across the country began rolling with a fine story of the death of the great leader, "by J. B. Sahne—International News Service Staff Correspondent." Martin never wrote a better story faster.

Not long after that Martin ran into an old AP friend, Charlie Grumich, who complimented him for the fine play INS had received in U.S. papers the day of the murder.

"Who's your man in India?" Charlie asked.

"J. B. Sahne," John said steadily.

"Of course . . . Sahne. I knew him well! First class."

John swallowed.

"I thought he was dead," he said.

Karl Von Wiegand was the last of his breed. He was a contemporary of and had been hired by W. R. Hearst, Sr., at some improbable time in the remote past. He broke one of the biggest stories of World War I: the German decision in 1916 to wage unrestricted U-boat warfare on all shipping. The decision, coming as it did a year after the sinking of the *Lusitania* (which claimed 1,195 lives, of which 128 were Americans) did much to end America's neutrality and send her into the war.

He had astonishing contacts in the Germany of that period. Many years later, Hal Boyle of the AP and I called on him at his estate, in the shadow of the pyramids, when the sun was low enough on the horizon. He was in his eighties, and almost totally blind, but still dapper, dauntless, aggressively goatee'd, and eager to relive his moments as an intimate of greats. It was not always easy to follow his train of thought because he assumed that his listeners had been on the same first-name basis that he had enjoyed with long-gone world figures. A treasured sample:

"I'll not forget the day Willie said to me, 'My dear Wiegand, tell Papa we've lost this war. Everytime I try to tell him, he gets furious at me.' "

I looked at Boyle and Boyle looked at me. One of us had to ask the crazy question.

"Willie who?" I said, weakly.

"Crown Prince Wilhelm, of course!" the old gentleman snapped impatiently.

Von Wiegand and his close friend Lady Drummond Hay made a spectacular trip around the world in 1929 in the Graf Zeppelin, commanded by Hugo Eckener and financed by the elder Hearst. The rise of Hitler in Germany gave von Wiegand so few qualms that INS clients began asking embarrassing questions about where his sympathies really lay. After World War II von Wiegand found Generalissimo Franco a figure deserving of weekly ovations in print, which offended liberal clients along the INS wire. Still later, when he moved to Cairo because he believed the sun and the dry heat would preserve his life indefinitely, von Wiegand commenced a lengthy infatuation with Nasser—which offended Jewish readers. And, worse, advertisers. After Seymour Berkson gained sufficient power in INS, he quietly dropped von Wiegand from the wire. His output during the last period of his life was airmailed, not cabled, and appeared in obscure sections of the Hearst Sunday papers.

Another star, spaced several million light years away from the run of us at INS, was Gobind Behari Lal, born in Delhi, one-time science professor at Hindu College, University of Punjab, hired by the elder Hearst in 1925 for the San Francisco *Examiner,* and co-winner of a Pulitzer Prize for science writing. His comings and goings as science editor of INS were scurries, not visitations. He would pop in, drop his copy on the news desk, smile timidly, and off he'd go. No one seemed to know where he went, or lived, but the legend grew that when he was not in the office, he affected a turban. And burned incense.

Then there was Les Conklin, much better known to one element of INS's readership than either von Wiegand or Gobind Behari Lal. He made our racing selections, even wrote a book or two on how to beat the races. Les lived somewhat less splendidly than the stereotype of a successful horseplayer. One night, after some formal function, Berkson dropped into the office to see how things were running. Les was sound asleep on a thin mattress he had spread on a table containing stories and flimsies either already filed or awaiting dispatch on the wire. Berkson's roar of indignation at this flophouse aura awakened Conklin, who had something about him faintly reminiscent of the wispy shabbiness of Charlie Chaplin. Les tried to explain, but Seymour thundered him into silence, then loudly berated the ever-patient Ferd Goodfellow for permitting such conduct.

Several nights after that, Carver spotted Berkson having a brandy at the Pen and Pencil, alone. That was always the best time to get through to Seymour, who was at most other times one of the most accomplished nonlisteners in history. Seizing upon this rare moment of mellowness, Lawton explained about Conklin: Les had worked out an arrangement for beating the high cost of drinking and low INS pay by making a deal with the Snug Bar and Grill down Forty-fifth Street from the office. He could drink all he wanted and eat periodically for a stipulated weekly amount. Certain, but insufficient, sleeping privileges were also thrown into the flat rate. Les bought a bedroll and would tote it each night from the Snug Bar and Grill to INS. When he had finished his racing selections and whatever else he had to do, he'd turn in for a few hours sleep at INS.

"Thereby making himself available for duty at all times," Lawton finished. Seymour ordered another brandy, and before the evening was finished, the whole arrangement seemed to make sense to him.

There was only one mishap in INS's career as a rooming house. One night Les rolled over in his sleep and squashed the spare pint of martinis resting in a paper container at his side. The cascade immersed a pile of flimsies ready to be moved on the wire. They had to be peeled apart and spread around various desk tops and even on the floor, to dry, before they could be discernible again. Held things up a bit, and when Faris heard about it, he shot off a memo to the desk stating that if things of this nature happened any more around there, well, there'd be some changes made.

In many respects our most remarkable man was Lou Alwell. He held half a dozen titles, including office manager, the vaguest of his portfolios. Lou's activities sometimes overlapped. He strolled into his friend Carver's sports department one night, shortly before it was converted into the ladies' room, and while the man on duty with the overnight work had his back turned, Lou put a match to the newspapers strewn all over the place. Then he walked out. So did the man on duty.

Lou was one of the first to return to the scene of the fire, and played a gallant role in putting it out. Inevitably, the next day brought a memo to Alwell—not as the arsonist but as office manager—asking for an estimate on the loss in flimsy "books" and carbon paper in the sports department fire. Alwell assessed the loss at less than a dollar and ordered posted still another memo about carelessness with matches.

Lou made the most interesting barroom bets in my experience: odd little wagers such as betting he could eat a dozen saltine crackers without taking a sip of liquid before Carver could run around the block and return to the bar. This turned out more spectacularly than planned. It was dead of night and Carver, lumbering up the deserted grade of pavement from Forty-sixth and Third to Forty-sixth and Second encountered a cop. The cop said "Halt!" Carver kept running. The cop gave chase. Carver couldn't explain. He'd need all his breath to win the bet. He was close to a heart attack, and perhaps a cop's bullet through the back, as he stumbled into the Pen and Pencil followed by the Law. Alwell was close to apoplexy. His eyes bulged. His mouth and chin were splattered with half-chewed cracker crumbs. He still had two crackers in his hand. When he tried to speak he made a sound like a man gargling ashes.

The cop settled for a beer. We heard later that he had resigned.

After a long lunch at the Pen and Pencil, one day when the rain was coming down by the buckets, the question of getting back to work was reluctantly brought up. That, naturally, suggested a bet to Alwell. He bet the magnificent proprietor, John C. Bruno, he could run all the way up Forty-fifth Street to INS, backwards.

"And on one foot," he added.

John swore excitedly that he would buy everyone in sight a drink if Lou achieved such a miracle.

Lou opened a borrowed umbrella with the flair of a circus tight-rope walker, gave a mighty leap backward on one leg, somehow retained his balance, and sloshed and slopped away on his mad race.

"He was doing great until he got a bad break," Carver later reported. "A cab splashed up to the curb beside him. Louie made the mistake of looking up. He found himself staring into Berkson's stupefied glare. This proved unnerving. Louie slipped and sprawled into a puddle, all snarled up with his broken umbrella. In a state of shock, Berkson ordered the cab to proceed, and Alwell came back to the Pen and Pencil to argue with Bruno over the bet. Alwell took the stand that he hadn't lost, really, because an outsider had interfered with his performance in a contest of skill and daring."

Alwell played an incomparable role at INS on national election nights. He set up a series of tables half as long as the deck of an aircraft carrier and divided the table space into sections reserved for returns from each of the states. Then he drew and tacked up an impressive chart which only he seemed able to decipher. He hired extra copyboys, laid in a supply of sandwiches, and kept the coffee-runners running. Our election headquarters lacked only one requisite: complete election returns. There wasn't enough of INS spread around the country to amass comprehensive tallies, identify trends, and obtain significant prognostications from the king-makers. We borrowed what we could from the *Mirror,* which had its own staff and a much more comprehensive coverage of AP and UP.

But somehow we held our own against these impossible odds— and sometimes we would breeze out in front. I wrote our night leads (for A.M. papers) for the 1952 and 1956 elections. Long before the polls closed in the West I'd yell across the room to Alwell, "Give me a projection, Lou." Lou would take his feet off a table, finish a soggy cup of coffee, riffle through the spiked flimsies of depressingly early returns from a few key states, look at his Rosetta stone chart, take a hot drag on his cigarette and say something like, "Ike by six million popular votes, and let's say four hundred fifty electoral votes." And I'd pound out a new lead. Lou was better than a Univac, and could run backwards on one leg to boot. Today's TV networks spend millions on what Lou gave INS for nothing.

I inherited that task of writing the election leads, something of an honor around our shop. The role had been played for some years previous by Bill Hutchinson, head of our Washington bureau, close friend of many national political figures, and one of the most sublimely pigheaded newspapermen I've ever met. His shouts and dark rages terrorized the Washington bureau. The only man there who was able to present even a slightly alternative point of view without being devoured was Art Herman. Most of the others, and they were good men, longed for friendlier fields in which to browse. But they stood in awe of Hutch's zeal and accomplishments as a lone wolf reporter and friend of the mighty on Capitol Hill, the White House, the FBI— and the Washington Redskins. The Iron Chancellor of INS-Washington was a slavering fan of that professional football team. He regarded owner George Preston Marshall's invitation to sit on the Redskin bench during a game as highly as he did his great newsbeats.

Hutch never worried too much about his troops' feelings.

He arrived in San Francisco in the heady spring of 1945 several days in advance of the opening of the assembly of fifty nations which cemented the United Nations, a not ill-considered verb. Jack Hanley whisked him to the hall, hard by the scene of the delegate meetings, where all the major news services of the world as well as all the great dailies and the news weeklies had leased space and set up on-the-spot bureaus. Hanley had wangled what all conceded to be the best space in the building. He had rented desks, typewriters, file cases, and had installed two teletype machines all geared and wired into the INS lines that reached across the land.

"Tear it out," Hutch said, in the sternly thin-lipped manner of a man who has just been grievously affronted.

"But Hutch, it's the best spot. . . ."

"Rip it up," Hutch thunderously ordered. "We'll work out of the regular bureau."

The regular bureau, housed in a forgotten wing of an almost as forgotten Hearst afternoon paper, the *Call-Bulletin,* was located on Howard Street. It did not matter that Howard Street lay in darkest Skid Row. Its bums had been netted by the police and placed elsewhere in escrow, so that delicate UN delegates from, say, Belorussia would not be offended by the sight of them. What mattered to Jack and the rest of us was that Hutch arbitrarily was screwing up our operation, making it even more difficult to compete with the better-manned, or at least more-manned, AP and UP.

Just as arbitrarily, Hutch changed his mind. There was a small marshmallow deep inside him, like the liquid core of a tough golf ball. It exerted itself in odd ways. He was very tough at the meeting he called on the first day he was in San Francisco. He laid down the law, and the assignments, to the Washington staffers who had come out for the story, and in the same tones that had given some of them ulcers and most of them shakes. Finally, he came to me, an outlander from INS-New York. He had given out all the possible assignments, including the job of writing the night lead, to his Washington staffers.

"What are *you* out here for?" Hutch asked.

It was a logical enough question, but I just didn't like the way he said it.

"To write the night lead," I said.

"The night lead, on a story like this?" he asked. "You're a sportswriter." He made it sound like a dirty word. So I went to the San Francisco Press Club, then unquestionably the world's best, to commune with its dollar steaks and twenty-five-cent Scotch.

The next morning at nine my phone at the Palace Hotel awakened me. It was Hutch. He was angry.

"Where the hell are you?" he demanded.

"In bed." After all, I had nothing to do but write a column, hours later.

"In bed! Don't you realize it's noon in New York and Washington and the A.M. wire is opening? Get the hell over here and start your night lead."

There was another day when Hutch made a greater mistake. He buzzed into the temporary bureau, leaned over the superbly groomed shoulder of Inez Robb as she was writing her column, and after a brief kibitzing job said, "What's *that* crap?"

Inez sprang to her feet, livid.

"How *dare* you!" she shrieked at what was probably the rudest man she had met in her newspaper life. Hutch flinched, genuinely startled by her reaction. Later he asked one of his Washington staff, "Why would she blow her top like that? What did I say that hurt her feelings?" He was flabbergasted.

Hutch was an incorrigible Republican, and that's how I wound up with his traditional job of writing the election leads. In November of 1948 he moved on New York with selected members of his Washington staff to handle the outcome of the contest between the overwhelming favorite, Gov. Tom Dewey, and the poor White House incumbent President Harry S. Truman. Hutch had no need for or confidence in the clairvoyance of Lou Alwell. Dewey would win—big. Hutch's leads reflected that conviction from the start, though INS prided itself in being as impartial as Charles Evans Hughes, once described by Bugs Baer as being so impartial that he even parted his beard down the middle.

I was assigned to cover Dewey's headquarters at the Roosevelt Hotel on the night of the election. I arrived at 8 P.M. and found things quite festive. Dewey workers were beginning to assemble in the ballroom for the victory celebration. There could be nothing less. The Democratic forces were hopelessly split among the President, former Vice President Henry Wallace, heading the Progressive ticket splinter, and Sen. Strom Thurmond, leader of the States Rights ticket.

Through much of the long night that followed, and as the orchids began to wilt on the fine committeewomen, some of whom surely had posed for Helen Hokinson, campaign manager Herbert Brownell made periodic descents from the candidate's suite aloft in the hotel to assure party-worker and press that things looked good. It seemed that every time he re-entered the elevator to be borne aloft, an AP printer that had been installed at the headquarters crackled out another bulletin indicating that Harry Truman, the 15 to 1 shot, was (1) not being swamped as the pollsters had predicted, and (2) was taking a pretty commanding lead.

No such heresy, of course, was getting on the INS wire. Hutch was in command. His leads had Dewey on the brink, verge, edge of a colossal triumph which would restore constitutional government, rout rascals, revitalize free enterprise, clean up the mess. And so it went through the night in a few selected circles, notably on the INS wire, at the Chicago *Tribune,* which went to press with a "Dewey Wins" edition that became a collector's item, and in the running radio commentary of H. V. Kaltenborn. At the Roosevelt, we knew differently. For one thing, Brownell had been commanded to make no more appearances. But more importantly, the photographers had ruled that it was all over. They staged pictures showing the night-charwoman shift tearing posters of the determined-looking candidate from the walls of Dewey headquarters, and other shots of brooms sweeping torn pictures and brave campaign quotes and pledges into trash bins. I kept the office alerted to these goings on.

Shortly before noon of the next day, Jim Hagerty, Dewey's press secretary, emerged from the elevator and headed for the crowded newsroom. He had a folded sheet of paper, like hotel stationery, in his hand. I picked up the phone that connected me immediately with the INS news desk. A voice said, "INS."

"Dewey concedes!" I said. "Flash it . . . bulletin it . . . something. Let's get going." I was conjuring a lead. After a moment I realized that there had been no rattle of activity on the other end.

"Did you get that?" I shouted. "Dewey concedes. Get cracking."

"Who's this?" the voice asked. I had been on duty and on and off the phone for sixteen hours. Alone.

"It's me—Considine," I said angrily. "Who the hell do you think it is? Now get going, goddam it. Dewey concedes." I could see Hagerty from where I was phoning. He was advancing into the mass of reporters and was obviously about to read whatever was written on the paper he held.

"This is Paul Allerup, Bob," the voice of INS said. "I just came on. I didn't know you. . . ."

"Paul, for Christ's sake get it on the wire: 'Dewey concedes.' "

There was an interminable delay, then Paul said, "How can we say Dewey concedes? Hutch's last lead has him out in front and. . . ."

I don't remember what I said, but it must have been a substantial enough oath to get Dewey's concession on the wire—three or four minutes after it might have been. The next week, *Editor & Publisher* carried a shameless INS advertisement, written by Berkson. It was one of those "First Again" blurbs which spread their bright pin-feathers through that pious blat. Glumly reading the ad, threaded with praise more fitted to describe a turn in the affairs of the Battle of the Bulge, I learned that INS had scored a "notable one-minute beat" over AP and UP on Dewey's concession. Berkson wrote something else about that time: a memo, as confidential as the recipe for the A-bomb, stating that thereafter the election leads would no longer be the automatic assignment of Bill Hutchinson. That's how I fell into, or rose to, the slot.

Hutch and Berkson had one strong trait in common: Either could inspire great wrath in a reporter, then turn it away. At five o'clock one afternoon at INS I decided that I had taken all I could tolerate from Seymour. I stood up, ready to do vulgar battle with him in the newsroom. At eight o'clock I was at his apartment at a black tie affair for some real or imagined client, and we were happily chatting over one of his most civilized martinis.

The day General MacArthur flew from San Francisco to Washington, where he was to make his "Old Soldiers Never Die" speech to the joint session of Congress the following day, I was one of twenty reporters invited by Rex Smith of American Airlines to "race" the General's Constellation across the country in American's first DC-6B. We covered MacArthur's speech and reception at San Francisco, then were rushed to the airport behind him, witnessed his takeoff for Washington, wrote our stories, filed them with Western Union, and boarded the DC-6B. It took off a half hour behind MacArthur, made what was then an extraordinary nonstop flight across the country, and reached Washington a half an hour before Col. Tony Story brought in the General's plane. It was still short of midnight in Washington. I realized with a slight shock that this was probably the first time on record that a reporter had covered two stories on opposite coasts within the same calendar day. I got to a phone and called INS-Washington. Hutch, of all people, answered. He was alone in the office, except for the teletype operator, for some unfathomable reason.

"Hutch, this is Considine. I've got a story I'd like to dictate about . . ."

"Get off the goddam phone!" Hutch bellowed. He seemed to be typing while he cursed me.

I tried again: a brief summary about what a unique gimmick it would be to have San Francisco *and* Washington datelines and by-lines by the same fellow, same day. . . .

"Will you get off the goddam phone?" Hutch shouted. It had been a long hard day for me. So I shouted, too. It was one of those senseless outbursts born of the twin devils of wounded pride and frustration. When I had finished, I could still hear typing for a time. Then Hutch spoke, and his voice was as tired as mine, but softer.

"Will you get off the goddam phone and let me finish the piece I'm doing under your by-line?" he asked. "We've been rolling with it since your goddam plane landed ten minutes ago."

Those two died like flashbulbs: one moment blazing, the next moment forever spent. Hutch, who was told little or nothing about the plan to shut down INS, read the abrupt announcement, went home, and died of a heart attack later that day. Berkson's heart gave off a warning skip not too long after that, but not particularly from any pang resulting from the death of INS. Seymour by that time had wired all of his built-in dynamos to the *Journal American,* as its publisher, and the paper was reflecting his tremendous drive and energy. Reluctantly, he consented to enter a San Francisco hospital for a check-up before returning to New York. On January 4, 1959, he called his assistant publisher, Charles Gould, with a long list of things he wanted done in the next day's paper.

"Seymour, for Pete's sake, I've taken care of all that," Gould said with a patient laugh. "Relax."

To ask Seymour Berkson to relax, really relax, was tantamount to telling him to get out of the news business, or roll over and die. Which is precisely what he did moments after talking to Gould.

"INS was a last frontier of the news business . . . free and easy, adventurous, awkward, short-handed, and constantly caught in money downholds," Carver elegized. Then he added:

> It was replete with all manner of harassments, including trends in office politics, and composed of an assortment of solid performers and misfits unsurpassed for talent and lack of it. Nothing made the slightest sense until you became accustomed to the contradictions. INS would spend thousands of dollars on a major story—"hit the big ones hard"—and then slash expenses in a panic so sweeping that Alwell would be confronted with a box of pencils only three-fourths used and berated for the office's extravagant waste.
>
> Berkson deplored office drinking, but learned to live with it as an epidemic he could not escape. Occasionally, he had reason to take a firm stand, such as the time our Western Union chief, Tom Walsh, enraged because Seymour had ordered some long story sent in by Postal Telegraph, deposited a large and very dead fish on Berkson's desk, with a thud. Another time he was vexed when, upon pulling out a paper towel in the men's room the rack flew open and a bottle of whisky fell out and hit him on the foot. He limped back into the newsroom letting it be known on all sides that if that ever happened again, well, disciplinary action would be taken.
>
> Drinking never seemed to interfere greatly with the flow of our wire. There was that Saturday afternoon when George Lait,

sitting in our Sunday desk with a monumental hangover, survived a shock that would have unsprung a lesser man: Gobind Behari Lal tiptoed out of his hiding place behind a file case and put down under George's nose at least a dozen books of copy. It was our science editor's pleasure to announce exclusively in this Sunday feature that science had solved one of mankind's most baffling puzzles: how to make practical use of urine.

George held his head in his hands for a time and prayed. He was also handling a bulletin story out of Washington, requiring New York follow-ups, and some big local story had burst in his face. George's staff, consisting of a cable-writer, wire-filer, and an officeboy to make up flimsy books, was two-thirds missing. Only the officeboy was visible. George ordered him to search the neighborhood bars for the cable-writer and wire-filer. The boy found them but he got drunk with them and didn't come back for a long time. Finally, people began drifting in, and George not only had his sparse Sunday staff but volunteers from the dayside, all pitching in. He borrowed two dollars from the sports department for dinner, drank it, returned to the office, and made a very touching talk. He said that this staff was undoubtedly the finest ever in any news-gathering organization. He vowed to call The Chief himself at San Simeon, first thing Monday morning, and get raises for everybody. Then he went to sleep peacefully, lulled by the fine sound of stories moving out on our teletypes.

The resourcefulness of INS men was seldom rewarded, but we rolled with the punches.

On his own initiative, and with his own money, Carver went to Boston once to play a horse he liked and to see his beautiful wife's relatives. While there, he wrote a superb feature about Don Meade, once a top jockey, then barred from the track "for life," but by this time attempting a comeback by the lowly route of exercise boy. Later that same day Carver attended a civic reception for Billy Southworth, who had been named manager of the Boston Braves, and persuaded him to write a signed story at no expense to INS. Lawton also wrote a couple of columns with a New England flavor, filed the whole batch, and an important client—the Yankee Network—sent a grateful wire to Berkson. When Carver returned to his New York desk the next day there was a memo from Berkson, congratulating him heartily on his string of exclusives. The memo had been sent via Faris' office, and Barry had added a P.S. It read: "Good job—*with some prodding.*"

The expense account Carver rendered after covering the America's Cup races off Newport was, of course, exorbitant. One item that repeatedly appeared was "Launch—$50." The account bounced through routine channels to Faris, who took one look at it and called Alwell.

"Louie, we've still got a horse on our books, bought by Damon Runyon when he was chasing Pancho Villa," Faris said. "We own an armed mule train Red Knickerbocker bought in Ethiopia. We're still carrying that Chinese junk Floyd Gibbons picked up in Hong Kong. Now Carver has added a fleet of launches. Looks like we're in the transportation business, mostly. Find out what it's all about."

Alwell found occasion to bring it up to Carver at the Pen and Pencil.

"The launch bit doesn't make any sense," he said. "Faris knows that you worked on the cutter the Coast Guard gave to the press. Remember me? I got your credentials for you."

"I still needed a launch every day," Carver said.

"But why?"

Lawton looked at his friend steadily.

"For shallow water," he said.

Alwell nodded sagely. And okayed the account.

INS covered several big and expensive stories in 1938, including Chamberlain at Munich, but one it skimped on turned out to be a triumph. Carver, about to cover the Poughkeepsie Regatta, was told that he must somehow get along without a wire at the finish line. Seems it would cost $150 to string it from a Western Union shack located on the Hudson shore about midway between the start and finish of the four-mile stretch. Resignedly, Carver chose the shack as the place he would work. He would not be able to see either start or finish of the eight-oared shell classic, but he could file into New York from there. And the AP and UP stories, sent from down at the finish line, had to come through there. With a little bit of luck . . .

Rain and choppy water delayed the race until near dark. Carver couldn't even see the crews as they swept past the Western Union shack. He went back to his blind spot and struck up an easy friendship with the shack's other occupants, venerable Western Union operators.

In time, two operators' old fashioned keys, using empty Prince Albert tobacco tins as amplifiers, came to life. AP and UP were flashing from the finish line: "Navy wins."

Carver looked over a cooperative operator's shoulder, sent the flash to INS on his own wire and began beating out a story about the big upset. Navy had not been given a chance by the experts. Either California or Washington would surely win.

Carver's story was rolling into INS-New York at a good clip when AP and UP had a violent change of heart at the finish line: "Kill Navy flash. California wins." A dismal silence then fell upon their wires. Carver sighed. Too much was too much. He continued with his story about Navy's dramatic victory over a storm-tossed Hudson in the face of stunning odds. Etc. What he was writing, in effect, was "To hell with INS" and its blind economies.

Then still another flash from AP and UP: "Kill California flash. Navy wins." Carver's story was so far along by that time and winning so many friends on the news desks of scores of client papers which also took AP and UP, that he had gotten down into the "color" of the victory: ". . . while the lights of battlecraft along the murky course blinked their salute. . . ."

Drenched, pooped, Carver returned to the office late that night, chiefly to type out a note of resignation. There was a memo in his typewriter. It was a flattering note from one of INS's most gifted writers, Walter Kiernan, who did not know Carver had been denied the advantage of a wire at the finish line. Kiernan's note congratulated Lawton for his "fast and excellent story written under pressure."

The *"under pressure,"* he figured later, was what prompted Carver to change his mind about quitting. He went to the Pen and Pencil instead.

INS lost some close ones, too.

On Monday, May 7, 1945, AP-London flashed the end of the war in Europe, followed by a two-hundred-word bulletin, and then a long and stirring account by correspondent Ed Kennedy of the surrender scene at the "little red schoolhouse" at Reims. It swept the world, sent millions spilling into the streets to celebrate. At San Francisco, the word was brought into the delivery room of the infant UN by a roly-poly Latin American delegate who disrupted a meeting by waddling up and down the aisles waving an Extra which had just spun off the presses of the *Call-Bulletin.* He kept shouting in incoherent and apoplectic Spanish. Joy reigned in the hopeful "parliament of man," and through the world. But not at INS. Or UP. Or any other news service. We had suffered a colossal beating. Only AP had the top story of the age.

At INS-New York, Jack Oestreicher, our foreign director, was in need of being tied down. He knew we had been double-crossed, but for an interminable two or three hours could not pin down the circumstances. The best we could do in the face of the masterful story by Kennedy was to speak of it on our own wire as an unconfirmed report and guardedly question its authenticity. That was not very convincing. Kennedy's story was complete, down to the names of the American, British, Soviet, and French officers who had presided over the surrender of the abject remnants of Hitler's general staff.

The most careful precautions had been taken and the most solemn assurances given on all sides before that to guard against a recurrence of Roy Howard's solo flight ending of World War I. U.S. editors had been told by Byron Price, the chief censor, that no announcement about Germany's surrender could be considered official unless it came either from General Eisenhower's SHAEF or a simultaneous broadcast by President Truman, Prime Minister Churchill and Premier Stalin.

Oestreicher had received a tantalizing message from Joe Smith, who was at SHAEF, several hours before the AP's bombshell. Smith messaged that Jimmy Kilgallen had left Paris. Period. Then Joe began a story that smacked of something much more significant than its subject matter, which, of course, had had to pass through the SHAEF censor's office. Joe wrote that Monday had dawned "almost like the birth of peace in Europe, with brilliant Spring sunshine flooding Paris." Shortly before Kennedy's story broke, Smith sent Oestreicher another pregnant message. It said simply that Jack could eliminate the word "almost" from his earlier story.

At San Francisco we gathered miserably around our INS printer, hours after AP's great beat. The word from Washington was that President Truman was about to make a statement. It could only be confirmation that the AP was right.

The bells rang inside the chattering machine. Then: "FLASH—WAR NOT OVER—HST."

We gave vent to a savage yell of joy. It was Inez Robb who brought us to our senses.

"What the hell are we cheering for?" she asked. Her husband, Ad Robb, was serving overseas.

When the official word came through from SHAEF the next day, it was a fat letdown. AP's promotion department crowed loudly over the scoop. But other sounds, shouts of betrayal, began to filter through from Ed Kennedy's colleagues. The full story pieced itself together as SHAEF censorship relaxed:

Seventeen correspondents, including our man Kilgallen, were flown from Paris to Reims May 6. They were permitted to watch Hitler's dream of a Thousand Year Reich end with the quavering signature of Adm. Karl Doenitz and the nervous silence of Adm. Gen. Hans Georg von Friedeberg, who was soon to commit suicide. The actual signing was at 2:41 A.M., May 7, Reims time. Brig. Gen. Frank Allen, in charge of the correspondents, briefed them pointedly on their responsibility. They could write their flashes, two-hundred-word bulletins, and as much of a story as they wanted to write. These could be deposited with Press Wireless at the Hôtel Scribe in Paris, to be held for release until SHAEF's consent or the aforementioned Big Three broadcast. All present gave their pledges.

Kilgallen and Kennedy, with their stories written and neatly enveloped, were in the first of the correspondents' cars that pulled up to the hotel late that morning of May 7, Paris time. The worthy competitors hit the curb before the car stopped rolling, burst through the door and headed across the lobby for the steps leading up to Press Wireless. Each wanted to get his flash, bulletin, and lead into the "Hold for Release" basket first—believing that the news would be moved on a first-come-first-served basis, when the time came to move it.

"Ed was gaining on me," Kil recalled a long time later. "He had longer legs than I did, which didn't seem fair. So I did a bad thing. I lobbed my typewriter at him, like a discus thrower. It was Faris' portable, come to think of it, but I knew he wouldn't mind. It caught Ed on the back of his legs and down he went. I shot past him, up the steps, and plunked down my story first: flash, bulletin of two hundred words, and thirty-one typewritten pages. Ed came in second, limping. I felt sorry about what I had done. They wouldn't allow that kind of thing at Aqueduct," the inveterate horseplayer was to muse in distant retrospect.

Kennedy exacted a terrible revenge. Learning (he said later) that the Flensburg radio had announced the Reims signing, Ed called AP-London through an Army switchboard, whose people had not been alerted to the lid that had been placed on the story, and dictated his flash, bulletin, and story from carbon copies he had made of his escrowed original. AP-London put a Reims dateline on everything and spread it through the world.

AP's pride of achievement was short-lived. Robert McLean, president and publisher of the Philadelphia *Bulletin,* and serving as president of the AP at the time, frigidly rebuked those in AP who permitted Kennedy's story to be released. AP-New York quickly cancelled its credit-taking promotion campaign. It pulled the red rug from under its conquering hero and cast him into exterior darkness. Years later, after serving out his time in a remote AP bureau and a quiet period on California papers, Kennedy met death most prosaically. He stepped off a curb and was hit by a car. The obits raked over his "shame." None of the dour last hurrahs that I saw got around to mentioning that if the AP had not chickened out on him, had stood by him as staunchly as, say, Faris stood by Kilgallen on the Hauptmann verdict, Ed would have been remembered as an intrepid reporter who saw his duty to his organization and answered the call.

If I could have afforded it, I would have paid INS to let me work for it. It was such a joy, over and above the frustrations. At INS, everything happened in Technicolor, and wide screen. . . .

We all trembled over Louella Parsons' bold announcement on the INS wire from Hollywood that Ingrid Bergman had an excellent reason for leaving hearth and home to marry her Italian director, Roberto Rossellini: she was pregnant by him. We trembled even more when there were indignant denials from the principals, the studios, and Louella's rivals. At the height of the tension, Louella returned home late one night to find her husband, Dr. Harry Martin, one of the most delightfully irreverent men in the nation, kneeling at his bedside reciting the Rosary. She dropped to his side, petrified that he was dying.

"Docky . . . Docky, what are you doing saying the Rosary?" she cried. "What's wrong?"

"Nothing," Docky said. "I was just saying a prayer that Ingrid *is* knocked up." *

INS had some homely reporters working for it, but not its girls. We had Inez, a good-looking woman who could type with her long

---

* She was.

white gloves in place, if the occasion warranted. And, whenever we could spring her from the *Journal American,* we had the services of Dorothy Kilgallen, whose face and style and keen mind were to be known to television's millions, too. We had Lee Carson, Phyllis Battelle, Dixie Tighe, and Peggy Diggins, all made to make men's heads wheel. And pert, pretty Rita Hume whose high school cheer leader looks and demeanor were misleading. She battled her way to Dongo, on Lake Como, on April 28, 1945, to see Mussolini, the life riddled out of him, strung up by his heels, and sent out the first story.

We had Doris Duke working for us briefly, too, for twenty-five dollars a week. The irrepressible Michael Chinigo, the Yale-trained Albanian who was the dominant figure in Roman journalism during his years with INS, put the richest girl in the world on the payroll and arranged with Col. Tex McCrary of the Eighth Air Force to get her to Berlin. There, at a dinner celebrating the short but sweet accord between the Soviet and American conquerors, Tex proposed a toast to a Russian woman tank-commander who was present. In response, the ranking Russian officer rose and proposed a toast to Doris.

"To a typical American girl," he said, probably the rarest compliment she was ever paid.

When our man at the Aly Khan-Rita Hayworth wedding, Irving R. Levine, filed the final words of stories of the nuptials by himself, Louella Parsons, Jack Lee, Elie Maissi, and whoever else we had buzzing around Cannes, he received a fond salute from Larry Klingman and Gerald Green, who handled the story at INS-New York.

"Mazeltov," they cabled him—a word breathed upon newly wedded couples by their Jewish relatives and friends which means "Good life." Faris appeared at their desk the next day, waving his "Mazeltov" flimsy and wanting to know what was going on around there. The boys explained that they were congratulating Levine and the others in simple, word-saving, money-saving Hebrew. Faris was pleased.

INS was sometimes accused by its jealous competitors of being edited by remote control, or osmosis. Actually, our stories were combed quite thoroughly, but never as completely as when the desk was manned by Paul Allerup. Hardly any lead ever really pleased Paul. Once, when an angry writer viewed a story Paul had dissected remorselessly, he cried, "You'd edit Shakespeare!"

Paul considered that for a searching moment. Then nodded.

"His stuff could have been tightened," he muttered.

But Paul did like at least one lead. It had been written for him without his knowledge by Klingman and Green as a gag, after they had wrapped up a story of a big plane crash in India. Before Paul came to work the next morning they slipped it into the pile of flimsies which had moved out during the night, sure that his eye would fall upon it. The eye did. It purported to be an eyewitness account of the crash:

By Ali Ben Ghouli

World Copyright, International News Service

The ways of Allah are mysterious indeed. . . .

"My God, what a great lead on this eyewitnesser," Paul exclaimed. "How did we ever get it from a guy in a rice paddy?"

We lost good men for bad reasons. Saul Pett left INS because Berkson insisted that the real lead of Saul's vivid account of the crash of a B-25 into the uppermost reaches of the Empire State Building was not the uniqueness of the collision but the number of persons killed: seven. Saul's fine work thereafter graced the AP wire.

Sid Eiges, a first-class man with responsible duties on the overnight desk, was being paid only seventy dollars a week. He asked Joe Connolly for a five-dollar raise. Joe mentioned it to Faris. Barry didn't like the chain of command Sid had used in his forlorn quest, and said so sharply to Sid. Sid quit, and eventually had to settle for a fifty-thousand-dollar-a-year job as a vice president of NBC.

One night Les Conklin failed to show up on time. Klingman called the Snug and learned that Les was asleep in his room over the bar, a room furnished mainly with a cot and his racing charts, past performance sheets, and losing parimutuel tickets. Larry called the police and reported that a man named Les Conklin was operating a bookie joint in bold defiance of the law in a little room over the Snug.

Les reported for work an hour later, carrying his bedroll, a carton of martinis, and his racing notes.

"Damnedest thing just happened to me," he said to Larry. "The cops busted in on me and accused me of running a bookie joint. They were going to lock me up until I managed to convince them that I worked for INS."

"How did you prove that?" Larry asked.

ABOVE: Bob Considine interviewing Henry Ford II
BELOW: With Gen. Douglas MacArthur

ABOVE: Considine and Gen. Jonathan M. Wainwright working on *General Wainwright's Story*. LEFT: Flying over the hump—India to China—June, 1945

RIGHT: Westbrook Pegler and Mrs. Franklin D. Roosevelt (*seated*); Deems Taylor and George Bye (*standing*). BELOW: Pat Morin, Jack Woliston, and Considine at Sing Sing prison to witness the execution of the Rosenbergs, June 19, 1953

ABOVE: Considine with Frank Conniff and William Randolph Hearst, Jr., interviewing Nikita Khrushchev, Moscow, 1957. BOTTOM LEFT: Considine and Babe Ruth celebrating the publication of *The Babe Ruth Story*. BOTTOM RIGHT: Boarding a plane with Toots Shor

ABOVE: President Dwight D. Eisenhower greeting Considine. BELOW: Frank Conniff and Considine discussing the latter's book, *It's the Irish,* with President John F. Kennedy, August, 1961

ABOVE: Considine and William R. Hearst, Jr., in a helicopter over the Mekong Delta, 1963
BELOW: Considine chatting with the Duke of Windsor

TOP LEFT: Watching an atomic bomb test at Yucca Flat, Nevada
TOP RIGHT: Considine with his wife, Millie. BELOW: And with his
daughter, Deborah

LEFT: Bob Considine at work. BELOW: Just before taking off at Bien Hoa, Vietnam, September, 1966

Les fumbled through his Chaplinesque suit and pulled out a small savings account book.

"I showed them this," he said, pointing to his balance. His balance was $1.40.

To stay abreast or even ahead of AP and UP frequently called for resourcefulness above and beyond the INS-ers' already considerable dedication. Good imagination also contributed. We were not above employing a jeep and a boxer dog named Butch von Hohenzollern to turn the tides of news-gathering battles with the opposition.

The jeep had been scrounged in some mysterious manner by Lee Ferrero, the only man INS had in Korea at one of the more critical phases of that war—the tug and pull of the late winter of 1950–51. Lee graciously shared his transportation with the AP and UP correspondents while covering the battling Third Division's activities in mountainous country that permitted little other means of transportation. Without warning or replacement, Lee was ordered to leave the Third Division and report thereafter from Eighth Army Headquarters in Taegu. There was no way he could take his jeep with him.

The thought of leaving all those good stories behind him was intolerable to Lee. So he made a hard but—in view of the circumstances—fair bargain with Sam Summerlin of AP. Sam could have the jeep if he kept Lee (and thus INS) informed about everything that happened to the Third Division. Sam rejected this shocking propositon. Lee shrugged. He said he was sorry, but he would be forced therefore to immobilize the jeep by taking its key and distributor head with him when he left for Taegu. That clinched it. Sam got his jeep, Lee got his news, and the word soon spread that INS was getting fine coverage out of that theater of war by means of a "talking jeep."

Butch von Hohenzollern and God helped INS score a fine beat when Robert A. Vogeler, the I.T. & T. official, was released by the Hungarian government after imprisonment on charges of spying for the United States. Barry Faris had become convinced that Marvin Stone, of INS's London bureau, had the inside track on all news about Vogeler because he was friendly with Mrs. Vogeler, a good-looking blonde who had made several dramatic pleas to the Communist government in Budapest to release her husband. Marvin made repeated efforts to assure Faris that he had no better "in" with Mrs.

Vogeler than AP or UP types assigned to the story. But when word came that Vogeler was about to be released and would be reunited with his wife and family at a villa she had rented in Vienna, Faris cabled Stone that he expected a clear beat.

As ever, AP and UP had much superior communications. Vienna was plugged into their European wire networks, with immediate transmission to London offices on tap. INS would be forced to use the overhead cable—RCA—to New York. That would take, conservatively, twenty minutes longer than the direct Vienna–London–New York wires of the competition.

Stone dispatched his one-man staff, John Fiehn, to the Austro-Hungarian border at Nickelsdorff. Fiehn got through to Stone in Vienna by phone and dictated a good story about Vogeler's release.

"How about AP and UP?" Marvin asked him.

"It's a dead heat at this end," Fiehn said. "They've got everything I got."

Resignedly Stone dashed off the story, filed it with RCA, and waited for the "rocket" from Faris—a rocket being a damning notice that the opposition had come through first. Most rockets end with a morale-shattering demand, usually, "How, please?"

One hour later, Stone received a cable from Faris. Expecting the worst, he was flabbergasted to read a message of congratulations. INS had had a clear beat of five minutes on the AP and ten minutes on the UP.

In the case of UP, a singularly precise bolt of lightning had hit and destroyed its telex antenna on the roof of the Wiener Kurier building. It had been erected to flash the news with the speed of light. Instead, the harried UP staffers had to raise Frankfurt by phone, which was time-consuming, and holler the story and details over a faulty line. It took UP thirty minutes to get the story to New York.

Butch von Hohenzollern delivered the coup de grace to the AP. Seems that on this momentous day the AP's Viennese secretary, one Effie, brought to work a particularly aromatic luncheon featuring bratwurst. She deposited the paper bag that contained the lunch at the side of her desk, resting on the telephone-connection box. A change in the wind communicated the presence of the tempting lunch to Butch, who had been asleep in INS's quarters several doors away from AP's room in the Kurier building. The boxer roused himself and went sniffing down the hall, entered AP, and made a voracious lunge for Effie's lunch just as the call came through from Nickelsdorff. In seizing the bag, Butch tore the phone box from its place, cutting off communication from the border for twenty-five minutes. AP was very angry at Butch von Hohenzollern.

"Ordinarily, that kind of stunning and undeserved luck on a story is enough to hold a man for a long time," Stone, now one of the editors of *U.S. News and World Report,* recently noted. "But in this case, we also came through with a tremendous photo beat, reflected in the full page the New York Sunday *Mirror* gave it while the Sunday *News* was dragging with some inferior shots. Ours was a memorable picture: the Vogelers reunited at the gate of their home with their two handsome boys, and the tears spilling from Vogeler's eyes.

"We had waited overly long for that picture and the oppositions had sped off to the airport with earlier stuff to make a BEA flight to Paris, whence they could radiophoto to New York. In those days there were no radiophoto facilities in Vienna. Well, we missed the BEA flight to Paris and had to put our undeveloped film on a later flight, direct to London. When New York was told that we probably would take a shellacking on photos, Sid Mautner, in charge of International News Photos, sent me a real tough rocket advising me that I was directly responsible for ruining INS's reputation around the world.

"A few hours later, however, up turned a cable of ecstatic congratulations from Mautner. Seems that the BEA flight had been grounded in some remote European airfield while our later flight sailed right on into London.

"So ended one of those rare days when, instead of putting your luck to work for INS and peanut pay, you should have been standing at the tables at Monte Carlo."

INS men *looked* right, when they had to, when nothing else would suffice.

No reporters were permitted on the clubhouse grounds one day in the early 1930's when Bobby Jones was invited to play a round with the Prince of Wales. But Tom Watson of INS-London easily made it. No one at the gate dared challenge him as he swept through in his rented chauffeur-driven limousine, smoothing his British Colonel's brush mustache, bowler cocked just so, spats, umbrella tightly sheathed, and face set in bored disdain. Phoned a fine account of the match to INS in Fleet Street.

INS was represented at the Lying In of George VI in 1952 at Sandringham, though the British and world press was specifically barred. John Carlova, whose principal claim to fame before he covered the Lying In was that his father had played piano for Helen Morgan, had the countenance of an honest choirboy. Scotland Yard's men at the Palace gate were touched when John showed up and shyly told them his story: He was an American GI who had hitchhiked for hundreds of miles to pay a simple soldier's tribute to the gentle king he had admired so greatly.

He filed his scoop to INS-London, including mention of the ruse he had used. Then with rare intuition he remained in the area. The next day Ed Korry of the UP appeared at the guarded gates and appeared to be well on his way toward being admitted, after telling a story strikingly similar to John's moist-eyed lie. Then the rug was pulled from under him. John appeared, beaming. And in good voice.

"Hi, Ed," he said, as his rival made his pitch with Scotland Yard, "how are things at the United Press?"

Rivals were always expendable, in the opinion of good INS men. But sometimes colleagues were, too. If the conditions were right, of course.

Marvin Stone was running INS's Far East operation from Tokyo when Operation Big Switch started in August, 1953, shortly after the armistice was signed wrapping up the Korean War. The one returning American POW everybody wanted to know about was Gen. William F. Dean, captured early in the war.

All communications from the press center at the prisoner-reception area were routed through the press center at Seoul and thence to the Tokyo offices of the wire services and other media maintaining offices there. There were, in addition, two or three so-called "official lines," presumably reserved for VIP's and UN personages. Stone instructed Rowland Gould, a displaced Englishman INS had picked up in Tokyo and dispatched to Korea, to try by hook or crook to get access to one of the "official" phones. It was the forlornest of hopes. But Gould apparently looked *right* to the guardians of the phones, strolled by them casually, picked one up, and called INS-Tokyo, immediately after the long press conference in which General Dean denied authorship of statements the enemy had attributed to him during his captivity and related the full account of his grueling experience. Sid White, on the Tokyo end of the wire, took ninety minutes of notes which were transformed, as they arrived, into a fine running story in money-saving cablese put together by Stone and Bob Schakne, shot to San Francisco to the waiting typewriter of bureau chief Howard Handleman, and on to the INS wire. Because all regular press lines out of Korea were hopelessly loaded down that day, INS had Dean's entire story on the desks of its clients about twelve hours ahead of the others.

When AP and UP complained about INS's unauthorized use of an official phone from Korea, Stone was called to Gen. Mark Clark's headquarters, Pershing Heights, Tokyo, on command of Lt. Col. Rodger Bankson, Clark's deputy public information officer. The following dialogue ensued:

Bankson: "OK, Marv, what'll we do about this?"

Stone: "I don't think you ought to do anything. We were just paying AP and UP back for some of their tricks in the past. And retribution is sweet."

Bankson: "I know, I know. But something has got to be done; they're asking for blood."

Stone: "Why don't you throw Gould out of Korea? After all, he hates being there. Secondly, I need him back in Tokyo. Thirdly, his wife threatens to divorce him if he doesn't get the hell out of there and get back home."

Bankson (sighing): "Officially, I didn't hear the last three parts of that statement. Okay, as of this moment, Gould has lost his Korea war accreditation until further notice. No, make that permanently. That ought to satisfy everybody."

INS had magnificent young men in the Korean War, after a bad start. And one of them had a flying machine.

In the early days there was a period of more than a week when Lee Ferrero's schedule went as follows: In the morning he covered the Eighth Army briefing at Taegu, filed his story, raced to the airfield where he had talked himself into the use of a light liaison plane, and flew to I Corps Headquarters on the Western Front. From there, after picking up the news, the plane flew Lee across the peninsula to Eastern Front Headquarters, where he mopped up more news, then the flight back to Taegu in time for the early evening Eighth Army

briefing. Lee finally cried out for help, and got it. Rival newsmen
wrote a song about him, set to the tune of "Mañana." A fragment of
the lyrics went:

> My name is Lee Ferrero
> And I work for INS,
> I always like to write the truth,
> But the lies come out the best,
> I asked for correspondents and they sent me Irwin Tress,
> My name is Lee Ferrero and I work for INS.

"Neither of the slurs was justified," memos Handleman, from his
U.S. News & World Report desk. "Lee's reporting more than stood
up. And Tress, a photographer, did a fine job doubling as a reporter.
In fact, Tress scored one of the greatest beats of the war—and
couldn't get it on the INS wire. He sent word to the Tokyo office late
in October or early November, 1950, that a handful of Chinese 'volunteers' had just been captured. The fear of China's entry into the war
had come true. But the young fellow who happened to be on the desk
in Tokyo that night spiked the story and told nobody about it because,
as he confessed after the oppositions had beaten our brains out on the
story, Tress was 'only a photographer.' "

By the spring of 1951 INS was able to field one of the finest teams
of young correspondents in wire service history: Frank Conniff, later
National Editor of the Hearst papers and now editor of the *World
Journal Tribune;* Don Schanche, who now edits *Holiday;* Bob Schakne,
with CBS-Latin America; Cecil Brownlow, with *Aviation Week;*
Rafael Steinberg, a leading writer on Far East affairs; Don Dixon,
production chief of National Educational Television; Irving R. Levine, with NBC-Rome; John Rich, a Japanese language officer in the
Marines at Kwajalein and Iwo Jima, now with NBC-Tokyo; Frank
Emery, a wonderful kid with a world of promise, who was killed; and
subsequently John Casserly, now with ABC-Washington; Ed Hymoff,
space expert and biographer of Lyndon Baines Johnson; Robert
Elegant, later with the *New York Times;* plus Bob Horiguchi, now
IBM's public relations chief for the Far East, and an astonishing group
of affluent and distinguished correspondents who became known as
"INS's guerrillas."

The guerrillas were of particular usefulness. They were loners, men
who commanded one-man Tokyo bureaus for their estimable news-

papers. When a man would pop over to Korea to cover the fighting, he needed someone back in Tokyo to handle his material and move it along to his editors. INS's Tokyo bureau was manned twenty-four hours a day by a magnificent staff of Handleman and Horiguchi. They worked twelve hours a day and perhaps another six hours of overlap. Gordon Walker of the *Christian Science Monitor* proposed to Handleman, out of the blue, that if INS would take his dictation from Korea and file his copy we could extract anything we wanted from his superb reportage. He was so pleased with the arrangement—INS was not only pleased, it was stupefied—that he urged other fellow loners to do the same, and under the same terms. As a result of his endorsement, INS soon had working for it, at not a penny's cost, such renowned correspondents as Lachie MacDonald and, later, Ward Price of the London *Daily Mail,* Bill Stevenson of the Toronto *Star,* and Denis Warner, then with a group of Australian papers. Without the gratis services of Warner and MacDonald, INS could never have competed with AP and UP on the fall of Taejon and the capture of General Dean.

Horiguchi was a marvel composed of equal parts of Japanese culture, Domei, the respected Japanese wire service that became a propaganda tool after he left it, and the University of Missouri's School of Journalism. Handleman recalls:

> Bob worked out a filing system that gave us an edge over the oppositions.
>
> All wire-service offices were on the second floor of Radio Tokyo. The cable head was a block away at the old Domei building—by 1950 called the Kyodo News Service building. By pure chance, INS was located closest to the Kyodo building. The other bureaus were strung out down a long hall in this order: Agence France-Presse, AP, and, around the corner, Reuters and UP.
>
> All copy had to be hand-carried to Kyodo—where it would be moved on a first-come-first-served basis. Official war communiqués were handed out at the door of the PIO office which was also on the second floor of Radio Tokyo.
>
> Copyboys fought like tigers to get their copies of the communiqués. It was a matter of pride—face—to grab the first copies. Our copyboy raced down the hall like a track man and relayed his two copies—like a baton—to our second copyboy crouched at the door of our office. That boy then ran through the office, dropping one copy to me at my desk in the middle of the office and the other copy on Horiguchi's desk next to the window. Then

he'd jump back to my desk, where I would be finishing the first short bulletin written on a cablegram blank previously addressed and signed. He'd snatch this, run it to Bob, and Bob would pencil-edit it, stuff it in a box and toss it out the window. We had a third copyboy waiting below. He had a bicycle, and off he'd go to the Kyodo cable head like an Olympic cyclist.

Our senior copyboys, Yoshikazu Ohmachi and Sadamu Hoseya, were remarkable kids. They spoke little English, but they taught themselves how to use our typewriters and later learned to operate the teletype machines we installed. They became so expert as teletype punchers that when the Communications Ministry finally installed teletypes at Kyodo our two boys were called on to teach the Ministry's people how to handle them.

The first time anyone in the office knew that the copyboys had learned how to type was when Ohmachi, without a word, handed me an envelope perfectly addressed to Barry Faris. He had looked over my shoulder to see who I was writing a letter to, and addressed the envelope for me. We learned a lot from our copyboys, too. There was the time I was doing a story about the Emperor, and how Japanese regarded him. Ohmachi, who could not have been more than fifteen at the time, answered several questions through an interpreter. Unwittingly, I asked a question he resented. The boy, who earned more at INS than his father earned as a laborer, squared his shoulders, stood at attention, and put his high-paying job on the line.

"You stupid foreigners never will be able to understand our love and reverence for our Emperor," he said. To Ohmachi, such a statement to the boss meant that he would be fired out of hand. But he was willing to accept that rather than remain silent after hearing what he considered to be a slight to his Emperor.

World War II's ending—or the announcement of it by AP's Ed Kennedy—shook INS. The ending of the Korean War produced an INS achievement which compressed within it all of the drive, ingenuity, and sheer delight that made it unique among the wire services. Handleman, Who Was There, remembers it best:

> It was July, 1953. Our INS suite in the Nadja Apartments in Seoul was crowded with competitors, shooting the breeze. Jack Casserly walked in, looking a little odd. After a bit he told me there was a fellow down at the bar who wanted to see me. When we got out of the room he told me what he had. He had the best

beat of the war, a locked-up exclusive that armistice terms had been agreed to.

Then began some play acting. The story had to be written in the room with all the competitors. My typewriter and cable blanks, carbons and so forth were there. Jack and I strolled back in and I sat down and started to write what I said was a little feature. I called Bob Elegant over to read the lead and asked him if he would word it the way I had. He suppressed his excitement, grunted something, walked slowly out of the room, then took off like a sprinter to find the Korean foreign minister. Ed Hymoff came in just then from Eighth Army Headquarters. He read what was in my typewriter, shrugged, and started a poker game as a diversion.

After the story was wrapped up—including confirmation to Elegant from the foreign minister—we got a gratifying payoff. Relaxed and happy and drinking beer, we saw four AP men race past our door toward the press office, single file, to pick up their rockets.

Time was rotten to us when we died.

It hurt us all so much that I tried to retort in my column. It went like this:

This is an open-faced letter to the young man—anonymous as a shady story—who wrote the obituary of International News Service in the Press section of *Time* magazine.

You poor guy:

You write, "On a Coronation story, editors could rely on the AP for the dimensions of the cathedral, the UP for the mood of the ceremony, and the INS (sometimes) for an interview with the barmaid across the way." There is also a reference to "splash-and-dash journalism." That's about all.

The men and women who sat in our silenced newsrooms and read that farewell nose-thumbing felt more than anger. Many of them were seasoned at their trade when you, in all probability, were making your first little jabs at a typewriter. Their anger was tempered by a pity for you; a pity born of the sadness that one feels in the face of flippant ignorance.

For one, I thought of Floyd Gibbons going down on one of the first ships torpedoed in World War I and surviving to write a brilliant story for INS. And of Jimmy Kilgallen tracking down Samuel Insull in Greece and practically bringing him back to trial, after turning him into a kind of legman for INS. And Inez

Robb in North Africa, and some years later in Texas City, being knocked flat by an explosion, and getting off the ground to get her story in to INS. And Davis J. Walsh who helped make sportswriting a profession.

I thought of Bill Hutchinson driving the opposition nuts at the Scopes trial and getting the great wartime beats on the capture and execution of the Nazi submarine-landed saboteurs, and the decision to retain Hirohito on his throne.

I also thought of Richard Tregaskis, Jack Mahon, and Bob Brumby, on Guadalcanal; of Pat Robinson in the New Guinea jungles; of Lee Van Atta, flying on so many bombing and strafing missions that MacArthur ordered him grounded. And of the incomparable H. R. Knickerbocker and irrepressible Sammy Schulman.

The memory of Pete Huss, Frank Conniff, Larry Newman, Graham Hovey, Joe Smith, Bill Hearst, Lee Carson, Joe Willicombe, and the others who went with the troops from the beaches to Berlin filled the cranial room where proud thoughts are stored. And of Mike Chinigo, crawling to a dead German sentry's phone on the beach in Sicily, making contact with the German commander whose artillery was shelling our landing troops, and (in perfect German) ordering him to cease—". . . We have driven the enemy back into the sea." (General Truscott put Mike in for the DSC.) And of Jimmy Young rotting in a Japanese prison, and Alfred Tyrnauer dumped into one of Hitler's death cells in Vienna for courageously writing the truth.

And of Clark Lee, who started the war with the AP on Bataan and ended it with INS in Tokyo. He and Harry Brundidge of *Cosmopolitan* magazine were the only reporters present when Tojo tried to kill himself. I thought, of course, of Runyon on a murder trial, or covering an execution, or describing the burning of the Morro Castle.

I thought of brave lads like Howard Handleman and Lowell Bennett, who was shot down over Berlin and not only escaped three times, but got the only stories out of Germany—INS stories, my poor friend. And of Tregaskis, who hungered to get close enough, walking down a mountain in Italy, his busted helmet in his hand, the top of his head left somewhere up on the hill. And of Larry Meier, wounded while covering the Dieppe raid. He never recovered.

I still don't think a wonderful friend I had named Jack Singer was getting an interview with the barmaid the day the Japanese

killed him. Death came to him in the wardroom of the carrier
Wasp, torpedoed into a funeral pyre. A young Navy pilot who
survived brought along the unfinished INS story Jack was writing
and finished it for him.

There weren't any barmaids on Okinawa the day John Cash-
man of INS was killed in action. John had lost an arm as a
serviceman, hooked on with our sports department, went back
to the wars as a correspondent, and died. The first reporter killed
in Korea was Ray Richards, INS, who might have been home
with his grandchildren. Four other INS men were killed there,
too.

Someday, son, venture out of doors and ask a couple of good
men like Frank Bartholomew and Alan Gould [Editor's note:
editors of UP and AP, respectively] what kind of a time they
used to have when they had even an undermanned team of INS
reporters competing against them on a big, fast-moving story.
Someday, son, if you improve, you'll be good enough to change
the ribbons on their beat-up mills.

It made some of us feel a little better.

But not much. Something dear and exciting had died in our business, never to resurrect itself.

5. *Moonlighting*

THE TOUCH of arrogance that is a part of every reporter's makeup frequently drives him into thinly related fields in which he has no marked competence. He seldom reads a book or magazine article or short story without feeling he could have written it better. He makes a note, sometimes on the back of an unpaid bill, to get cracking on some "outside work," as he likes to call it. If he carries through with his intention, he finds the going a little rougher than anticipated.

He knows in his heart (and for good reason) that he knows more about news than a vast majority of the golden-voiced, beautiful news-givers on radio and TV. But the sight of a mike or the relentless glare of a klieg light fills his soul with doubt or dread. During the 114-day newspaper strike in New York, stretching through the winter of 1962–63, the local TV and radio stations made considerable use of the city's better-known newspapermen. We were, by and large, simply awful—especially those who held the lowest opinion of electronic journalism.

I don't think I ever met a reporter who agreed that Hollywood was capable of turning out a bona fide screen reporter, or a true picture about a reporter's life and times—or anything else.

The above is presented merely as prelude to experiences I've had in all three of those fields. I've grossed a million dollars moonlighting, but only have been able to save the memories.

The person who practices daily journalism and tries writing magazine articles on the side tends to wind up doing one or the other. Doing both becomes a bloody chore, even for the prolific. Paul Gallico's success in "outside work" caused, or forced, him to close his successful sports column in the New York *Daily News*. Others who left the daily grind and did well in magazine work—men like Stanley Frank,

126

Charles Einstein, Quentin Reynolds, and Stewart Alsop—never hankered to return. They had conquered greener pastures. But for every successful foray there have been countless failures and blizzards of rejection slips.

Runyon rode the two horses well, turning out his daily sports column by day and his fiction about even more fictional Broadway characters by night. Bob Ruark scored very well simultaneously with his columns, slick magazine pieces, and with books as flaky as *Grenadine Etchings* to such impressive and challenging undertakings as *Something of Value* and *Uhuru*. His posthumously printed *The Honey Badger* should have been interred with his bones. His newspapering had long since withered and died.

Most reporters who just know for certain that they've got a book in them, lurking somewhere between the pituitary gland and the liver, find it appallingly difficult to "give to airy nothingness a local habitation and a name." The endlessness of a book presents the spot-news reporter or 750-word columnist with the predicament of an Olympic one-hundred-meter sprinter suddenly called upon to run the marathon. There are just so many words stoked in a writer's gut each day. If he uses them all on a PTA meeting, or the death of God, he cannot then come home and find any more words for his book. If he has taken an advance against royalties from the publisher, a transaction which he was still celebrating when the money ran out and the publisher began writing and calling for action, he will feel sad about the whole deal, particularly after a third martini.

I returned the advances on two books, both of them complete in typescript form. The editors of Dodd Mead & Company considered my book on St. Patrick's Cathedral lacking in merit, substance, and general interest. I agreed, not heartily. It is very trying on a writer's frayed nerves to give back spent money, especially to a publisher. A book I did about the Christian Brothers of Ireland, for P. J. Kenedy & Sons cath pubs, as the firm is listed in the Manhattan phone book, might be called a remorse of a different color—a play on words fit to sicken even Bennett Cerf, who has been kind enough or unguarded enough to publish four of my books. I worked hard on the Christian Brothers book, made two trips to Ireland researching it, spent a great deal more money than the Kenedy people dared advance, and then gave back the advance. Moreover, I've never tried another publisher with the book.

What caused the cath pubs to gulp and wish out was a substantial section of the book which dealt with the efforts of jealous and entrenched Catholic Orders in early nineteenth-century Ireland to crush the congregation of teachers being fashioned by a well-to-do sports-minded merchant of Waterford, Edmund Ignatius Rice. Rice was a widower with a daughter. He and the first fellow monks he gathered, for an assault on the ignorance and delinquency of maverick boys of the city, were accused of homosexuality. How they erased the smear, and not only survived but expanded in a climate of British persecution and the hostility of fellow religious, seemed to me the heart of the book.

But it was a bit too much for conservative elements among the Brothers' leadership, though all of the material was selected from Vatican archives where it has been filed in the continuing effort to secure beatification for Rice. An unexpurgated Life of Rice must not be sold to the students of Irish Christian Brothers schools on five continents! The Order withdrew its support of the project; when Kenedy asked that its advance be returned, I borrowed the dough and swore a mighty oath never to write another book related to my faith.

As was once the case with the price of refrigerators west of the Rockies, the above oath is subject to change without notice.

Radio can be an easy and substantial buck, if you get a break, as I did.

I got into it by default. At the pit of its misery in the early 1930's the Washington *Post* arranged with radio station WMAL to provide a five-night-a-week news show—fifteen minutes. Volunteers were called but few answered. There were two reasons for their reluctance: (1) there would be no pay for this extra duty, and (2) what self-respecting newspaperman wanted to be caught red-handed in a radio studio? Radio was for "Amos 'n' Andy," not news.

When the final head count was taken of the volunteers, it showed only Harris Hull, our aviation writer (who much later became an Air Force general) and the paper's high school sports reporter and tennis columnist.

Harris and I divided the agony. There was never any thought of "taping" in advance; indeed, there was no tape as yet. Everything was "live" and, in my case, ill-prepared because of my time-consuming work in the sports department. One night, reading the hurriedly pasted-together script, I found myself recounting the AP's story of the arrival in Britain from Australia of the heroic over-ocean flier, Amy Mollison. Never given to believe the AP could possibly have a typographical error on its wire, I found myself saying, "As she stepped from her plane, the crowd shouted: 'Hurrah for our British Army!' "

I came to a ghastly stop, and so did WMAL.

"I don't understand why they were cheering for the British Army," I said after what must have seemed to management an eternity. Then, obviously crazed by the experience, I heard myself saying into the microphone, "Oh, I see. It's a typo. They must have yelled, 'Hurrah for our British *Amy!*' " Somehow, I escaped alive.

Then there was the night of February 15, 1933. I was fumbling my way through the pablum of a bland script when to my astonishment the station's announcer, Warren Sweeney, slid a hastily scrawled note to me. The *Post*'s telegraph desk had phoned an urgent bulletin to WMAL. An attempt on the life of President-elect Roosevelt had just been made in Miami. There were no further details. Should I promptly blurt the flash? Could it have been the fiercely competitive Washington *Herald* that had phoned a phony to me? Torn, I kept reading the immensely lesser news and then, as a final item, heavily qualified ("there is an unconfirmed report, etc. . . . ."), the richest morsel of all.

WMAL was a good, safe last in the race to get that vital information to all those teeming hordes out there in radioland.

I still get a little ill every time I hear John Philip Sousa's "The Washington Post March." It was our theme song.

The first remuneration I ever received from radio was a quart of Chickadee Rye. Too many bottles of too many rare and rotten whiskies have clinked and clanked into me over the years. But that quart of Chickadee is unforgettable. Prohibition was still in effect, so far as the hard stuff was concerned. This was "prescription" whiskey from the private reserves of People's Drug Stores, Inc., which sponsored a fifteen-minute sports show featuring Arch McDonald, the classy country boy from Chattanooga who came to Washington in 1933 to broadcast the Senators' games and set a pennant-happy city singing his theme song, "They Cut Down the Old Pine Tree." A death in Arch's family sent him back to Chattanooga for a week during the winter of 1933–34, and he asked the several Washington baseball writers to substitute for him. Wholly inadvertently, we gave Arch's listeners a fuller appreciation of just how good he was. I was a terrible substitute, when it came my turn to step up there and make radio history. Shirley Povich advanced Arch's reputation, too. Six or seven minutes into the fifteen-minute show, Shirley said, "Well, that's it, sports fans. Good night." A tall, thin, black-browed announcer at WJSV (which we used to say stood for Will Jesus Save Virginia?) vaulted to the microphone Shirley had abandoned and talked smoothly about this and that for the remaining minutes. His name was Robert Trout.

But there was nothing much that Trout, the glibbest of them all, or anybody else could do when Dick McCann of the Washington *Daily News* stepped up to bat for Arch. Dick had prepared a witty script and had timed it down to the proper length. The "on the air" light blinked on, Trout introduced him, and Dick opened his mouth to speak the first word.

Nothing came out.

Nothing. The lips moved, the face contorted, the spasm of the born orator seized Dick. But for the first two minutes of The Arch Mc-Donald Show the only sound that went out from WJSV was the rattle and rustle of the script in Dick's palsied hands.

Notwithstanding Arch presented us with our bottles of Chickadee. Each bottle came enclosed in an oval tin can featuring a garish painting of, what else?—a chickadee. How could one conceivably forget a drink that had to be challenged first by a kitchen can opener?

Radio paid better, once a fellow got to New York. But to the menace of a critical audience was added another factor not calculated to give a performer added confidence: the sponsor. He, or it, had to be pleased enough with the person's ability to sell his product on the air that he was willing to stand for the costs. Moreover, he or it had to remain pleased—or else.

My first brush with a sponsor was unnerving. Bill Corum, Caswell Adams, and I were invited to a Brooklyn brewery to lunch with its principal directors. They obviously wanted to see what they had been urged to buy in the way of a three-man radio sportscasting team. During the luncheon, glass after glass of beer was poured into glasses bearing the brewery's name and emblem. Bill, Cas, and I were loud in our praise of the beer. None of us noticed a subtle stiffening on the part of the beer barons.

"So," said the director who looked more like a pig than the others, "you like our beer, hey?"

We swore it was a beer fit for higher echelon gods.

"Well, chentlemen, we have been serving you the beer of our worst competitor—Rheingold!" he said contemptuously. "And you, chentlemen, didn't know the difference."

We lasted thirteen weeks.

There were random radio jobs during the war, including a stint on BBC, a two-season stretch giving General Electric's "institutional" pronouncements during lulls in Fred Waring's Show, and then one of those breaks for which there is no accounting. William J. Brooks, a first-class newsman and bureau chief for AP, had become vice president of NBC in charge of news and special events. He left repeated messages for me at my office and apartment before I overcame my lunatic reluctance to return phone calls. Bill's patience somehow weathered the apparent insult.

"Forgive me for bothering you," Bill said, "but I have a fifteen-minute spot for you on NBC radio each Sunday at 6:15."

In 1951, shortly after Bill provided me with this showcase, I was called by Morris Jacobs, former Omaha newsman and by then head of the Bozell and Jacobs advertising agency. His principal client, Mutual of Omaha, had instructed him to look about for a network radio and TV show. Jacobs said he had several types of show in mind and that he'd like to look me over. I invited him to lunch at Shor's.

If Toots likes you, he's a great asset when you're trying to impress a guest. He will see that you get one of the best tables, a lot of attention from the captains and waiters, the bowl of celery and radishes, and, from time to time, his own overwhelming presence for a brandy-and-soda "and set up a fresh one for these fellows."

All preliminaries were attended to. Morris was impressed by the position of the table, my somewhat studied ease with the captains and waiters, the friendly waves of patrons he recognized, and the service.

"Where's your friend Tooooots?" Morris asked.

I said I guess he had been detained somewhere and would be in a bit later. Just then, Toots appeared. There was no question that he had been detained—in a brandy vat. He fell into the seat opposite Morris and before I could get to the introduction, Toots said, "Who's this creep?"

I explained that my guest was one of the most distinguished citizens of Omaha, a great fund raiser for worthy charities, a prime mover in the city's inter-faith circles, the King of Ak-Sar-Ben, and a first-class gent.

"Nice to know you, Tooooots," Morris said. "I have an important client who is looking for a radio and TV personality, and I'm thinking seriously of recommending your friend here for the job."

"Why you four-eyed so and so from no place, who the hell you think you are, coming in here and insulting my friend Considine by saying you're going to do him some big favor. You're nothing but a piece of raisin cake."

It wasn't one of Toots's better days.

Morris was not going to take that sitting down. He began to talk just as tough as Toots, and at one point picked up a knife. I've always meant to ask him which he intended to stab: Toots for giving him such a hard time or me, for introducing him to Toots.

Subsequently, they became fast friends. Also, shortly thereafter, Morris offered me to Mutual of Omaha, and the world's largest health and accident insurance company accepted the package: fifteen minutes of prime network time on NBC-TV with the format left up to me, and fifteen minutes of radio time. The salary, embarrassingly enough, was almost commensurate with that of the president of Mutual of Omaha, V. J. Skutt, whose genius had built a parochial institution into international importance.

It was much too much for a fellow whose main job was to turn out six columns a week for INS, plus coverage of major stories at home and overseas, and the creation of a certain difficult series of special articles. The latter included about that time the first in-depth interview with Frank Costello (arranged by Toots Shor), a long, hard look at Las Vegas and what and who made it tick (which won a Sigma Delta Chi Award), and a progress report on cancer research (which won a Lasker Award).

But I managed, somehow, to serve both masters, W.R. and V.J. Mostly responsible for this trick was Ann Gillis Slocum, a frail but incredibly durable NBC producer. Ann had had much to do with the development of John Daly during his early days in Washington and made many important contributions to the success of Bob Trout, Morgan Beatty, Edward R. Murrow, and John Cameron Swayze. Now she took me in hand, taught me how to keep my hands out of my pockets on camera, personally edited out of my radio tapes every last "er" and "ah" until I sounded as if I spoke that way in real life. Few figures in public life, particularly during the 1952 political campaigns, resisted Ann's invitation to appear on my shows. They were uniformly better than I, having had much more experience, and I learned a lot from them. Particularly from a Senator from Texas named Lyndon B. Johnson.

The instant I finished asking L.B.J. the first question of the interview, his eyes darted here and there to the three cameras, latched on to the one whose red light was on, and gave his answer to it, not me. Thereafter, whichever camera director Martin Hoade chose to carry the action, L.B.J. faced it instantly and gave it the full impact of his answers. I interrupted him once, by nodding. It seemed dishonest to take the money for that particular show.

Averell Harriman was a memorable guest. He proposed to run for the Democratic nomination at Chicago and thus oppose his longtime friend, Gen. Dwight D. Eisenhower.

"I could beat Ike," he said on the air.

"What makes you think so?" I asked him.

He seemed surprised by the question.

"Because I'm a Democrat," Harriman said.

That was a chancy sort of interview. The Harrimans had me in for dinner at their mansion in Washington on the night of the show. It was a fine dinner and the after-dinner talk was so interesting that we lost track of the time. A slightly horrified glance at my watch showed that we had scarcely half an hour left before air time. I hurried the distinguished public servant toward his front door, explaining that it would take at least fifteen minutes to reach the NBC studios in the Sheraton Park Hotel, after which we would have to be made up, the lighting would have to be arranged for, etc.

Honest Ave sometimes doesn't hear too well. He pulled on a brocaded butler's cord and sent the man off to a pantry as we stood near the front door. The butler returned presently, bearing a fifth of Johnnie Walker Black, ice, and two large old-fashioned glasses.

"I usually like a little drink before I go on the air," Ave said, pouring me a triple and himself a tipple. We drank, straight and fast. Then to my dismay, he poured another for himself and for me. We drank and fled.

We reached our chairs on the TV set about one minute before NBC would have had to announce, coast-to-coast, "Sorry, neither fellow showed up." Ann whipped out a powder puff, hit us each in the face, smeared it around a bit and jumped out of the picture just as our announcer, Bob Denton, began his introduction.

Harriman was excellent throughout the fifteen minutes, clear, concise, coherent. Then, as was her practice, Ann changed microphones, seated us in more comfortable chairs, and gave me the signal to go ahead with the radio version of the interview—to be played two days hence. The strong TV lights, the closeness of the studio, and the relaxation of tension built up before and during the TV show combined to give full sway to the whiskey in our systems. We wandered and meandered through twenty-eight minutes of tape, at the end of which time Ann sighed and said, "I guess that'll be enough for a fifteen-minute show."

It took her many hours of painstaking editing and re-editing, and the floor of the editing room was littered with probably the greatest number of *"Well's . . . Er's . . . Ah's . . . I Dunno's . . . Maybe's"* plus grunts and reflective pauses ever discarded. But when the patched tape went on the air, we sounded briskly letter-perfect. Ave called me after he heard it.

"Bob," he said, and he was serious, "you're the only fellow knows how to interview me."

I don't have a strong enough personality for TV. In a day when there was only black and white TV I perfected another color—gray. My guests found no difficulty whatever in forgetting me, sometimes when we were on the air. I had what I thought was a most interesting interview with Sen. Robert Kerr one night. He called me Bob, and was real down-to-earthy in a best-pal manner throughout the show. Two mornings later, Shor and I, en route to the Kentucky Derby, got off the plane at Cincinnati to pick up a fast beer during the short stopover. There, in front of the terminal, stood my dear friend Senator Kerr, surrounded by a group of admirers.

"Hi, Senator," I called out to him.

He turned and looked right through me. He had never seen me before.

Toots laughed all the way to Louisville.

It was this certain grayness, I feel in retrospect, that made it almost impossible for me to shut off a TV interview on time. I marveled at my superiors who could slice into a guest's prattling like a guillotine and end things in time for the last commercial and the credits. I was always afraid of hurting the person's feelings or causing him to take a punch at me.

Ann got me out of an interview with Baseball Commissioner Happy Chandler on time by arranging for her brother-in-law Frank Slocum of the commissioner's office to toss a baseball to me from the corner of the set. The startling act rendered Happy speechless, a condition which he had never experienced before or since. He was mute just long enough for me to say, "Thanks, Hap. Good night, folks."

"The best way to get off on time is to frame a question and answer in advance," Ann told me. "Then tell the guest that when you ask that question he'll know that this is the end of the show; that he gives the rehearsed answer and that's that."

It worked pretty well, but then came the night when my guest was Gwen Cafritz, the Washington Hostess With Almost the Mostest. Before air time we agreed on the climactic question and answer:

Q: In the old days, Dolly Gann had a lot of trouble seating people properly at Washington dinners given by her brother, the Vice President. Do you have such protocol headaches?

A: Of course not! This is a democracy.

All went beautifully. As the second-sweep hand on the studio clock hit the predestined moment, and the No. 1 camera came inching toward us, I casually asked Mrs. Cafritz a question I had apparently plucked from the wild blue yonder.

"In the old days, Dolly Gann had a lot of trouble seating people properly at Washington dinners given by her brother, the Vice President," I said. "Do you have such protocol headaches?"

"I've been thinking about that since we talked it over before the show," I heard Gwen say, as if in a nightmare. "I don't have troubles because I stick to the rules. Now, let's say I have the Chief Justice. I put myself on his left. On his right, I put the wife of—"

"Thank you, Mrs. Gwen Cafritz, famous Washington hostess, for coming all the way up here to New York to—"

"On *my* left I usually have the dean of the Washington diplomatic corps while on *her* right I—"

"Sure grand of you to come all the way up here to New York—"

"Next to the dean on my left, and to his left, I put. . . ."

The floor director had, in deadly succession, held up his right index finger, meaning that we had one minute in which to wrap up the show; then had crossed that finger with his left index, meaning thirty seconds, then had clenched his fist, meaning time's up, than had slashed his right index finger across his throat, meaning get the hell off. The camera was in quite close on us now. Bob Denton, at his desk on the other side of the set, bore the puzzled look of a man wondering how best to explain to Mutual of Omaha why he had been unable to sell any insurance due to a last-minute reseating of The Last Supper.

"On *her* left, I put. . . ."

I reached for Mrs. Cafritz's leg, figuring I might be able to break it. Surely, the camera was by now so close to us that it was televising us only from the chest up. Alas, the red light blinked out just then, and I swiftly learned that the cameraman was using his wide-angle lens. The Mutual of Omaha show had gone off the air, for lack of time, showing its commentator lewdly grappling for the shapely leg of a fine woman who had come all the way up from Washington to do him a favor.

Mutual moved me to radio not long after that. V. J. Skutt is a very patient man. The *J* in his name must stand for Job.

I have come on from a lot of odd places, mostly via radio, over the years: London, Paris, Rome, Madrid, Moscow, Berlin, Brussels, Cairo, Monaco, Tel Aviv, Mexico City, Buenos Aires, Rio, Brasilia, Anchorage, Honolulu, Hong Kong, Tokyo, Seoul, Melbourne, Dublin, from Pope Paul's Alitalia jet between Rome and New York . . . and from Topeka, Kansas.

The last named was on opening night of one of the most ambitious and disastrous TV news shows ever concocted, NBC's "America After Dark." It was a noble effort to bring live TV to the arid reruns and old movies that clog America's screens late at night. It replaced the "Steve Allen Show" and preceded the "Jack Paar Show." It lasted six hazard-strewn months.

The sterling cast of commentators included Earl Wilson, Hy Gardner, and myself in New York, Irv Kupcinet in Chicago, Paul Coates and Vernon Scott in Los Angeles—and anybody who happened to be awake and around other NBC stations that late at night. If everything worked, we could cover anything from a prison break in Fargo to a midnight funeral in New Orleans, and live, man, live.

There were grumblings at NBC when I said I could not appear on the opening show because INS had assigned me to talk to a Rotary in Topeka that very day, at the request of one of our badly needed client papers. Then someone connected with the show slapped his knee and declared—and I use his very words—"This could be a plus!" My presence there would show the skeptics, provided they were still awake, that "America After Dark" could indeed fulfill its pledge to cover the darkness, live, from coast to coast. Pray, what better proof was needed than to switch to Topeka in the dead of night?

We lined up a dandy Topeka sequence, starring a prize-winning drum majorette, Alf M. Landon, sheepishly wearing a huge sunflower button like the ones that stampeded Maine and Vermont to his cause in his 1936 race against F.D.R., and Dr. William Claire Menninger, all live. My role before introducing them was to stand on the roof of the hotel that housed us, point out into one of the deadest nights Topeka ever had, and talk for thirty seconds about Topeka, the Chisholm Trail, the Atchison, Topeka, and the Santa Fe (which was picking up the line charges), and whatever other goodies came to mind.

On signal, I went into my bit like St. Vitus imitating a semaphore. After thirty seconds the red light blinked out on the camera and the local director ripped off his headphones with a gesture of disgust.

"No audio," he said. "Somebody forgot to throw a switch when Scott, in Los Angeles, turned it over to you. Made you look like a damned fool, standing there yapping and gesturing and not a sound coming out of you."

When the ghastly night ended, I called my mother-in-law in Kansas City, who had been sternly alerted by her daughter to watch the show.

"How did you like it, Mom?" I asked her.

"You were pretty good," she said. "But I couldn't hear a word you said at the start. Speak up, son, when you're on the air. Don't be bashful. You're as good as any of them."

"Something called the audio went wrong and. . . ."

"Never mind that," Mom Anderson said. "You just speak up and you'll be all right."

I spoke up repeatedly over the next six months, but it didn't stay the slow but sure death of the show. The unions began to get personal about the appearance on the show of such stars as Jimmy Durante, who did a number or two from the Chez Paree in Chicago, gratis, because his old friend Kup asked him to. In a valiant effort to stem the inevitable, Earl Wilson had his hair dyed bright red, live, at an all-night beauty salon patronized largely by chorus girls and insomniac prostitutes. Somehow, the fact that the show was in black and white detracted from this self-sacrificing show of *esprit de corps*. Hy Gardner and management stopped speaking because of a demented system of time allotments which turned his in-depth interviews into surface scratchings. The news department of NBC became upset with me for opening my five-minute spot news slot with, "Sorry, but there isn't any news tonight." (Jack Gould of the *Times* liked it.)

Our most steadfast critic was Jack O'Brian in the *Journal American*. He called the show "America *in the* Dark," hammered away at it like Gutzon Borglum chopping a new head on Mount Rushmore.

America After (or in the) Dark lived six months. The next to last item on its final show was a remarkable shot of a fire raging in Boston, live, which I described on the air as a dramatic, if belated, confirmation of the program's original premise. The final shot was humiliating. It showed a big moving van filled with the show's cast and some of its accouterments slowly pulling away from the curb in front of NBC. Jack Lescoulie, our M.C., smiling as bravely as he had on opening night, announced that he and the others were headed for Cain's warehouse, traditional boneyard of Broadway flops.

I wouldn't lend myself to the finale. Too stuffy for that sort of self-ridicule, I guess. Ann and I walked around the corner to Toots's. He was waiting.

We had a few.

I was a bit player in what I feel was Hollywood's last Golden Age, the period that reached from a point near the end of World War II until 1947 or 48. Television had not drugged the nation. The studios made great sums of money with pictures that had nothing to do with perversion, dope addiction, seduction, incest, sodomy, murder-for-kicks, and miscegenation. All was right and decent in the picture world, and L. B. Mayer was in his heaven. So were Sam Goldwyn, who chartered Robert Sherwood to write *The Best Years of Our Lives*, Jack Warner, Darryl Zanuck, David O. Selznick, Cecil B. DeMille ... and other giants, authentic geniuses, court jesters, knaves, and fools. The knaves and fools had more intrinsic class than most of today's screen tycoons, who are little more than glorified smut peddlers bent— as are their bankers—on filming any tawdry tale that might lure the televiewers from their nightly spells. Our newspapers compound the felony by printing lewd advertisements of such pictures and all the paid-for, lascivious words, while at the same time editorially deploring the decline in juvenile moral standards.

When I was in Hollywood, the intent of most film makers was to turn out pictures that had some meaning, some social significance, some hope of enduring. Whatever their backgrounds and penchant for emulating Julius Caesar, these men possessed all but indestructible taste. And a passion for detail that expressed itself in ways as varied as DeMille commanding the dusty charge of an army of extras to Goldwyn crankily supervising the proper mixture of developer in the darkroom where that day's film was being processed.

There were "hawks" and "doves" in the paradise of Hollywood in those days, but of a different nature. The screenwriters, by and large, were intensely liberal: Russia could do no wrong. They had a few cohorts among the directors, most of them foreign-born. The executives, on the other hand, were preponderantly Republican. L. B. Mayer could expound for an hour on the nation's need for Douglas Mac-Arthur in the White House.

But there was laughter, too, and remnants of the hell-raising that had marked previous Golden Ages, and splendid pride in achievement. One night in Mike Romanoff's a conversation I was having with John Lee Mahin, one of the finest writers extant, was rudely interrupted by a complete stranger. He had recognized Mahin.

"The trouble with you goddam Hollywood writers is that you're all alike," the man said, poking Mahin in the chest with a punctuating forefinger. "Whenever one of you writes a religious story it's about one of two things. It's about a goddam Catholic priest who can sing like a bird, play baseball, and knock out the town bully, or it's about a goddam Jewish rabbi who is always so sweet and gentle and gets up the mortgage money to save the Catholic school.

"This is a Protestant country, goddam you," he continued loudly. "This is the greatest goddam Protestant country in the world. Now for Chrisakes why don't you make a movie about a Protestant minister?"

John put down his drink and looked at the fellow.

"One of the greatest pictures ever made in this town was about a Protestant minister," he said quietly.

"That's a goddam lie," the boor brayed. "Name it!"

"Rain," John said.

On most of my half-dozen raids on Hollywood I hitched my modest wagon to a wobbly star, MGM's mercurial old producer, John W. Considine, Jr.

On occasion, usually while drinking, we claimed a state of cousin-ship whose genealogy became mired in a peat bog in County Clare, whence sprang (or were driven) both our paternal grandfathers. But if there was a relationship, it was a tenuous one. John grew up in Seattle under the stern domination of a father who was tough as nails (killed a foe in a close-range duel), shrewd enough to amass a fortune out of the Sullivan-Considine vaudeville circuit, humanitarian enough to found the Loyal Order of Eagles, and foolish enough to think he could shape his son into his exact image and likeness. John, Jr., was the kid who lived in the big house, had a cart and pony, was packed off to the best prep school, then Stanford, Yale, and a year at Oxford after World War I.

He had a story to fit every stop he made in life: "An embarrassing thing happened to me just after I was mustered out of the Navy," he'd say. Then, self-cued, he'd continue:

I decided that since I was overseas at the time I might as well go up to Norway. I had never seen the fjords. Well, there I am, a handsome young and virile bachelor, alone on a cruise. Then I saw her at dinner. I've known a lot of beauties around this town, and in a few other places, you might say. But I never saw anything like this before or since. When I learned she was trav-eling alone, it was almost too much to bear. I worked on her as quietly and unhurriedly as I could, but she was an iceberg until the last night aboard ship. Then all the woman in her surfaced and she said Yes, Yes, indeed, she would meet me on the top deck that night.

You should have seen me in those days, hard as a rock from head to foot, no belly, just beautiful. And this was my night. To make sure she knew from the start that I was all man I decided to wear my lieutenant's uniform. I had had it made in London, of course.

Well, there I am in my cabin, smelling like a rose after my bath, putting on my uniform, whistling away. But then a strange thing happened. When I buttoned my collar it was uncomfortable. I wondered if I was putting on a little weight without knowing it. But that was impossible. I loosened it for a moment and felt better. Then I buttoned it again, and I felt worse than I did the first time. I began to sweat and it was only then that I realized that I was becoming seasick—me! a representative of the great navy of the United States.

It just couldn't be; it couldn't be happening to me on a night when I was going to score with the most beautiful girl in the world.

I straightened my shoulders, finished dressing, and started for the big tryst. She would be waiting, I knew. There would be a few preliminaries, then back to her place, or mine. It was a two-deck climb to the top. Inboard. When I cleared the last of the first set of steps, one deck below, I knew the awful truth: I was going to be very sick very soon. I stumbled down the passageway, looking for a men's room. There was not one in sight. Then I saw a cabin whose door was open. I lunged into it—its lights were out. There was a fine-looking Gladstone bag on a bag-rack. It was open and partly filled, I could see from the light in the passageway, with beautifully laundered shirts.

I put my head in the opened bag and, well, I've never been sicker. When there was nothing left in me I staggered weakly out of the cabin and leaned against a wall. Then I heard footsteps approaching. I fled back to the landing of the staircase, stood behind something, and looked down the passageway. My dining room tablemate, a retired British colonel who wore a Sherlock Holmes deer-stalker, was coming down the way. I knew, sure as hell, that it had to be *his* cabin I had been in.

Sure enough, he turned into it. I leaned against a wall, too weak to move. And then it came, a roar that must have sounded over half of Norway: "GOOD GAWD!"

I was too weak to make it to the top deck. She looked right through me at breakfast the next morning. But my tablemate didn't. "Glad to see you, old chap," he said as I sat down. "Been wanting to talk to someone. The most extraordinary thing happened last night when I was taking my constitutional. Some bounder fouled my luggage!"

John Considine was one of the finest producers the film industry ever knew. His taste was impeccable, when sober. His imagination was boundless, drunk or sober. Traveling east on the Union Pacific one day, he stepped off the train at Omaha, picked up a copy of the *World Herald,* returned to his drawing room, and read it cover to cover. Somewhere buried in its depths he noticed a tiny story about a talk given the previous night by a local priest named Flanagan who operated a haven for homeless and rudderless boys. The talk was titled "There Is No Such Thing as a Bad Boy."

That single atom fissioned into MGM's *Boys Town,* starring Spencer Tracy and Mickey Rooney. John assigned Dore Schary to do the script. It was a tremendous success, propelled the priest to an international reputation, and expanded the school to its present dimensions with students from all parts of the nation.

John was the producer of many MGM moneymakers, including a very good tough-guy picture named *Johnny Eager* with Robert Taylor, an early *Born Free* named *Sequoia,* and *A Yank at Oxford.* I shared only in his defeats, and they were as monumental in their way as his triumphs.

MGM had him either on probation or off the payroll during my times with him. He waged through that period as desperate a battle against the bottle as I've ever observed. On days (or parts of days) when he was good, he was very very good. On days when he was bad, he could be a totally different person. There were in-between periods when his wasting system struggled to clear itself of the vapors. These were the saddest times of all to share with him. They were spent for the most part in endlessly recounting stories of his father. It was a complex any psychiatrist worth his salt would have paid to listen to.

"My father used to say. . . ." and off he would go, a trace of sweat on his forehead, hands fluttery. I lost track of the number of times he said "My father used to say that the worst drink a man can take is his first."

The first was John's worst. He grew up in a hell-raising period in Hollywood, long since departed, but would never touch a drink. But one night at a dinner party at the home of Joan Bennett another actress, somewhat the worse for wear, commandeered the table conversation with a shrill interrogation of John on the question of his sobriety—which offended her.

"If you've got any guts, take a drink," she said to him.

He gave her his handsome, virile smile and said, for the dozenth time, "I'm sorry, but I don't drink."

"You're yellow," the woman said, and a depressing silence fell on the room.

John looked at her for a time, then turned to Joan's butler.

"I'll have a drink," he said.

"What shall I serve you?" the man asked, his composure ruffled. "Doesn't matter," John said.

The butler returned with a Scotch, and John drank it, looking over the glass at the woman.

I worked as a writer on three of John's best nonproductions: a sequel to *Boys Town* and a brace of projects titled *The Church of the Good Thief* and *Gripsholm*. The pay ranged from minuscule to nothing because during the course of the three separate labors John was under suspension by MGM and his handsome salary of $3,250 a week cut off. He alternately proposed to produce them independently, interest other studios, or sail back to MGM basking in the radiance of their potential. I wrote reams of script, but not one foot of film ever emerged.

There were novel extenuating circumstances.

The *Boys Town* sequel was pursued by John in the face of odds which only he seemed unable to see. There was no chance that he could ride back to MGM on it; Metro had worked that claim dry. No other studio seemed interested. We took a trip to Omaha where I was to soak up enough Boys Town lore to etch a story line, while John was to hold a series of summit meetings with Flanagan and his advisers, notably Ted Miller, the wizard who headed Boys Town's mail solicitation, sale of stamps, booklets, and souvenirs. It was a distressing visit. Miller, who had grown quite well-to-do on the percentage he took of each contribution to Boys Town, made no effort to camouflage his contempt for John's proposition which, I learned to my embarrassment, was to have Boys Town provide the capital for the film. Father (by then Monsignor) Flanagan was impervious to John's plans and pleadings in an amused way. John and I attended his Vespers one bitter, ice-clad evening, and that turned out to be the saddest part of the trip for me. The honors that had come to him firmed up his image as the gentle shepherd of an unruly and pathetic flock of boys. He was the good man welcoming the kid standing in the snow carrying a kid almost his size. ("He ain't heavy, Father, he's my brother.")

During Vespers, conducted by a curate, Monsignor rose from the first pew on the left of fine Boys Town church where he had sat in solitary splendor. Then he walked slowly toward the rear of the church, pausing first on this and then on the other side of the center aisle, to gaze benignly at the boys and lay a hand on a scruffy head.

"Beautiful, wasn't it?" John said later at the Blackstone over his alarmingly receding case of Haig and Haig Pinch.

"No."

He was surprised. "No?"

"No. Didn't you notice that as he passed down the aisle every kid's head turned and looked at him in wonder?"

"So what?"

"So he hadn't done it before. He was putting on an act for us."

John plunged into his next nonproduction, *The Church of the Good Thief* with sporadic vigor. I arranged to take a short leave from International News Service, trained to California, caught him on a good day, and soon shared his vision. John had found (or vice versa) a priest named Ambrose Hyland, chaplain of Clinton State Prison at Dannemora. The upstate New York jug was as tough as Alcatraz and bleak as Siberia. But its inmates of all creeds, or none at all, had built a house of God within the prison's high walls. The priest had had to remove many barricades erected by state and church, and raise much money, before the erection and consecration of *The Church of the Good Thief*. The good thief so honored was not the prison's most distinguished inmate, Lucky Luciano. It was Dismas, the repentant hood who was crucified with Christ. On the day of dedication the warden learned for the first time why somebody had stolen the glass from the stop lights of his official car. They had been incorporated into the church's stained glass windows.

John dispatched me to Dannemora to soak up the atmosphere, after a few vaguely troubling meetings with Father Hyland on the Coast. Father was a swinger who didn't seem to care a great deal if we ever left Chasen's. I spent a couple of days around the prison and came to know some of the willing craftsmen who had built and decorated the church. Two, at least, had rechanneled their criminal trades in interesting ways. A convicted counterfeiter and forger produced some very good copies of the better-known sacred art. A burglar famous for his work with a jimmy and other tools turned out to be a fair sculptor. Prison and inmates took such redemptions in stride. Once, when a Dannemora warden's office safe went out of kilter and resisted efforts to open it by twiddling the combination the warden just called in a prominent safecracker he had in custody—and presto!

The day I left Dannemora the incumbent warden took me for a little ride around the reservation. In time we hove into a rare sight

in those days of steel-rationing. The framework of a very large struc-
ture was being erected with all the clatter which attends such creations.
I asked him what was going up.

"New cell blocks," he said, proudly. "Plenty of 'em."

I was puzzled.

"But you told me just a minute ago that Dannemora is only half
full," I said.

"That's right," he said cheerfully. "But we've got to be ready for
the boys coming home from the war, don't we?"

When I felt well enough to think, I thought it might be a good idea
to expose the State of New York for the infamous precautions it was
taking at the patriotic taxpayers' expense. But cooler thought prevailed.
If I wrote it for INS, it would be picked up immediately by the Japanese, and good men fighting a terrible war in the Pacific would be
further taunted by Tokyo Rose.

I swallowed it. Almost simultaneously, John swallowed *The Church
of the Good Thief.* He had had a falling out with Father Hyland, he
explained weakly over a transcontinental telephone line.

"What happened?"

"I'm afraid the good padre drinks," John said, passing irrevocable
judgment on the damned.

Gripsholm, which was to have been the story of that great white
ship's merciful services to refugees and POW's, ran into an early
snag. John made the long train trip from California to join me. The
ship was in dock, steady as a rock. John was something less. He was
ruefully unable to sign his name to the form which the security guard
insisted we fill out before permitting us to board. He was unmoved by
a long story John told which commenced, "My father used to say. . . ."

Things were better the next day and for a number of days after
that. We mapped out a misty story line: Japanese diplomats and
merchants we picked up after Pearl Harbor was bombed and sent
to the Greenbrier, White Sulphur Springs, West Virginia, are seen
enjoying their golf, tennis and good food; Americans rounded up in
Jap-held lands are seen living in great want and bravely enduring vile
justice; Lap Dissolve. Mournful sound of *Gripsholm's* great horn:
"Ooooooooooooooooo . . ." Jap diplomats bow politely as they and
others leave U.S. to be exchanged for Americans, then turn despotic
and dictatorial as neutral ship leaves U.S. territorial waters. Ragged
Americans come aboard at Goa. Pathetic. "Ooooooooooooooooo . . ."

Big buffet table on sunny deck. Starvelings attack it as if playing giant xylophone. Charley Ruggles type keeps trying to say, "May I have a drink first?" and/or "Where is the bar?" but is drowned out each time by "Ooooooooooooooooo." Intrepid correspondent files story to his paper about U.S.-educated Jap prison official who had kicked him in groin; story saying U.S.-educated Jap had privately castigated Hirohito, Tojo, etc. and was secretly rooting for U.S. victory. Sort of steal from *Address Unknown.*

John returned to his headquarters-redoubt, set up on the second floor of his fine home on Canon Drive, Beverly Hills, and informed me by wire that things were moving along fine: He had retained the directorial services of his old friend and mine, Norman Taurog. I should rush out and, with his guidance, shape up the script.

I checked into the Beverly Hills Hotel and called John. He was not available, so I called Norman. He said he had just heard from John.

"What did he say?" I asked.

"Ooooooooooooooooooo," Norman said.

"Anything else?"

"No, that seemed to be it."

John and I had some productive sessions on *Gripsholm,* particularly early morning meetings. But things had a way of becoming derailed before the sun was high enough to cut the smog. One morning I was busily typing away on the script, copying down some fine dialogue his wonderful mind was concocting, when without prelude he said, "Look at your shoes!"

I thought I had stepped into something on the walk from the hotel to his home. But they looked about the same.

"What's wrong?"

"What's wrong? When did you last have them shined? Or repaired?"

I apologized and said maybe it would be better to wear the pair of size thirteen tennis shoes John had borrowed for me from his good friend Walter Pidgeon. But the dialogue had chased his muse from the house, and we both had to wait for a better morning.

It came, of course. No one with John's talents could stay unproductive for very long. One morning we worked together so well, so productively, that I—a good touch-typist—could scarcely keep up with the flow of words and ideas. It was a joyful creativity I had seldom before experienced, and I marveled once more at the skills of this battered but still brave genius. For a precious period that morning I would have bet my arms that John stood on the brink of a comeback that would shake the industry to its gizzard.

"Excuse me a moment," he said, interrupting the torrent of his talent. He left the room. I continued to type, trying to catch up with what he had dreamed. He was back in a minute.

"Answer the phone," John said in a voice that was oddly unlike the one I had been listening to during the morning.

I assumed I had not heard him correctly.

"Okay, let's go, John," I said, putting a fresh sheet in the typewriter.

"I said answer the phone, goddam it," John said with terrible intensity.

I suddenly felt drained.

"It's not ringing, John," I said, looking at him as if we were utter strangers.

He got up impatiently and snatched the phone off its cradle. I could hear the dial tone.

"Yes, Admiral," John said into the phone.

It was too much. I went down to his bar. There was a little shot glass sitting next to the bottle of Scotch. I poured myself one or two, as John had moments before, and went back to his office. He had finished his nonexistent dialogue and was relaxing in his favorite chair.

"It was Admiral Ernest King again," he said. "He keeps calling, asking me to be Secretary of Navy."

It seemed as good a time as any to go back to work with INS. Millie and I had dinner with Norman and Sue Taurog the night before we left. Norman mixed a drink for us. He touched glasses with me.

"Ooooooooooooooo," he said, affectionately.

It was much more profitable—$2,500 a week, actually—writing scripts that were produced, but not nearly as entrancing as working with John.

Shortly after the A-bombs fell on Hiroshima and Nagasaki, and I had finished a stint for INS that involved interviews in Washington with Lt. Gen. Leslie R. Groves, Col. (now Judge) William Consodine, top security officer of the incredible organization that created the Bomb, Dr. Robert Oppenheimer, and others involved, I received a call from MGM producer Sam Marx. Sam was enormously engrossed with the subject of the Bomb's creation, application, and the morality of the act. He assigned me to write the script of MGM's *The Beginning or the End*. Jim McGuinness was the executive producer, Taurog the director. Comdr. Spig Wead, the paraplegic former Navy test pilot who did the screen play for *They Were Expendable,* was assigned to help me write a filmable script.

It was my first brush with the "story conference." We'd all meet in Jim's big office, and after an exchange of pleasantries I'd read aloud what I had written that day or the day before. As the lowest man on that particular totem pole my words were expected to move up through channels. I recall one sequence where our young nuclear physicist, who had been virtually torn from the brink of his connubial couch by an order to proceed immediately to Oak Ridge (then Los Alamos, then Tinian) says to his forlornly unfulfilled bride, "Well, with us I guess it's a case of touch and go."

Spig, the next man up on the totem pole, chuckled appreciatively. "Good line," he said.

"That'll play," Norman said.

"I'll buy that," Sam said.

All eyes turned to Jim, the executive producer. After a bit he shook his head.

"It has a dirty connotation," he said.

"Let's hear it once more," Sam said.

"Well, with us I guess it's a case of touch and go."

"I think Jim's right, we shouldn't risk it," Sam said.

"On second thought, I'm not sure it *would* play," Norman said.

"Here's a better line," Spig said.

Some months later I went through L.A. with Frank Conniff on the way to Bikini to cover the A-bomb tests against captured Japanese and obsolete U.S. ships. Sam Marx was kind enough to ask us out to MGM to see some of the rushes of *The Beginning or the End*. One particularly alarmed me. I had patiently researched and worked into the script an important, at least to me, step in the development of the Bomb. Included in the research was a trip to Stockholm to talk with Dr. Lise Meitner, who had been an important part of the little research team that had proved at the Kaiser Wilhelm Institute in Berlin in 1939 that uranium-238 when bombarded by radium emissions showed, under chemical analysis, that portions were transmuted into barium and krypton, whose combined weight on the nuclear scale was just short of the weight of the uranium atom involved. Therefore, atoms had been split, and every book on physics had to be rewritten. Something had escaped in the form of energy.

Dr. Meitner had been expelled from Germany shortly after the staggering discovery on the ground that she was part Jewish. She made her way to Denmark and divulged the news to her friend Niels Bohr, who had won the Nobel Prize in Physics for related studies and theories having to do with the enormous potential of atoms historically considered unsplittable. Providentially, Dr. Bohr was about to depart for the United States on a lecture tour. He alerted his friends in the nuclear physics community and a small group that included Enrico Fermi greeted him at the pier upon his arrival in New York. The men proceeded immediately to Columbia University and there proved, as Albert Einstein had proposed years before, that Energy really does equal MC square.

Now there were half a dozen or so in the Free World who knew that man was on the verge of unleashing stupendous power. But they were mostly men who had little knowledge of the workings of the American system of give and take. There was, for example, Fermi, the genius who had refused to take his brilliant Jewish wife Laura and their children back to Fascist Italy after he won the 1938 Nobel Prize for his experiments with radioactivity. And the Hungarians Leo Szilard and Eugene Wigner. Suffice it to report that in time one suggested that the terrible secret they shared should be presented to President Roosevelt. But how?

Then a thought: Why not call upon Professor Einstein, inform him that he had been right all along about matter being converted into energy beyond the dreams of avarice, and urge him to present the findings to the President? After all, was he not the world's foremost scientist?

A group visited Einstein in July, 1939 at a cottage he had rented near Spring Lake, N. J. He listened to the presentation but said, when he had heard it out, that he could not possibly ask for an appointment with President Roosevelt. The President would not know him, the Father of Relativity protested. As a compromise, he would write a letter. He did that, explaining the research that had been done, alerting the President to the fact that Dr. Meitner's associates,

Otto Hahn and F. Strassman, were still around in Germany, that Hitler was showing a deep interest in the uranium-bountiful pitch-blende mines of Czechoslovakia. He, the ultimate pacifist, proposed that it was theoretically possible to manufacture what he, of all persons, called an atomic bomb. He envisioned it as something so huge that it would have to be transported by ship into an enemy harbor, whereupon the crew would light some form of fuse, abandon ship, and the whole thing would blow up—either knocking down or contaminating the adjacent port or town.

Anyway, as I brought out painfully in my script, Einstein and the other scientists decided that it was not safe to trust such a letter to the United States Post Office. It must be delivered by hand. A friend of the group, Alexander Sachs, Russian-born economist and science buff, volunteered to hand-deliver the crucial letter to the President. It took him some time to arrange an audience, whereas Einstein would have been granted an immediate hearing if he had asked for one.

The rushes of *The Beginning or the End* followed this entire sequence superbly—to a point. The scientists did not call on Einstein at his summer cottage. They trooped into his Princeton home in dead of winter, as attested by the swirls of ersatz snow that greeted their arrival at the great man's digs.

"It was summertime, Sam," I said to my leader in the darkness of the projection room.

"Shhh," Sam explained.

Then the actor who played Einstein, portrayed shivering near a blazing fireplace and bundled to the gills, gave an interesting reason why he would not make the short journey to Washington and tell President Roosevelt, who was actually very much impressed by him, that we had knowledge of a potential superweapon that must be fabricated before Hitler built his own.

"Why won't you go?" I heard an actor playing the role of a nuclear physicist ask on the sound track.

"I have a bad cold," the actor portraying Einstein said.

The lights came on in the projection room.

"Sam," I said after a time, "I worked pretty hard running down the story of how the men got through to Roosevelt. Now, the only reason I did the business of Einstein was to show how modest this great man was. Roosevelt was delighted to save his letter for the autograph alone. Why did you change the season, and the reason that he didn't go to Washington. The picture makes him sound like a nutty hypochondriac."

Sam shrugged.

"The actor looked better in a muffler," he said.

Then there was *The Babe Ruth Story,* produced by Allied Artists, directed by Roy Del Ruth, no relation, and starring William Bendix as the Babe. I tried to get Paul Douglas for the Ruth role. Paul was an athlete, knew Babe, looked like Babe. But Paul was not yet a star and naturally could not induce the casting department of the Allied Artists bank to vote for him. The department was happy to underwrite the film so long as Bendix played Babe.

I met Bill in the office of a decent Hollywood fellow named Steve Broidy, a very uncomplaining sort. I had the film's technical adviser, Pat Flaherty, with me. Pat, who had played big league ball for Mc-Graw's Giants, was a man no studio could do without if it ventured into baseball. He could not only teach actors how to handle themselves in a baseball uniform and in position, but could appear in bit parts with them and tolerate their utter ignorance. The day he first went out to work as adviser/actor for Sam Goldwyn's *Pride of the Yankees* he said to Gary Cooper, cast as Lou Gehrig, "Let's loosen up a bit, Gary." He tossed a baseball at Cooper, and it hit the actor in his chest. Pat thought he was clowning. But Cooper failed to catch the next few easy tosses.

"I'm sorry," Cooper said in the end. "I never played baseball. You see, I fell off this horse when I was a kid and did something to my pelvis and, well, I never got around to playing baseball. Then I came out here and. . . ."

"And what?" Pat asked after a long pause.

"Well, don't tell anybody," the actor said, "but I've never even *seen* a ballgame." As it turned out, Coop *became* Gehrig under Pat's tutelage.

Now, in Broidy's office, Pat and this time myself were appraising the Ruth book I had ghosted with the help of Fred Lieb, and whose script I had written. In came our hero, Bendix. He looked about as much like Babe as I looked like Elizabeth Taylor, a virginal kid who had just made *National Velvet.* The talk turned naturally to hitting styles, and Pat and I commented on Babe's magnificent posture, right-leg-tuck-in, weight-on-left-leg, body-turned, ready-and-waiting stance.

"That's wrong," Bendix said. "I know all about the way the Babe used to hit. I was a batboy at the Polo Grounds when he played there with the Yankees before the opening of Yankee Stadium. Here, I'll show you."

He picked up the *Herald-Examiner*, rolled it into a makeshift bat, took his position at the side of an imaginary home plate, studied a mythical pitcher, then ran several steps forward in the direction of that pitcher, and swung the newspaper.

"Babe always ran a few steps toward the pitcher before he swung at the ball," Bendix said.

Pat looked thoughtfully at the ceiling, I at a passing Good Humor truck. There wasn't anything to say.

Everybody concerned seemed satisfied with my shooting script. It was an easy one to write, of course. Just about everything Babe did in life was dramatic: early hardships around his father's saloon, the rough and tumble days at St. Mary's Industrial School (where the monks decided he might make a good shirtmaker), the discovery by Brother Matthias that the kid was a ballplayer in a million, the move to the old Baltimore Orioles, the trade to the Boston Red Sox, the pitching heights he reached there, the great sale to the New York Yankees, dazzling home runs, living it up, shooting his money out of a cannon, the slow decline, frustration over not being named a manager, the cancer he refused to believe he had, the croak-voiced farewell in Yankee Stadium. . . .

I went back to work at INS. Perhaps a month later I received a note from Joe Kaufmann, Allied Artists executive. A staff writer had "made a few changes," Joe wrote. He was sending me the new script for quick approval before the filming began.

The new script had everything but dancing girls in the Yankee locker room. I sent it back with a note:

"Very interesting, but who is it about?"

Joe called. Would I come out to Hollywood again, at $2,500 per and all expenses, including car, and make the script "right" again? I did and restored it to its original form.

They filmed the other one.

I took our son Mike, then twelve, to see the preview. He had hung more or less breathlessly on the fashioning of each word of the book, and the prospect that the book would become a moving picture was of great importance to him. "Pop," he said, when I turned in the script, "please arrange for a screening at our school. It'll make me the biggest kid in the whole place."

He was silent for some time after we left the preview. Then he said, "Pop, don't bother about showing it at the school. I'd hate to see you lugging all those heavy cans up there."

I went through Hollywood once more, this time in my more natural role as a reporter. There was good news about John. He had shaped up and through the intercession of his good friend Neil McCarthy, who was close to L. B. Mayer, was back at work in MGM's Thalberg Building—known less respectfully as the Whited Sepulcher. John invited me to lunch with him the next day in his office suite. He sounded just fine.

He was late for the appointment, but that meant nothing. What mattered was that he was stoned, and drenched with self-pity. The handsome suite, he said, was an insult to him.

I said I thought it was swell.

"Come here," he commanded. "You call that swell?" He pointed out the window to a nearby mortuary. "They put me on the side of the building nearest the undertaker, that's what they did!"

Just then, several waiters from MGM's excellent commissary arrived bearing luncheon, kept warm by great silvery covers. I was hungry, particularly for the rich chicken soup which L.B. insisted be on each day's menu—as a reminder that in his youth he had dreamed of such soup but could not afford it.

The waiters were setting the spotless table under John's critical eye when suddenly he roared, "Get out, and take that junk with you! Out! Out!"

As they fled, dropping things, John said to me, "Why should I eat here when all those incompetent horses' asses are eating in the Executive Dining Room? Come on, I'm taking you up there with me."

It didn't matter, all of a sudden.

It was a slightly terrifying, but oddly magnificent, scene. John, his fine gray hair askew, flung open the heavy doors of the lordly dining room. MGM's brass was all there: L.B., Sam Katz, Eddie Mannix, Marvin Schenck. . . .

They froze.

"We're having lunch here, hear me?" he said. "My cousin *Bob* Considine and I, see? You can insult me, John Considine, all you want to, but nobody's going to insult *Bob* Considine. Nobody in this room!"

Several of the executives got up and left quietly. Marvin Schenck said cordially, "Come in, Bob and John. Have lunch with us."

All gone now, John . . . L.B. . . . the beauty and the flaky chivalry . . . crushed under the hooves of TV.

I miss John the most. I often wish I could remember some of the things *my* father said. He died when I was ten, and the only thing I can remember hearing him say is, "Boy, remember this: Never shake hands with an undertaker."

6. *Intrusions*

Sometimes you wish you had chosen Diesel engineering, say. Sometimes you feel like a vulture, hovering.

"Stop looking at me, you dirty sons of bitches," the accused murderess hissed at several of us who had been permitted to go into the cell area of the dismal jail at Snow Hill, Maryland. She was sitting on the side of her cot behind the formidable bars of her cage. Her great dark eyes blazed with indignation. She had been a beautiful and spirited woman, surely. But now she was a trapped animal, charged by corn-pone Eastern Shore police with the shotgun slaying of her husband. They had made a national case out of the ugly business by making her submit to a then novel test. They had dipped her hands in paraffin and deduced that the impurities the wax had sucked from her pores were caused by the acridly smoking gun used in the killing.

"Who the hell gave you the right to stand there, looking at me?" she said. Every word was a knife.

Who, indeed, gave us the right?

I have no memory of a more poignant scene than that at the graveside of a girl named Beverly Burda, one of ninety-five children burned to death in the tragic fire that leveled Chicago's Lady of the Angels parochial school in December, 1958.

"The services for the girl will be held in advance of the mass burial ceremony," a windblown and shivering young priest said to us as the pathetic white casket was placed on its lowering apparatus. "It would be too much of a strain on the family to wait until the others arrive."

And so, while one after another funeral procession snaked into

155

the bleakly frozen and terribly misnamed Queen of Heaven Cemetery, the last rites of the Catholic Church were given to this little girl alone. The Burda family and friends came forth, trodding the imitation grass and sorely stricken. The mother, a short woman whose rough woolen scarf was a frame for a searing portrait of grief, was supported by two larger women who wept loudly. The mother was silent. Behind her spellbound eyes was the question that had lain heavily on all the bereaved: "Why?"

But it was not Mrs. Burda with her inexpressible grief who commanded the thunderstruck attention of those nearby.

It was the father of the dead child. He had no visible face of human skin. Instead, he wore a startling leather mask that extended from his hairline to his sensitive mouth. Out of the right side of the mask, at eye level, protruded what seemed to be a jeweler's eyepiece with a pinpoint opening instead of a full lens. He stood there, erect and silent, on the arm of a male member of the mourning party, oddly aloof to the wails of the women supporting his wife and the even louder cries of other women farther back in the group immobilized at the graveside.

The priest from Our Lady Help of Christians droned into the familiar ritual. I could not take my eyes off the shocking leather mask. Another priest saw my rude consternation, and above the weeping, the Word, and the marrow-freezing wind he whispered:

"He just came from the hospital against the doctors' wishes. Had an operation for detached retinas a few days ago. He's been told that if he cries the salt of his tears will enter the open incisions and destroy his sight for good."

There this man stood, surrounded by tears, alone in his midnight at noon, and I, too, wept to see him fight for control of his exposed chin, wept to watch him try not to weep. The service went on and on, mixing as of old the melancholy fact of death with the promise of life hereafter. The mortal remains and the soul of the schoolgirl were urged to rest in peace. But what of the benumbed mother? What of the father who must not cry? I found myself praying other prayers than those for the repose of the little girl, prayers that Burda somehow would not do the most natural thing in the world—and let free his scalding blinding tears. I watched the telltale jaw, for there was no way to know what agony lay expressed behind the harsh leather mask. It was not the jaw of a fighter or a male model. It was just the ordinary jaw of a poor man who worked hard and had been visited by more woe than human spirit could endure. Once the jaw trembled, then firmed up, fluttered again, and recovered.

It was time to go now. The weeping women led the stumbling mother away. The man at Burda's arm pointed him down a narrow line between open graves. His head was high, as if he were reaching for his breath. His jaw was like a rock.

The Secret Service, Boston Police, and guards at the hospital ordered the lobby cleared of all reporters and cameramen. President Kennedy was momentarily due to come down from the room where he had spent half an hour with doctors who had been given the impossible task of saving the life of Patrick Bouvier Kennedy. The infant had been brought to the hospital earlier that day by police-escorted ambulance from Otis Air Force Base, where he had been born the day before and where his mother was recovering. A last-resort decision had been reached. The baby would be given emergency treatment inside the hospital's monstrously large "iron lung," as big and as ugly as a section of a submarine. There was little or no hope that the first son born to an incumbent American President in 68 years would live to know he had moved millions of hearts great and small. I had flown from New York to cover.

In the confusion of clearing the hospital lobby, I was either overlooked or forgotten. Whatever, I was there alone when the President came out of the elevator with Jim Rowley and another Secret Service man. Jim directed the President's attention to me. He crossed the lobby with a smile and shook hands.

"Hi, Bob," he said, "what are you doing here?"

It knocked the wind and all composure out of me. I could not answer.

"Are you on vacation?" he asked.

I clutched gladly at that. "Yes, oh yes," I said, eager to lie. "Vacation."

"Have a good time," the President said, shook hands again, and moved through the door to the waiting press, the bulb-popping cameramen, and the sympathetic crowd.

The baby died at four-thirty the next morning, August 9, 1963. The President, summoned from a room he had returned to in the hospital, was outside the great pressure boiler when the end came. He asked to be alone. For ten minutes he rested his forehead on a small porthole that commanded a view of the infant's bed inside the brightly lighted apparatus. Then he walked out, silent, and a much older man than he had been.

In the press room at the hospital a doctor gave me a signal to join him outside the room. I followed him by a circuitous route to the building that held the pressure chamber. The baby's body had just been removed. A doctor, dejected and exhausted, slumped in a chair near the chamber, smoking a cigarette under a large No Smoking sign. Inside the boiler, another doctor and two interne assistants were lying on the deck, undergoing decompression.

"Didn't work, this time," my doctor-guide said, looking at the evil thing that filled the room.

About a hundred of us gathered later outside the plain, barracks-like base hospital at Otis, watched the President enter to join his wife, and settled down to wait for him to reappear.

But after a bit, it seemed so obscene, so indecent for us to be standing there like grave-robbers.

"It *is* obscene," our White House correspondent Marianne Means agreed. We were walking toward her Hertz rental to drive to Hyannis Port, where there would be a briefing still later in the day. "Terribly, terribly obscene. But most of them will stay on, in fear of being beaten on the story."

There was a period when the death sentences imposed on the Rosenbergs seemed patently proper. Just. Had to be done. They asked for it, see?

But then there came a night at Sing Sing. . . .

At the beginning of any scrutiny of the Rosenbergs, their lives, crimes, legalistic gyrations, propaganda roles, electrocution, and red-labeled "martyrdom," it should be stated that theirs was essentially a clear-cut spy case.

They violated the provisions of Title 50, Section 32, the United States Code, by funneling atomic, fire-control, submarine-detection, and other guarded U.S. military secrets to Soviet Russia. They were caught, indicted, tried, and given the maximum sentence: death.

The Rosenbergs, parents of sons then nine and five, might have died in comparative obscurity during the originally assigned week of May 21, 1951, and been remembered chiefly as the first persons ever sentenced to death for espionage by a U.S. Civil Court and the first to die in Sing Sing by federal decree.

But shortly after the couple stoically heard the death sentence handed down by Federal Judge Irving R. Kaufman, the Communist Party made a discovery which must have impressed even the most avid Red.

The Rosenbergs were "safe." They were not only willing but determined to go to their deaths without revealing the names of others who worked with them in the Communist apparatus set up to steal American military information for the Soviet Union. They would not "talk" as did other atomic spies such as Dr. Klaus Fuchs, Harry Gold, and Sgt. David Greenglass, Mrs. Rosenberg's brother, whose remorseless testimony helped send her and Rosenberg to the chair.

Their fellow Communists had kept their hands strictly off the Rosenbergs during the trial of the New York couple. For example, the *Daily Worker* did not cover the trial or display any interest in their arrest and indictment.

But, once convinced of the Rosenbergs' complete loyalty to the Soviet Union and their eagerness to die for it, the Kremlin itself filtered word down to party functionaries to launch a sweeping propaganda campaign against the United States, its judicial system, etc.

In the end, the campaign exceeded even the Kremlin's virulent "germ-warfare" line in its open animosity and violent rupture of known truths.

The once-mute *Daily Worker* seethed with grotesque panegyrics about the Rosenbergs, letters the unrepentant couple sent from the death house, sobbing features about the sons, and protests from Communist fronts, left-wingers, and fuzzy humanitarians from all over the world.

The purpose was to invest two not overly bright espionage agents with the dignity of martyrdom, an estate which the Reds hoped to trade upon in the future. The Rosenbergs entered wholeheartedly into the macabre plan.

According to prison sources, they were "happy to die for the cause," though they obviously had enough Communist training to realize they were being used as few condemned persons in history have been exploited.

The Russians used them in a variety of ways. Gullible areas of the world and captives of Communist-dominated countries and organizations were repeatedly told, for example, that the Rosenbergs were condemned to death because they were Jewish. This was an effort to fan hatred of the U.S. and to help take the curse off the newly ordered wave of anti-Semitism in the U.S.S.R. It blithely overlooked the fact that Julius Rosenberg forsook rabbinical training to become a Communist. It ignored such facts as that Judge Kaufman was also Jewish, as were U.S. Attorney (now N.Y. State Supreme Court Judge) Irving Saypol, Chief Prosecutor, and Judge Jerome Frank of the Court of Appeals, who upheld the verdict.

The Russians used the Rosenbergs also to tell countless millions that the U.S. judicial system was corrupt. Half-clothed primitives in parts of darkest Africa may still mull over reports, received from Red infiltrators, that American witnesses and such agencies as the FBI indulge in mass perjury.

The Rosenbergs were not tried as Jews, nor because "they spoke for peace," nor because they were members of the Communist Party. They were tried under a statute which Congress laid down in 1917.

This statute, boiled down, states that any person who in any way delivers or conspires to deliver to a foreign country any information of any kind relating to U.S. national defense shall, in time of peace, be sentenced to prison for not more than twenty years. If espionage was committed, as in the case of the Rosenbergs, at a time when the nation was at war, the maximum penalty becomes death.

Julius Rosenberg and his wife, three years older than he and even more immersed in Communism and its requirements for regimentation, inhaled secrets as avidly as a vacuum cleaner gulps dust. Julius stole a complete proximity fuse from the Emerson Electric Company. This fuse—a device that exploded a shell or bomb with deadly effect near a target and without contact—was one of America's most jealously guarded World War II secrets. He and she gathered information about the latest U.S. Navy sub-detection devices, processed bizarre data on a man-made satellite to be rocketed beyond the gravitational pull of the earth, acted as paymasters and patrons of lesser wartime spies, and continued their activities after it became abundantly apparent that Russia was no longer an ally.

As Judge Kaufman put it, Ethel Rosenberg was a "full-fledged partner."

It was their work in the field of the atomic bomb, however, that was the principal cause of the death sentence imposed by Judge Kaufman, a gravely concerned man who spent many hours of contemplation and prayer in his synagogue before rendering the hard verdict.

In gathering and submitting to their Russian superior, Soviet Vice Consul Anatoli Yakovlev, a treasury of atomic information via their willing dupe, Sergeant Greenglass, the condemned Rosenbergs committed a crime which Judge Kaufman denounced as "worse than murder." In passing sentence, the federal jurist, shaken physically by the experience, said:

"It is not in my power, Julius and Ethel Rosenberg, to forgive you. Only the Lord can find mercy for what you have done."

Judge Kaufman was subjected to enormous pressure after imposing sentence. The full scope of that pressure probably will never be known. But he never wavered, never failed to give the Rosenbergs' defense counsel, Emanuel H. Bloch, recourse to every available avenue of appeal.

When every legal facet was explored and exhausted, from the setting aside of the judgment to a reduction of the sentence, the case was sent to the White House.

It was to no avail. Execution inexorably awaited this couple who, until a few years before, were hardly distinguishable from other New York couples of moderate means, eager to improve their lot in life. Yet veteran court attendants agreed they were the "coldest fish" they had ever seen.

Julius and Ethel sang "Good Night, Irene" and "Battle Hymn of the Republic," and smiled fondly at each other as they were taken away from Federal Court in New York City after hearing themselves condemned to death.

At forbidding Sing Sing, while she waited to be the eighth woman to die in the prison's electric chair and the first ever to die as a spy convicted by a U.S. Civil Court, soft, little Ethel Rosenberg was no trouble to matrons assigned to her.

While pickets paraded before the White House and before U.S. embassies and consulates throughout the world, demanding that she and her husband be spared, the placid woman continued her reading and wrote an occasional letter to her sons Michael and Robert or to her doomed husband in another wing of the death house.

Sometimes she played handball for exercise. She ate regularly, slept well, and took pains with the soft brown curls that framed her round face.

Julius kept up a heavy correspondence, much of which found its way into the *Daily Worker*. He was quite indignant when the prison librarian, either by accident or design sent him several books about the growth, glories, and humanitarianism of the United States.

"I will not crawl," he assured the *Worker* in his next message. He regarded the selection of the books as another effort by U.S. authorities to persuade him to gain clemency by naming co-conspirators in the wartime espionage apparatus and by giving details of its workings.

Rosenberg, a neat bespectacled man whose engineering training was received at the College of the City of New York, evidenced no outward emotion when he described the electric chair and its operation to his two curious sons, come to visit him in prison. He, too, played handball within what amounted to first-bounce distance of the room in which he was due to die.

"Their lips have remained sealed and they prefer the glory which they believe will be theirs by the martyrdom which will be bestowed upon them by those who enlisted them in this diabolical conspiracy (and who, indeed, desire them to remain silent)," wrote Federal Judge Irving Kaufman in denying their application for a reduction of sentence.

The Rosenbergs sprang from desperately poor Lower East Side, New York, families. Intelligent, ambitious, and seemingly devoid of harmful complexes, they went their separate ways through the public school system, grade school and junior high, and met at Seward Park High School.

Julius went on through CCNY and graduated in 1939 as an electrical engineer. Ethel became an accomplished stenographer who dreamed of being a singer. They were married in the summer of 1939 and for a time she supported him, while he looked for work, by clerking in the Census Bureau in Washington, D.C.

The record is vague on why they became Communists, though Julius probably was recruited by friends at CCNY. But each embraced Marxism with zeal and in time prepared to die in its name. They labored mightily to spread Communism among their friends and relatives. Most of their prospects shied away; but one who did not was Ethel's younger brother, David Greenglass.

He stood in dumbfounded awe of the learning of his sister and brother-in-law. And he was grateful for the gifts Julius would bring to him—occasional tools, elementary machinist manuals, and always some Communist literature. He was delighted to join the Communist Youth League when the Rosenbergs assured him it was the "right" thing to do, just as he later considered it "right," as a sergeant at Los Alamos, to give them the atomic secrets they passed on to Russia.

By 1942, Julius Rosenberg had ingratiated himself enough with his superiors to become a semi-official leader of Communistic or left-wing government employees connected with the Federation of Architects, Engineers, Chemists, and Technicians. He was by then a civilian expert assigned to the Army Signal Corps.

By November, 1944, Julius had reached his goal. He had moved on beyond his cell and his recruiting activities to the status of spy. He was no longer reporting to fellow American Communists. He was reporting directly to Russians who obviously had satisfied themselves as to his loyalty to the U.S.S.R. To them, among other things, he had delivered the proximity fuse, audaciously carried out of the Emerson plant in his briefcase after an inspection tour in his Signal Corps capacity. The fuse was subsequently used against U.S. and UN aircraft in Korea.

Julius and Ethel were now ready for the biggest job of their lives, and they laughed at how easy it was going to be.

Poor, naïve David Greenglass—on a million-to-one shot—had been sent by the Army to Los Alamos, New Mexico, to work on the very weapon Russia wanted most of all—the atomic bomb! Rosenberg was delighted with the information Greenglass sent back, and still more pleased when Greenglass arrived in New York City, January 1, 1945, on furlough.

Rosenberg easily persuaded Greenglass to write down everything he knew about the project. The notes were retyped neatly by Ethel, who was accustomed to her brother's bad writing. Among the information revealed was a description of the "lens" device which is the heart of the A-bomb, the mechanism through which explosive fission is achieved.

During the furlough Greenglass was introduced to a Russian and, during a twenty-minute automobile ride through deserted New York slums, told him all he knew about the bomb. Greenglass borrowed the car for the occasion and was its driver.

Before the furlough ended Rosenberg introduced Greenglass to a

Russian courier named Ann Sidorovich at the Rosenberg apartment and told him to be on the lookout for her when and if she came to Albuquerque—where, it had been decided, Mrs. Greenglass would set up an apartment to be paid for by Rosenberg's Russian friends.

To make sure of the proper identification, Rosenberg took an empty raspberry Jello box, tore off one side of it, cut it in half in irregular style, and gave one part to Mrs. Greenglass for safekeeping. The other part, he explained, and the salutation, "I came from Julius," would properly identify any agent who called on the Greenglasses.

On the first Sunday in June, 1945, about six weeks before the A-bomb was tested, Harry Gold arrived at the Greenglass apartment in Albuquerque with the Jello tear-out. It had been given to him by Rosenberg's superior, vice consul, Anatoli Yakovlev. So had an envelope containing five hundred dollars, which Gold—now serving thirty years for his part in the conspiracy—gave to Greenglass after the latter had turned over sketches of the "lens mold" and other data. Yakovlev eventually told Gold that the Greenglass material was "extremely excellent and very valuable."

In September, 1945, shortly after V-J Day, Greenglass was given another furlough. With him this time he brought sketches of the improved "trigger" used in the Nagasaki bomb and the makeup of the bomb itself. Ethel typed an eleven-page report from his revelations.

Julius, who had by that time been secretly awarded the Soviet Order of the Red Star and had been given a special console table designed to facilitate the microfilming of other secret documents and plans he was receiving, gratefully pressed two hundred dollars on his brother-in-law.

Rosenberg strongly urged Greenglass to apply for civilian work at Los Alamos when it came time to be mustered out, so that he could continue his spying. But Greenglass took his honorable discharge as a sergeant and returned to New York to enter the machine-shop business with Rosenberg.

Rosenberg had by then been fired from his Army Signal Corps job. The FBI discovered a record of his membership in the Communist Party and the Army promptly dismissed him. Rosenberg entered a fuming protest but told intimates he was secretly relieved. The FBI report made no mention of espionage, just party membership.

Julius and Ethel were happy people as 1950 dawned. In addition to other favors from their Soviet masters they could now point to handsome watches, and they could bask happily in the shock of horror that had swept the United States when President Truman announced that Russia had successfully completed and tested an atomic bomb.

But one day in February, 1950, the Rosenbergs were struck across their faces with a shattering headline. Their world was beginning to collapse. Klaus Fuchs had been arrested in London. Worse, he was talking. Rosenberg raced to the miserable cold-water flat of the Greenglasses on New York's Lower East Side to tell him the significance of the news.

David Greenglass did not know Fuchs. But he had met and had passed atomic information to Gold.

What Rosenberg did not know was that Fuchs never knew Harry Gold's name, his profession, or his place of business. Fuchs knew Gold only as "Raymond." From a casual description Fuchs gave of the meek-looking Gold, an obscure Philadelphia chemist, the FBI tracked him down by May, 1950, one of the more masterful manhunts in the history of crime detection.

The three-month period between the arrest of Fuchs and that of Gold was a frantic time for Julius and Ethel. They had had personal troubles with Greenglass. The machine shop in which he had become a partner with Rosenberg was doing badly; Julius appeared to be the only one prospering, and Greenglass had repeatedly asked for just recompense for his work therein.

Now, as he urged Greenglass to leave for Mexico immediately, in the wake of Fuchs's arrest, Rosenberg promised to pay the ex-sergeant's debts. He made inquiry of a doctor about the "shots" the Greenglasses would need, ascertained the least conspicuous place to pick up travel cards, and outlined the path they would travel to safety behind the Iron Curtain.

Greenglass would not budge. When the newspapers announced Gold's arrest, Rosenberg took more positive action. He gave Greenglass one thousand dollars and promised that an additional six thousand dollars would be forthcoming. The Greenglasses were to go first to Mexico, thence to Sweden, Czechoslovakia, and from there to Moscow, where a job would await David. There were bizarre instructions as to how he could recognize Soviet agents while passing through the escape route.

On May 30, 1950, Greenglass finally stirred. He had six sets of passport pictures taken of his little family and early in June accepted four thousand dollars from Rosenberg. He wavered again, to the horror of the Rosenbergs, and delayed his departure. He turned the money over to another brother-in-law, one Louis Abcl, for safe-keeping.

Harry Gold was by then "singing" one of the longest confessions in U.S. crime annals. In time he came to Greenglass' role. Greenglass was taken into custody and appeared to be relieved to tell what he knew.

He quickly agreed to become a Government witness, and because of his complete cooperation—which brought his sister and brother-in-law to the death chair—he drew only a fifteen-year prison sentence. Mrs. Greenglass, chiefly responsible for persuading her husband not to attempt to flee, at a time when the family might have made a clear getaway, was given no sentence.

The arrest of Greenglass caused Ethel to call immediately on Mrs. Greenglass and promise to shower her with gifts if she could prevail upon her husband not to implicate the Rosenbergs.

For reasons never properly explained, the Rosenbergs tarried in this country for weeks after sounding their first alarms to the Green-glasses. It was not until late May or early June, 1950, that the Rosenbergs appeared at the photo shop of a Ben Schneider, at 99 Park Row, and had passport photos taken of themselves and the children.

Schneider, a stunning surprise witness produced by the government at the end of the Rosenberg trial, who was permitted to testify over the protests of defense attorney Bloch, said that he recalled the Rosenbergs because they came in on a Saturday—usually a bad day for him—spent nine dollars, their children acted up, and Mrs. Rosenberg volunteered that they were traveling to France to pick up a bequest left to her.

The government used Schneider's testimony to prove to the satisfaction of the jury that the Rosenbergs contemplated flight. And the jury ruled that this act was, indeed, "an indication of the consciousness of guilt."

The historic three-week trial of Julius and Ethel Rosenberg suffered a partial eclipse of an improbable nature. It conflicted in dates with the less significant but more sensational Kefauver Committee hearings involving Frank Costello, Joe Adonis, Virginia Hill, and former Mayor and Ambassador William O'Dwyer. I covered that ham-ridden farce, as well as the Rosenberg drama, and marveled that the meaning and nuances of the spy trial were consequently lost on millions of Americans captivated solely by the sight of Costello's knuckle-kneading on their television screens. Overseas, the Rosenberg trial took clear precedence. So vast and effective was the spread of Communist propaganda about the trial that the U.S. State Department felt forced to send a lengthy review of the case, outlining the charges and the evidence presented, to forty U.S. diplomatic missions throughout the world.

There followed also one of the most vigorously appealed cases in U.S. criminal history. First the case was sent up to the Court of Appeals—composed of Chief Judge Thomas Swan and Judges Harrie Chase and Jerome Frank—and the verdict was unanimously upheld in February 1952.

Petitions for a rehearing in the Court of Appeals were denied in April, 1952. The Supreme Court then declined to review it because the high court seldom, of course, reviews any case that has no bearing on the Constitution. There were appeals and upholdings through the fall of 1952 and the early part of the winter, and finally one which sought to set aside Judge Kaufman's judgment.

Kaufman himself was assigned to judge this but withdrew and Chief Judge John C. Knox referred it to Judge Sylvester Ryan. On December 10, Judge Ryan denied the application. Judge Ryan's decision was argued before the same Appeals judges. Then defense counsel Emanuel Bloch went back to Judge Kaufman for a reduction of sentence. It was an emotional scene.

"Tell me where I erred," Judge Kaufman said to Bloch at one point. "I'm anxious to know." He had been the target of thousands of wires and letters from all over the world, many of them parroting phrases and distortions which followed the known Communist line on the case.

"When the day comes when we are swayed by pressures, we might as well close the doors of justice," the deeply concerned jurist said in this respect.

"You have in your hands the fate of two human beings," Bloch told him with muted passion. ". . . Your Honor should have witnessed the scenes with the children.

"The Rosenbergs are soft, sweet, tender people whose hearts are no different than yours or mine—what is it that causes them to say 'we are innocent'? Why don't they take the easy way out and confess if they are guilty? What stops them?"

Judge Kaufman broke in soberly. "I have pondered that over and over," he mused.

"Is it fair to forfeit these lives when you have some doubt?" Bloch appealed. "Any doubt—one little iota of doubt? It's such a terrible thing to take the lives of people who stand up in the shadow of death and still say, 'We are innocent!' knowing that if they came to this court now and said, 'Guilty!—have mercy!' you'd commute their sentences. Millions cry, 'Don't kill these people!' All humanity cries out against it.

"Once the current passes through the bodies of the Rosenbergs nobody can ever right the wrongs done to them, their children, and American justice.

"God, your Honor, you have a heart! These are parents! They love their children as you love yours. Please think. Please consult with your conscience. You'll never be able to look in a mirror again, or at your children. . . ."

"If I felt that way for an instant," Judge Kaufman said evenly, "I'd change."

In denying the clemency appeal and opening the door to the Rosenbergs' appeal to the White House, Judge Kaufman wearily explained that the espionage act of 1917 gave him no opportunity to hand down a verdict of life imprisonment. It had to be a prison sentence up to thirty years, or death. He found death in any form heart-rending, he said, and he was "deeply moved by considerations of parenthood." But, he added, "My personal feelings or preferences must be pushed aside, for my prime obligation is to society and to American institutions.

"This court," he observed near the end of a remarkable document, "has no doubt but that if the Rosenbergs were ever to attain their freedom they would continue in their deep-seated devotion and allegiance to Soviet Russia, a devotion which has caused them to choose martyrdom and keep their lips sealed."

Then the little man who had resisted perhaps incomprehensible pressures in an effort to make him change his mind looked around his courtroom—packed with Rosenberg cohorts who had hissed U.S. attorneys in the corridors—and quoted from the English novelist Mary Ann Evans, who called herself George Eliot:

"There is a mercy which is weakness, and even treason against the common good."

Julius and Ethel, particularly Ethel, died bravely. I was one of three wire-service reporters permitted to see them go. Guards frisked us for hidden cameras, and even took away our fountain pens. I never again wore the expensive wrist watch I used that night at Sing Sing to measure the last seconds of their lives. I threw away some of the clothes I wore, for they stank of death.

As in life, Ethel was stronger than Julius when death came toward them.

He went first, but not from choice. He had spent the last afternoon, Saturday, June 20, 1953, in Ethel's wing of the death house. The cell that had been given to him there was closer to the chair room's door than that of his wife. This meant that if Ethel were designated to be the first to go she would have to pass his cell en route to the chair. Sing Sing recoils from that sort of salting of wounds. So it was Julius who led.

His familiar black mustache had been shaved away. He was the picture of a soberly stricken but silent man as he walked behind Rabbi Irving Koslowe, of Mamaroneck, New York. He seemed to be trying to keep step with the Rabbi's sonorous Biblical quotations.

Rosenberg had been told that two "open" telephone lines, one to Attorney General Herbert Brownell and the other to the governor's mansion at Albany, were at his disposal—if he wished to name fellow conspirators. The big ugly switch on a nearby wall would not be activated if he spoke out.

Julius did not utter a sound. He was strapped to the chair, rather roughly gagged with a black cloth, and the current was applied. He quivered under his bonds, and his neck seemed to grow several sizes. Three charges killed him. Dr. George McCracken, a jaunty-looking old political appointee in a sports jacket, applied his stethoscope to Julius' chest and confirmed his death. The body was unstrapped and wheeled off.

Then Ethel. Her little procession into the shockingly silent and bright room was led by Rabbi Koslowe, who had retired after leading in Julius. The Rabbi's resonant voice had sounded the coming of the macabre parade before a coatless guard opened the huge oak door that leads to the chamber.

Now, somber in his vestments, the Rabbi walked in quoting from the 15th and 31st Psalms. His voice replaced the eerie silence of the room. . . .

"Who shalt sojourn in Thy tabernacle . . ."

Ethel wore a Mona Lisa smile. Her little minnow of a mouth was curled at the edges in the faintest possible way. She was dressed in a dark green print of cheap material, a prison dress that revealed her plump legs below the knee.

Her dark brown hair, apparently freshly washed, was set in an almost boyish manner. Her head had not been shaved, only clipped short on the top. Like Julius, she wore brown cloth slippers.

Just before she reached the chair, for which she showed no revulsion, she turned and looked at the two dumpy, gray-haired matrons who had followed her into the room.

With an impulsive gesture she reached out her right hand to them. It was taken by the elder of the two, Mrs. Helen Evans, who had guarded her for two years. Ethel's iron composure melted briefly as she took Mrs. Evans' hand and pulled the woman into a quick and affectionate embrace.

She kissed Mrs. Evans on the left cheek, but even as she turned away to retrace her steps toward the chair, the tight little smile came back to her lips.

Ethel was cooperative with the little swarm of death-house attendants now collected around her. She stretched out her hands along the arms of her ghastly throne to facilitate their buckling on the black electrode straps. She cocked her head in such a way as to help those who were fitting the monstrous crown. She tucked in one fat leg to help a guard adjust its strap.

Only once did she change her expression before the mask came down over her eyes. That was when an attendant roughly adjusted the electrode that reaches down through the center of the hood and makes contact with the scalp.

But her face quickly regained its composure. As the hood was lowered over her eyes and the black strap placed across her mouth, she was looking straight ahead, almost triumphantly, her gaze directed at the wall over the heads of the ashen reporters sitting on hard benches before the chair.

Executioner Joseph Francel, a wasp-waisted little man as innocuous-looking as his regular pursuit might indicate—he was an electrician in Cairo, New York—walked quickly into the little alcove which contained his switches and meters, stared pensively across the room at the grimly enthroned woman, and without a change of expression went about the grisly work for which he was paid three hundred dollars.

As the torrent of electricity swept through her body, Ethel braced herself. Slowly, surely, the index finger of her right hand rose as if in silent rebuke. From every pore of her body there seemed to emanate a strange, unearthly sound made up almost exclusively of the letter Z. Now she seemed about to stand. Her hands contracted into fists. Thus she sat, lifted off her seat as far as the straps would permit, and I had the startled feeling that she would break those bonds and come charging across the floor, wielding those tight little fists.

Out of the left side of the gear that covered her head rose a heavy cloud of blue-gray smoke that ascended straight up in the deathly room until it flattened out in an ugly cake against the skylight overhead.

Slowly and majestically she began to descend again in the chair, as if the executioner could no longer conquer the law of gravity with his switches. The smoke continued to rise from her head. From the chair there continued the sound of the skillet.

It was a three-second jolt. Francel left his instrument board and, hand on hip, speculatively studied the smoking figure in the chair. He shook his head, went back to his panel, and shot the second jolt into her—a fifty-seven-second surge. The woman's index finger rose again, then slowly subsided.

There was a stir in the room now. The executioner had signaled that the woman had received a sufficient charge to cause death. Dr. McCracken and a younger assistant, Dr. H. W. Kipp, moved over to Ethel and pulled at the front of her round-collared dress.

The collar was not large enough for them to introduce their stethoscopes. They ripped it. An attendant unleashed the black strap that had been tied tightly across her breasts. Other attendants unbound her arms and a leg.

The doctors hovered over Ethel, stethoscopes attached to the white skin beneath the sleazy dress. Then they stared at each other dumbfounded, held a whispered consultation, and beckoned to the executioner.

Francel seemed surprised. He came over to them, lips pursed. "Another?" he asked, vexed.

"Yeah," one of the doctors muttered.

Now the business of restrapping her had to be attended to. Two more fifty-seven-second jolts went through her. The plume of smoke reappeared, and the room was heavy with the smell of electrocuted death.

She could relax now. What had been a woman who once dreamed of the operatic stage and settled for espionage, sat there loosely composed. The doctors advanced again, listened and agreed.

"I pronounce this woman dead," said Dr. Kipp.

They took the mask off Ethel Rosenberg now and her face possessed the same quizzical half-smile that had been painted upon it minutes before. She was freed of her straps. Two guards picked her up and placed her on the wheel-table and pushed her out of sight. Ethel's right leg was flexed in an easy and almost nonchalant posture.

Relman Morin of AP, Jack Woliston of UP, and I were bundled into a paddy wagon and taken back to the Visitors Room of Sing Sing, where thirty-eight reporters from half a dozen countries waited for details. All three of us were supposed to brief them, but neither AP nor UP cared to do so. It was left up to me. I was put behind the elevated desk that commands a view of the screen-separated tables where inmates normally converse with their visitors from the outer world.

It was a trying experience for a reporter, particularly when the first question asked—after blunt details had been given—was a shrill one from a lady reporter.

"What did Mrs. Rosenberg wear tonight?" she called up to me.

It just seemed so damned callous.

There are other sins of intrusion. . . . Killing is so damned impersonal, in the electric chair or a war like Vietnam.

That's the second reaction you're likely to experience after flying in the back seat of an F-100F on a combat strike.

The first reaction, of course, is a swarming surge of relief that they didn't shoot you down. Now you can unpeel about sixty pounds of flying gear: suit, gut-corset, parachute, life jacket, survival-vest kit, pistol, knife, head-shrinking helmet, and suffocating oxygen mask. And you can stand up, rub your aching butt, and slip into a cold beer.

The second reaction hits you as soon as there is an evaporation of the bubbly elation of still being alive, still having a chance to make something of yourself in life's miserably short span. It is a sobering reaction. You realize that you were a kibitzer to a killing.

At least, you suppose it was a killing. You don't see anybody spin and fall. But Viet Cong were known to be lurking in the patch of woods Capt. Carl Young of Towson, Maryland, hit with two 750-pound canisters of napalm, two 500-pound bombs, and only God and the VC know how many slugs of 20-mm. shells during what seemed like endless low-level passes over the target at 450 miles an hour.

In the course of a seat-grinding zoom-out after Captain Young dropped his bombs, I heard his airborne spotter come on the pipe with his molasses drawl and say, "Would you believe it? A secondary explosion." There were two such detonations in the wake of the strike. Apparently, something the VC had dragged into their cover had blown up, perhaps killing some of those who planned to use it to blow up others.

For Captain Young, father of two sons, Pat and Mike, and veteran of twelve years of Air Force service, it was just another day's work. This was his 220th sortie since he went into action at this base nine months ago. With a little bit of luck he'll fly dozens more during the remaining three months of his tour.

For me, well, it wasn't quite routine. I walk around ants to keep from stepping on them. The epitaph my stone will bear is "Here lies a bum who never swatted a fly."

So come along and share the experience of an uneasy greenhorn.

There was an infernally prolonged prelude. This teeming air base is less than twenty miles from Saigon along the best road in Viet Nam, but it took well over an hour to reach it. The maze of traffic around Saigon is all but impenetrable and ranges in nature from growling fifty-ton tanks to lovely bicycling Vietnamese girls in gossamer garments that float like butterflies.

Lt. Jim Farley, an Air Force flack who drew the gloomy task of delivering me intact to the Third Tactical Fighter Wing of the 308th Tactical Squadron, made interesting small talk as we inched toward the field.

"I've been over here eight months, but the war never hit me until last night," he chatted. "I dropped by a mortuary in Saigon, and there were these thirteen soldiers stretched out on slabs. Dead," he explained.

Now even the turtle's pace decelerated. On the right-hand side of the road, a mop-up crew was doing something about what was left of the Sealand Motor Pool. It had been hit several hours before by VC mortars, grenades, and rifle fire. There were still some bodies among the sixty battered vehicles.

Suiting up for a ride in an F-100F takes another hour if you're my size and girth. This is a slim, flat-bellied war. But they found a stylish stout in the limitless inventory, and an airman named Jones went to work on me.

First you strip down to your shorts and climb into a long-zippered jumper that looks like Churchill's "blitz suit." Then you are ornamented like a macabre Christmas tree. The gut-corset, designed to hold your insides during dives and pull-outs, is strapped around you tight enough to shape you like a dumbbell.

Then everything else is piled on. In time, you can hardly move. You're bent over like an old man, the crotch-straps of the chute having been tautly pulled.

With all this goes a running commentary about what each bit of equipment means—how to unzip, unbuckle, unsnap, and uncrank in case you must bail out. After a bit you stop listening. You know in your heart that you'll either not remember or be too petrified to un-anything.

Now, everything is taken off you except the jumper suit. This was just a fitting, so to speak. Besides, a monsoon weather has settled over the target, and there will be a delay. A briefing fills part of the void.

"We've lost five birds in the past twenty-four hours," the young briefing officer said briskly. "I guess you've heard about Jerry. His F-One-hundred ran into a wall of fire, and he never pulled out of his first dive. Watch it. Your MIG alert call today is 'Phillies,' and you are Sabre Two. Any questions?" When there were none, he compressed his pointer like a retractable radio antenna, put his map under his arm, and went off on some other mission of good cheer.

Captain Young was doodling a problem on his pad. Now he looked at his two wing men, Capts. Gerald D. Cannon, of Tremonton, Utah, and Charles W. Bradley, of Goff, Kansas.

"You should have a hundred twenty-nine knots after three thousand feet of roll, and go off at a hundred eighty knots and sixty-one hundred feet," he murmured. Then he turned to me and said, "We've got ten thousand feet here at Bien Hoa. With the help of the braking chute, we can still stop in time if something goes wrong at a hundred sixty knots with four thousand feet to go."

Then a bewildering account of the various switchings that would have to be made from one radio band to another. One band would tell him more about the weather, another would give him general details about the target, and still another—the band reserved for the daring young man in a tiny plane who would find the target and lead us to it by dropping a phosphorescent marker-bomb squarely on it.

"FAC [Forward Air Controller] will give us additional information," Captain Young said casually. "Oh, such as the best places to bail out if we get shot up—places where there are more friendlies than VC, let's say." He turned back to the pilots.

"I want each of you guys to come in at different angles than the one I'll use," he said, drawing a sketch. "If you come in on my tail, they are ready for you, and they shoot you down. Make them guess where you're coming from. Make as many dry runs as you need. You've got to do that sometimes to make it good when you finally drop. One-second bursts with the guns. No more. Save thirty rounds, enough to cover one of us if he goes down. That should hold them off until we can get a chopper in for a rescue."

Another hour dragged by. The pilots dropped off to sleep on their chairs, as effortlessly and peacefully as children. Lt. Col. Ed Derryberry, Information Officer, had something for me to do.

He led me to the next hut, that of the 510th Tactical Flight Squadron, to see its mascot. The mascot was asleep on top of a partition that formed a briefing room. It is a python, nine feet two inches long. A pilot reached up and rubbed what I assumed was its belly. It stretched contentedly.

We rode through the sullen rain to the Officers' Mess and were having a cup of coffee when in from the downpour, shaking himself like a wet terrier, came one of the bravest hands in aviation history— Col. Chuck Yeager, first man to fly through the sound barrier. After years of test-piloting at Edwards AFB, California, and training Air Force astronauts (among them Jim McDivitt, Frank Dorman, Mike Collins, and Dave Scott), Chuck is working as Wing Commander of the 405th Fighter Wing based at Clark AFB, Philippines.

"Are you going to fly while you're here?" Colonel Derryberry asked him.

"Me?" Chuck snorted. "No sirreee! They don't pay me enough."

A phone rang in the Ready Room. Captain Young said something into it very quietly and hung up. "Let's go," he said.

You're redressed at the side of the F-100F, and you weigh a ton as you climb the ladder and wriggle into the little seat. An airman attaches all the straps and plugs you in to the oxygen and communications system. The Pratt and Whitney J-57 you're squatting on bursts to life with a convulsive shriek, the canopy comes down and locks in place, and pretty soon you're rolling down the runway faster than you've ever moved before on the ground.

Then up through the dirty overcast like a rocket and into the blue. And suddenly, as intimately as if he were sitting on your lap, the easy voice of FAC.

"Good afternoon," FAC said with disarming cordiality. "I have some news about your target. I'm over it now. I'm over to your left at nine o'clock. I have red wingtips. There was a big operation around here couple days ago, and the only place Charlie could have gone is back into these woods. Target elevation sixty feet. The houses in the woods are considered friendly. They are unoccupied. We don't want to hit them. If you're ready, I'll go in with the smoke."

"That's fine," Captain Young said. "I'll make a dry run just to be sure."

We sluiced down four thousand feet through a small hole in the cloud cover. It was like jumping off a cliff. Just about the time and altitude where it seemed likely that I had become a silent partner in a suicide pact, Captain Young flattened us out, and I was pushed down into my seat as if a thousand pounds had been dropped on my shoulders.

A mile or so ahead of us a creamy cloud rose from the woods and hung there. We raced at it at about two hundred feet altitude, shot past on the right, and knifed sharply up and away. I wondered what it would be like, going right through the bottom of the F-100F.

The next time was for keeps. The fighter-bomber shuddered as explosive charges punched the big streamlined napalm bombs from the underside of our wing. As we went through the hamburger grinder of the pull-out and getaway, FAC spoke—as if he were in the jet with us.

"Right on it!" he applauded. "Beautiful. Now for snake eyes [the two 500-pound bombs]. I'd like you to come in a hundred meters to the left of the napalm."

"Thank you," Captain Young said. "But I'll try a dry pass first." He switched from FAC to me. "A dry pass at this stage tends to change their minds about popping up and shooting at us," he said.

We did the dry pass. It tends to make the throat dry, too. Then FAC was back.

"I'm over the target now," FAC remarked laconically. "The friendlies have moved out of the way."

"That demonstrates the importance of tactical airpower," Captain Young commented. "There's been criticism back home, I understand, but we can work very close with people on the ground, clear out enemy positions maybe fifty meters in front of friendlies."

And so it went—airpower and comparatively small talk—for the next half hour. There were belching thrusts of 20-mm. fire from the four guns. And FAC was on and off.

FAC was full of gossip about the target. In addition to the two secondary explosions there was some kind of fire raging that interested FAC. "I can't tell what it is," he said, "but it's burning real good. White smoke."

We sprang up and away from the business at hand, our wings free of the awesome and ugly bombs, the arsenal of 20-mm. shells down to the minimum thirty rounds. The F-100F was about a ton and a half lighter. It was a jaunty fighter again; not a lumbering fighter-bomber. With Captains Cannon and Bradley alarmingly close to his wing tips, Captain Young reached for the deep blue overhead, as if hungering for its cold, antiseptic absolution.

We went over the top at thirty thousand feet, and then down. Captain Young switched on his afterburner, and five thousand more pounds of thrust surged through the engine.

"You won't notice much when you go through sound," he said. "Maybe a little nudge."

Sure enough, there was a nudge as the needle touched Mach 1 and moved on to Mach 1.1. Captain Young switched off the burner, and though we were in a steep dive, it seemed as if we had run into a thick layer of transparent gelatine. We were flung against our shoulder straps but leveled off in time, and were talked back to the field through the gray potage that lay just over the trees and paddies.

Colonel Derryberry was there at the bottom of the ladder. He had a can of beer ready.

"Thing like that can vitiate a fellow," he said.

The judgment in the debriefing session, back in the rickety office, was that it had been a successful mission. Eventually, somebody among the friendlies would venture into the woods and count the dead, if any.

Somebody else, Lt. Jim Farley, let's say, would write a little piece about it, which none of the newspapers would use. It would be, at most, a footnote in the endless annals of war, memorable only to those who were hurt, and to a kibitzer to a killing.

7. *It Broadens One ...*

... sometimes in the wrong places.

The first long trip I remember was to Chesapeake Beach, Maryland, a resort a few miles out of Washington. Tension ran considerably higher than, let's say, a subsequent Sabena jet flight which involved breakfast in Moscow, luncheon in Brussels, and dinner in New York. Minutes before the train for Chesapeake Beach huffed into action (it looked like the one that carried Lincoln to Gettysburg) my brother-custodian Charles got off to buy a bag of peanuts. When the train began to move and he had still not returned, I panicked. I went to the platform of our car and sat down on the steps that led to the ground, now slipping by faster and faster. I was abandoned, penniless, in the alien corn. I thought of trying to jump off, but the dizzy acceleration of the train warned of disaster. So I just sat there and wept.

Charles and a conductor found me in that position and condition. My keeper had gotten back on the train by way of another car and was somewhat concerned to find our seat empty. The meeting between Stanley and Livingstone could not have been more emotion-filled. I was led back to our seat somewhat the worse for wear. Between tears and cinders (whatever happened to railroad cinders?) my face was a surrealist painting in black and white. One cinder stuck in my eye the rest of the day, eluding what was the open-heart operation of that day, pulling the eyelid down as far as human tissue permitted and groping for the snug little obstruction with the saliva-moistened and twisted corner of a handkerchief.

It was a day to remember.

There were other great voyages in my youth but none to compare with the annual outing at Marshall Hall, Maryland, engaged in by the families of St. Aloysius parish.

179

That one took a lot of preparation. There was money to raise by means of selling old papers and scrounged scrap to the neighborhood junk yard, by delivering repaired shoes for an old Irish cobbler who lived down the street from us in the Swamppoodle section of Washington, and running errands for Laddon's drug store at the corner of Third and H Street, Northeast. A fellow needed a pretty good pile to do Marshall Hall correctly. The roller coaster cost a nickel a ride and though breathtaking beyond description, wasn't a very long ride.

The voyage was made by ship. The *Charles McAllister* was a noble white sidewheeler with a fine black rocker-arm on its top deck and a steam-horn that made us clap hands to our ears and dance with joy. My father had been one of the organizers of these yearly adventures, usually staged on August 1. After he died, my mother carried on the tradition of attending and provisioning us. She would make the fried chicken and the baloney sandwiches the night before, and the hard-boiled eggs, and see to it that there were tomatoes and pickles and even potato chips. I'd help squeeze the lemons into a Ball-Mason jar, to be made into lemonade with iron water pumped out of the earth of Marshall Hall's picnic grounds the next day.

We'd eat and play ourselves into exhaustion, then back to the *Charles McAllister* for the long, sleep-filled twenty-mile voyage back to the pier at the foot of Seventh Street. If the night had turned chilly as we stretched out across the ship's canvas chairs, our mother would cover us with newspapers.

I've sometimes wondered since if osmosis was involved.

The first time I journeyed all the way to New York was to play in the National Indoor championship. At that time the Pennsylvania Railroad maintained a station-platform in adjacent Jersey called Manhattan Transfer. When the conductor stuck his head into the coach and bellowed its name, I hurriedly put on hat and coat, grabbed bag and tennis racquets, and labored down the aisle, convinced that the train would start again before I could get off and I'd be carried to some hostile place farther to the north, say, Albany. The conductor's contempt was withering as he told me that Manhattan Transfer was not Manhattan even though many transfers were made there. Equally flabbergasting was an examination of the Manhattan phone directory which I opened immediately after reaching my room in the then brand-new New Yorker Hotel. I turned to the McIntyres. There was a small forest of them listed in the book. But no O.O. I wondered how in the name of God the writer whose every word about New York was gospel to me couldn't afford a telephone.

The big war gave wings to a lot of us who had never dreamed we'd see far-off places. Americans spread around the earth like a blessing or a plague, depending on the viewpoint of the hosts. For this reporter, sometimes, and wrongly, regarded as the "travelingest," there is no substitute for travel, no comparable adrenalin. And one is not likely ever to forget his first important break with immobility. . . .

"Step outside, sergeant," the portly lieutenant colonel at 90 Church Street in New York crisply ordered. The enlisted man retired and added to the mystery by closing the door as if it were mined. Then and only then did the light colonel lean across the desk he had commanded so faithfully.

"Pier 90," he whispered. "Be there no later than 1800. Destroy that note you just made! Dress in civilian clothes, not your correspondent's uniform. Don't take a cab all the way to the pier. Get off two or three blocks away and walk the rest of the way."

It was the early summer of 1943.

I kissed Millie and Mike and Barry good-bye and patted the one in the oven—who turned out to be Dennis six months later. Mike, who was seven, gave me the first and only salute I ever rated as a correspondent.

I did as my leader had commanded, though it made no sense. All those German spies who followed me in black limousines with drawn blinds must have suspected that something was up when they saw me get out of the taxi and begin lugging my gear—including helmet and gas mask—in the direction of the *Queen Mary*. I clanked like a pots-and-pans peddler. It was a blazingly bright 6 P.M. The ship's proud bow and nameplate hovered over a busy West Side Highway. The spies' lingering doubts may have vanished completely during the night. An entire division marched aboard to the accompaniment of a brass band. The next noon the *Mary*'s horn rattled windows as far away as New Rochelle while tugs nuzzled her on her way. As we edged down the river toward the sea, thousands waved handkerchiefs from skyscraper windows. Tugs honked a farewell. Thus did we surreptitiously slip out of town.

"Attention! All men on deck!" the brass-lunged public address system boomed. Thousands cluttered to the decks.

"Face inboard!" we were ordered. The *Mary* was passing through the antisubmarine nets strung across the Narrows. They must not be looked upon by us who were about to die.

Later that first day out I was startled to hear myself being paged and asked to appear immediately at the purser's office. A young British officer in immaculate whites, with shorts, was looking vexedly at an immigration declaration I had filled out earlier.

"I'm sure you've made a mistake here, old boy, under 'Nationality,' " he said. "You've put down 'American.' "

"I am an American," I said, vibrating with an inner orchestration of "Yankee Doodle," "Dixie," and "The Battle Hymn of the Republic."

He looked at me as only the British Navy can.

"Are you a Red Indgeon? They are the only Americans."

I said, "That would come as a big fat surprise to the fourteen thousand guys on this ship who are going over to fight for you."

He ignored that, handed me a pen, and said, "Under 'Nationality' please write 'U.S.A.' "

At sea we zigged and zagged with metronomic monotony. Even an incurably cockeyed U-boat commander could not have failed to send us to the bottom. But nothing violent happened, except the day a big Negro kid blew his stack and began throwing his equipment overboard, yelling incoherently as he did so. A Negro sergeant as old and wise as Jersey Joe Walcott walked up slowly and said, almost soothingly, "Boy, don't do that." The kid wheeled and reached for his knife pocket, but he never got it out. The old sarge, who had been sucking on a bottle of Coke, hit the boy across the face with it and it cut him like the swipe of a machete. There wasn't any trouble after that.

A couple of the blacked-out nights we sat wherever possible, including the side of the bathtub, in the cabin I shared with Lt. Col. John Staige Davis, Air Force doctor, while Willie Shore and his USO troupe sang a song soft and low and, somehow, poignantly. A handful of Red Cross girls dropped by for these sessions, including Taty Spaatz, daughter of the Army Air Force general, and Kit Kennedy, cheerfully freckled daughter of the former ambassador to the Court of St. James's.

We debarked at Greenock while a Spitfire, a breathtakingly beautiful fighter when first (and last) seen, rolled over us beneath the low, gray overcast. The train to London took all day and well into the dark. A truck awaited us at the terminal and carried a full load of us—

standing and reeling—through the shrouded streets to the faintly lighted doorway of the Savoy. Dr. Davis and I had confirmed reservations there for the night, as did our fellow shipmate and truckmate, Walter Rothschild, the Brooklyn merchant prince and philanthropist who was a dollar-a-year man in Government service.

"As bedraggled a group as ever entered this lobby," observed a gaunt, gray, black-caped, black-suited old man whose cigarette ashes flowed like dry lava down his clothing. Turned out to be the beloved eccentric of Fleet Street's critics, Hannen Swaffer. We were to become good friends in the ensuing months, but that first meeting left something to be desired. So did the first meeting with the desk clerk the Savoy must have ordered from Madame Tussaud's. He introduced us to the most implacable expression of that period of austerity in Britain.

"You've had it," he clicked when I asked if we could have supper. The train had been foodless, and, foolishly, I mentioned that. He shook his head. "You've had it," he repeated, meaning an assortment of things: We were too late to be served, we had had such luxuries in the long ago past, we should be nourished by memories of better days. . . .

The only lodging available at the Savoy was a magnificent suite. John Staige Davis had three small cans of rations. I drew the beef stew. We held our repasts under the hot-water tap, and Walter somehow opened the cans with his penknife. We ate with our fingers, perhaps the first time that lack of couth had been seen in a Savoy suite since Henry VIII week-ended.

John Staige went off to his airfield in the Midlands the next day, and Rothschild disappeared on one of those unspelled-out dollar-a-year missions. The man from Tussaud's, or one just like him, moved me into more sensible quarters in the hotel. I was just settling in for the night in my pitch black room when the air-raid sirens went off. I was frightened, experiencing an alert for the first time, particularly after the anti-aircraft guns in Hyde Park began to cough and mutter and vaguely shake the deeply hooded windows. The rules of the hotel were that all guests must retreat to the air-raid shelter in its venerable bowels, but there was scant hope of finding it in the dark. At least, I must dress. No sense being blown out of one's room in pajamas. It was surprisingly difficult to find the necessary bits of clothing in that strange inky room. Halfway into them, with doom now swiftly approaching, I remembered more sobersided counsel given to me by the desk-flying lieutenant colonel back at 90 Church. He had put me through a crash course in how to don, secure, and operate my gas mask.

"Those Krauts will be using poison gas before very long," he said as he helped me through the incomprehensible.

Now, trapped in my posh cell, pants at half-mast and a left shoe on my right foot, I somehow found the mask. But it had been folded and packaged so ingeniously that I could not have opened it within a week. I was still struggling with it, using Braille, when the "All clear" sounded.

Thereafter, it seemed simpler during raids on London late at night to put a pillow over your head, pull the covers up around your shoulders, and go back to sleep.

This was hardly sheer bravado. This was the period between the Battle of Britain and the coming of the V-1's and V-2's. "Look at it this way," a correspondent with more experience put it. "Suppose the Germans dropped a half dozen fifty-dollar bills on this city of seven or eight million. What do you think your chances would be of catching one?"

Reactions to air raids were manifold, I soon found. Elderly ladies in London tended to have upset stomachs on mornings after emphatic raids. The Ministry of Health professed to have diagnosed the reason for this. If the bombing and cannonading grew menacing enough, the dear old girls would get out of bed, repair to the pantry, and eat some carefully harbored luxury item, long since disappeared from London's better grocery shelves: tinned deviled lobster, say. These were riches one *could* take with him to the grave.

One of the older cocks at INS, which ran a tight little bureau at 78 Fleet, found his long-dormant sexual prowess rejuvenated whenever the sirens sounded at night. Conveniently, he shacked up with another type of siren: a big blonde Scandinavian suspected of wishing that the Luftwaffe would bomb more often.

From Italy came still another report on the antics of the reflexes when bombs are dropping. Former heavyweight champion Jack Sharkey and the fabled Yankee pitcher Lefty Gomez were caught one night in a raid while doing a USO job. All hands were ordered to hit the slit trenches on the double. Sharkey dived into one head first, a belly flopper, and Gomez landed on top of him. The racket of the raid grew intolerable.

"We're going to die in this rotten place," Sharkey mourned into the dirt that pressed against his face. "We're going to die."

"You think so?" Gomez asked, his lips close to the former champion's ear.

"I know so," Sharkey muttered.

"If that's so," Lefty said, "may I ask you a question?"

"Heluva time to ask questions," Sharkey growled. "What is it?"

"Did you go in the tank for Carnera?"

The most senseless bomb that fell on England while I was there in 1943 was not meant for the target it hit. It was the one-bomb blitz against East Grinstead on July 1. A German bomber pilot fleeing home after an ineffectual daylight raid on London apparently shook loose a five-hundred pounder that had jammed in its release mechanism and was slowing down his escape. It fell into the thick overcast and plunged through the roof of an East Grinstead movie house that was showing a Western. Most of those killed or wounded were children. Nearly every family in the town was affected by that one bomb. But there was no time for mourning. The people of East Grinstead had to be cheerful.

On the edge of town sat the Queen Victoria Cottage Hospital where a wizard plastic surgeon from New Zealand, Archibald McIndoe, remade the faces and arms and hands of badly burned RAF men. There had been trouble at the hospital before the catastrophe of the movie house. A patient had committed suicide in the room later assigned to me. The bullet had passed through him and torn an unrepaired chunk out of a wall. He had looked at himself in a mirror for the first time since extensive surgery and grafting and found his noseless, earless, scorched face, hung with wattles of flesh from other parts of his body, too much to bear. Mr. McIndoe forthwith ordered all mirrors removed from the hospital. But then he gave a second and stunning order which must be obeyed: All patients able to walk must stroll through the streets of East Grinstead each day as part of their psychological therapy. No man, however ghastly, was excused—if he could walk.

Mr. McIndoe had prepared the people for their ordeal. They must not stare at the macabre strollers. They must not turn away. By all means, they must not become ill. They must make these horribly disfigured young men welcome. They must show them that normal people wanted them to come back to a normal life. They must invite them in for a spot of tea, or something stronger. On Saturday nights the pretty girls of the town and magnificent young nurses from the hospital would dance with these effigies of young men.

"Nursey, you'd never know it but I was a good-looker and the girlies couldn't get enough of me," a faceless and all but fingerless Spitfire pilot croaked with a jaunty laugh one day as I passed through his ward.

The girl came over to him and put her hand on what was left of his.

"Don't I know!' she said. "That's what the whole lot of them tell me." And here and there in the ward sounded ghostly chuckles.

Then the bomb. Heartbreaking, but the town must rise above it. There was work to do.

I spent some time with Bob Hope on that trip, writing a Sunday feature on how he managed to keep going with his entertaining all day and most of the night. I never found out, and still haven't. But trying was interesting. At the end of a backbreaker of a day Bob and his writer-friend, Hal Block, who was to mean so much to the early success of television's "What's My Line?" would kick fresh gags around, weighing them, making notes to put the good ones into the next day's inventory. Sometimes they'd finish at four in the morning and have to start for the car or the airfield at six, headed for another round of camps and hospitals.

In the course of that trip Bob asked me to accompany him to the funeral of his British grandfather who had died one month short of his one hundredth year. I wondered if his presence in the little village might not eclipse the day's main event.

"Not a chance," he laughed. "I went back to the old place just after making it big on Broadway. My grandfather MC'd a show they put on in my honor. Nearly everybody in town turned out. He had them in stitches all the way. When I went on I gave them the full routine, everything that had made me big in New York. Laugh?—I thought they'd never start. In fact, they didn't. Then my grandfather introduced a couple of bell-ringers in bloomers—locals—and they broke up the joint."

At the old homestead a cousin led Bob into the little living room where the body lay in an open coffin.

"He looks better than I do," Hope said, and may have had something there.

One day Bob took over the controls of a small twin-engined plane provided for us by the RAF, and for the next few miles I felt I was on an invisible roller coaster. Holding on with one hand I scribbled a note to him with the other. It read, "Stop ad-libbing!" It led later to a revealing side of his labors overseas. The subject of insurance came up from nowhere. It reminded me of a bleak fact I tried to forget throughout the war: that if I were killed my insurance was worthless and Millie would be penniless. I asked Bob about his infinitely larger insurance.

"I'd blow it," he said with a shrug.

With other members of his troupe—Frances Langford, Tony Manero, and Jack Pepper—Bob showed up the next dawn at a field near Londonderry. The plane that was to take us to Belfast was the saddest-looking B-17 imaginable. It was patched like a clown's coat and gave every appearance of running on tired blood rather than gas. A sleepy airman in a shack of a terminal looked at Hope, unshaven, and pooped, did not recognize him, and handed him the usual chilling form the Air Force reserves for civilian passengers. Under "Person to be notified in case of death" Bob wrote:

"Louella Parsons."

We brought a precious cargo back to London from Belfast: two dozen real eggs. My quota was four. The eggs were the first I had seen in weeks. The Atheneum Court, where I lived by that time, was no different from any other war-rationed hotel in London. Its eggs were powdered, its sausages had only the barest acquaintance with meat, and its Spam was endless. It was imperative that the real eggs arrive in London unscathed. However, upon landing at tiny Hendon, there was a bad minute or two when we as well as the eggs seemed about to be cracked. The bucket-seat Lockheed Lodestar hit the short runway with a wallop, bounced crazily a time or two, and then the pilot gave his engines full throttle. We staggered off the end of the runway and somehow cleared the chimney pots of a residential area just beyond. We were all alarmed and terribly silent as the plane swung around for another landing attempt. I was sure the first one had mortally ruptured our landing gear. I looked across the tin aisle at Hope, sitting bolt upright among his shillelaghs, his blackthorn walking sticks, his bottle of Irish whisky, and his eggs. He was looking at me intently.

"What sort of billing do you think you'll get in the story of our crack-up?" he asked.

We landed safely, smuggled our loot into the egg-beleaguered city, and in gratitude for having survived the rough landing, I gave away three of my four. The fourth and last egg spent a peaceful, chilled night on my windowsill.

Next morning the floor waiter came in aglow with news.

"No Spam for you this morning, sir," he said. "We're serving real by-con. It's the first we've had in a long time."

I told him that the gods clearly had chosen this day to stand out like a star in the annals of wartime Britain's cookery. I fetched my egg off the ledge (the Luftwaffe had been thoughtful enough not to bomb the night before) and handed it to the waiter like the Kohinoor.

"Sunny side up with my bacon," I said.

He looked stricken.

"Sorry, sir, it's against regulations to have by-con and aig on the same dish," he said.

"But it's my egg. . . ."

He sighed. "There's not a thing I can do about it, sir. Regulations. I can fry your aig for you, but no by-con if I do. Or I can serve the by-con alone."

It was a somewhat less majestic compromise than the Missouri. In came the bacon and when the man was gone I locked the door, put my treasure in a glass and let the not-quite-hot-enough bathroom water run on it. After half an hour I had the first one-minute egg I ever sucked. Ghastly.

The greatest hero I interviewed while in England was Sgt. Maynard Smith, a B-17 waist-gunner inevitably called Snuffy, after Billy De Beck's testy little comic strip hillbilly. Col. Tex McCrary, the intrepid mission-flying Eighth Air Force public relations officer, arranged transportation so that I could be present and write something about Snuffy's sublimest hour. Turned out to be an unnerving hour, too, for Snuffy wasn't precisely the type the Air Force was featuring on its enlistment posters. He didn't fit the public's image of a Congressional Medal of Honor winner, which he was about to become in a glittering ceremony at Bassingbourn Airdrome, Cambridgeshire. Indeed, he'd be the only one in the whole ETO.

There was no question that he rated the highest decoration a grateful nation can offer. On his first mission over Germany, the previous May 1, his B-17 was jumped and set afire amidships by German fighters. It turned for home without fighter escort and was harder hit. Snuffy's fellow waist-gunner, the bombardier, the navigator, and the belly-turret gunner bailed out. Snuffy manned first one and then the other waist-gun position and shot down two of the enemy. Between times, he beat on the flames with his gloved hands or rolled his body against them. The tail-gunner crawled up to Snuffy's fiery section, shot through a lung. Snuffy gave him first aid and positioned him so that the lung would drain. He went back to firing his .50 calibers at the fighters again, but the fire grew hotter. He picked up the portable latrine and flung its contents on the fire.

Miraculously, the B-17's pilot and co-pilot coaxed the scorched wreck across the Channel and landed on an RAF grass strip at the water's edge. As the fire engines and ambulances arrived at the ravaged bomber's side, Snuffy was observed dousing the remaining flicker of flame by urinating on it.

Throughout the century and more of its existence there has never been a bestowal of the Medal of Honor quite like the day the hallowed ribbon and medal was hung around Snuffy's neck. Twelve generals including Ira Eaker, commander of the Eighth Air Force, and Jacob Devers, commander of ETO ground forces, lined up beside Secretary of War Henry L. Stimson, old in the service of his country but proud to be present on such a momentous occasion. Old Glory never fluttered better, airmen never marched in review with as much cadence, and a dozen B-17's drummed low over the noble scene.

The only one who seemed to be out of uniform was Snuffy. He had been roughed up in a happy free-for-all in a public house in Oxford the week before, made the constables very mad at him, was turned back to the Air Force, and drew a most unusual punishment for a man on combat: KP duty, peeling potatoes. A larger sergeant loaned him his coat for the great occasion, Snuffy's having been ripped beyond fast repair in the Oxford caper.

When it was all over, I met Snuffy. He had been given the short pin-on ribbon of the award and the rosette. But he was still wearing the round-the-neck ribbon and its dangling medal. After a few routine questions and answers, I asked him if he would like a drink.

"Are you some kind of a nut? Of course I would."

It was a good half-mile walk to the Nissen hut where I had a cot. Halfway there I noticed an Air Force captain striding in the opposite direction. He obviously had missed the ceremony, didn't know Snuffy, and was excessively salute-conscious. As the gap closed, his right arm stiffened, ready to return Snuffy's salute. Snuffy ignored him, continuing to talk to me. They were abreast now. The captain stopped and glared at Snuffy, his right arm now half-up.

"Buzz off," Snuffy said to him. We kept walking, with Snuffy chatting as if he did not share my expectation of our both being shot in the back by the flushed and angry officer.

"There's a bum who don't know history," Snuffy remarked. "I guess he never heard that no Congressional Medal of Honor winner ever has to initiate a salute. The other guy salutes the Medal, first."

We had a drink out of the bottle and then Snuffy said he must be getting back to his Nissen to see his fellow noncoms and go to chow. I walked back with him, taking more notes. He lay down on his bed and lighted a cigarette.

" 'Ten-shun!" an airman barked near the door of the hut. A bird colonel entered. Every man leaped to his feet and stood at attention. Except Snuffy. The colonel walked to the foot of Snuffy's cot and reddened as Snuffy lay there and regarded him indifferently through an exhalation of cigarette smoke.

The colonel braced and saluted the reclining figure of Sgt. Maynard Smith.

"General Eaker's compliments, Sergeant Smith," the colonel said. "The General would be pleased to have you at the officers' mess for lunch."

Snuffy looked at the proud and distinguished officer for what seemed an eternity. Then he spoke, ever so casually.

"Tell him I'm busy," Snuffy said.

The colonel turned and marched out faster than he had entered.

"You shouldn't have done that, buddy," I volunteered after the hut had relaxed with a wheeze of admiration.

"Why not?" Snuffy asked with great honesty. "I didn't make the rules. Everybody's got to salute the Medal, salute me first. Eisenhower's got to salute me."

That was hard to top, but I tried.

"MacArthur doesn't," I pointed out.

"Yeah? How come?"

"He's got the Congressional Medal of Honor."
Something died in Snuffy.
"Oh, rats!" he said.

Unbeknown to the poor slob, the American taxpayer (circa 1944–45) underwrote some of the most senseless expeditions in the history of transportation. I should know. I was both a taxpayer and a beneficiary.

I had felt until the junkets of 1944–45 that the war's high point in useless expenditure would remain an exercise in England in the early fall of '43. Mr. Churchill called it Harlequin. Thousands, maybe tens of thousands, of troops were trucked, trained, bussed, flown, and marched to embarkation points, along with all their gear. Some never-revealed number boarded ships and troop carriers, headed for what was then never called Festung Europa, but made U-turns about a mile out in the Channel and came back to port. That whole section of England seemed to shake under the roar of planes just before daybreak. They, too, returned to their bases. Coastal anti-aircraft batteries blazed away, shooting blanks.

Harlequin, indeed.

The realization that it was just a show, a sham, somehow increased the chill in the air as I stood with a group of British war correspondents on a windy promontory at Newhaven, Sussex East. A great slash of pink began to show its lovely face in the east. We watched the rebirth of day in silence and wonderment. That is, all but one of us.

"Bugger the rosy-fingered dawn!" a British correspondent muttered.

It remains one of the worst obscenities I've ever heard.

Harlequin (which was said to have greatly annoyed Stalin, who was pressing the Allies hard for the opening of the Second Front) at least could be condoned as a dress rehearsal for D-Day. I was never able to discover the true purpose, if any, of an Air Transport Command visitation to the North country in November, 1944. ATC billed it as a trip which would prove for all time that no degree of Arctic violence could stay those winged messengers from the swift completion of their appointed rounds, occasionally rounds of drinks. Arctic Safety Trip; that was the way our orders were cut.

The Safety Trip got off to an interesting start. Our bucket-seat C-46's port engine burst into flames shortly after takeoff. The pilot put the flying gas tank (there was a big one inside the cabin, too) into a sharp 180-degree turn. We limped back into the landing pattern on one engine, with the other one smoking like a chimney on its gas-heavy wing. We hit hard about one third down the runway. I caught a blurred view of several pieces of fire-fighting apparatus and an ambulance giving chase. The pilot gave his craft all the brakes it had, and when they proved insufficient he managed to bring us to a stop by making a 180-degree turn at the end of the runway.

"Out!" someone ordered, as if the whole business was about to erupt in one vast fiery belch.

We moved as fast as we could to the now-open door in the rear. The last wisp of smoke fluttered from the engine, which the pilot had immersed in the fire-throttling chemical foam with which planes are equipped. Just then the first fire truck drew up with a screech of brakes. A boy dressed in what looked like a deep-sea diver's outfit made of asbestos, head encased in a weird cylindrical helmet with a glass peephole, leaped off the still-moving truck, pulling a hose behind him. He pointed the nozzle of his fire-fighting weapon at the burned and foam-flaked engine. His gloved fingers twitched on the nozzle's trigger. But there was no fire left to put out. He took off his helmet and looked at the former fire in disgust.

"Shit," he said.

It seemed like such an unusual reaction that I sought him later— while someone in charge was ordering another plane—and asked him to explain.

"I been chasing planes ever since I got in the service two years ago," he said. "Something always happens at the last minute, and I don't get to squirt my hose. Today looked like the day more than any other time. Then just as I got there the goddam fire goes out. It's driving me nuts."

There wasn't much to do except apologize and go to the new plane, a C-47. The Safety Trip began all over again. All went well until we arrived at LaGuardia, where our group was transferred into another C-47 bound for Presque Isle, Maine. ATC's handling of the group's typewriters left something to be desired. They were put on a plane going somewhere else. There was another jarring note. Just before the pilot buttoned up the C-47 and prepared to taxi away for the takeoff, a general arrived with his staff and all their gear. The pilot remonstrated as vigorously as he dared that the plane was already overloaded and not another pound could be carried without endangering all hands. The general outvoted the other forty of us by a healthy majority of 1 to 40.

ATC could fly in the teeth of the Arctic's iciest gale, perhaps, but it couldn't get off the ground at Presque Isle for forty-eight hours because of a slight drizzle. During the wait, somebody back at headquarters concluded that perhaps it might be better to spring a better airplane for that increasingly restless platoon of reporters. We drew a four-engined C-54. It took us to the U.S. airbase at Stevenville, Gander, where another chapter was added to the saga of the Safety Trip.

"Anything happening around here?" Carl Levin of the New York *Herald Tribune* asked an airman as we deplaned.

"Nothing much," the kid said, "except the crash."

"Crash! What crash?"

"Oh, a '54 like the one you're on. It pranged a mountain out there last night, trying to find the field."

Unluckily, the Air Transport Command had deposited a whole plane load of reporters at a point near a crash which, under normal wartime conditions, would have attracted, at most, an obscure paragraph. It was not the kind of story ATC wanted spread at any time; now countless thousands of words began pouring from our reclaimed typewriters. The tour's ATC public relations officer, Maj. Lynn Mahan, a decent man, made the lot of us what a few of us considered a fair proposition: ATC would supply all the details of the crash, names of the dead and names of the survivors. In exchange, he asked us to spare the feelings of the next-of-kin of the dead by limiting the more grisly details of the crack-up and concentrate on the good job done by rescue forces who climbed the wild peak and saved lives. It was depressing to hear several of our number accuse him bitterly of trying to throttle the free press.

I never wondered again why so many good public relations people hate our guts.

The by now numb Safety Trip reached Bluie West 8, Greenland, just in time to be present when an Army Air Force officer who had been stationed there a bit too long blew his stack in front of some of us and launched into the worst condemnation of ATC we had ever heard. Printable portions made some of the papers represented in our group.

There seemed to be no statute of limitations on the trip's bad luck. One of the officers assigned as our keepers got himself pleasantly involved with a six-foot version of Ingrid Bergman within ten minutes after our arrival in Reykjavik. He was deeper involved three days later as we prepared to leave. The massive rosy-jawed beauty came to the airport to see him off. One hazarded a guess, judging from appearances, that they had not spent all of their time together discussing U.S.-Icelandic cod-fishing treaties. Our roué stood several inches shorter and fifty degrees colder than his girl. She enveloped him in a great hug and cried on the top of his head in the course of the most one-sided farewell since Rhett Butler took leave of Scarlet O'Hara.

It was time to go. Our man, who couldn't wait for the propellers to start turning, broke away from a last kiss, with the noise of a rubber suction cup pulled off a glass pane, patted her paternally on her buttocks, and spoke the line that was used more often and less sincerely than any other sentence uttered overseas in World War II:

"Good-bye, honey," he said. "If you ever come to the United States, be sure to look me up."

On Christmas Eve the following year, our hero was assembling the toys after tucking in the three kids for the night. His ever-loving wife, about to have their fourth, was knitting contentedly in her chair. There was Peace on Earth in cozy little Peaceful Glade, Virginia, for men of such good will.

There was, at least, until the phone rang. Our man picked it up and—as was his wont—officiously announced his name. Then he froze.

"Dolling!" a deliriously happy Icelandic voice crackled in the phone. "It's your Poopsie. I'm here!"

The China-Burma-India theater was a bypassed arena of World War II by mid-summer of 1945. Japanese forces still held most of the China coast, but there was little fighting. Chiang Kai-shek's armies and those of Mao Tse-tung, ostensibly allied in the common cause of casting the Nippon devils out of China, were busily engaged instead in caching arms against the inevitable postwar day when they would fight for possession of the world's most populous country. In Burma and India there was hardly a memory of the war. Each was more concerned with the kind of postwar world it would inherit or be forced to accept.

China was America's problem child, exasperating but tolerated, expensive but endured. If any American in or out of public office at that time suspected that one day China would be considered a major menace to the welfare of the United States, he held his tongue. Its excesses were conversation pieces, but hardly alarming. There were dozens of reports that Chinese recruits being transported like cattle in C-47's across the Hump to India, for training, occasionally would throw one of their number out of the plane's open door for laughs. Tons of Chinese paper currency, printed in the United States, were jettisoned by cargo planes experiencing engine trouble, it was said. Everybody seemed to accept the story that Chinese co-pilots on Hump-flying runs made fortunes trafficking in penicillin, Parker 51's, and Scotch. It was unquestionably true that Chinese farmers along the fuel pipeline we built from the Persian Gulf to Kunming regarded it as their own. They'd occasionally crack it open just to fill a primitive lamp with a few ounces, and let the precious stuff gush for hours, sometimes days, until U.S. repair crews could find the precise breach and patch it. Other Chinese would break open the pipe at night, light the spilling gas, and gather around to enjoy the impressive flames. The fuel was estimated to cost twenty-five dollars a gallon by the time it attempted to slip past the Chinese farmers.

Chinese military and civil officials sometimes unnerved and shut up indignant Americans who protested against Chinese robbers by seizing the robber, or a reasonable facsimile, and chopping off one of his hands. Exhausted Hump fliers learned to sleep fully clothed in their Kunming bunks after their more trusting buddies had been virtually stripped naked by Chinese while sleeping off the rigors of flying aid to the same Chinese. In July, 1945, the United States presented the Generalissimo with a C-47 whose interior had been fitted to serve as his combination airborne headquarters and executive suite. The plane was named the Mayling, for Madame Chiang. It reached Kunming too late in the afternoon to risk continuation of its ultimate deliverance on Chungking's unlighted side-of-the-mountain airstrip. So the U.S. ferry crew parked it at Kunming for the night. Chiang, pleased over the present from the grateful democracy on the other side of the world, flew in his honor guard to police the plane through the night. The next morning, when the American crewmen reported to fly the plane to Chungking, they found it stripped of most of its furnishings. Even the springs in the seats had been carried away. Obviously, the honor guard had rifled it.

Still, China was preferred to India, almost equally poor but much more forlorn about its status. There was always something antic about China. The fierce regimentation eventually imposed on it by the Communists was nowhere in evidence. In India the poor shrank from an American's efforts to be friendly. In China the people met you half way, with a smile and often a prepared plan to relieve you of your shirt at the earliest opportunity. They laughed. The Indians and Burmese preferred heavy sighs. The consensus was that the Chinese would be first-class allies forever if they patched up their petty political differences. Toward that end, the United States insisted in time that Chiang integrate Mao people into his Kuomintang government —with historically disastrous results.

Chiang's younger son by his first wife tried to be helpful during our stay there. He had trained in Arizona as a flier and had picked up many American ways and expressions which he tried, with lamentable results, to implant in his father. I was witness to one setback in his attempted Americanization of the Gimo. In the course of a luncheon Chiang gave us at the graduation ceremonies of China's "West Point," near Sian, I related to young Major Chiang a story Pat Hurley had told me not long before. I asked Hurley how he, an old soldier and politician, sank into diplomacy. He answered with a typically thundering anecdote. Seems (he said) he was caught in a Japanese bombing raid on Port Moresby, New Guinea, early in the war. While running for a slit trench he was hit in the back of the head by a bomb fragment.

"I was unconscious for two or three days, and when I woke up I was a diplomat," he told me. Young Chiang enjoyed the story much more than it warranted.

"You must tell that to my father just the way you told it to me," he insisted, and would brook no protest. "Don't worry about the language problem," he said. "You just tell it to him, and I'll interpret as you go along. He'll love it."

It laid an egg. A five-hundred-year-old Chinese egg. As I reached the pallid punchline, young Chiang was laughing so robustly he had trouble sputtering his words. He slapped his knee with joy and searched his father's face for a reaction. So did I.

Chiang's face remained an inscrutable mask throughout. His luminous black eyes never left mine as I spoke. An infernal ten seconds or so after his son's laughter and the translation had died away, Chiang muttered a few words in Chinese, still with no change in expression. His son sighed and led me away.

"You know what he said?" young Chiang asked me. "He said, 'I trust General Hurley was not injured badly.' "

I often think of Sian and wonder if its pleasant people still water down its wide and dusty streets each evening to keep the dust at bay. It was the thriving capital of the Ch'in dynasty, which gave China its name, 250 years before Christ. For me, it provided two enduring memories. I lay ill and homesick in a rickety hotel there one afternoon when the door was flung open by Bob Rodenberg, an old friend I had worked with on the Washington *Herald* ten years before. Bob was stationed nearby at an OSS camp, had wandered into Sian, spotted one of the correspondents with our group, and, making small talk, remarked that he had a friend who was a reporter—name of Considine.

"He's at that fleabag down the street, dying of the crud or something," Rodenberg was told. He took me to the OSS camp and nursed me back to health with repeated applications of Four Roses and apple pie.

Harry Grayson supplied my other indelible memory of Sian. One day the neighborhood shook with the approach of a brassy band playing the "Wedding Hymn" from *Lohengrin*. Behind the musicians followed four Chinese carrying a sedan chair whose curtains were drawn. We followed it to the site of the wedding, a public room in our hotel. The bespectacled and extraordinarily homely groom was waiting. The bearers put down their burden near him and out stepped one of the loveliest creatures I've ever seen, a shy but radiant young Chinese in her wedding robes.

It was a beautiful wedding, somewhat marred by my friend Grayson. "Poor son of a bitch," he'd say from time to time, chewing his cigar. Harry felt sorry for the groom for getting married. Hooked, Harry said.

It is difficult to equate the Chinese I came to know in 1945 with, let us say, the Chinese who have nuclear weapons, the Chinese who underwent without audible protest the "cultural revolution" of 1966 which was hazily delineated in Peking's *People's Daily* as follows:

> China's masses of workers, peasants, and soldiers and revolutionary cadres and intellectuals have started to criticize the old world, old things, and old thinking on an unprecedented scale, using as their weapon the thought of Mao Tse-tung.
>
> We criticize the system of exploitation, the exploiting classes, imperialism, modern revisionism, all reactionaries, landlords, rich peasants, counter-revolutionaries, bad elements, and rightists.
>
> We criticize the representatives of the bourgeoisie and bourgeois "scholars and authorities." We criticize the bourgeois conception of history, bourgeois academic theories, pedagogy, journalism, and theories of art and literature, and all bad plays, films, and works of literature and art.
>
> In sum, we criticize the old world, the old ideology and culture, and old customs and habits which imperialism and all exploiting classes use to poison the minds of the working people; we criticize all nonproletarian ideology, all reactionary ideology which is antagonistic to Marxism-Leninism, to Mao Tse-tung's thought.

. . . Poor son of a bitch.

In the summer of 1946 the United States produced a nuclear spectacular which, if presented today, would bring down on its head the frowns and fulminations of much of the civilized world—excepting France and Communist China, which would wish for such an entrepreneur's role. We tested two twenty-kiloton A-bombs at Bikini Atoll in the Ralik chain of the Marshall Islands. Their targets, securely anchored, were rusty relics of World War II's naval engagements: obsolete American, Japanese, and German warships, plus complements of laboratory animals, mostly rats but also goats and pigs. The project was named "Operation Crossroads," into which some of us on hand tried to read a certain significance. It engaged 42,000 men from the Army, Army Air Force, Navy, and Marine Corps, some of them against their wills. It was a time when most servicemen wanted out of uniform. It was also a time when the national conscience was first being pricked by the massive horror we had rained on Hiroshima and Nagasaki (and would have flung down on Tokyo, which was to have been the target of Bomb No. 3). On the "Big Apple" (as our ship was called) and elsewhere there was mirthless jesting about the possible effect of the Bikini bombs on visiting genitals.

We had a monopoly on the Bomb but were hardly adverse to demonstrating what it could do. Eleven nations accepted our far-flung invitations to send observers, as did the United Nations Atomic Energy Commission, members of Congress, representatives of the scientific community which had produced the weapon, and a motley army of newsmen. The latter journeyed from Oakland to Bikini aboard the *Appalachian,* a communications ship noted for its abominable communications. The Navy insisted on the ship as the very least it could contribute to an experiment designed primarily to show the uselessness of having a surface Navy in Year One of the Atomic Age. We ploughed westward for many days at eight knots, followed by an eight knot wind which thus lay on us like an oven's continuous breath. Some were driven to drink and, surprisingly, did not find it hard to get. Sensing the probable need for such relief, the Navy had been unusually clement in the language in which it couched our orders. Our papers read that alcoholic beverages were strictly forbidden aboard all U.S. Navy ships, but for Operation Crossroads there would be no baggage inspection. Thus, many reporters brought two bags aboard at Oakland: one for clothing, one for comfort.

Still, it was an infernally long voyage. The "Big Apple" had never before been asked to carry as undisciplined a party. The executive officer, a ludicrous martinet, was soon reduced to a perpetual rage at the sight of our lolling about the decks for days on end, dropping cigarette butts on his spotless craft, and ordering ice brought to our stuffed cabins as if we were aboard a bloody *Queen.* Powerless to do anything about us, he spent his venom on the crew. They chipped a vast fortune in paint during that trip, and several times each day they were forced to line up in front of us for a spit and polish review in which the exec set new U.S. Navy records for lint-picking. We urged the crew to mutiny against him and set him adrift in an open boat with a pint of water and two breadfruit, but they never took this excellent advice.

A Russian reporter, whose bunk was on the lowest level of a four-tier job in the largest and most crowded cabin, pinned the picture of a hula girl on the bottom of the mattress of the bunk just above him

and would lie for hours looking up at it, two or three inches above
his nose. Now and then on the long first leg of the trip he was heard
to mumble "Havaii . . . vimmen!" But the pleasure of expectation
must have been diminished by his need to throw up again. He was
our only seasick newsman, but generously made up for the rest of us.
In the same gamy cell a fine-looking young reporter who had been
shot up during the war haunted the evenings with his nightmares. In
his torment he would call for his mother like a frightened child in the
dark.

Honolulu was a happy respite, save for the man from Tass. He
remained too ill to accomplish the dreams that had sustained him for
2,200 miles at eight knots. My friend Red McQueen, sports editor of
the Honolulu *Advertiser,* and his dear wife Glenn adopted a good half
of us and made their pleasant waterside home in the Kahala area
ring with hospitality. It was interesting and enlightening, too, to meet
Clark Lee's wife—incongruously called Baby—a robust and fullback-
sized granddaughter and heiress of the last Queen of the Hawaiian
Islands, Liliuokalani. I arrived at their palatial home bearing a lei
and commenced the pleasant ritual of draping it about her shoulders.
"Please," Baby said, waving it aside, "I'm allergic to leis."

Sometimes one must go a great distance to learn a small thing.
The long second leg of the trip to the bomb-test area was a case in
point. One learned, for example, that the U.S. Navy will not stop one
of its ships—specifically, the "Big Apple"—to retrieve a medicine
ball erratically heaved overboard during a game. When we lost the
third and last of the ship's supply, we exercised our talents instead of
our tired blood. We wrote a theme song, to be sung to the easiest-
remembered melody of Gilbert and Sullivan's *H.M.S. Pinafore.* We
dedicated it to the patrician officer in charge of us, Capt. Fitzhugh
Lee, U.S.N., named for his illustrious grandfather, the Confederate
cavalry general who so well served his own uncle, Robert E. It was
a poor verse, but there was little else to do at eight knots:

> We are the boys of Fitzhugh Lee
> We hate the Navy and we hate the sea
> We hate the Army and we hate this ship
> But we're all signed up for the atomic trip.
> (We're all signed up for the atomic trip.)
> We're all signed up and ready to go
> To offer up our testicles for UNO.

There was a verse near the end that poked fun at the two most distinguished science writers aboard, Howard Blakeslee of the Associated Press and William L. Laurence of the *New York Times,* who had written about the explosive properties of uranium as far back as 1940, was the only journalistic witness of the Nagasaki bombing, and the sole pool man for the entire development of the Bomb. The verse had something feckless to say about the impressive scholarship of the two men, made so bold as to doubt if they knew what they were talking about, and ended with what we all felt was a superior rhyme, composed by two of our better wits, Steve White and Tom Priestly. It went (still to the rhythm of Messrs. Gilbert and Sullivan):

> Oh, the goddam thing will hang in midair
> And Energy will never equal MC square!

Once at the scene, which had overtones of a grisly Gauguin depicting natives being moved away to avoid contamination with radioactive fallout, all newsmen aboard the "Big Apple" became painfully aware they were the helpless victims of Navy communications. Most of our early stories elicited starts of surprise from stateside offices. They arrived in badly garbled condition or out of sequence. Clark Lee and I, along with our counterparts with AP and UP, offered our services to the Navy as impartial wire-filers who could keep the stories in order and pass them along in proper sequence to the ship's teletype operators. Navy was hurt. Navy said the ship's communications center was off-limits to civilians. Navy said it had been handling messages since long before Admiral Farragut's "Damn the torpedoes! Captain Drayton, go ahead! Jouett, full speed!" How that ever emerged without its syntax scrambled, though it passed through Navy hands, remains a mystery.

But Fitzhugh Lee presented a comforting compromise. He issued an order to the ship's communications center to turn the story-basket upside down, when the transmission period began, and thus the story that was first in the basket would be the first to be sent.

The day before the first test, a freelance type nobody seemed to have much respect for—probably because he wore a black homburg with shorts and aloha shirt—handed me ten typewritten pages and asked me to read them. It was a lurid, eyewitness account, or vision, of the next day's event. It had borrowed heavily from Bill Laurence's Pulitzer Prize-winning descriptions of the first A-bomb test at Alamogordo, New Mexico, and the Nagasaki detonation—without credit. Our hero portrayed himself as having been knocked to the deck by the concussion, following which (I read on) he shook off the terrible blow of twenty-thousand tons of TNT, fought his way back to his post at the rail of the *Appalachian,* and beheld an enormous conflagration "brighter, more dazzling, than 100 suns." I laughed when I finished it, but he was serious.

"Laugh all you want," he said, "but I just filed it. My newspapers will have it in hand, in type, and ready to go as soon as the flash comes in that the bomb has been dropped."

He must have read my face.

"Okay, it ain't ethical," he said. "But it'll get through."

The bomb was dropped on schedule, July 1, 1946, from a B-29 passing over the chained flotilla at thirty thousand feet. Its aim left something to be desired, but it sank five of the ninety target ships, ignited an escort carrier's deck, further scorched an already crisp and ugly Japanese battleship, gutted the superstructure of a sub, and ruptured the boilers of the handsomest of the doomed ships, the German pocket battleship *Prinz Eugen.* From where we tried to watch it wasn't nearly as exciting as Black Homburg's story, by now snugly arrived at its several destinations. We were positioned fourteen miles from the blast and our vision was almost completely blacked out by welders' glasses. As for the sound of the bomb, it was like the sound of a discreet belch at the other end of a bar. But there was a torrent of activity on our typewriters. A blizzard of stories hit the communications center almost simultaneously.

Captain Lee's orders were scrupulously obeyed. The first story placed in the basket that day ran six pages. The seaman in charge of impartiality turned the filled basket upside down and handed the six pages to the seaman assigned to send it. That seaman, obeying the order as he understood it, sent the story in just that order, beginning with Page 6 and persevering backwards to Page 1. I wrote fifteen pages. I learned later that Page 15 was the first to arrive at INS-San Francisco. My "lead" came in the next day. A patient man named Harry Bergman, at INS-San Francisco, put together the scrambled stories he received from me and from Clark Lee, updating mine for the morning papers along our circuit, Clark's for the afternoons, as we used to say, dropping the apostrophe. "My" stories, liberally laced with Lee's words, won INS's George R. Holmes Award, named for the late great head of our Washington bureau. That's show business.

Forty-eight hours after the shot Bikini lagoon was judged safe enough for correspondents, and vice versa. Our tour of the damage was made memorable by our leader, Captain Lee. For reasons comprehensible only to Annapolis graduates, he was cheered by what short-sighted newsmen considered a pretty beat-up array of targets.

"Good as ever!" the captain boomed as we tooled slowly past a submarine that looked, in retrospect, like the fish in Hemingway's *The Old Man and the Sea* just before it docked at Havana. "Any good crew could have her under way in short order," he pronounced as we passed the wavy-decked and flaky escort carrier. Maj. John Moynihan, the Army Air Force public relations man who had been all the way with the Bomb, from the tinkering stage to Tinian to Hiroshima and Nagasaki to Bikini, had a hard time getting in *his* word. His word was that an unlucky thing happened to the bomb as it slid out of the B-29's bomb bay. It scraped, or something, and one of its several chubby tail wings was knocked off, which compromised its true aerodynamism, or some such. Instead of detonating smack over the ugly old Japanese battleship, which deserved nothing more, it blazed immediately over a light Japanese destroyer and crushed it like a sardine can, which may have been the inspiration of its designer.

The second test put the Bomb in a more properly somber perspective. It was our first underwater experiment with a weapon whose proliferation would haunt all mankind. It regurgitated a monstrous fountain whose falling waters contaminated everything they touched. It ripped the guts out of nine ships. The *Prinz Eugen,* which seemed to have been spared, later plunged to the bottom of the sea while being towed to the United States.

I haven't the foggiest notion of how many plane trips I've taken in search of news or to cover a story. But I have a clear memory of a flight I did not take. In 1949 I received an invitation from Lynn Mahan, by that time doing public relations for The Netherlands, to join a press junket he was leading to Batavia (Djakarta) for a last look at Dutch colonialism before it succumbed to Sukarno. I was the first to accept the invitation. But Barry Faris came up with other plans for me. He assigned me to Germany for the last runs of the Berlin Air Lift and the birth of the Federal Republic of Germany. The KLM Constellation carrying Mahan and his press group, including the legendary H. R. Knickerbocker, crashed at Bombay and killed all aboard.

My borrowed time has been spent gratefully.

There was that touch of Korea, circa 1950, in the stunned early weeks of the war.

("What's on the other side of that hill?" I asked a dog-tired, sick-of-retreating GI. "Another hill," he said.)

And getting to know MacArthur at one of the most tempestuous periods of his life as a folk hero. He had just shaken Washington, and London, and the UN by flying to Taipei without President Truman's permission to engage in what appeared to be war talks with Chiang Kai-shek. There might have been fewer jitters back home if the full text of the Supreme Commander's remarks had been printed.

("Tony, look at the leg on Madame Chiang," he whispered to his aide and pilot, Colonel Story, as he stood ramrod stiff at the top of the plane steps while the band played and the Chiangs waited to welcome him. The wind was doing little tricks with Madame's beautifully tailored split-gown. "The leg of a girl of twenty . . .")

And a productive swing through Europe in 1951, with a stopover at Villa Taverna for a TV interview with Ambassador Clare Boothe Luce.

("Where shall we set up the camera?" I asked. "Let's case the joint," Her Excellency said in her grandest manner.)

Then back to Korea in '52, this time with President-elect Eisenhower. Our departure was spooky. Ike was spirited out of his Columbia University president's mansion in the dead of a cold November night, after the Secret Service had tricked the mansion's sentry, a New York cop, into going around the corner to an all-night beanery for a cup of coffee. As soon as the cop was out of sight, Eisenhower, who had been waiting behind the door, stepped outside and trotted to the limousine parked down the street. The car's headlights had been killed. The little bulbs inside the car that light up when a door is opened had been unscrewed, so no mortal eye could recognize the figure who stepped into the shrouded car and was swiftly driven away. For days thereafter, John Foster Dulles, Secretary of State-designate, appeared at the mansion with an impressively stuffed briefcase and, upon leaving hours later, calmly told reporters he had had another stimulating meeting with the President-elect. The getaway of the press pool was equally clandestine. The Secret Service would not let us alert our offices as to takeoff time.

But nobody was pulling the wool over the eyes of Bob Rodenberg. Trust an old OSS man to find a weak link in what appeared to be the strongest security chain since the gestation of the A-bomb. By accident, Bob called our apartment at some unconscionable hour the morning of the takeoff. Deborah, then three, was the only one awake. She had only recently discovered the telephone.

"Hello, baby," Rodenberg said patiently. "Let me speak to your daddy."

"He's not here," the cunning little spy lisped. "He's flying to Korea with General Eisenhower."

There was an odd little scene at Iwo Jima, where we took a two-day breather after pausing only long enough at Hawaii, Midway, and Wake to refuel. The commanding officer of Iwo's air base laid on a string of jeeps to carry Ike and his party to the Marine memorial atop Mt. Suribachi. It was a hot day filled with the island's stench of sulfur and swarming with tiny, indigenous black bugs that hit like pebbles. Ike, in fresh khaki, collar spread open, strolled from his Nissen-hut quarters toward his jeep. Gen. Jerry Persons stepped up close to him and whispered something that caused Ike's face to become a sternly upset mask. He turned on his heel, reentered the hut without a word, and reappeared minutes later wearing a necktie —and a sorely put-upon look.

"Dammit," he muttered as he climbed aboard his jeep, "one of these times I'm going to do something the way *I* want to do it."

If I had gone with Lynn Mahan, as I had wanted to, I would never have seen the gloriously girlish smile of Elizabeth II at the end of her incredibly taxing coronation in '53. Or Khrushchev's childish pushing and shoving of Bulganin, in order to enter the Soviet limousine ahead of the premier at the Geneva Summit Conference of '55. And I would have missed the vintage year of '56.

In the spring of that year the Defense Department let the world in on the test of an H-bomb, for the first and presumably the last time. Repeated delays kept us in the Bikini-Eniwetok area for most of the month of May. This time, the entrepreneurs wanted to be sure. Two years earlier an unexpected shift in the wind carrying a giant radioactive mushroom across the Pacific from its point of birth at Bikini had changed the hot cloud's course and its fallout pattern. It seriously contaminated a stretch 240 miles long and 40 miles wide, struck and sickened 236 Marshall Islanders and 31 U.S. test personnel on Rongelap and Utirik islands, and dripped its "ghastly dew" on the 23-man crew of the *Fukuryu Maru* ("Fortunate Dragon") which was tuna-fishing 85 miles from Bikini. The Japanese were hospitalized for a year, and when one died the relations between the two countries reached their lowest ebb since the War. The miscalculation cost the United States millions in reparations and incalculable face.

Now in May of '56 a bigger and hotter bomb was to be tried, the first hydrogen bomb to be dropped from a bomber. One of the postponements, made necessary by a last-minute weather reading, occurred while the B-52 bearing the H-bomb was airborne and all hands on the observation ships had been told to prepare to put on their protective glasses. The bomber returned its megaton monster safely to Eniwetok, but from somewhere out of the night a two-man B-60, one of the jets scheduled to flirt around the edges of the radioactive cloud and scoop in samples of its poison, plunged into that forlorn area of the Pacific. Our press ship, the *Mt. McKinley,* joined in the fruitless twenty-four-hour search that followed. On what amounted to the second night of the hopeless hunt our restless searchlight spotted something glowing in the water. The bullhorns gave a breathtaking command for a boat to be lowered. I strained my eyes against the night, praying that the tantalizing glow would become a flashlight held by a man, two men, on a raft. Nightmarishly, throughout this throatcatching scene, a claptrap movie blared on deck and commanded the absolute attention of perhaps a hundred officers and seamen.

The glow in the water was a reflection from a tin can.

The test was a deeply moving experience. Just to sense that the ship's loudspeaker system said, "Bomb away," not "Bombs away," was to dwell moodily on how science had miniaturized and neatly packaged the art of overkill. Each with his own thoughts, we sweated out the long seconds of the bomb's fall. We were forty miles from the islet intended for extinction, but one could toy with the possibility that the bombardier had lost his bearings. . . .

And then our whole world became a hell that erupted on the predawn horizon and engulfed us in its fiery spell. Instinctively, our heads dropped and our shoulders hunched, as if bracing against and warding off a blow we could not comprehend. Instant and alarming heat swept over us. But the light, the indescribable light, was worse. It was a scalding thing, condition, presence. It permeated, pierced, and nothing could stop it. It plunged through welders' glasses, through our clothing, our skulls, our marrow.

I raised my head and beheld through the black glasses a conflagration I knew I could never reduce to words, a huge and tormented and boiling and seething and flaming Thing that now was reshaping itself as it rose against its gray-black backdrop. For a moment it became a flaming red arm bloodily holding aloft a white-hot sword, the bottom of the arm encased in a huge lace cuff tailored of the boiling and steaming sea. And then the thing was a huge brazen ball ascending and sucking behind it that part of creation where it had been born. It seemed safe enough by now to look upon it without protective lenses. Something warned me as I raised the left side of my black glasses to direct my gaze downward at my typewriter rather than at the Thing. It was just as well. The light from the bomb was still blinding to the naked eye.

There was still no sound. It was still en route. And in that eerie silence, like a film that has lost its soundtrack, a seaman said in a voice that went boyishly off key, "Christ. Suppose that had been my home town. . . ."

In time the white mushroom cloud grew and spread until it measured one hundred miles across its crown. Jets flying so high that only their vapor trails were visible, slender as slim white woolen threads, stitched at the edges of the great cloud as if trying to sew it to the blueing sky.

"I'd say it was two or three megatons," remarked a scientist at the ship's rail.

Bill Laurence, our doughty dean, held up a separated thumb and forefinger, peered at the departing cloud through the aperture, and ruled, "I make it at least five megatons."

This learned dialogue was too much for Ed Lahey of the Knight papers.

"Megatons schmegatons, it was one hell of a bomb!" he snorted.

It would have been hard to find a greater change of pace than the following month's assignment to cover the wedding of Grace Kelly to

Prince Rainier. It was the difference between malevolent muscle and merry meringue, the difference between the scalding light of the H-bomb and the cool chic of having tea with Dorothy Kilgallen at a table off the bar at Hotel de Paris. Dorothy and the Kelly clan were not on speaking terms for the nonce because of a misunderstanding over something Dorothy had written in her column. Coupled with the fact that Rainier was not speaking to anybody, including his own family, this made news scarce.

"I've never known such a dearth of news," Dorothy said, staring moodily into my teacup, which had been drained down to its tea leaves. I put my hand over the cup.

"Stop reading my notes," I said.

It was an antic time, hardly likely to happen again. The original cast could never be reassembled: eccentric Lady Docker, playing Ping Pong on her yacht and denouncing both the Kellys and the Grimaldis for slighting her . . . the hefty Matt McCloskeys of Philadelphia being robbed of their jewels . . . French cops beating photographers with their fungo-sized billies . . . Irwin Tress, our International News Photos photographer, who ran his car over a French cop's toe for revenge, and was promptly jailed . . . Conrad Hilton, representing President Eisenhower . . . the breezy conjecture around the town's bars over whether Rainier could forget Gisèle Pascal . . . the story mischievous George Schlee spread at the Hotel de Paris bar that it would be a double wedding with Rainier's estranged father, Count Pierre de Polignac, marrying Gloria Swanson . . . Art Buchwald's pieces about the ancient feud between the Grimaldis and the Buchwalds, culminating in his not being invited to the wedding and their not being invited to one Becky Buchwald's wedding in Brooklyn . . . Rainier, handsome as John Gilbert in an old Garbo movie, chain-smoking as he swept out of the picture postcard harbor of Monte Carlo to fetch his bride-to-be from the S.S. *Constitution,* and his return with her at his side on the white honeymoon yacht, while church bells rang, ships' horns sounded, and Aristotle Onassis' yellow seaplane from his huge *Christina* bombed the Rainier yacht with pink carnations.

"I think I'm going to cry," announced a stout lady from New Jersey I happened to be standing near. And she did. On me.

Only five of us were permitted to cover the civil wedding performed at the palace by Chief Justice Marcel Portanier. It was limited to INS, UP, AP, Reuter's, and Agence France Presse. It was a most uncivil

civil wedding. Rainier was angry, for reasons unknown. He stared straight ahead at the judge throughout the barren ceremony, ignoring an occasional and ever-so-entreating look from the beautiful Philadelphia girl who sat at his side in an identical ceremonial chair-throne. The ceremony finished, Rainier marched his bride out of the room, gave Conrad Hilton and other dignitaries in an anteroom a curt brusque-off, and started down a long second-story gallery toward his apartment. Grace walked shyly at his side, chastened by his moody silence. There was nothing in my invitation that urged me to join the newlyweds after the ceremony. But the father of the bride, Jack Kelly, was a good friend. I found myself walking with him and chatting as he and all the Kellys and a sprinkling of Grimaldis strolled along twenty paces behind the forbiddingly silent couple whose great romance was being heralded around the world. AP and UP eyed me warily, torn between the clear call to duty—writing the story of the wedding—and the nagging fear that I, or INS, was moving toward some bigger story under the protection of Jack Kelly. After a bit of agonizing soul-searching, they decided to tag along, too.

Just short of the entrance to his lost-bachelorhood lair, Rainier stopped and shook off whatever it was that was bugging him. He turned to Grace, gave her his most dashing smile, and they embraced happily. An audible wheeze of relief was exhaled by the Kellys. Jack lost the somewhat preoccupied look in his eyes, stopped rambling about sports, as he had been, and said something direct, hearty, and nice about his new son-in-law. The Dom Perignon soon popped like vintage corn.

The religious ceremony in the nineteenth century cathedral the following day was part God, part Schubert. Rainier was in full military dress, down to an ancestor's sword; Grace was a vision. Every available crowned head was on hand, and at least one uncrowned one. Farouk filled part of a front pew like a sad, beached whale. Halfway back in the cathedral, some guest, if that he was, read a newspaper through the early part of the wedding Mass, turning its pages from time to time with a loud rustle. At one point Rainier appeared on the verge of going back into his saturnine slump, but snapped out of it. On the whole, it came off much better than the civil wedding. It, too, had its interesting aftermath: the unforgettable sight of Dorothy Kilgallen, bless her, busily beating out her story in the strange headquarters INS had established near the cathedral. She was surrounded, in all her bouffant glory and magnificent raiment, by the regular product of the place: sample water closets and bidets.

Later that same entrancing year I saw peace break out. That had happened seldom before in my life as a reporter, and never since. Peace broke out on the final day of the Olympics in Melbourne. The Games had opened in the traditional manner: the parade of the chauvinistically segregated teams, each behind its flag and banner, each aloof of the others. Much the same ceremony was planned for the final day, but sheer inspiration intervened. On signal, at the parade-assembly area beneath the crowded reaches of Olympic stadium, the teams happily scrambled. Flags and banners and identification cards were put aside, and when the athletes of most of the nations of the world marched on to the stadium's running track they marched arm in arm, short, tall, fat, lean, white, black, brown, yellow, Communist, Socialist, Democrat, Republican, Jew, Christian, Moslem, Buddhist, agnostic, atheist—all their competitive fires doused, furies spent; no cares, no Big Brother watching. The crowd of 100,000 began singing the bitter-sweet "Waltzing Matilda," which can be as enspiriting as "Dixie" and as hauntingly sad as "Greensleeves." The athletes picked up the chant and sang, or hummed, or whistled it. And the whole place was one.

Peace lasted a good ten minutes. It was glorious.

I was covering the 1958 World Series between the Yankees and the Milwaukee Braves when Frank Conniff sent me winging on a more somber mission. Pope Pius XII, eighty-two years old, lay dying at Castel Gandolfo. Several years before that, he had survived another serious claim on his life, a prolonged and nearly fatal siege of hiccups. Upon recovery he informed members of his hierarchy that during his periods of unconsciousness he had been visited by and had been spoken to by Jesus. Now, once more unconscious, there was no thought of divine intercession. The time had come for aristocratic Eugenio Maria Giuseppe Giovanni Pacelli.

His mission had ended. He had lived through one of the most trying reigns since Peter's.

If the Roman Catholic Church maintained a Central Casting Office, it would have selected Pacelli as its future Pope from the time he began his studies for the priesthood at age fourteen. He was born of a mother who was a marchioness and a father who was a prominent Vatican attorney. He was the favorite grandchild of Marcantonio Pacelli, founder of *L'Osservatore Romano.* He was top man in his class at Gregorian University, the State University of Rome, and the Papal Atheneum of the Apollinare. With his doctorates showing, he brought his priestly scholarship and zeal into the Vatican's Secretariat of State, which soon expanded his horizons by sending him to London to present to Edward VII the sympathy of Pope XIII upon the death of Queen Victoria. In time Pacelli was being depended upon as the Church's chief pact-maker, but it was a time when pacts were not easily arranged. He failed badly when he tried to convince Kaiser Wilhelm to end World War I in 1917 before America's entrance—a failure which cost the United States 126,000 dead, 250,000 wounded, and direct and boldly indirect veterans' benefits which have amounted to billions of dollars. A comparatively young man of fifty-three, Pacelli, as papal nuncio, was dean of the diplomatic corps in Berlin in 1929, when he was called back to the Vatican to be consecrated a cardinal by tough-minded Pius XI. In February, 1930, three months after being given his red hat, Pacelli was named papal secretary of state, then archpriest of St. Peter's Basilica. He was author/architect of the daring ploy which saw Monsignor Francis J. Spellman spirit out of Vatican City Pius XI's statement accusing Mussolini of violating the Lateran Treaty. The future cardinal archbishop of New York called in key correspondents, once he reached Paris, and distributed the bombshell.

Pacelli was voted Pope by the sixty-two cardinals of the conclave that followed the death of Pius XI. The election came on March 2, 1939, his sixty-third birthday. It was reached on the third ballot, and the legend firmed up that the margin of victory was 61 to 1; he voted against himself. Nevertheless, he was the first cardinal secretary of state elected to the papacy since 1667, and he had taken over an awesome job at the brink of the biggest war in history. His conduct during that war was accepted by the antagonists as that of a humane neutral. But after his death he was the target of a play, *The Deputy,* and a book, both of which condemned his silence in the face of Germany's treatment of Jews. Vatican denials were timid and tentative.

Actually, Pius XII was a good friend of oppressed Jews. When the Nazis took over Rome from their halfhearted Italian allies in 1943, Pius opened Castel Gandolfo to fifteen thousand Jews living in Italy and gave shelter, food, and clothing to thousands more inside the Vatican walls. In September, 1943, the German commandant of Rome demanded a million lire from Dr. Israel Zolli, chief rabbi of Rome. If it were not paid by noon of the following day, along with one hundred pounds of gold, the Jews who had not put themselves under the Church's wing would be "dispersed." Dr. Zolli, unable to raise but a fraction of the money and gold, appealed to Pius. The ransom was paid on time. Melted sacred vessels helped provide the demanded gold. A month later the Nazis broke the pact, smashed and looted Jewish homes and shops, broke up families, and dispatched hundreds to concentration camps. Pius protested and, astonishingly, many Jews were returned to Rome. A month after the Allied liberation of Rome, Dr. Zolli praised Pius' good works and not long after that was received into the Catholic Church.

I ended Pius' noble life forty-eight hours earlier than God chose, which may have seemed presumptuous to both. My scoop will not be remembered with Roy Howard's unilateral shutdown of World War I some days before the November 11, 1918, Armistice. But I'd wager I suffered greater pangs of remorse because of my false report, which was never printed, than Howard suffered during the chaotic week that followed his great gaffe, for Roy had a tremendous amount of "Aw, to hell with it!" compressed in his hide.

What happened in my case was a combination of unpardonable gullibility and bad reporting. I was working on a piece at the Hearst service's office in downtown Rome after being assured at Castel Gandolfo that the Pope was still battling, when John Casserly came in to report that the Pope was dead. Jack, head of our diminished operation in Rome, now that INS had folded, still retained an Italian wire service. It was the Italian wire which flashed the Pope was dead. With Jack translating, I wrote a long piece about Pius' death and not a little about his life, and we sent it off to New York, via Radio Stampa, at urgent rates. Then I suggested that we go to Stampa Estera, probably the worst press club in Christendom, to salute the late-lamented pontiff with a drink.

There was nobody at the bar and very few correspondents in the workroom upstairs. Moreover, there was a stunning reason for this: The Pope was still alive. I rushed back to Radio Stampa and sent through a kill on my story, despairing of its ever getting to New York in time to repair the damage, then back to Stampa Estera, which has a phone service, and put through a call to New York.

The circuits were busy.

"Three . . . four hours," the lady who booked calls at the club said. She couldn't have cared less. Romans, most of them professedly Catholic, have about as much interest in Popes as do delegates to a Baptist convention in Philadelphia, Mississippi.

It was one of the worst sweats of my life as a reporter. I could see the presses at the *Journal American* crunching out hundreds of thousands of copies with my florid blunder spread across the front page. But with the phones clogged, and the wireless completely irresponsible, so far as back-and-forth communication was concerned, there was no way to stop this nightmare, this Niagara of wrongness emblazoned with my by-line.

At long, long, long last my call to New York came through. It was late enough in New York by that time for the *Journal American* to have completed most of its run. But I felt I could salvage some of the final thousands of papers with a correction. I had it, all of it, on the tip of my tongue, ready to dictate.

"Kill the story I filed hours ago," I shouted into the phone, one of Marconi's first. "I have a new lead . . . the Pope's still alive. Ready?"

"Relax," a voice from the *Journal American* said, across the ocean. "When AP and UPI didn't confirm, we decided not to use your death story." It was the only insult I ever welcomed.

I did not go directly to the bar on the floor below. I paused on a marble step at the head of the staircase, knelt down, and breathed a "Hail Mary." *Then* I went to the bar.

First things first.

As soon as the word came officially that the Pope had died, Casserly and I drove to Castel Gandolfo. The pleasant little square in front of the papal summer place was filled with newsmen. The limousines of cardinals and other dignitaries were drawing up solemnly, disgorging distinguished mourners. I settled down with the others for the long wait, until that distant hour when the Church's public relations division, which has not been noticeably altered since the Inquisition, awakened to the fact that perhaps the entire world might be interested in Pius' postmortems.

Then, a chance in a million. A bustling, black-haired monsignor emerged from the main gate of Castel Gandolfo, which faces the square. He seemed bent on facilitating the entrance of some distinguished mourner.

"That's your friend Paganuzzi," Casserly said. "He celebrated that Mass for the Hearsts and you when you came through Rome last year on the way to. . . ."

We were at his side in a moment. To our complete consternation and troubled delight, he led us past the guards and through the great gates. I could feel the glares of dozens, hundreds, of restrained colleagues on the back of my neck. I also became acutely aware that I was wearing a light, excessively noisy blue-checked sports jacket—donned earlier with little thought of attending a Pope's wake.

All that remained of Pope Pius XII, the most graceful world figure I ever met, lay on the simple brass-barred bed in which he had died. The ghastly black tubes which his reprehensible doctor, Galleazzi-Lisi, had inserted in his nose and mouth before death, and then photographed for profit, had been removed. The dead Pope looked as sparse as a sparrow in robes that seemed to have been summoned by the papal household as an afterthought. His head was covered by the kind of tam o'shanter in which pontiffs of the Middle Ages posed for papal court artists. His hands, which *Time* likened in life to two fluttering white doves, had become the alabaster holders of Crucifix and Rosary. At each corner of his bed stood a young priest. Several grief-stricken nuns knelt on the sparse-rugged floor of the bedroom, hammering their beads. A beautiful Italian woman in her sixties, swathed in black, knelt on a prie-dieu in the center of the room and did not take her great, sad eyes from him while we were there. The room was heavy with candle fumes. I felt like an outrageous intruder, in my obscene sports jacket.

"Kiss his hands," a voice whispered, interrupting my silent recitation of my Rosary. It was Paganuzzi. He was looking at Casserly and at me. We hesitated.

"Kiss his hands!" he repeated in a louder tone.

I got up from my knees, went to the bed, and bent over it. It was a three-quarter bed. The body of the Pope was directly in the middle of it, necessitating something of a stretch or reach. One couldn't very well cock a leg up on the mattress, for balance. To compensate, I leaned on the side of the bed with my hands, momentarily expecting to tip it and wind up on the floor with the late Vicar of Christ on Earth on my lap.

His hands were as cool and white and graceful and sad as the hands in Michelangelo's Pietà. I can never forget what they felt like on my lips.

On the way out, Paganuzzi told us touching stories about the Pope's final hours. We took the Great Circle route around the waiting correspondents in the square, slipped into a Radio Stampa mobile transmitter, and I riffled the keys of the van's typewriter. Alas! It had the European keyboard, not a suitable arrangement for any typist ever turned out of Business High School Night School, Washington, D.C. So in quiet desperation I fell back on the hunt and peck system, which to a touch typist is as tedious as pushing a peanut up Pike's Peak with one's nose. I tapped out: "Castel Gandolfo, Oct. 9."

Jack was watching over my shoulder. He had not served INS in vain. Or vice versa.

"Don't you think the dateline should be 'At the Pope's Bedside'?" he asked in a way that would reach any INS man. And so that was the way it went out. It won the Overseas Press Club of America's award that year for the Best Foreign Correspondence from Abroad. It also won a sobering comment from Red Smith, the thinking man's sports columnist.

"It was a pretty good story but I kept worrying as I read it," Red said at Shor's one night not long after.

"Why?"

"Well," Red said, "I had a vision of you typing away on a typewriter you had put on the side of his bed."

I promised him it would never happen again.

Pius XII's successor, John XXIII, came as a big surprise to about 300,000 gathered in St. Peter's Square—300,001, actually. I had kept a vigil atop the roofing of the Bernini Colonnade for hours during the third day of the balloting, watching more black smoke emerging from the Sistine Chapel's chimney than the old engine that took me to Chesapeake Beach. So as the dusk of another day gathered over Rome, I sought the counsel of an adjacent bishop who assured me that nothing more could happen that day; the old cardinals were probably hungry, crotchety, obviously divided, and feeling for their pasta and bed. That was enough of a horse's mouth for me, so I started down the endless flights of steps toward the square, cunningly bent on getting a taxi before the exodus started. Surprisingly, I saw Bill Hearst and Frank Conniff coming up the same staircase I was descending. They

had heard that the election was imminent. Patiently, I told them what
I had heard from a bishop, no less, and went my way, feeling a little
let down by their stupidity.

I threaded through the dense crowds in the square to the head of
Via Conciliazione, where sat a Radio Stampa trailer, fully staffed with
technicians but empty of correspondents save for an American priest
who said he hoped to write an article, eventually, for his diocesan
newspaper. He could speak Italian.

"Why do you suppose the crowd is still sticking around?" I asked
him.

"They must know something," he said. "Vatican Radio just broadcast that there won't be anything more tonight. But they stay."

I was about to go on in search of a cab when an enormous shout
went up from the crowded square. A light had appeared in the vast
ceremonial salon that stretches the width of incredible St. Peter's
and opens on to the familiar loggia that soars over the main entrance
to the basilica. Now more lights shone and the roar swelled.

"They've got a Pope," the American priest said.

"But the smoke has been black. . . ."

"They've got a Pope."

I asked him to ask the Radio Stampa man to get me a circuit to
New York.

It came through like magic. I requisitioned the only typewriter in
the trailer. Incredibly, it had the style of keyboard that fitted my
touch-typing. Now the great doors leading to the loggia were lighted
and opened. Members of the household appeared and draped a huge
papal banner over the stone railing of the loggia. Immediately, the
balcony was filled with what appeared to be doddering old men groan-
ing under the weight of their vestments. They had a Pope all right,
and said so.

"What's his name?" I asked the American priest.

"Roncalli. Angelo Giuseppe Roncalli," he said, then held up a
hand for silence, when the papal chamberlain droned on toward the
name the strange new occupant of the Throne of Peter had chosen.

"He'll be John XXIII," the priest said. "I have some dope on
him. . . ."

I beat out the story as fast as my fingers could fly over the keys,
but there was time to wonder, too. Why did they select an old fellow
like that—seventy-seven!—so different in size and shape and looks

from the image—Pius XII's image? He couldn't speak English and had spent much of his career in places like Turkey and Bulgaria. And why did he choose the same name as one of the worst scoundrels who ever laid claim to the papacy?

(Baldassare Cossa, the original John XXIII, was an on-again off-again pope from 1410 to 1415. He apparently had done well as a pirate, though he came from a good Neapolitan family. He led a dissident group of Romans in and out of the Church who withdrew their support of Pope Gregory XII *and* the current anti-Pope Benedict XIII. He was largely instrumental in convening the Council of Pisa which elected a third reigning pope, Alexander V. But Alexander died in 1410 and his followers elected Cossa pope. Thereafter, he was largely in flight, protected first by one king and then another. He was incapable of inspiring confidence or obtaining succor for any great length of consecutive months. The Council of Constance, which he called in 1414, excommunicated him as one who was *scandalizator ecclesiae.* He was jailed in Germany for three years, came back to Rome as a layman, threw himself at the feet of the now legitimate and uncontested Pope Martin V, and asked for mercy. In 1419, Martin V made him cardinal bishop of Tusculum, just southeast of Rome where the rich had had their summer places since Nero's time. Cossa lived only a few months thereafter. He is remembered chiefly today for the magnificent tomb in Florence which Cosimo de' Medici ordered to cloak his last remains.)

The new John XXIII answered the question of his choice of papal designations and many other questions in the swift four and a half years of his astonishing reign. He took the name John XXIII, he said in effect, to cleanse the numerical succession and perhaps inspire some pope of the future to carry it onward without misgivings. He set out on the first Sunday of his stewardship to visit the least of his flock in his secondary role of Bishop of Rome: the raucously pious jailbirds in Rome's main jail. "I, too, am a prisoner now," he told them. For all his age and avoirdupois he proved himself an industrious pedestrian, and, having been something of a fancier of wines at an earlier age, was said to be delighted when he learned that Romans—who usually don't like popes too much—were beginning to refer to him as "Johnnie Walker." Unlike his predecessor, a man of infinite dignity and sceptered mien, he liked to laugh, joked about his homeliness, occasionally would look about—as if searching for someone else—when he was addressed as "Your Holiness." Pius XII was by El Greco; John XXIII by Rubens.

In 1901, when Roncalli was a country boy from Bergamo studying in a Roman seminary and faceless as any other seminarian, Pacelli was a patrician young priest with the Congregation of Extraordinary Ecclesiastical Affairs, an important division of the Papal Secretariat of State. Pacelli went up; Roncalli went into the Italian army for three years, emerged as a sergeant, returned to the seminary, and was ordained a priest in 1904. Almost simultaneously, Pacelli was becoming a monsignor, a leading authority on canon law and a professor of law at the Academy of Ecclesiastical Nobles. He was the regal papal ambassador to Germany in World War I while Fr. Roncalli, once more in uniform, was medico-chaplain in trench warfare.

In short, John XXIII came to the Throne of Peter as much more a man of the people than was his predecessor, and people in general were quick to recognize that this man was no mere seat-warmer until a true successor of Pius XII could be found. On January 25, 1959, he removed all remaining doubt. He announced that he would convoke an ecumenical council to "open the windows of the Church to fresh air." It was to draw to Rome the Fathers of the Church and observers from most other religions, and to promulgate changes, reforms, concessions, and guidelines without precedent in the centuries-old Church. The last of John XXIII's encyclicals, *Pacem in Terris,* issued two months before his death on June 3, 1963, was the first papal social document addressed to the world in general. It was much more encompassing than his surprising first encyclical, *Ad Petri Cathedram* ("Unto the See of Peter") which invited the "separated brethren" to return to the Church of Rome. "Peace on Earth" rang bells not only in the capitals of Christendom but in Moscow, Peking, Mecca, and Jerusalem. The encyclical called for a nuclear-test ban, disarmament, rights of minorities, support of the UN, freedom of conscience, and cooperation between the Communist and free countries to alleviate poverty, disease, and ignorance; and it preached the brotherhood of man more ardently than any previous pronouncement from the Vatican. As it was being prepared for release, "Good Pope John," as he had come to be known, received in audience Aleksei Adzhubei, Khrushchev's son-in-law who edited *Izvestia,* a journal not known for its deference to popes. Roman conservatives complained bitterly that this single act of brotherhood resulted in a million in-

crease in the Italian Communist Party's vote in the next election. But
the effect it had on lessening world tensions and its appeal to basic
reason far outweighed parochial setbacks.

John's agonizingly prolonged death touched hearts and minds never
before moved by any event of the papacy. When at last it was official,
there was relief as well as fond sadness. He had suffered enough. His
last prayer, "May they be one," has not been answered. But they are
more "one" than they were when he came out of nowhere, so far as
the world knew, and pried open stained-glass windows that had been
locked for centuries.

Count Enrico Galeazzi, the elegant "Mayor" of Vatican City, provided me with a credential that permitted me to view the body of
John along with the diplomatic corps attached to the Vatican. Em-
balmment, Italian style, had rendered the jolly red-faced man a dismal
green. The flat catafalque was tipped to a daring 10 or 20 percent
grade, suggesting that strong ropes attached to it beneath his excessive layers of unduly (for him) crusted sacerdotal robes prevented a
downhill slide. It was an unreal scene, until a woman in deep mourning a few people ahead of me in line genuflected and kissed the sandal
of the good man that death had turned into an effigy. All who followed her did the same, and for the first time there was meaning to
this ritual.

The chief surprise about the election of Giovanni Battista Cardinal
Montini was that it took all of three ballots. The irreverent betting
around the pizzerias had made him an overwhelming favorite. This
was made painfully apparent to him at the solemn Mass of the Holy
Ghost, always celebrated in St. Peter's just before the cardinals retired
into the purdah of the conclave. The number of pictures taken of him
by photographers of the world press approximated the margin of the
edge he held over the others. He was visibly perturbed by the attention.

My own luck held. With INS gone, there was no longer any way
for me to get through to New York in a hurry. Radio Stampa was
perpetually swamped with the endless words of hundreds of newsmen
on hand. There were hours-long delays on trans-Atlantic phone calls.
Just for the Heaven of it, so to speak, I booked a call to the *Journal
American* early on the morning of June 20. The operator at the
Cavalieri Hilton said she could not even guess as to when there would
be a circuit available. I went back to bed. At 11 A.M. an old St.

Peter's bell sounded quietly. Just once, it seemed, but I jumped up and switched on the television. White smoke was coming from the Sistine Chapel's skinny chimney.

I was trapped. If I went to St. Peter's square and the Radio Stampa van was engaged, as it would most certainly be, there would be no way to get my story in. If I found a cab and we were lucky with the impossible Roman traffic, I might be able to get from the hotel to downtown Radio Stampa in forty-five minutes or an hour, during which time I'd be out of contact with what was happening at the Vatican. I picked up the phone and inquired about the status of my earlier call to New York. Sorry . . . it might be several more hours. I felt as frustrated as an old firehorse tethered in a firehouse while a four-alarm blaze roared on the other side of town. The smoke from that blaze continued white.

I called my friend Luca Salvatore, public relations director of the Cavalieri, and asked him if he would come up to the room and act as my interpreter of the event that would soon be taking place on the loggia. There wasn't much I could do about sending a story, but at least I wanted to *know*.

Three things happened simultaneously. Just as Luca walked in the TV camera switched to the loggia and its great doors began to open. And my telephone rang! The *Journal American* was on the line, clear as crystal. Al Robbins, the fastest and best man we had, was ready. I spread my reference books on a bed, pulled up a chair facing the TV set, and said, "Let's go, Al. It's coming now. . . ."

I dictated for an hour and a half, the news, the background, the significance. Everything fell into its exact place. Every fact, date, reference I needed literally sprang from the books spread on the bed. It was just one of those times, one of those impossible successions of breaks, that warm a reporter's memory the rest of his days.

"How did you do it? You were from five to eight minutes ahead of the wire services," *Journal* Editor Paul Schoenstein asked me later, plainly expecting some whispered admission of a popish plot.

"The phone happened to ring," I said. It didn't sound very heroic. Richard Harding Davis would have been made uncomfortable.

Paul VI turned out to be a remarkable combination of the two opposites who immediately preceded him. He looked like and spoke like his mentor, Pius XII, but his words and viewpoint were those of

John XXIII. Vatican II would continue. The fresh winds would continue to air out the Church.

He was to make his revered mentor and predecessor appear sedentary and timidly sequestered by comparison. He flew to the Holy Land, India, and New York. On the Mount of Olives he embraced the towering and holy Patriarch Athenagoras I, and, as the Patriarch told me with simple eloquence the next day at a meeting arranged, extraordinarily enough, by Spyros Skouras of Twentieth Century-Fox, "We wept over divided Jerusalem." It was the first such meeting between a pope and a patriarch of the Orthodox Eastern Church in eight hundred years. In Bombay Paul was mobbed by countless poor peoples of other faiths among whom the word had spread that he was a saint of sorts from a remote part of the world, come to Bombay to distribute food and favors. In New York, he drew several millions to the sidewalks, spoke before the UN, had warm exchanges with celebrities as varied as Jacqueline Kennedy, Soviet Foreign Minister Andrei Gromyko (who later called on him at the Vatican), and President Johnson, celebrated a Mass for eighty thousand at Yankee Stadium, took in a portion of the World's Fair, and flew back to Rome the same day he had left it.

I carried a spear in the small armies of reporters who followed him to Jordan and Israel early in 1964 and to New York in the fall of 1965.

As mad an hour as I ever expect to experience was that at Damascus Gate the evening of the Pope's arrival. Perhaps a montage approach would best describe what it was like:

Dusk, and a chill the TV and newsreel kliegs could not diminish. . . . A torrent of unruly Jordanians surging through police and military barriers, screaming like dervishes. . . . Land Rovers and troop carriers prodding into the packed and shoving thousands in front of the gate, with troops beating the people with canes and sticks. The helpless inability to breast the human tide, the fight to keep from being knocked underfoot. . . . The holy men of several faiths, so bearded and serene only ten minutes before, being tossed around in the chaos like everyone else. . . . A nun no bigger than your arm being crushed against a wall as old as time (I muscled my way to her, braced my hands against the wall over her head, and pushed back as hard as I could against the insensate mob. It was like trying to hold back a ten-ton truck in low gear). . . . Then, more sensed than seen, Paul VI was convoyed through the center of the jam, a frail white bark led and flanked and followed by burly black-suited ice-breakers in the form of his Italian security guard and a few Jordanian officers and police who had kept their heads . . . and all the while, overhead, the deep-voiced young ruler of the Hashimite Kingdom of Jordan, Hussein, swept back and forth in his chattering helicopter.

Inside the Old City, just as one enters or is propelled through the Damascus Gate, it is necessary to take a sharp left to the street that leads to the Via Doloroso—along which the Pope proposed to retrace the steps of Jesus carrying His cross to Calvary. The human avalanche that burst in through the closing gates just behind the Pope managed to make the left turn, but could not then make the right turn into the narrow street that winds into the center of the city. Tons of flesh and bone spilled through the primitive windows of a fruit store, disentangled itself somehow, picked the glass splinters out of its composite hide, and plunged on. Oranges spilled from the showcases and were trampled and squeezed under successive feet. In the crush, as I was pressed along like a log in a millrace, I felt an empty shoe beneath my foot and momentarily expected to find myself involuntarily walking over the ankle, shin, thigh, torso, and head of some poor soul invisible underfoot. But it was just a shoe. Somewhere up ahead of me its owner was hobbling along the cold cobbled street with no chance of reversing his course. The shoe owner, like me, was going where the crowd took him.

Paul VI strove like a saint to meditate and pray at the Stations of the Cross. But it was not feasible by any stretch of piety. At one point a photographer's flashbulb exploded near his face and peppered him with glass needles. At another he had to seek the shelter of a doorway to avoid going down under a new tidal wave of humanity that swept the mob in his wake. And in the midst of the solemn ceremony that followed at the Church of the Holy Sepulchre, a badly wired TV light short-circuited and threatened to set fire to the holiest place in Christendom, as if it did not already have its share of troubles, having been quarreled over for centuries by Franciscans, Copts, Syrian Jacobites, and Gregorian Armenians.

Paul's trip to India later that year for the Eucharistic Congress saw his life endangered by Turkish air-force fighter pilots who playfully buzzed the Alitalia DC-8 bearing the Pope and his suite as it flew over

Turkey en route back to Rome. By comparison, his flight from Rome to New York was as uneventful as it was historic. The fifty-five of us who were aboard to report it were snugged into the tourist section of the Alitalia charter. The Pope's party, cardinals, aids, and Alitalia officials, occupied the center section of the plane, as aloof from us as the Pope was from them. Paul VI had a compartment to himself in the forward area behind the flight deck. In tourist, through the night and into the dawn of the New World, we saw quite a bit of the flying Princes of the Church in a new and highly informal light. The only gentlemen's room they could attend was at the rear of our ghetto. It was interesting to see them thread their way down the narrow aisle in their rustling silk, bent on the commonest of man's poor but rewarding endeavors.

We had no hopes that Paul VI would come our way. But as the jet swung near Newfoundland on its long parabola reaching for New York, the plastic gate that segregated us from the rest of the passengers was pulled back a foot or two and an Italian head poked itself through the opening. It was one of the Alitalia types.

"Il Papa!" the head said. The eyes of the head seemed to be saying, "What the hell does he want to see *you* people for?"

The accordion barrier was retracted, and there stood the Pope looking quite relaxed about the ordeal of invading our lair, a lair cluttered with typewriters, cameras, clusters of lights, tripods, half-eaten meals, and half-finished drinks. Lights blazed, microphones were extended toward him, and cameras whirred as he moved down the aisle. He added a few words in English to a tape Walter Cronkite, Irving R. Levine, Serge Fliegers, and I had made for CBS, NBC, Mutual, and ABC, respectively. Then he was gone as suddenly as he appeared, only to return to us about an hour later to give each of us a silver medallion commemorating the flight.

I thought once more of Harry Grayson's ultimate accolade to another pope: "That guy's okay."

President Eisenhower's trips at the end of his White House stay probably were the costliest goodwill voyages ever undertaken. But anyone who was lucky enough to go along would have been a fool to complain. What man, what economist, what computer can put a price on goodwill . . . or would be daft enough to try?

The first trip, December 3 to December 22, 1959, covered 18,520 miles. It remains a magnificent blur, in Technicolor.

Rome: Rain. Scrawled insults on wet walls suggesting that our leader go home. The colors of welcome banners, running. The meaningless communiqué after the meeting with John XXIII. Seems they discussed peace, and both were believed to be in favor of it.

Ankara: Ataturk's stark mausoleum, and a swarthy trumpeter's single, piercing, frightening note as Ike laid a wreath on the grave. Ike (reading): "If I couldn't be an American, I'd be proud to be Turkish. . . ." The Turkish official beamed. He was executed in 1965.

Karachi: Gorgeous, maybe a million in the streets, brassy cymbaled bands, splendid Sikhs in superb turbans, red-coated horsemen right out of Kipling roaring through the superb exercise of "tent-pegging," and, always at Ike's shoulder, President Ayub Khan, impeccably Sandhurst—and slightly annoyed when Ike looked at his watch and said he guessed he'd have to leave the bloody boring cricket game before the tea break.

Khyber Pass: U.S. helicopters fluttering over the invasion routes of Alexander the Great, Tamerlane, Baber, Mahmud of Ghazni, and Nadir Shah, prospecting the weather for the jet of the President of the United States of America, his $6,000,000 reserve jet, the C-130 and C-54 supply planes, and the crowded Pan Am Boeing 707 press plane wherein beautiful stewardesses, for whose favors Alexander and the others would have given minor kingdoms, moved up and down the aisles ladling prebreakfast Bloody Marys.

Kabul: Crazy, awesome Afghanistan. Marrow-freezing cold. Russian-built jet strip of great octagonal cinder-blocks. MIG's, always sinister to regard, roaring off boisterously to escort the President's jet. Roughest-looking honor guard on record. Mad ride in busses and trucks over inconceivable roads into the dung-colored capital, with veiled women peering from roofs and windows like caged animals. Crowds that allowed only inches of freeway for the open car—a Mercedes convertible—bearing the President, wearing his anachronistic black homburg . . . crowds that hit him repeatedly in the face with wads of confetti at point-blank range. He was up to his ankles in the stuff by the time his car pulled up to the modest palace of King Mohammed Zahir Shah for lunch. When he tipped his homburg to a reception group, a small and varicolored Niagara spilled from its brim. He was spitting confetti and finding the patented Eisenhower grin a bit hard to summon as he entered. A wild ride back to the airport in the press busses. The driver of our bus kept dozing at the wheel, waking up just in time to avoid plunging bus and us down some nameless rocky gorge. "Give him a cigarette," somebody suggested. The driver accepted it gratefully. Then he ate it.

New Delhi: Nehru, fussing like a hen over the exact placement of this and that official he had appointed to the reception committee at the airport. He moved them like obedient chessmen, scolded them shrilly if they did not move fast enough. Ike's jet swept in silhouetted against an incomparable Indian sunset, but it was pitch dark as the procession began the long crawl into the capital. Nehru, determined to have India outwelcome Pakistan, had emptied every village along the parade route. Their people came to the side of the route by foot, bicycle, bullock, cart, and car. Paced at regular intervals were human lamp posts, holding garish butane lights aloft. Barefooted men and boys ran crazily through the narrow and dangerous gaps between the cars and busses of the entourage. Dozens climbed the walls of the bus I rode in. You could hear their bare feet and sandals scraping on the roof. Now and then the driver would apply his brakes savagely, for no other reason than to catapult a few rooftop passengers off their perch to the roadway. A twenty-mile blanket of dust hung over the parade route in time. As the car bearing the President and Nehru neared the outskirts of the city, the crowds spread across the road in impenetrable bulk and would give way and make room only when Nehru would leap agilely from the car and angrily demand that they do so. The first thing Ike ordered when he reached the haven of his quarters was an oxygen tent.

Agra: Blinding sun. Perfect blue sky. Nehru, proud, arranged it so that he and his distinguished visitor would not behold the Taj Mahal until the last possible second—for the sake of exquisite impact. Ike, unaware of this presentation, was engrossed in a monologue about U.S. wheat surpluses and the problem of reducing them. "There she is!" Nehru interrupted, gesturing gracefully to the most beautiful edifice on earth. Ike squinted at it. "Pretty," he said, and went back to wheat.

Tehran: Our ugly press bus, so far behind the President's car that a brace of camels and a wine truck were ahead of us, crunched over a million dollars worth of superb Persian rugs spread in the dirty street leading to Shah Mohammad Reza Pahlavi's digs. It seemed a regrettable waste, if not a sacrilege against artistic craftsmanship.

Athens, Tunis, Paris, Madrid, Casablanca . . . peace to you, King Paul, and you, your Excellency President Habib Bourguiba, and you, dear General, and you, Generalissimo, and you, too, Your Majesty Mohammed V—and if it doesn't offend you I don't think I'll have another serving of chocolate-covered goat.

Things didn't go as well on the next trip, in February, 1960: Brasilia, Rio, Sao Paulo, Santiago, Montevideo, Buenos Aires, Mar del Plata, San Carlos de Bariloche, and Laurance Rockefeller's Dorado golf club near San Juan, Puerto Rico.

At Brasilia, as spectacularly lonely as Lhasa, President Juscelino Kubitschek was late arriving at the muddy airport to greet Ike. Then with Ike still aboard, tapping his foot, a brilliant red carpet was unrolled from the temporary air terminal of that day to the steps of the plane. Alas, either the plane was too close to the terminal or the terminal had been built too close to the plane. The roll of carpet was still a yard thick when it reached the bottom step, presenting the leader of the Free World with the problem of needing to vault to the receiving line. A disgusted-looking airman from the President's plane leaped over it, pulled his knife, and chopped it to the right length.

At Rio, U.S. Ambassador and Mrs. John Cabot asked the U.S. Marine Band, which was making a concert tour of South America at the time, to fly a contingent to Rio for the scheduled Eisenhower reception. Its plane collided with a Brazilian airliner over Sugar Loaf and all were killed.

At a housing project outside Santiago, a haggard young Chilean woman carrying a pathetic baby broke through police and Secret Service lines during a politician's speech about how well things were going, held out the baby to Ike, and cried, "Cure my baby!"

At Montevideo, police with armored water-squirting trucks and tear gas were needed to break up a violent pro-Castro demonstration as the President's car passed the university.

Trout the size of fireplace logs and golf on a course as lush as the Masters were prospects dangled temptingly before the President by what amounted to the Chamber of Commerce of San Carlos de Bariloche, Argentina's spectacularly colorful Swiss-like mountain and lakes resort. It was a long flight for what turned out to be a few fingerlings and a rocky, alpine course.

At least, we all said, the exhausting trip would end pleasantly for Ike. He'd get to play Dorado, justly rated one of the world's finest courses. Our jets made a record, nearly four-thousand-mile flight up through the wild heart of South America from Buenos Aires to Ramey Air Force Base in Puerto Rico. And bright and early the next day the nearly one hundred newsmen on the trip piled into buses for the long ride from the air base to the Rockefeller pleasure dome.

Everything was laid on for him, the President learned to his disgust. Several hundred guests of the resort were gathered around the first tee when he arrived, all armed with movie and still cameras.

He had always loathed playing golf in front of a crowd, and this day was no exception. His tee shot, which he hurried in order to separate himself from the crowd, was a humiliating pop fly into the palmettos on the right.

"Take a Mulligan, Mr. President," said his friend and golf mentor Ed Dudley, the pro who had flown there from Colorado Springs to be his partner for what had now become a most involved little round. Ike, very angry, accepted the invitation. This time he tried to kill the ball. It followed the same dismal trajectory as the first shot and may be remembered with it as among the most-photographed bad shots in the game's annals. Ike stalked to his golf cart and sat down. Dudley drove a long one down the fairway, followed by the adequate drives of Maj. John Eisenhower and his partner.

Dudley slid into the cart seat next to the President, and what since has always seemed to me a slightly poignant procession began: Ike still brooding over his bad beginning in front of all those damned newspapermen and tourists, with three carts bringing up the rear. In the first of these sat John and his partner. In the next cart, riding alone, came Gen. Howard McC. Snyder (ret.), long-time personal physician, carrying a few simple first-aid items: oxygen, glycerin, and, inevitably, his number-one remedy for every Presidential ill from coronary to ileitis, milk of magnesia. In the fourth cart rode two strapping fellows who did not look like golfers, though the cart carried two golf bags on its rear deck. They were Secret Service men. The bags contained a few token clubs, but the main contents were (1) a machine gun, for use in case of ambush, and (2) a walkie-talkie tuned to call in the reserves. An Air Force Sikorsky hovered noisily over the Presidential party. At each spot along the course where trees and/or heavy vegetation grew close to the edge of fairways, uniformed members of the Puerto Rican constabulary faced the suspect foliage, guns at ready. Ike's game was off kilter that day. . . .

The President's last grand tour was a shade short of grand. A pall was cast over it before it could get underway. White House press secretary Jim Hagerty, advance man for what was to have been a triumphant Presidential visit to Tokyo, ran into trouble at Haneda airport two weeks before the President's expected arrival in mid-June, 1960. Wilder members of the Zengakuren (All Students League) massed against Jim's Embassy limousine and threatened to turn it over. It took the downwash of the blades of a helicopter to disperse the rock throwers. The protest was against the signing of a treaty the previous January under the terms of which the United States would guarantee Japan's security and maintain military bases on her soil. The pacifist students demonstrated their objections in a most warlike manner.

For safety's sake, the government of Premier Nobusuke Kishi endured great loss of face and asked the President not to come to Japan. It then resigned under heavy attack from Leftists and neutralists.

It was a great disappointment to the President. But there was balm for his hurt in the fine welcomes he received at other points of the farewell flight: Anchorage, Manila, Taipei, Seoul, and Honolulu.

Okinawa was difficult. The U.S. military and their wives on hand as Ike's jet whistled up to the Tarmac at our great air base at Naha were as loyal and loving as could be expected. But just outside the field's guarded gates the President's entourage encountered unexpected hostility. Little knots of grim-faced Okinawans, liberated from Japan at the cost of much American blood and treasure, held banners reading: "GIVE US BACK TO MOTHER JAPAN," and, worse: "GO HOME IKE."

Four of the nine Ryukyuan councilmen elected under our patiently taught system of government refused to appear at the official welcome ceremony in the council hall. The chants of the crowd that assembled outside made it difficult to hear the exchange of cordial remarks. The Secret Service and Air Force Security took the President out a rear door to a waiting jeep for a fast and bumpy ride to a waiting helicopter and thence to his plane.

It was distressing. Hot, dirty, and not a little indignant, the reporters and cameramen climbed aboard the Pan Am charter. My seatmate, Rene MacColl of London's formidable *Express,* a great foreign correspondent in the old tradition, was fathoms deep in brooding silence until the girl brought the martinis. Rene downed one in a swallow, turned to me, cocked a thumb back in the direction of Okinawa, and said something so right I'll never forget it. "If that's a sample of your outpost of Empah," he said, "I'll take Poona!"

President Kennedy's trips, a saga as slim as Blake's verse and as eloquent, presented an entirely new cast of characters and mostly new backdrops: Vienna (where Khrushchev misjudged him badly enough to presume Cuba could become a strong Soviet base), Paris (where he introduced himself as the fellow who was touring Europe with Jacqueline Kennedy. And where a cartoonist depicted General and Mrs. De Gaulle asleep in their double bed, with de Gaulle dreaming of Jackie), Berlin (*"Ich bin ein Berliner!"*), Rome (and Paul VI), Naples (for a much warmer reception than blasé Rome wished him), and, of course, Ireland.

Ireland was a green loving cup, overflowing wherever he ventured there. He was Prince Charming and Brian Boru combined, home to reclaim his lands in freedom.

Everybody on the press plane wished to find the proper words to pin down the scene, and then gave up. The *Irish Press* of Dublin had said it all:

> Ireland welcomes you, Mr. Kennedy, President of the greatest Republic in the world's history. You have come to the home of your forefathers and history fulfills itself in your journey and your arrival, and in the welcome from the heart that the Irish people offer you.
>
> It is a mere forty-four years since President De Valera crossed the Atlantic to appeal to the United States as the President of the Irish Republic at a time when the chosen government of the people had been declared a dangerous association and prohibited and suppressed.
>
> Your great free land then welcomed and aided our country's cause. They expressed by their welcome the longings and aspirations, even the just anger of generations, driven out by hunger and injustice, who had sought freedom and opportunity under

the star-spangled banner of a new world. In the person of the President, those who came to support him saw the hope that the dreams of dead generations would become real, that the Irish Flag might fly in freedom east of the Atlantic as the Stars and Stripes did in the West—and because of their support it is possible today for an Irish President to welcome to Ireland a President of the United States who is the great-grandson of an Irish exile.

Today, visiting the homeland of your people, you stand for almost two centuries of turbulent and always valiant endeavour. You join together as no man has ever done before the stories of this country and of that vast nation to which Ireland has made so many contributions, including that important one in the name of Kennedy.

Ireland—North, South, East, and West—joyfully welcomes you; from the rocks of Connemara and the Western ocean to the streets of Dublin, from the Glens of Antrim to the Reeks of Kerry, from Donegal to Cork and to your own Wexford, where the statue of the great sailor—Barry—looks forever out at the sea he was to sail in the name of freedom.

It was not a long way from Tipperary . . . but, by God, it was some distance and some years from a train ride to Chesapeake Beach.

It is hard to top traveling with a President, unless the President in question prefers Johnson City, Texas. But if you will bear with me, it is even harder to top traveling with a man named Hearst.

8. *Task Force*

THE HEARST TASK FORCE, which has won journalism prizes from the Pulitzer down, was built on the thoroughly improbable proposition that someone named William Randolph Hearst, Jr., could get through to the men in the Kremlin. The risk would have given Lloyd's of London pause. Hearst, senior, waged total editorial war against Bolshevism/Communism from the day of its birth in the Great October of 1917. He numbered Stalin among the infamous mass murderers of history, never tired of writing (or ordering written) uncompromising frontal attacks on the ideology and its disciples abroad and at home. He did not consider the U.S.S.R. a true ally in World War II, said so repeatedly, and was pilloried as a hopeless—if not seditious—reactionary.

His namesake son made an effort to get into Russia in 1945 through the Army Air Force's shuttle-bombing missions: takeoff from England or Italy, bomb deep in Germany, and fly on to Russian-held fields. Bill also sought the good offices of U.S. Ambassador Harriman. All seemed in order. Bill then informed his father and ran into a veto. The elder Hearst cabled his war correspondent son that Stalin had only recently ruthlessly liquidated the survivors of the Warsaw uprising against the Germans to clear the way for the scheduled takeover of Poland by the Lublin Government, yet had received no real censure from Washington and London. Therefore, why would he not just as callously liquidate someone named William Randolph Hearst, Jr.?

That ended that. But in December, 1954 (Hearst, senior, had been dead three years) the chief of the Hearst bureau in Washington, Dave Sentner, urged Hearst to think again about a Russian trip. Stalin had been dead a year, his heirs were generally unknown and just might be willing to talk—preferably to a popular American newspaper chain

231

totally aloof from ideological involvement. Hearst was willing to try, and go if permitted. His wife, mother, and members of the company's hierarchy were not amused. One member of the Establishment, J. D. Gortatowsky, most trusted of the trustees, predicted that if Hearst ever got to Russia he'd wind up burning the Communist flag in Red Square. Everyone joined in the laughter over that absurdity.

On December 23, 1954, Sentner sent a special-delivery letter to Konstantin G. Fedoseev, counselor of the Soviet Embassy in Washington. It read: "W. R. Hearst, Jr., chairman of the editorial board of the Hearst Newspapers, has requested me to take up an important matter with His Excellency, Soviet Ambassador Zaroubin. I would like to have a preliminary discussion of the matter at your convenience."

Fedoseev called Sentner on Christmas Eve and suggested that the next day at noon would be a good time to get together. They met in the otherwise empty National Press Club bar. The only witness to the conception of the Hearst Task Force, which was to set a wholly fresh pattern in reporting, was a bartender.

Fedoseev said after a drink or two that things had changed in Russia since Stalin's death. Dave asked if they had changed enough to allow a person named Hearst to obtain a visa.

"I don't see why not," the Russian said. "Permit me to say that I think it could be arranged."

Dave permitted him. It was arranged, miraculously enough. But before accepting a prized visa that many newsmen had been seeking for years (the application of the *New York Times*'s C. L. Sulzberger had been on the waiting list for seven years), Hearst asked for two additional visas for Kingsbury Smith and Frank Conniff. After much grumbling and presumably a great deal of coded cabling, the additional visas were produced. Shortly thereafter, Hearst, accompanied by Conniff, was received in audience by Ambassador Zaroubin at the Embassy on Sixteenth Street. While they were waiting to be admitted through the locked iron outer door, Conniff waved at the National Geographic Magazine office building across the street.

"What's that for?" Hearst asked.

"I wanted the FBI to get a better picture of us than one just showing the backs of our necks," Frank said.

Zaroubin's butlers spread the good caviar and vodka before the Ambassador's guests, and the Ambassador, apparently expecting to be thanked, informed them that in addition to all other courtesies being extended the Embassy had plotted their itinerary. They would fly toward Moscow first by Air France as far as Prague, then transfer to Aeroflot for the rest of the voyage.

Hearst said no. He and his associates would fly to Moscow via Paris and Berlin. What he did not tell the Ambassador was that he wanted a final briefing from U.S. intelligence and diplomatic and military people before taking the next big step.

The trip turned out spectacularly. Doors that had been shut for decades creaked open at the precise hour of dramatic change in Soviet policies, portfolios, and personnel. A single question aimed at Molotov, artfully composed by Smith and blandly asked by Hearst, elicited an answer that led to the withdrawal of the Red Army and Allied forces from Austria. A brusque command by Khrushchev—to the effect that he would accept no telephone calls while being interviewed by the Hearst team—was the world's first inkling that this relatively unknown First Secretary of the Party had no superiors among Stalin's heirs.

Marshal Zhukov, bristling with eight rows of medals, three Hero-of-the-Soviet-Union stars, and gusts of good humor, was happy to see the Americans whose interviews with Molotov and Khrushchev had filled the entire front page of Pravda. He recalled affably, over tea in his office, his last meeting with General Eisenhower in 1945 during which each man pledged with a handshake that his country would never attack the other. Conniff, who teethed on a hard-cover edition of Clausewitz, asked him two questions that drew forth in masterful brevity explanations which subsequent historians felt required a million words.

"What was Hitler's greatest strategical mistake in the invasion of Russia?" Frank asked.

"The decision to invade Russia. He launched an operation for which he never had the necessary means. The conquest of Russia was simply beyond the means at his disposal."

"What was Hitler's greatest tactical mistake?"

"His dependence on aircraft at the expense of artillery. The Luftwaffe was a very formidable instrument, certainly, but there would be days at a time here in Russia, even weeks, especially during the winter months, when airplanes couldn't fly at all. Then he missed the artillery, which could function in any weather, and which we had in abundance."

The Task Force was present in the Supreme Soviet when Malenkov abruptly stepped down as premier and Bulganin—at Khrushchev's suggestion—was unanimously elected in his place. The team saw the new premier, heard him express the hope of a rapprochement with the United States. Before the remarkable trip was concluded—it covered less than three weeks—the trio entertained and were entertained by Galina Ulanova, Maya Plisetskaya, Yuri Zhdanov, Nicolai Fadeyechen, and Georgi Orvid, hitherto unapproachable Bolshoi greats, were permitted to see and talk to Stalin's daughter Svetlana (who wept when Hearst asked her whatever became of her brother Vassily, once a top-ranking commander in the Red Air Force), and spent some time with Patriarch Alexei and the sequestered monks at Zagorsk. Dmitri Shostakovich recanted all over Conniff.

It was a trip that could never be topped, but Hearst set forth again late in 1957, this time with Conniff and myself as his spear carriers (Joe Smith had moved upward and onward to general manager of INS). The timing of the trip was again exquisite.

Khrushchev, having denounced Stalin, had narrowly survived a power play aimed at ousting him and had emerged stronger than ever and banished Molotov, Malenkov, Kaganovich, and Shepilov, the prime conspirators. On top of this, he then made an unperson out of his friend Zhukov, whose skillful employment of Red Air Force transport planes had rounded up enough members of the far-flung Central Committee to give Khrushchev the vote of confidence he needed. This was a perfectly sensible move on Khrushchev's part, I was told later, because when Zhukov had demonstrated his ability to save Khrushchev he had thus demonstrated his capability to destroy him!

Sputnik I had startled and alarmed the world in early October of '57. Sputnik II, weighing a then awesome half a ton and carrying Laika, the immortal dog, went up on November 3 of that year while we paused in Rome on our way to Moscow. The word reached us as we were being given a tour of St. Peter's by Monsignor Paganuzzi, a good friend of the Hearst family who had just celebrated Mass for us at the tiny altar near the Tomb of Peter in the depths of the basilica. I have been judged (falsely) a pious person, but it was a genuine relief to be done with the good monsignor and be on our way to atheistic Prague later that sunny Sunday.

Prague was a study in gray depression. Hungering as I was to dig my typing fingers as deep into Russia as they'd be permitted to plunge, I found every Czech hour a burden. It wasn't so much the grayness of the old city as it was the grayness of its people. The people who had known the wand of Woodrow Wilson and been stirred by the Masaryks and Benes seemed to have surrendered abysmally without even token struggle—a crude generalization, I'm sure, but one which subsequent visits tended only to strengthen. Our three days there would have been farcical if pity had not enveloped the laughter. Whenever we ventured from the Alcron Hotel for a walk, day or night, we were followed by two ludicrous security agents, burlesques right down to their greasy raincoats, slouch hats, and squeaky shoes. When we whipped off one night in a car to file a story with the couple who represented Press Wireless, a security car followed us and remained parked at a distance while the saddened couple took our copy and served us coffee and slivovitz. At the Alcron bar, better attended by the three imperialists in town than by Playboys of the Eastern World, the bartender George liked to regale us with accounts of his adventurous travels. He had been all the way to Paris. But Paris had nothing on Prague, he would conclude strongly if there were other Czechs at the bar. Late one night there was just us and George. It was my birthday, as good a time as any to ask him to have a drink. He poured it carefully, marked it down on our check, drank it, looked around, then leaned over toward us.

"Myself, I am a Catholic," he confided in the voice of the confessional. We felt like promising not to turn him in.

Katherine Clark of INS took us to the airport through the early morning smog the first day, followed by the two clowns assigned to tail us. There sat the rakish TU-104, a jet transport we could not match at that time. It had been built as a Bison, the Red Air Force's medium-range bomber, and only modestly altered to enter commercial servitude. The plexiglass nose compartment had exchanged its bomb-sight for navigational equipment. But being a plane buff I found it enchanting and couldn't wait to get aboard.

The seventy Moscow-bound passengers moved restlessly toward the terminal's proper gate as the scheduled time of departure neared. But the gate remained closed. There was no announcement when the departure hour came and went, nor could the Czechs behind the counter give us any reason for the delay. Hearst, the Compleat Traveler, is not a man to tolerate such indignities. He flushed a Scandinavian Airways man who surmised, sotto voce, that one or two factors probably were involved: (1) The weather in Moscow was bad and the Russians didn't want to admit it. (2) Aeroflot might be sweating out the arrival from other places of Communist VIP's ticketed for that particular flight.

The passengers remained in that bleak, cushionless, foodless terminal until nearly dusk without information. Then a Czech behind a counter rapped for attention.

"Tomorrow," he announced helplessly.

The next morning, dull and early, we thought it best to inquire before making the long trip to the airport.

"Certainly the plane is leaving this morning," the Alcron's travel desk man said flatly. "It is scheduled to go, so it will go." He gave the appearance of a man talking for the benefit of a concealed "bug."

We vegetated at the airport all day. When dismissed again, Hearst braced the Czech behind the counter and asked him why he hadn't made his announcement hours earlier.

The poor man said, "The Russians won't tell us *anything.*"

The next morning, November 6, the fortieth anniversary of the Great October and a day of tumult and shouting and marching and missile-brandishing in Red Square, dawned with a deluge in Prague. We seemed doomed to spend another unbearable day far from the action and the news. We went to the airport more from habit than lively anticipation and to our astonishment were told we must hurry—the TU-104, cascading rain, was primed and raring to go. First, however, we must obtain exit permits. We found our way to the right bureaucrat's desk and restlessly watched as he made out the endless forms without which the whole Communist world would collapse. When he had finished, the man behind the desk held onto the permits and said that the cost would be seventy-five korunas—about ten dollars at the official rate. Our leader dug in his pocket, a familiar movement for him, and produced the seventy-five korunas. The man shook his head and held on to the permits.

"We are not permitted to accept Czechoslovakian money from persons leaving Czechoslovakia," he said by rote. "It must be in American dollars." Hearst said something defamatory about korunas in general and Czechoslovakia in particular and paid in dollars.

Now we were outside under a leaking shelter of sorts; a Czech girl in uniform was calling out the names of those permitted to proceed to the TU-104. We discovered that all passengers were members of official delegations en route to the meeting of the clan in Moscow. France's Duclos and Italy's Togliatti swept past us with their suites when called. After fifteen minutes the girl obviously had begun to scrape the bottom of the barrel.

"Deligazie Sudanese!" she shouted. That group of towering Africans stiffened to attention and filed past us into the rain. Each seemed seven feet tall. They had protected themselves against the raw day by wrapping scarves around their heads from chin to crown. On top of the scarves they had balanced their cheap little fedoras. They resembled the Harlem Globetrotters in a comedy routine.

"Regards to Abe Saperstein," Conniff said to them as they went by us.

"Deligazie Hearst!"

Our friend from SAS appeared out of nowhere and hurried us through the rain to the steps that led to what turned out to be the rather plush first-class section of the jet. We had just settled down happily in the three remaining empty seats when a heavy-set hostess loomed over us and gave us the brusque signal used by umpires to indicate that a runner is out. We retreated in disarray to the narrow-aisled tourist class of the classless society's jet and squeezed into seats designed especially for passengers with one-cheek bottoms and six-inch legs. And after an alarmingly long run down the semi-inundated runway the jet's two huge engines flung us aloft. We were still climbing when a hostess plopped lunch in front of us—a small portion of cold veal, vegetables too sodden to offer ready recognition, and a small glass of red wine. The wine made it a happy ship. One by one the heads of delegations aboard would rise in his place, make his voice heard above the considerable roar of the engines, and shout a toast to the U.S.S.R. and Comrade Khrushchev. I had the empty feeling of being a long way from home. I touched my glass to Bill's and Frank's and said "The President of the United States," and we had our separate (but equal) sip. Then Conniff rattled a spoon against his glass and a silence fell on nearby comrades as they readied their glasses for his toast.

"To the president of the National Association of Manufacturers!"

Frank sang out. It must have sounded like a newly formed Soviet industrial front to most of the comrades around us, for they drank to it.

The early night had fallen on Moscow, the parade had gone off to wherever Russian parades disappear. But a carnival air prevailed in Manezhnaya Square when we pulled up in front of the National Hotel, where Hearst and his troops had stayed on their first trip. The chambermaids on our floor were delighted to see Hearst again. *"Gospodin Gearst!"* cried the biggest of them and threw her arms around him. She was saying "Comrade Hearst," or, stretching the point a bit, "Citizen Hearst." The Russians have as much trouble with *H* as the Cockneys, but in a different way. *H* becomes *G*. Before our trip ended we were to hear many strong denunciations of Adolf *G*itler, but none of *G*erbert *G*oover.

Bundled in his wraparound camel's hair coat and muffler, Hearst led us into the living room of the four-room suite from the balcony of which Lenin once harangued throngs as dense as those which now populated gay Manezhnaya and, just beyond, Red Square. It was one of the most entrancing moments of my life: the gaudy Czarist suite with its ceiling painting of peacocks pulling a cushiony nude's troika, "people's" music thundering in from flung-open French doors, the invigorating rush of wintry air that accompanied the music, the huge illuminated pictures of Party leaders hung from the walls of neighboring buildings and spotlighted on captive balloons, the formless symphony of sound of the mobs just below, and the clucking and shoulder-dusting of the elephantine maids. The delirious, delicious cacophony was pierced suddenly by the urgent ringing of the living room's antique telephone. Hearst snatched it off its cradle and a torrent of cackling Russian bombarded his ear.

"Speak American, we've taken over!" he shouted into the phone, and hung up. Beautiful.

He and Conniff showered, shaved, dressed, and went off to the formal reception given that night to the visiting Communist delegations in the great George Hall inside the Kremlin walls. For want of a ticket, I remained in the suite with Serge Fliegers, INS's Man in Moscow, a remarkable young correspondent with a gifted command of a half dozen languages coupled with a driving curiosity and an ability to write well whatever he witnessed or heard. He had taken extensive notes on the day's parade, particularly on the missiles displayed and the first appearance in the forefront of Marshal Rodion Malinovsky, who had replaced Marshal Zhukov.

As I began to stitch the story together on my typewriter later that night, Hearst and Conniff piled in with more news: The two stars of the big reception had been Khrushchev and Mao Tse-tung. Bulganin, still premier, looked gray and tentative—had laughed nervously when Hearst asked for an audience and said, "No, it is Khrushchev you should see." Khrushchev had danced up a storm, had bussed a giggling matron or two, and had joined the Red Army chorus during one of its virile numbers.

It was an easy and colorful story to write: Red Summit, clank of military might, dancing in the streets, bygone saints exhumed, corks popping under glittering George Hall chandeliers. . . .

Serge's phone call to INS-London went through just as I finished the first page. I handed it to him and he began to dictate, as his predecessor, Charles Klensch, had during Hearst's earlier trip. But he had hardly begun before a loud click sounded through the system. London had disappeared. The voice on the phone now spoke Russian. Fliegers listened for a bit, then broke into an angry torrent of Russian himself. We couldn't understand a word, but it was clear he was losing the argument. Finally, he hung up.

"We're not permitted to file out of here by phone," he said. "Everything must go through the censor's office at the Telegraph Building."

Suddenly, I realized it was very late. The streets and squares had emptied their multitudes. The loudspeakers had fallen mute. The lights were going out, accentuating the bloody Red Stars that protruded into the night from the parapets and towers of the Kremlin across Manezhnaya Square. A night that had started as a glorious lark had descended into ominous silence, and doubt had taken the place of doughtiness.

Obtaining interviews with top Soviet officials can be a humbling pursuit. You just don't call up one of them and put in the request, any more than a Russian reporter visiting Washington could ring the White House or the State Department and ask for the man in charge. But at least that hypothetical Russian reporter would have the satisfaction of knowing that the phone on the other end of the line rang. Russia has not discovered phone books as yet. Phone numbers of even some of the office buildings which house newsworthy Russians are difficult to obtain.

But we did get through to the commissar of the foreign press, Leonid Ilychev, on the morning of our first full day in Moscow. Interviews? Why, that was out of the question; everyone was too busy with the meetings and celebrations of the Fortieth Anniversary. Premier Bulganin said you should see First Secretary Khrushchev? Well, he'd look into that. In the meantime, write a letter explaining why we had come to Moscow.

The hotel produced a Cyrillic alphabet typewriter, Intourist provided a typist, Bill composed the letter, and Serge dictated it to the girl. Bill signed it, sealed it, and Serge deposited it where Ilychev had dictated—in a mailbox hung on a Kremlin wall.

If that was utterly baffling, the next ten days were equally as deflating. True, there were pleasant distractions. Intourist chose as our official keeper a relentlessly cheerful and efficient little woman named Zoya Novikovo. As do all Intourist guides, she made us feel like Cossacks as she shepherded us past long and frozen queues of true aficionados. She steered us unerringly into *Swan Lake* at the Bolshoi, where Khrushchev and Mao Tse-tung sat together in ordinary orchestra seats while Anastas Mikoyan occupied alone the huge royal box on the mezzanine. She had the password and the last-minute tickets for such perennial sellouts as Moscow's unforgettable one-ring circus with Popov and a monstrous hippopotamus which mingled with front-row patrons like a lap dog. She knew the best way into the puppet show, the museums, into any place except the places we wanted to go: to the offices of newsmakers.

We spent a depressing number of hours shamelessly waiting for Ilychev to call. I began to wonder about the incidence of stir-craziness. But this was averted largely by two diversions: (1) Hearst's daily breakthrough against the impenetrable language barrier, and (2) an eerie fulfillment of the prophecy of J. D. Gortatowsky.

One of the hardest things to obtain from the room-service waiter at the ice-bound National was ice. We couldn't get through to him even with such overwhelming documentation as our English-Russian Dictionary:

ice *sb* лёд *m* (1d)[1) thick
то́лстый, thin то́нкий, hard
кре́пкий, clear чи́стый, transparent прозра́чный, artificial иску́сственный, slippery
ско́льзкий, dry сухо́й; 2)
breaks лома́ется, melts та́ет,
cracks трещи́т; 3) cut ру-
би́ть, crush кроши́ть, break
разби́ть, melt растопи́ть];
the river is covered with ~
река́ покры́та льдом; she
slipped / fell on the ~ она́
поскользну́лась / упа́ла на
льду́; they fished through
holes in the ~ они́ удили
ры́бу подо льдо́м; the water under the ~ was cold
вода́ подо льдо́м была́ хо-
ло́дной; put some more ~
in your glass! положи́те
себе́ в стака́н ещё льду!;
your fingers are as cold as
~ у тебя́ па́льцы как лёд.

Our leader cracked the code. He faced the puzzled waiter and
called for his careful attention. Then Bill flung his arms around himself, did a jig, shook his head, rattled his teeth and said:

"Br-r-r-r-r-r-r-r!"

The man marched out immediately and returned with a pitcher of
ice.

"Eggs" were as bewildering to the waiter as "ice" had been until
Bill squatted on the fine Persian rug of the living room, made a series
of faces indicating pain, then beamed beatifically and began to cluck.
Thanks to Hearst, Conniff and I could have our eggs boiled as we
wished. For example, he would stand in front of the waiter and point

to the glass or pitcher he was holding. Then he'd do "egg" again (the deep knee-bends kept him in excellent condition), tenderly deposit the "egg" into the receptacle and wiggle his fingers under its bottom. That, of course, was "fire" or "flames." Then he'd hold up, say, three fingers and point to Conniff. And Frank would get his three-minute eggs.

We ate better when Serge was present. All waiters moved on the double when Serge—who looks as if he posed for Van Gogh's pork-pied *Young Man*—snapped orders in Russian. He was generally at our sides at the endless rounds of diplomatic receptions whenever a story might be afoot. I always marveled at his command of one of the world's most difficult tongues, but never more keenly than the night he lost his way while driving to a party at the Liberian Legation—an indication of the condition of our desperation. Serge spotted a Moscow policeman standing his lonely vigil on a remote side street, pulled over to the curb, reached past me in the front seat to open the window, and engaged the fur-hatted man in what turned out to be five minutes of animated dialogue. There was much gesticulating on the part of the officer as he apparently told Serge when to turn left, right, and do an outside loop. Gravely impressed, I sat between them in the eye of a hurricane of lively exchanges, using neck muscles that had lain dormant since my days as a tennis reporter. Finally, Serge rolled up the window and we were again on our way. He started to laugh.

"Did you ever hear such an atrocious accent as that?" he asked *me*.

As for Gortatowsky's curse:

"Hey, we're on fire!" Hearst announced one night in the suite. Conniff was in his neighboring room taking a bath. I was engrossed in my typewriter attending the birth of a column by Caesarian section.

Hearst pushed open the doors that led to the main balcony and the suite was instantly filled with the music and crowd noises of the continuing Great October celebration . . . and smoke.

We *were* on fire. The big Hammer and Sickle flag that adorned the balcony of a man named William Randolph Hearst had drooped its tail end low enough to become enmeshed in a neon sign that hung just below our balcony. The sign, one of the most familiar in Moscow, read "Ресторан," meaning (and more or less pronounced) "Restaurant." The flag's tail, wet from the day's rain and snow, short-circuited the sign. The sign sent out a small fireworks display of sparks and the flag burst into sullen smoke and flames.

Hearst dashed across the living room, picked up a pitcher of drinking water, sped back to the balcony and heaved the contents upward and outward at the unnerving blaze. I found a bucket in one of the bathrooms, filled it, and let fly. Hearst was right behind with another pitcher full. We weren't quelling the blaze but we were certainly risking a bad electric shock, for the tail of the flag was still enmeshed in the sputtering wiring. Moreover, we discovered with a jolt, we were making a lot of Muscovites mad at us. We had forgotten the milling crowds in the street below. Every time we missed with the water, they got it on their heads. There seemed to me to be shouts of rage mixed somewhere in the ear-splitting street music that swept the mad scene. A few shook their fists up at us, blaming us for either setting fire to the Hammer and Sickle during a most hallowed anniversary period, or giving them an unrequested bath.

Bill and I were still playing energetic firemen when Frank Conniff entered the smoky living room with naught but a towel wrapped around his middle. He was delicately fanning the smoke away with his hand.

"Fire? What fire?" he asked, addressing his remarks to what we felt was the "bug" in the ceiling nude's navel. "I don't know anything about a fire. When the secret police arrive, I'll be given a clean bill of health."

Help arrived. It wasn't very friendly help. A swarm of chambermaids, porters, and probably electricians stormed into the living room like a pandemonium scene from the Winter Palace, circa 1917. The fire was doused, the desecrated flag lowered and bundled, and then for good measure they took the other flags off our proud balcony and trundled them off, with many a dark look. Serge wasn't around to explain the whole thing, and Bill couldn't come up with a quick pantomime depicting a sodden and drooping flag, short circuit, smoke, flames, valiant effort, so sorry. . . .

More deadly days of waiting, and then the logjam stirred.

We were permitted to see Andrei Gromyko, the first interview he gave after being named Foreign Minister. He was much more relaxed and affable than during his years at the UN in New York. He asked with mock alarm if Bill Hearst's compact tape recorder was a bomb, listened to it for a moment, and then said, "It doesn't tick. It keeps saying 'bleep . . . bleep . . . bleep.' " That was the sound of Sputnik I, and we still had nothing to match it at that time. Gromyko laughed at his joke and was chatting agreeably about New York in his flawless English until one of us asked him the first question of the interview.

Immediately, he switched into Russian. Presumably, he was "bugged" too and wanted to make certain that whatever answers he gave to us thereafter were clearly understood by superiors who presumably would add the tape to his dossier. He didn't say enough to fill three sticks of type. The next bone we were tossed was Yuri Zhukov, a crude oaf who had previously edited *Pravda* and was now staggering under the title of Chairman of the Soviet Union's Committee on Cultural Relations with Foreign Countries. He explained why the U.S.S.R. was jamming Voice of America broadcasts: "There is an old Russian proverb which goes 'When a man is trying to throw a stone into your window you try to protect your window. You close your blind.' "

That was the last day we had Serge Fliegers' services as our official interpreter. At one point in the interview, Zhukov's interpreter translated into English a Zhukov reference to Anthony Eden: ". . . but then, after certain events that took place in Hungary, the Conservative Eden . . ."

"Mr. Zhukov didn't call Eden a Conservative, he called him a Fascist," Serge spoke up. Filled with surprise, confusion, and anger, Zhukov acknowledged that he had. Thereafter, we were minus our miraculous linguist during formal interviews. And by coincidence or design, Serge was ordered out of Russia some months later.

Khrushchev bounced into the reception room of his modest suite in the Central Party headquarters building. He shook hands all around, giving each of us penetrating looks not quite in keeping with his feckless gold-toothed smile. The little glacial eyes paused a bit longer on me. He clearly remembered Hearst and Conniff. Bill explained that I had replaced Kingsbury Smith on this trip. Khrushchev muttered in Russian and laughed. Victor Sukhodrev, the testiest of Khrushchev's interpreters, also laughed as he translated:

"He's bigger than Smith, but is he as good?"

At last we were gathered around the big table of his inner sanctum. The hour I had actually prayed for, but doubted would ever come, was at hand. We arranged our scores of questions in front of us, carefully selected during hours of work back at the hotel. All the major INS bureaus in the world had contributed to our treasury of pertinent and impertinent inquires. But first the ice must be broken. Our icebreaker moved into the barrier.

"It *is* the same office as the last time, isn't it?" Hearst asked, scanning the inevitable picture of Lenin and Khrushchev's memento-laden desk.

"Of course," Khrushchev said, through Sukhodrev. "We don't change in this country as you do in yours."

Hearst started all over:

"Frank Conniff and I have noticed a lot of changes in Moscow since our visit of two years ago. For instance, there are many more cars on the streets. . . ."

"We're not interested in automobile production," Khrushchev cut in when he got the gist. "It has no important role in our country."

We weren't getting out of the batter's box, and this predicament obviously pleased Ilychev. The mean little man was silently laughing at us.

"Now, about these questions . . ." Khrushchev said, picking up the bundle we had sent him on Ilychev's telephoned demand. He looked at them with impatience showing, pushed them aside, and said, "Ask me whatever you wish."

He gave us three hours and thirty-five minutes.

It was one of those once-in-a-lifetime exclusives. The man's grasp of the spectrum of human events and crises was phenomenal. Only once during the crammed session did he refer to his notes, in order to quote accurately a portion of a speech President Eisenhower had delivered several days earlier in Oklahoma. The rest was off the top of his head, or lower. It ranged through war and peace, mutual suspicions, integral differences in the two ideologies, the arms race, Russia's ability to kill tens of millions in the United States with its ICBM's ("Your cities and bases could be stricken from the earth"); NATO, West German rearmament, Hungary ("It could have been different"); creature comforts, consumer goods, the need of East-West trade, hybrid corn, Soviet pre-eminence in space, aspirations of the workers of the world, disarmament, inspection. He left no base untouched. His words were weighed around the world by government leaders and policy makers. Popularly, however, the chief impact of the interview emerged from an area in which apparently he had never been questioned. I asked the question that loosed the little avalanche:

"You have made several references to God, the human soul, and spiritual freedom under Communism. How is it that any man who might believe in all those things is denied advancement in the Communist Party?"

Surprisingly, Khrushchev rose from his place at the conference table and started toward the rear door of his office. I feared the question had guillotined the interview before we had exhausted all the darts in our quivers. But he stopped at the door, poured himself a glass of his country's noxious seltzer water, and strode back to the table. He was angry but in full control.

"Because the situation is incompatible," he said, "We are atheists! Certainly we use the name of God, as in 'God's truth,' but it's only a habit, an expression. We could just as easily say, 'I give you my word.' We are atheists, but we have a tolerant attitude toward all religion. There is no contradiction in this attitude."

Then he hit the table with his fist. Pencils bounced.

"But if the acceptance of religion is intermingled with political activity that works against the Communist Party, that's different. If they intrude on political activity, that is against our constitution. It is not permitted. We are not going to fight for God's body. We don't fight for an empty coffin so that other coffins, filled, will cover the world. That's what the Crusades were fought for."

The mood interested Hearst, who is hardly gulp-prone in the presence of any world leader, however menacing. He told Khrushchev that no great country or civilization had ever risen without deference to or dependence upon some form of divine guidance and dared him to deny it.

"Let them believe what they want," Khrushchev said, sweeping the previous affairs of man to one side.

"That's the basic difference between us," Hearst said. "When we give our word, we consider it is a pledge to God. In your case, the pledge remains on paper only." It was a slap Khrushchev obviously never expected in his own office or anybody else's. In the tense silence that followed I wondered idly if we'd get out alive.

"We set high value on our pledges and on our word," Khrushchev said, picking up a blue-handled letter opener and wagging it at Bill. "We Communists, we atheists, are fighting actively to prevent another war. We mean it when say we are doing everything possible in order that there will be no new war. That is where the discrepancy lies. Such people (religious) seek to present things as if their activities really proceed from divine commands. In actual fact, they contradict the very principles of humanity and, consequently, of the whole of human society." He was getting louder.

"Your John Foster Dulles wears the mask of God, but behind the mask is the Devil. I've seen pictures of priests throwing holy water on tanks, guns, blessing these weapons that murder innocents and enslave the colonial peoples. Your priests brought the Cross and the Bible to strange lands and peoples and took their riches, leaving only the Cross and Bible." He hit the table again with his chubby fist, then calmed.

"I recall a story I once heard," he said, "about robbers who killed a man. Among the loot they took from the victim was a chunk of fresh ham. After a time, the robbers stopped to rest and eat the ham. They had distributed it among themselves when one asked what day of the week it was. He was told it was Wednesday or Friday—I can't remember the exact day named in the story. He declared he couldn't eat the ham, for his Church prohibited meat on Wednesdays and Fridays.

"You see how it is! The robber killed a man, took his life and everything he had, but didn't eat the ham taken in the loot for fear of committing a sin! Don't the deeds of certain Western statesman remind one of the sacrilegious people mentioned in the story? For they, shielding themselves with the name of God, quite often do things which bring death to thousands and millions of people."

When it was over and we were back in the hotel we compared our books of notes and I sat down at the typewriter. I wrote for nearly seven hours, never wanting food or drink. When the two long main pieces, the feature on his religious tirade, and a column on what it was like were finished, Serge read proof on the thick stack of material and took it to the censor's office in the Telegraph Building. A woman behind the counter stamped the original and carbon, to note the time of arrival, and carried both through a door beyond which no newsman ever was permitted to pass. Hearst got through to New York by phone that night—a Friday—and sketched the scope of the interview for the promotion department. He ordered the first of the two main

articles to be released in Sunday papers. Consequently, the Hearst
Papers and a great many INS clients the following day, Saturday,
carried the following blurb:

KHRUSHCHEV SPEAKS

For three hours and 35 minutes—in one of the most significant
interviews of our times—the dominant figure of Soviet Russia
has answered the questions of three famous newsmen.

No subject was out of bounds, no holds barred as William
Randolph Hearst, Jr., Frank Conniff, and Bob Considine explored Khrushchev's views on war, peace, coexistence, science,
satellites, missiles, nuclear power, and the probable directions
of Soviet policy. Don't miss it. Sunday!

There was one fly in the ointment, we discovered when we woke up
Saturday morning after celebrating the completion of the big coup.

Every word, comma, period, dash, and exclamation point was still
being held by the censor's office. Nothing had moved, nine hours
after Serge had delivered it for approval and transmission. At 10 A.M.
we made an aborted effort to reach INS-London and dictate it. The
call never got beyond the nearest Russian switchboard. At 11 A.M.
we craftily put in a call for Communist Prague, where we knew the
two courageous Press Wireless people would take it. We were cut off
before we could start. Just before noon it appeared that Hearst would
be forced to tell our papers and clients in the United States and elsewhere in the world that the stories would not be forthcoming until,
let's say, the publishing of our memoirs.

But at the stroke of noon, with Serge pacing back and forth near
the counter in the censor's outer office, a woman emerged from the mysterious door with the stamped and approved carbon copy of everything. Not a word had been changed. The entire works was on its way
to New York. We were given to understand later that Khrushchev
had asked to see a translation of the material that Saturday morning
and had personally passed it.

The Hearst team saw more of that remarkable rogue between this
time and his downfall. The meetings were never nearly so productive,
but they were lively. Hearst and Khrushchev were as separated as
the earth's poles, but instinctively enjoyed a rapport. Each time the
Russian spotted Hearst, sometimes as just another face in the crowd,

he greeted him cheerfully, if sardonically, with such as "Ah!—my old monopolistic friend." Hearst once said to him, a bit ruefully, that he wished the Hearst papers *were* monopolies here and there because they were taking a financial pounding from the determined opposition in those markets. Khrushchev obviously didn't believe him, judging from his laughter. At the end of their first meeting, which had been heated at times, Khrushchev patted Hearst on the shoulder and said, "When you return to America and are called before the McCarthy committee investigating subversion—and you are sure to be after sitting down for hours with a Communist leader in Communist head-quarters—I am prepared to testify for you that you defended your country's position well and ably." In the course of their long second meeting, after Khrushchev had expounded at length on what he called the plight of the American working class, Hearst said, "I've heard everything you've said and don't believe a word of it." Khrushchev was more amused than offended by being called a liar. Tapping his letter opener's blade on the conference table, he beamed and said, "When the time comes when the United States worker will say, 'I am the boss. I create all the values, and I will vote in the interest of myself and other members of the working class,' don't be afraid. We who will be in overall charge then will tell the leaders of the working class in the United States, Mr. Hearst, that you were not a bad capitalist at all."

"Gee, thanks," Hearst wheezed.

There were shrouded chapters in Khrushchev's life that suggested strong evidence he might be among the most ruthless hatchet men of the twentieth century. He was in at least partial command of putting down lawlessness in his native Ukraine after World War I. He was again there on orders in 1924 with his boss, Lazar Kaganovich, to wipe out Trotskyism. He was part of the prosecution in the for-gotten but bloody purge of 1932 which led to the suicide of Nadyezhda Aliluyeva, Stalin's wife, which facilitated the dictator's marriage to his mistress Rosa Kaganovich, sister of Khrushchev's patron. Khru-shchev was moving fast within the Party. Stalin was amused by his rough-hewn manner, barnyard humor, unquestioned loyalty, and the aggressive manner in which he danced the native *gopok*. He made him political overseer of the engineering endeavor that is still one of the man-made wonders of the world, the Moscow subway system. Of that phase, Edward Crankshaw, one of the foremost Western authorities on the Soviet Union, wrote searchingly: *

> With his cloth cap, his sloppy clothes, his brash, overbearing manner, and his ability to coax disgruntled workers and jolly them along as well as to bully them and lash them with his tongue, he was the practical man who knew how to get things done. High office and a host of sycophantic subordinates at his command had not changed him. As in his early days . . . he still liked to get out into the field and face his problems on the ground instead of keeping his boots clean and operating from behind a barricade of paper. At the same time the talent for intrigue, for smelling out heresy, for paying out rope in the most calculated manner until his enemies stumbled and a short, sharp twitch of the halter broke their necks, put him in the front rank of Party hatchet-men.

Eugene Lyons, longtime student of the U.S.S.R., testified before a Congressional committee just before Khrushchev's visit to President Eisenhower in 1959: "He was sent in 1937 as Stalin's trusted killer (to the Ukraine). . . . His first move was to summon a conference of the entire Ukrainian government, staged as a social occasion. The gathering was surrounded by the secret police, arrested en masse, and most of his 'guests' died in the cellars of the Kiev and Moscow secret police. When his two-year Ukrainian purge was over, an estimated 400,000 had been killed and terror gripped the whole population."

During World War II Khrushchev held a number of important jobs that were never mentioned in dispatches: military commissar for the Kiev area, commander of a partisan force in the Ukraine, and he was at Kharkov and Stalingrad with the rank of lieutenant general. In the postwar years he nimbly kept his balance in the face of Stalin's senile rages and outfoxed and outmuscled his fellow heirs when Stalin died.

Still, there was no noticeable demonstration of joy when his luck and his gall ran out and he became an unperson, another faceless member of his society's living dead. Indeed, he seemed to have sympathizers in the West, persons who had grown accustomed to his wacky ways and preferred him to his solemn-faced and unplumbed

* *Khrushchev: A Career.* The Viking Press. Copyright © 1966 by Edward Crankshaw.

successors, Leonid I. Brezhnev, Aleksei Kosygin, and the always mysteriously well-placed "theoretician" Mikhail Suslov. In the United States many felt they knew Khrushchev, could guess his future moves quite accurately from such risky and ridiculous past performances as planting missiles in Cuba and then chickening out and removing them, pounding his shoe in the UN, giving the Allies "notice" in West Berlin and then conveniently doing nothing about his ultimatums, expressing shock over the scantily dressed chorus line on the *Can-Can* set at Twentieth Century-Fox, complaining shrilly about not being permitted to go to Disneyland.

A lot of Americans remember him with mixed emotions . . . notably Richard Nixon.

Before he flew to Russia on a trip which for a time at least seemed a solid stepping stone to the White House, the Vice President invited the Hearst team to fly to Washington and brief him on the temper of the man he was to face.

We assured Nixon that Nikita Sergeyevitch (or Sergeivich) was tough as nails, rough as a cob, sharp as a tack, smart as a fox, mean as a razorback . . . and exciting to be around. I suggested to him that he collect a series of good waterproof American proverbs before he set foot on Soviet soil, for he'd surely be assailed by sentences beginning "There is an old Russian proverb which goes. . . ." Khrushchev used proverbs not only to sum up his arguments but conclude them triumphantly.

Actually, there was little that anyone could do to steer Nixon through his Russian trip without turmoil. In the first place, his credentials lacked distinction. As President Eisenhower assessed them, they called on Nixon to pay a visit to the U.S.S.R. and officially open the American Exhibition in Moscow's Sokolniki Park. This would repay the visit to New York the year before (1958) of Khrushchev's First Deputy Frol Koslov, who had opened the Russian fair at the New York Coliseum.

"It is a goodwill gesture, and we wanted to have a prominent American to officiate at the opening of our exhibit," the President told a news conference. The feeble fiat offered Nixon precious little armor for his inevitable brushes with Khrushchev and other assailants. The Hearst group and seventy other United States correspondents found themselves fending for Nixon as best they could, cheering him on his uncharted path, giving him a "press" back home that removed much doubt that he would be the GOP nominee in the following year's presidential campaign.

He needed every friend he found. Early on July 24, 1959, his first full day in Moscow, Nixon decided that he'd jump right into the life of the city. With a Secret Service man at his side, he left U.S. Ambassador Llewellyn Thompson's residence, Spaso House, and set out on a brisk constitutional. In time, the pair came upon a market-grocery, Danilovsky's by name. The inveterate politician compulsively entered, waved to customers and clerks, and sought out the manager. The manager and others recognized him, to Nixon's keen pleasure, and there was enough English afoot to pursue a dialogue. He signed a few autographs and smiled for the Secret Service man, who had brought along his 8 mm. home-movie camera.

All would have gone well if the manager of the store had not remarked that he and many others were unable to buy tickets to the eagerly awaited American Exhibition. Nixon, not knowing that Soviet officials had limited ticket sales to thirty thousand a day to suppress excesses of public endorsement of the fair, assumed the manager meant that he and others could not afford the price of admission tickets.

"I'll see to it personally that there are tickets for everyone here in the market," he announced generously. He had not picked up any Russian currency as yet, so he borrowed a hundred ruble note from the Secret Service man and offered it to the Russians to buy tickets. They laughingly protested that it wasn't a question of being unable to afford to go, and some applauded him as he left the place. But the next day's *Moscow News,* an English language tabloid, berated him pitilessly for his "insult" to well-paid Russian workers and accused him of bringing along a photographer to make a propaganda film.

Later that first morning he met Khrushchev in the latter's office in the Kremlin. Echoes of the introductions had barely died away when Khrushchev began to question Nixon sharply on a resolution passed in the U.S. Senate a day or two before expressing sympathy for the "captive nations" behind the Iron Curtain. In the course of its passage, several Senators from states where large numbers of refugees and others tracing their roots back into Eastern Europe lived and voted, attacked Khrushchev as an arch despot.

Khrushchev demanded to know whether this resolution marked an official change in American foreign policy. Nixon attempted to explain that there is a difference between a resolution and a fact of policy. Then why, Khrushchev wanted to know, was it passed just at this time when Nixon was embarking on a good-will tour? Nixon said that something of this nature was voted on at the tail end of just about every Senate session. But what does it *mean?*

Distressed, on his own, hoping to get his tour off on the best foot, Nixon said in a roundabout way that the Senate resolution didn't mean anything, despite the fervor of its language and the publicity it got.

Khrushchev was genuinely puzzled for a time.

"You mean it is just horse shit?" he asked incredulously.

Nixon nodded and the tension disappeared. Khrushchev skipped over to his desk, scooped up a miniature of Sputnik I, and brandished it before Nixon like an old child braying proudly over a new toy. His gamesmanship was showing badly, but Nixon saw nothing to do about it, then. They rode to the fair together in Khrushchev's limousine.

John Daly, then chief of news and special events at ABC, and I were luckily positioned at the entrance of the Exposition grounds as Khrushchev and Nixon arrived, followed by Mikoyan, Klimenti Voroshilov, the powerless president Khrushchev pointedly ignored, Kozlov, and bumbling Yuri Zhukov. Khrushchev, wearing a cheap little white hat with a brim that was in contrast to his breadth, beckoned Mikoyan to his side and gruffly introduced Nixon.

Determinedly polite, Nixon shook hands warmly and enthused, "Oh, yes, I met Mr. Mikoyan when he was in Washington. In the United States we have great respect for Mr. Mikoyan's ability as a trader. Everybody in our country recognizes Armenians as the greatest of traders." Through his interpreter, Khrushchev barked, "Then your country has forgotten how to trade. Mikoyan couldn't make a single deal while he was there." With that, Khrushchev led the way to heavy wire gates behind which at least a hundred cameramen fired away. Nixon turned to Daly and me as the procession began.

"Maybe I shouldn't have gotten into that," he said of the abruptly demolished talk about U.S.-Soviet trade.

There wasn't a kitchen in sight when the famous "kitchen debate" began. The wrangle between the temporal tsar of all the Russias and the man from Whittier, California, began in RCA's color TV pavilion. The schedule called for Nixon to show it off as an American scientific marvel, make a brief video tape with him, and move on. But Khrushchev noticed that the glassed-in gallery that looked down into the studio where they paused was crowded with attentive and admiring constituents. The prospect of appearing on a tape that would be seen on American TV a day or two later also struck Khrushchev as a lively challenge. The camera's red light glowed. A floor director nodded to Nixon. He was on. He had just plunged into a description of color TV for Khrushchev's benefit when Khrushchev grumpily said that Russian scientists had developed the same thing years before. And from that curious springboard he launched into a sputtering attack on U.S. overseas bases. Before Nixon could speak (Khrushchev's words were already being applauded by Russians in the gallery), the dictator also charged that the United States was deliberately fomenting a war over Berlin.

It was embarrassing. Nixon's smile became a grimace. Once he tried, "Now back to color TV . . ." but that's as far as the bullying monologist in the crazy white hat would let him go. Nixon was being held personally responsible for the lag in U.S.-Soviet trade, continuity of cultural exchanges, and what Khrushchev decreed was the average American's contempt for all Russian achievements. The camera was still on.

Clearly, it was then or never for Nixon. Suddenly he jabbed his right forefinger at his truculent guest.

"Just a moment," he said, louder than Khrushchev had been talking. "You're trying to dominate this talk. You would've made a good lawyer. Don't give *me* your ultimatums."

"Who is giving ultimatums?" Khrushchev spouted through his interpreter.

"This is hardly the time and place to hold a debate," Nixon beefed, looking around the studio at the litter of the scheduled plans.

"Why not now?" Khrushchev dared. He looked up at his fans and when they got the translation from the monitors placed strategically in the gallery, they cheered. Khrushchev tried a new tack.

"You will forgive me for raising my voice?"

Nixon turned to his own interpreter, Alexander Akalovsky, supplied by the State Department.

"Tell him not to worry. Tell him I've been insulted by experts."

"Will this exchange be broadcast in the United States?"

"Yes, it will."

"It will be so edited," Khrushchev declared, "that it will hardly be recognizable."

"It will be played just as it has been done here. I give you my word on that. But will it be shown to the Russian people?"

"Of course," Khrushchev said expansively. "If you show it, we'll show it. But I have reason to worry about how much of it you will show. You suppress."

"We suppress! Listen, for every word you print in your papers from a speech by our President, we print a hundred words of your speeches."

I found myself suddenly shouting, "That's telling him, Dick!" a most lamentable lapse in reportorial impartiality. I was not alone.

"So you will show it all?" Khrushchev repeated.

"Of course we will."

Khrushchev suddenly reached his right arm straight up, brought it down like a semaphor, seized Nixon's hand, and pumped it like a handle.

"Shake," he said, somewhat redundantly.

Khrushchev acted just as rudely later in front of the kitchen exhibit in the model American home. There was a preposterous exchange that grew out of a misinterpretation of the word "dictate." Nixon took advantage of a semicolon in one of Khrushchev's nonstop sentences to observe piously that no country, however strong, should attempt to dictate to a lesser nation. Khrushchev replied heatedly that he resented being called a dictator.

"We will answer your threats with threats," he shouted while reporters and cameramen jostled in the dense crowd around the antagonists. "We have means at our disposal which can have very bad consequences for you."

"We have, too!" Nixon answered toughly, poking him in the chest.

Subsequently, the GOP distributed tons of copies of that stirring picture of the nominee "standing up to Khrushchev." But not enough tons, apparently.

It was not much of a fair we spread before the visitors to Sokolniki Park, but they loved it. The eyes of stolid housewives were moist but enormously proud as they accepted their free shampoos, sets and hairdrys. A large head of Abraham Lincoln commanded the same bovine attention one observed at the mausoleum in Red Square. Shoes, pots and pans, vacuum cleaners, toasters, refrigerators, stocked deep-freezers, textiles, and carpentry sets created a constant chatter of admiration and bashful (or fearful) inquiries as to how such wonders might be purchased. The library, although pruned of 150 volumes the Russians considered offensive, was a top attraction. Several Russians were arrested by covertly deployed Soviet police for attempting to spirit books out of the exhibit. The weight of the law also fell on a group of Russians employed by the Pepsi Cola exhibit. One night when no one was looking they drank the thick, gagging Pepsi syrup-concentrate.

A carefree lull before subsequent and most ominous storms—the U-2 debacle, collapse of the Eisenhower-Khrushchev-de Gaulle-Macmillan Summit, and the Cuban missile crisis—permeated Moscow with Nixon and the Exposition on view. Moscow was "in" that summer for the more adventurous American tourists. Newsmen were everywhere, among them that noteworthy anachronism on the fabled scene, Westbrook Pegler. That's how far the bars had been lowered in the U.S.S.R. of that vintage year of '59. I wrote a column about him that started: "Moscow—Westbrook Pegler and I picked up our copies of the London Daily Worker today and hurried off to 10:30 Mass."

We did, too. Peg's prime cause of choler, Franklin Delano Roosevelt, had wrung a modest concession from Stalin in exchange for U.S. diplomatic recognition of the Soviet Union in 1933: One American priest would be allowed to maintain residence and chapel in Moscow. The Assumptionist Fathers were selected to staff this outpost. Peg grumbled a bit about going to Mass. He hadn't been since shortly after the Council of Nicaea, or thereabouts. But once we were on the way his interest quickened. I alerted him to be on the lookout for the Russian cop stationed in the phone booth/pill box near the entrance of the eight-story apartment house and office building on whose top floor was hidden the tiny chapel and living quarters of Fr. Louis F. Dion. Peg gave the cop a comprehensive sneer.

Father Dion, a large man who is now president of Assumption College in Worcester, Massachusetts, was delighted to meet Peg. He showed him his tiny domain: a tight-fitting sanctuary just big enough to hold the small altar, a good-sized wall ikon of the Virgin and Child, and himself; an adjoining room which could seat a congregation of perhaps eighteen or twenty on two divans and folding chairs, and a small bedroom and kitchen in the rear. The heady scent of a coffee pot percolating on the stove was Father Dion's favorite incense. He weaved and bobbed into his vestments and was off about his holy business. Peg and I took the two remaining chairs and tried to lose ourselves in certain old truths by now wholly alien to the land around us.

Pegler's somewhat surprisingly reverent reverie was dissolved by the arrival, late, of an attractive young woman—probably from one of the Latin embassies—and her son of three or four. Peg rose in his courtliest manner and offered his seat to her. She gave him a brief but dazzling smile, but put the child on the seat—whereon he squirmed and fretted and made a general nuisance of himself for the remainder of the service. On the way back to the huge, homely Hotel Ukraina Peg was still warmed by the morning's experience and uncommonly mellow.

"Isn't that something, persevering like that priest does?" he asked, not expecting an answer. "And how about that beautiful girl? Imagine a beautiful thing like that stuck over here in Russia." I began to worry a bit about my friend, and wondered if he was feeling well. But the worry was soon erased.

"How about that kid?"

What about the kid?

"The goddam kid the mother plunked down in my seat instead of sitting on it herself," Peg said, letting winter back into his eagle eyes. "The Catholic Church is wronger than Hell on its stand against birth control."

Now Nixon and his camp followers were given unprecedented permission to advance en masse on Novosibirsk, the largest industrial center of Siberia, and Sverdlovsk, chief heavy machinery complex in the foothills of the Urals and (when it bore its original name, Ekaterinburg) scene of the mass execution of Czar Nicholas II and his family by the Bolsheviks in 1918. It was a journey that could be called tensely hilarious.

Mir i druzhba! ("Peace and friendship") was our slogan and just about exhausted our knowledge of the language. At times the motto lacked meaning. Yuri Zhukov was our shepherd and set out each day to wring the neck of any peace dove which might flutter into view. His people had been sent out in advance to choose and brief the "typical workers" Nixon would be steered to. During his tour of a Novosibirsk plant Nixon found himself blocked by a "worker" who asked him a question which must have constituted Topic A at night around the samovars of every worker's hovel in the city: "When will the United States cease atomic tests, which imperil the peoples of the world with fallouts of strontium 90?"

There was seldom any effort made to answer the planted questions because the interrogators had been trained only to ask, not to engage in subsequent dialogue. Usually when Nixon tried to answer he'd be interrupted by another question on a wholly new subject, and that, too, called for no reply. The *Tass* and *Izvestia* reporters who accompanied us dutifully filed stories about the American vice president's inability to find honest answers to the searching questions of peace-loving workers. One day at Sverdlovsk a man who identified himself as a foreman stopped the Nixon party and proclaimed in a loud voice, "Look at the lovely sky! Do you see any Iron Curtain keeping you from getting through?"

Browned off, Nixon blazed, "Yes, I can. Let's take radio, for instance. We can listen to your broadcasts. But you can't listen to ours because your government jams them."

This was not the way his script was written, so the man started a different question. Nixon wouldn't let him finish. Tough and audible he now said, "Mr. Khrushchev says many things we don't like, see? Such as his statement that our grandchildren will live under Communism. But those things are printed in our country and are heard on our radio. We expect our people to listen, to read, and make up their own minds as to whether this is a fair prediction. We believe sincerely that you've made great progress in the Soviet Union. But we also believe that you would make greater progress if you had, or were permitted to have, a full exchange of ideas."

When he had his interpretation the foreman came up with an answer indicative of the futility of *mir i druzhba*. His reply was, "What you say about our progress is correct. But how you say it is a dirty slander."

Occasionally, a member of Nixon's official party would come to his aid.

"What about your rocket bases?" someone in a crowd of workers taunted as Nixon passed.

"What about *your* rockets?" a sharp and commanding voice retorted. It was Vice Admiral Hyman Rickover, who had been doing a slow burn since his arrival with the Nixon group. He strode up to Nixon's heckler, armed with an interpreter, looked him over with contempt and said, "You're not a worker, you're a politician." The admiral made it sound like a bad word. "I don't want to talk to politicians." As he turned and started to walk away, the man protested that he was not a politician. Rickover turned again.

"Then you're a Communist," he said, sizing him up.

"No," the man said, "I'm just a candidate for party membership."

"All the same thing," Rickover said, breaking it like a stick. "I don't want to talk to party members either. I want to talk to the people, if we can ever find them."

But there was laughter, too, and a fresh look at life in the Soviet hinterland.

The press hostel at Novosibirsk was a bit Spartan for the tastes of the American newsmen. The lone rusty toilet and cold-water sink at the end of the corridor of tiny rooms produced an unhappy queue in the mornings. One morning James Reston of the *Times,* having braved the primitive plumbing, strolled back to his crib past a line of his waiting confreres. He spotted George Healy, New Orleans *Times Picayune* editor who had recently conducted a campaign that resulted in the confinement in a mental institution of Louisiana Governor Earl Long.

Reston stopped and regarded his friend Healy, standing there in Siberia in his pajama bottoms, holding a ragged little towel, and waiting his turn to use a water closet that wouldn't flush.

"And you called Earl Long crazy," Reston said, shaking his head.

One night in Sverdlovsk the big band at the hotel's dining room and cabaret drew an unexpected guest drummer, William Randolph Hearst, Jr. The band's repertoire offered no problems to him. All the arrangements were from Glenn Miller, Tommy Dorsey, and other American maestros whose works had been pirated by means of short-wave radio and laborious counterarrangements. Another night Conniff and I discovered that we could drink a massive amount of vodka if we sat all evening with the mayor of the oblast. Conniff would pour a drink, neat, all around, we'd click our little glasses, say *"Mir i druzhba!"* and down the hatch. Then I'd pour one around and we'd do the same. Then the Mayor. It was the only thing we had to say until closing time, but Hearst had something to say after closing time. He said, "Watch it, you two. You were hitting it awful heavy tonight." He was unaccountably serious.

We wished him a cordial *mir i druzhba,* and were immensely relieved the following night to find him back in the drum section, flailing away at "Tiger Rag."

The homestretch of the Nixon visit was a trial to him and a time for sober assessment of Soviet ways on the part of those with him. John Daly worked long and hard to provide Nixon with proper technical aids for his appearance on Soviet TV. But just before air time two of the three studio cameras suffered suspicious power failures. Daly was somehow able to browbeat the remaining camera's crew into changing the angle from time to time to give variety to Nixon's discourse.

It remains the bluntest talk the Kremlin ever permitted its peoples to hear from a foreigner's lips. Simultaneously interpreted by Akalovsky, Nixon said in part:

"Both of our peoples want peace, but both of us also possess great strength, and much as we want peace, neither of us can or will tolerate being pushed around. . . . If you doubt that the American government and the American people are as dedicated to peace as you are, look at our record and you can reach only one conclusion, that only aggressor nations have anything to fear from the United States of America. . . .

"Why do we maintain military bases around the world? Well, let's look at the record. We disarmed rapidly after World War II. Then came a series of events which threatened our friends abroad as well as ourselves. The Berlin blockade and the war in Korea are typical of the actions which led the United States and our allies to rearm . . . Whenever the fear and suspicion that caused us and our allies to take measures for collective self-defense are removed, the reason for our maintaining bases will be removed. The only possible solution of this problem lies in mutual rather than unilateral action leading to disarmament. . . .

"Let us expand the concept of open skies. What the world also needs are open cities, open minds, and open hearts. Let us have peaceful competition not only in producing the best factories but in producing better lives for our people. Let us cooperate in our exploration of outer space. As a worker told me in Novosibirsk, 'Let's go to the moon together.' Let our aim be not victory over other people, but the victory of all mankind over hunger, want, misery, and disease."

There was no way to calculate the number of TV and radio stations that carried the broadcast. But one indication that it may have had widespread impact was the last-minute decision to have Frol Kozlov make a twenty-minute speech at the airport when Nixon departed a day or two later. Kozlov's speech rehashed everything Khrushchev had been saying, with a little of Stalin thrown in for good measure. It was an insulting farewell. The newsmen were given something of a grilling, too, before they were permitted to board the TWA Boeing 707 they had chartered to take them out into the free world. The closer they came to leaving, the cooler the Intourist guides became. In Novosibirsk the four rather prim young ladies from Intourist who had been assigned to us blossomed in much more feminine suits and dresses, took a drink and even danced with us. Alexander Rogow, manager of the big Intourist bureau in the National Hotel, became the soul of conviviality once we had put some distance between ourselves and Moscow. But at the airport Rogow had become stiff and stern, and it was "Mister" here and "Mister" there instead of "Bill" or "Frank." Three of the four girls disappeared into the rotting woodwork at the terminal and the survivor seemed petrified by some nameless dread.

Our passports were held up for an unnervingly long time. Then a dozen or so were returned to their owners, who promptly proceeded to board the waiting jet while the rest of us sweated matters out in Customs and Passport. But after a time those who had boarded the plane were ordered to return to the terminal. They had to yield their passports once more for further mysterious scrutiny. We concluded that somebody was attempting to make a break for freedom in the general hurly-burly of our noisy leave-taking, and the Russians were out to thwart his/her/their plans.

At long last, passports repossessed and clutched in our hands, we walked to the steps of the jet. But there was still another barrier. At the top of the steps, blocking the door, stood three Russian police who would have had to be cast as turnkeys in the darkest dungeons of Lubyanka prison. The goon in the middle demanded my passport. He opened it to the identifying picture, and then he and the other two glared at it, then at me, then at it, then at me, grunted, shoved it back to me, and opened up enough room for me to enter. In all my travels, it was the only time I ever felt happy about looking like my passport picture.

The pattern of the Hearst Task Force remains unique. At the start of its operations, Kingsbury Smith and Conniff presented Hearst with a format that made our subsequent newsgathering unlike any method that had preceded. Hearst would be presented to the celebrity who was to be interviewed as an equal rather than as one of several story-seeking reporters. He scoffed at the notion at first but came to realize that his name was a most effective door-opener, and in just about any chancellory in the civilized world. From that posture of equality ensued a writing style which sets a Hearst Task Force interview apart from all others. I have lost track of the number of stories, written under my by-line, which began: "Prime Minister so and so told William Randolph Hearst, Jr., today that . . ."

This tacit rapport between Hearst and the personality being interviewed has additional advantages. It enables Hearst to ask tougher and meatier questions—questions which if asked by one who is known simply as a reporter might antagonize the person being interviewed. During some of our interviews I've detected that the figure being interviewed—no matter how unapproachable and clam-mouthed under ordinary circumstances—went out of his way to reveal or explain first-rate stories to Hearst. Intuitively, Hearst is at home with any world figure. Moreover, he comes endowed with a low boring point. That can be a prodding force. In our 1957 Khrushchev interview, his most illuminating information was given to us after the first hour, at which precise point Bill had looked at his wristwatch and said to Conniff and me, "Isn't that about enough?"

Hearst's status in our reportorial apparatus was perhaps best recognized by Sukarno, who gave us one of his rare interviews at his palace in Jakarta in the fall of 1963. He welcomed Hearst with open arms as we entered, then piercingly inspected the editor-in-chief's companions.

"What was your name again?" he asked me. I repeated it.

"Considine . . . Considine . . . what kind of a name is that?"

I said it was an Irish name springing chiefly from County Clare. Astonishingly, the man knew Clare and its foremost product, Eamon de Valera, and excitedly recalled how he had emulated de Valera's revolutionary tactics.

He turned to Frank and repeated the question he had asked me. "Conniff . . . Conniff . . . and what kind of a name is that?" Conniff told him Irish. He beckoned us into comfortable chairs around his desk, pried the top off a round tin of Gold Flakes, and lighted one. He exhaled happily, looked at the cigarette, and said, "The only good thing about the British—their cigarettes."

For the next half hour the jaunty popinjay sprayed a stream of invective over just about every subject from Malaysia to motherhood. He let us know when he had finished by snapping his fingers to a waiting guard and saying, "Tell my Cabinet to come in."

It entered, an odd mix of civilian and military, intellectual and thug. Some were executed in the purge of 1966. Hearst, Conniff, and I stood up. Sukarno remained sprawled comfortably in his chair. He held out a languid hand for each Cabinet officer to touch or shake. When they were all present and accounted for, Sukarno put the identity of the visitors in focus for his ministers.

"Gentlemen," he said, "I want you to meet the very distinguished American journalist, William Randolph Hearst, Jr. And two Irishmen."

Task Force memories do not lend themselves to orderly sequence, nor is it invariably the headlines that linger.

I think of Henry Cabot Lodge, starchy in his air-conditioned embassy in ovenlike Saigon, assuring Hearst, Conniff, Warren Rogers, and me that when we called on Ngo Dinh Diem the next evening, as scheduled, we'd find a broken man who had lost his hold. Diem turned out to be enormously vigorous and positive in his plans ("We won't need your American troops after the end of 1965"). He defended his sister-in-law's right to act like a female. He said he had no intention of acceding to demands from Washington that he fire his brother and political adviser Ngo Dinh Nhu. ("What would be President Kennedy's reaction if Vietnam asked him to fire Robert Kennedy?") Diem further demanded that Lodge turn over to Vietnamese authorities a Buddhist rabble rouser then being given asylum in the Embassy—one Thich Tri Quang. The Embassy refused. On a subsequent trip to Vietnam to cover the Constitutional Assembly elections, the Ambassador told me that he felt Tri Quang would have been killed if he had been turned away the night he burst into the Embassy, hotly pursued by police. The following day Lodge was instructed by the State Department to keep the monk indefinitely. Lodge, informed of the impending CIA-supported coup to unseat Diem, made two attempts to persuade the doomed President to accept asylum at the Embassy. Diem refused, insisting that he would be able to cope with any threat to his position. Lodge then wrung from Maj. Gen. Duong Van Minh, soon to take over, a pledge that he would guarantee Diem and his brother safe-conduct out of the country. They were murdered while in the custody of Minh's men.

I think of Jawaharlal Nehru elegantly descending the great staircase of his residence in New Delhi, delicate rosebud peeping from an opening in his impeccable tunic, snow-white Congress Party cap cocked just right, great dark sultry eyes set in his ascetic's head. He was approaching seventy-four, yet had spent most of that day inspecting Indian Army positions, on foot and without added oxygen, along the 11,000 to 13,000 foot Ladakh front facing the Red Chinese Army. He led us to an elegantly decorated sitting room, clapped softly for tea, and tried patiently to explain to his highly skeptical friend, Hearst, that (1) he felt there was an opportunity for the generally hated Krishna Menon to make a comeback in government; (2) that the aggression by the Chinese had not altered India's determination to remain a neutral and unaligned power; and (3) if Red China's name came up for membership in the UN, India would vote affirmatively.

I think of Walter Ulbricht, goateed chairman of East Germany's Council of State, giving us the full treatment in East Berlin: conference room, lights, cameras, beaming fellow puppets, hearty handshakes for the East German TV newsreels, and the booming voice with which he began reading his statement. Hearst stopped him. "We didn't come here for a statement," he said. "We came to ask questions." The lights began to go out, one by one. Ulbricht grew unhappier with each question. It ended on a ludicrous note. He declared at length that West German forces were secretly armed with atomic weapons whereas East German troops and their Red Army colleagues had only conventional weapons. I remembered Khrushchev had bragged to us that his troops in East Germany packed every known modern weapon. So I stopped Ulbricht in mid-flight and with mock shock asked, "Are you calling Comrade Khrushchev a liar?" That put out the last light.

I think of *Der Alte,* Konrad Adenauer. As we marched into his office in Bonn we were Hearst, Conniff, Fliegers, our UN chief Pierre Huss (who had known Hitler before the war), and four West German press officers. Adenauer looked at the group, eyes smiling through the wrinkled iron mask that was his face. "Who's to be shot?" he asked. I remember his mild condescension toward Khrushchev: "He's not a Communist, he's trying to be either Ivan the Terrible or Peter the Great. He doesn't have nearly the naked power Stalin had." And I can still hear the old man say, "Someday, and I will not be alive, China will attack Russia with millions and millions of troops, and whoever rules the Kremlin at that time will turn his face to the West and cry out, 'Save us. We are white. Save us from this Yellow horde.'" The old man was quiet for a moment. Then he added with a weary chuckle, "And you will."

I think of the pomp and circumstance of our interview with Franco. It had more of the trappings of an audience than a press conference. We were led through a series of ornate salons and galleries all but as impressive as those that lead to the throne room of the Pope. The generalissimo wore his sunburst of medals, insignia, lower chest medallions and sword. He said that some of his best friends were Americans. He told of resisting great pressures brought to bear on him by Hitler to persuade him to permit the panzers to sweep through Spain and attack Gibraltar. Ideologically, he had become disillusioned with Hitler. The fact that Hitler had deigned to do business with Stalin, even for a brief period, stuck in Franco's craw and he told him off at great risk. Would he mind letting us see the correspondence with Hitler? Yes, indeed, he would mind. He'd mind very much.

I think of the following day in Lisbon. The tin gate to the modest residence of Antonio de Oliveira Salazar, premier since 1932, was guarded by two drowsy policemen, whereas the long driveway leading to the doors of Franco's palace had been double-lined with gorgeously uniformed mounted guards. The drowsy Portuguese cops swung back the door and our car crunched across a pebbled drive to the little flight of stone steps leading to a green front door straight from Main Street. We rang and a painfully shy rosy-jawed maid showed us into a dim, drab sitting room. Everything was as gray as a funeral parlor. After five minutes alone we were joined by a gray-faced, gray-haired, gray-suited, and slightly harried man, obviously some sort of clerk in the dictator's office. He stuck out his hand toward Hearst. "Salazar," he said.

I think of Generalissimo Chiang Kai-shek, and brittlely brilliant Madame. They couldn't wait to see us, that late afternoon at their pleasant summer place in the hills up from Taipei. They had moved the interview up twenty-four hours because two days before in Tokyo Premier Hayato Ikeda had told us (and we had reported) that nobody any longer took seriously Chiang's wordy pledges to liberate mainland China. Madame hardly waited for Hearst to blow on his tea. She quietly blazed, "This Ikeda person you give so much attention to is a nobody, a nothing. Why, he was a *clark* in Manchuria when my husband was a general. Why did you publish such an interview?" Hearst said he published it because it was news, but that made Madame angrier. "And I say you should not have," she said indignantly. Chiang sat through the exchange with the set, uncomprehending smile of a polite old man. Bill looked at him, and then at Madame. "Looky," he said to her, "I'll run my newspapers; you run your country."

There are so many other memories, born of the wondrous fact that Hearst cared enough to be a reporter as well as an editor, publisher, and rich man's son.

An ominous roadblock across a hazardous Tunisian highway, at night. Premier/President Habib Bourguiba had sent out word to stop Hearst's car! And invite him back to Tunis for a late dinner. . . . A strange omelet served to the Task Force and their wives at a luncheon given by Venezuela's President Romulo Betancourt. "What's in it?" Mrs. Hearst asked sweetly as we all chewed tentatively. "Many flowers," Betancourt said proudly. We all stopped chewing, our mouths filled. "He means many *flavors,*" the President's interpreter laughed. Chewing resumed. . . . An open window in the Elysée Palace, commanding a view of the magnificent gardens. Charles de Gaulle, having peremptorily ended a general press conference, had marched out of the conference room. Now he appeared in radiant profile, moving past the window like a newsreel. Fliegers cried out to him to pause and meet *le journalist plus grand,* William Randolph Hearst. De Gaulle reached his hamlike hand right past Bill and shook hands with me. Aghast, Serge tried again. Once again de Gaulle's big mitt came through the open window. This time he seized and shook *Serge's* hand, and moved off like a huge wound-up doll.

With Winston Churchill, who had once worked for W. R. Hearst, Sr., Bill always had it made. The old man tended to hate reporters in his later years. But he always made a point of seeing Bill in the wake of a Task Force venture. He'd be damned, however, if he'd see any of the rest of us.

Just Bill.

Just Our Bill, a kind of one-man Navy whom you can join and see the whole blinking world.

9. *The Fraudulent Art of Spooking*

ONE OF THE more lugubrious callings within the literary stockade is ghostwriting. As in other reaches of the supernatural, there are good ghost-writers and bad ghost-writers. The bad ghost-writer inflicts his own words, thought patterns, philosophy and morality on the facade of another man's story. The good ghost-writer emulates a sheep dog who merely keeps the flock cohesive and headed in the proper direction, and he never yearns to join it.

The *Concise Oxford Dictionary* makes no such distinction. Its fourth definition of *ghost* (*gō-*), *n.*, & *v.t.* & *i* glacially states: "Artistic or literary hack doing the work for which his employer takes credit."

That's not quite true, or adequate. The employer, whose by-line dominates the book or article or speech prepared for him by the spook, does not automatically take credit in the wake of publication. It all depends on how the offering was received by the audience. If it is praised, all's well and good. He wonders why he needed a ghost in the first place; he could just as easily have done it all on his own. But if the effort with the bogus by-line is condemned or, worse, ignored, then there is no vestige of credit-taking. The ghost is to blame. He didn't capture the *real* me, the employer will swear all the way to his distant grave.

There are other complications that tend to militate against the integration of ghosts and their masters. When Zsa Zsa Gabor failed to marry her ghost, Gerold Frank, at the climax of their literary rapport, I, as a paid-up member of the ghostly guild, was willing to wager that never would the twain, between hack and employer, meet.

Gerold Frank is a self-effacing wraith, perhaps the best in the strange business. Others are not so selfless. Insensitive hacks who produce win-

268

ners for their inarticulate employers can sometimes make themselves quite obnoxious. I've known spooks who thought they were worth as much as a one-third financial interest in a succesful book they wrote under a nonwriter's name. One such boor is said to have had the bad manners to show up at a New York Herald Tribune Book Luncheon honoring the author-of-record. Another put in an appearance at NBC one bleak dawn to offer to help his straw man answer Hugh Downs's distressingly searching questions about a book. Worst of all, certain ghosts have been known to get stoned late at night in public houses and loudly reverse the pattern of the Concise Oxford's No. 4 definition by taking all the credit themselves.

One would think that the relationship between spook and master would smack of the cozy togetherness of the confessional. Not so. There is always a certain reserve, particularly at the beginning. In the days before I was exorcised of my spook quotient, I'd generally try to evade the assignment altogether.

"Try writing it yourself," I'd say as earnestly as I could. "You're the only person in the world who really knows what happened to you, or what you want to say. So do it."

"But I can't *write*," was the standard complaint.

"Then speak it into a tape machine, hire somebody to transcribe it, and, presto!—you'll have your book in your own inimitable style, your kind of words."

They never believed me. Looking back, I'm glad some of them didn't, for they enriched my life.

I felt throughout my ghosting days that the doer of the deeds to be chronicled deserved to feel that he was a cut above the scrivener he had fetched to put the glorious saga into high-school English at least. Douglas MacArthur would have agreed with my outlook. In his forgotten but gorgeous report to a probably confounded Calvin Coolidge, after commanding the victorious 1928 U.S. Olympic team, MacArthur dipped his pen deep into his purple inkpot and wrote:

> In undertaking this difficult task, I recall a passage in Plutarch wherein Themistocles, being asked whether he would rather be Achilles or Homer, replied: "Which would you rather be, a conqueror in the Olympic Games or the crier who proclaims who are conquerors?" . . . I can but record the bare, blunt facts, trusting that imagination will supply the magic touch to that which can never be forgotten by those who were actually present. . . ."

MacArthur was writing about a reporter's plight in this case, of course. But a ghost is a reporter of sorts. He is an interviewer who is expected to give the employer—ugly word!—his head, see what he can do to make the story sing like a high-tension wire, and provide protective covering for all exposed feet of clay.

Ghosting is a major industry in this country. A vast majority of all statements, proclamations and communiqués which shower down on the public from high places is written or polished by obscure professionals. The nation has been blessed with a large number of responsible Presidents, particularly in times of national and international stress. But only a handful were able to write their way out of a wet paper bag: Jefferson... Lincoln... Teddy Roosevelt... Wilson... Kennedy. I would think the list ended there.

The more stirring phrases of Franklin Delano Roosevelt, trumpets that heralded a new social order and a call to arms to protect it in a great war, were his thoughts filtered through the golden vocabularies of pros like Robert Sherwood. The poetry that laced John Fitzgerald Kennedy's public utterances was a reflection of the man himself, but also adorned with the clean glitter imparted by Arthur Schlesinger, Jr., or Ted Sorensen.

The two worst deliverers of good ghosted material in my time as a member of the White House Correspondents were Harry S. Truman and Dwight D. Eisenhower. Each gave the impression that he had never seen the document at hand before plunging into the cold water of its first sentence. Neither had the foggiest notion about when to pause for audience reaction; each always looked up impatiently from the text when their audiences exercised their constitutional right to applaud. By that time, each would have charged well into the next sentence.

Emmett John Hughes, who can write like a sexy Walter Lippmann when the moon is full, composed many memorable speeches for President Eisenhower. But if Emmett had written another Gettysburg Address, Ike could still have made it sound like a 4-H Club's silage report. Like Truman and some of the others, Ike read speches for his own amazement. In the thick of the 1952 campaign, he appeared to start with surprise when he announced that, if elected, "I will go to Korea."

President Johnson wants no traffic with what he clearly feels were the dude words put in his predecessor's mouth by the Harvard hacks, and thus has gathered to his court spooks closer to his style and gait. His style is John Wayne waiting, steely-eyed, for Geronimo to start playing dirty again. His gait, one would estimate without ready recourse to a tracking station, is Dr. Billy Graham. In slow motion.

I once ghosted a speech for Herbert Hoover which, I like to think, contributed something to his latter-day image as one of the mellow fellows. The occasion was a sports rally at Madison Square Garden to raise funds for Finland, at that time giving the Red Army an inspiring pasting in the ice-caked forests of the Karelian Isthmus. Sports columnist Joe Williams of the New York *World Telegram* and other Scripps-Howard papers was chairman of the affair and thus in a position to order me, a simple spear carrier on the lengthy committee, to compose something to put on Mr. Hoover's tongue.

Thousands at the Garden marveled at the former President's keen knowledge of Paavo Nurmi, and the David-like Stanley Ketchel's courage the day he flattened Goliath-sized Jack Johnson. No ghost is ever completely satisfied with the way a person reads his words, but the thirty-first President's delivery was better than average. We once had a New York mayor who, in the course of reading a ghosted speech to a distinguished audience at the Waldorf, lunged into a passage which began:

"All of which reminds me of the story of Pat and Mike. One fine day while walking past St. Patrick's Cathedral, Pat said to Mike. . . ."

The mayor's voice trailed off absently and died away, and the surprised audience beheld him silently scanning his script.

Suddenly, he burst into loud laughter. He had never read the joke before. Looking up, he seemed startled to find he had company. Then he plowed onward with his speech.

Herbert Hoover never knew who wrote his brave-little-Finland speech. Other famed Americans exercised much closer control over my ghosting services.

One was Gen. Jonathan M. Wainwright, author of *General Wainwright's Story* (. . . edited by Robert Considine, the dust jacket stated).

The fine old soldier had suffered through nearly four harrowing years as a prisoner of the Japanese. He was beaten, starved, humiliated. But his most constant worry during all that time was that he had let his country down by surrendering. He kept a sketchy diary during

his years as a POW, a thin three-by-four-inch notebook in which he
inscribed, in a script more suited to the head of a pin, certain events
and disasters of his confinement.

Long periods, sometimes months, might be encompassed in a single
terrible word, such as "hungry." Other abysmal trials went unrecorded,
such as the quarrel among the distinguished senior officers in his POW
billet. One of them was accused of not sharing the worm he had discovered in his bowl of dirty rice. Such was the craving for protein.

The longest passages in the general's notebook dealt with his soul-
searching explanation of why he considered it better to surrender than
fight to the last man. He had said it all in his last two messages from
Corregidor, one to President Roosevelt, the other to General Mac-
Arthur in Australia.

The message to the President on May 6, 1942, read:

> With broken heart and head bowed in sadness but not in shame
> I report to Your Excellency that today I must arrange terms for
> the surrender of the fortified islands of Manila Bay.
> With many guns and anti-aircraft fire control equipment de-
> stroyed we are no longer able to prevent accurate bombardment
> from the air. With numerous batteries of heavy caliber emplaced
> on the shores of Bataan and Cavite the enemy now brings dev-
> astating crossfire to bear on us, outranging our remaining guns.
> . . . There is a limit of human endurance and that limit has
> long since been passed. Without prospect of relief I feel it is my
> duty to my country and to my gallant troops to end this useless
> effusion of blood and human sacrifice. . . . With profound regret
> and with continued pride in my gallant troops I go to meet the
> Japanese commander.
>
> Good-bye, Mr. President.

The message to MacArthur was more personal, for MacArthur had
repeatedly urged him to hold on. It read, in part:

> American and Filipino troops have engaged and held the enemy
> for nearly five months. . . . We have done our full duty for you
> and for our country. We are sad but unashamed. I have fought
> for you to the best of my ability from Lingayen Gulf to Bataan
> to Corregidor, always hoping relief was on the way. . . .
> Good-bye, General, my regards to you and our comrades in
> Australia. May God strengthen your arm to insure ultimate suc-
> cess of the cause for which we have fought side by side.

Wainwright was haunted throughout his captivity by the thought that the messages may not have gotten to their destinations, or been given short shrift if they did. By an unnerving coincidence he was interviewed one day in the worst of his several prison camps by a Domei correspondent whose first question was, "Do you think you will be court-martialed if you ever returned to the United States?"

Instead, Wainwright was promoted to four-star rank, given a hero's welcome when he reached home—gaunt as a skeleton but straight as a sword. President Truman pinned the Congressional Medal of Honor on his chest at the White House, King Features Syndicate paid him $155,000 for newspaper rights to his story (plus $5,000 to me for writing the forty-two part series), and Doubleday gave him a $25,000 advance for the book rights.

It was a memorable experience.

Each morning for a month, that saffron autumn of '45, I'd climb the hill to his cottage overlooking famous old Greenbrier, White Sulphur Springs, West Virginia, then known as Ashford General Hospital. He would be seated on the porch if the weather was fine, lean and spent in his fresh khaki, coatless, shirt open at the collar, Adam's apple bobbing with a courtly "Good morning." A few yards away, in a quiet corner of the porch, Sgt. Archimedes Giacamantonio, the sculptor, shaped a blob of greenish clay into an increasingly taut likeness.

I would bring with me a first draft of what he had related the day before and which I had put through the typewriter the previous night. He'd put on his glasses, take a stubby pencil out of his breast pocket, and carefully read the material. He used the pencil more as a scanning tool than an editorial implement, I was always relieved to notice.

Indeed, during the entire time I spent with him, he made only two changes, each time wetting the little pencil's point in his mouth before applying it to the script.

The first of these changes had to do with the vanity that is in all who have a story to tell. MacArthur had willed Wainwright two jars of shaving cream and a box of cigars before leaving Corregidor for Australia. On April 28, 1942, having enjoyed a shave with the cream, Wainwright breakfasted in the convalescent mess inside Malinta Tunnel and then headed for an exit to breathe some fresh air and inspect a nearby battery.

About forty feet short of the barrier that protected the mouth of the tunnel, Wainwright stopped to light up one of the precious Mac-Arthur cigars. The decision saved his life. If he had continued walking he would reached the barrier just as it was struck by a 240 mm. Japanese shell.

Wainwright's left eardrum burst and the right ear lost much of its hearing. Armed with those facts, I had written, ". . . as a result I have been quite hard of hearing ever since." Actually, questions to him often had to be half-shouted.

The general drew a line through that phrasing and in his neat hand replaced it with ". . . and the right ear since then has never been up to its old standard."

The other change he made was an addition, a touching assessment of a scene that can have had no parallel in American military history, his departure from Corregidor in defeat. This is how he told it to me:

> Under guard, Colonel Haba led me and five of my staff officers out of the Tunnel's west end. And again we passed through my captured men. They were standing there in the blazing sun in the area where I had seen them the night before. Obviously, they had not been fed or given any water during that terrible time.
>
> They were in very bad shape. But as I walked through them they all got to their feet. Some stood at attention and saluted as I passed, and I raised my hand to my old sun helmet. Others just stood, took off their hats, and held them across their chests.
>
> Again I felt the tears welling up in my eyes and could do nothing to stop the emotion.

The general read the section without comment. Then, after priming his pencil, he slowly wrote:

> I am a student of the Civil War, but not until then did I know how General R. E. Lee felt after Appomattox.

Wainwright was among the less formal World War II generals. "Call me Skinny," he said cheerfully, the day we met. "Everybody else does except Douglas [MacArthur]. Douglas calls me Jonathan. Only man in the world who calls me Jonathan. So call me Skinny, Bob."

It was "Skinny" and "Bob" until the chronological narration reached that point where the general told of the first of several beatings he suffered. Under prodding, he described the scene: the grim prison compound at Karenko, on Formosa; the attack of beriberi which had stripped him to the bones, the drudgery on the prisoners' truck farm, the starvation . . . and a trip one night to the vile latrine. As he was returning to the barracks, a young Japanese sentry shouted at him. Wainwright related that he dutifully stopped, bowed, and waited for whatever it was the sentry had in store for him. Other prisoners "froze" nearby, silently watching the confrontation.

"The Jap swung very quickly and slapped me across the face," the general said calmly as we sat on the hushed porch. Mrs. Wainwright came out, sat near him, and composed herself.

"It was a stinging blow," he continued, "and in my throat I felt a rising gorge of hate and despair."

Suddenly, tears rolled down the old soldier's lined and weather-crusted cheeks.

"I stood there," he went on. "Encouraged by what he had done, the Jap slapped me again, then again, and then a fourth time. Each time he hit me he shouted, 'For Japanese in America!'

"The blows made my legs weaker, but I was determined not to fall at the feet of a rat like that. He saw that I was not going down, so he took a lunge at me and hit me on the left jaw with his fist. And then I fell. I was only half-conscious from the blow, but the part of my consciousness that was alive told me that this was the very pit of my life."

The general stopped talking. Mrs. Wainwright cupped her sad face in her right hand. I felt tears in my eyes.

"That dirty son of a bitch," I sympathized. But the reporter in me recognized that this was a moment when I must extract every last drop of the doleful episode.

"What else went through your mind as you lay there, Skinny?" I asked tenderly.

Wainwright slowly stiffened in his chair. His shoulders, which had dropped as he told his story, squared off. He fetched a newly laundered handkerchief from his pocket, dusted the tears from his cheeks and eyes, blew a thunderous blast from his nose, and regarded me coolly.

"I'll tell you what else went through my mind as I lay there, Mr. Considine," he said curtly. "And this is it: a private should never strike a lieutenant-general!"

I never dared call him Skinny again.

There were other exchanges which, like this one, did not get in the book. It soon was apparent to me that Mrs. Wainwright did not share her husband's dogged, if sometimes humor-tinged, loyalty to MacArthur. At dinner on two occasions, Mrs. Wainwright left the table at the first glowing reference to the Supreme Commander. It was abundantly clear that she felt MacArthur easily could have selected her husband among the fifteen top aides he took with him to Australia, along with Mrs. MacArthur, young Arthur, and the boy's amah.

"She always does that," the general explained the first time his wife departed. The second time he shouted, "Dammit, cut that out and come back to dinner!"

For all his admiration, Wainwright could poke fun at MacArthur, too.

"One day Douglas came over to Bataan to see me," the general recalled with the trace of a smile.

" 'Jonathan, where are your 155 mm. guns?' he asked. I told him where the six of them were, and since two of them were fairly close, I suggested that he walk over with me and take a look at them.

" 'Jonathan,' he said, 'I don't want to *see* them. I want to *hear* them!' "

He chuckled and remembered another one, which he did not want in his book:

"After the surrender ceremony on the Missouri, Douglas invited me to return to Yokohama with him on the destroyer that had brought us to the battleship. On the way he said, 'Well, Jonathan, I hear that you've been offered a lot of money for your memoirs.' I said that was true. 'Bully!' he said. 'You write them, then send them to me and I'll check them and send them on to the War Department.' "

Wainwright glanced sideways at me, smiled tightly and whispered, "I didn't do any such thing."

Only once during our long days together did Wainwright show even the faintest tinge of bitterness toward the man whose orders had caused him so much grief.

In the last days of the Battle of Corregidor, President Roosevelt sent a message to MacArthur in Australia, which was to be relayed to Wainwright "if you concur." Wainwright's radio people intercepted the message, said to have been written by Robert Sherwood. It read:

> During recent weeks we have been following with growing admiration the day-by-day accounts of your [Wainwright's] heroic stand against the mounting intensity of bombardment by enemy planes and heavy siege guns.

In spite of all the handicaps of complete isolation, lack of food, and ammunition you have given the world a shining example of patriotic fortitude and self-sacrifice.

The American people ask no finer example of tenacity, resourcefulness, and steadfast courage. The calm determination of your personal leadership in a desperate situation sets a standard of duty for our soldiers throughout the world.

In every camp and on every naval vessel soldiers, sailors, and Marines are inspired by the gallant struggle of their comrades in the Philippines. The workmen in our shipyards and munitions plants redouble their efforts because of your example.

You and your devoted followers have become the living symbols of our war aims and the guarantee of victory.

FRANKLIN D. ROOSEVELT.

Wainwright waited several days. MacArthur did not forward the tribute.

"Naturally, I was burned up," the general told me in retrospect. "So I repeated the entire Roosevelt message in a wireless to Douglas, and at the end of it I added one sentence: 'Apparently you did not concur.' "

MacArthur apologized briefly in a message to Wainwright in the final hours of the bloody defense of Corregidor, pleaded that the pressure of work had caused the oversight, and urged Wainwright to do his best to hold out.

Publication day, as always, was a happy one. The general had regained some of his weight and looked fine. The teeth that the sentry had knocked out had been replaced. He was at peace with the world. I hovered on the fringe of the admiring crowd which came forward at the party to ask him to autograph their copies of the book. When the crowd thinned out, I handed him my copy and asked him to sign it.

He did, in his firm hand. I treasure what he wrote:

"To 'The Gost'. . ."

The Pentagon presented no problem in the case of the Wainwright book, in contrast to the roadblocks it erected earlier in the path of *Thirty Seconds Over Tokyo,* by Capt. Ted W. Lawson, and "edited by Bob Considine."

I met with Ted the first time at the Mayflower Hotel in Washington in the Fall of 1942. He had participated in the Doolittle Raid the previous April as pilot of one of the sixteen B-25's used and lost on the mission. He had crashed just off the China coast after bombing Tokyo and been spirited out of the clutches of the occupying Japanese forces by friendly Chinese. His gangrenous left leg, gashed when he burst through the windshield of his plane—the bomber was prophetically named *The Ruptured Duck*—was amputated by the mission's flight surgeon, Capt. Thomas R. White, in a primitive Chinese hospital. But he lived and made it home in time to be near his wife Ellen when their first child was born.

Ted told the whole enthralling story in a couple of hours, without embellishment, painstakingly careful not to make himself sound heroic. But, bare as he outlined it, it had (as *Time*'s review stated much later) all the ingredients of an epic.

When he finished, I called Charles Colebaugh, editor of *Collier's*, and asked him to wait in his office until I could get to New York. I couldn't tell him over the phone. The Doolittle Raid's details were still top secret, months after the fact.

I had to return to New York by train, airplane seat priorities being what they were at the time. During the four-hour ride, I wrote thirteen single-spaced typewritten pages from the several pages of notes I had typed while Lawson relived his adventure. Colebaugh was alone in the big editorial room when I arrived at 250 Park Avenue that night. I read him my notes in the otherwise stilled and blacked-out place.

"Forget about doing it as an article," he said when I finished. He was quite touched. "It'll be at least six articles, I'd say, and of course it'll be a book." I hadn't thought of that.

I wrote it in less than a month, dictating parts of it and continuing on my typewriter when the stenographer took off to transcribe her shorthand. There was also the necessity of writing my daily sports column for International News Service, and feature assignments.

As the story took shape, my association with it weakened. Bennett Cerf of Random House had been tuned in and wanted rights to the book so keenly that when I suggested he give Ted a five-thousand-dollar advance he said, "Nonsense! I'll give him seventy-five hundred." But other publishing houses got wind of it. One approached Ted with two suggestions: (1) unload Random House, and (2) dump me. In respect to the second suggestion, the publisher said (and I was inclined to agree) that this was the kind of saga that needed the sure touch of Antoine de Saint-Exupéry.

I had a friend at court, however, in the person of Teddy Hayes.

The former trainer of Jack Dempsey, and U.S. Commissioner at the New York World's Fair of 1939–40, had met Lawson during the time Ted was undergoing painful additional surgery on what was left of his left leg. They became fast friends. Teddy kept me in the picture.

When I had written everything Lawson had told me I asked him to search his memory for some last little fact about his story. He furrowed his brow.

"I forgot to tell you about a funny thing happened to me at Walter Reed," he said with a laugh. "You see, I hadn't told Ellen I was back in this country, hadn't told her I had lost the leg. What I wanted was to get my face fixed up, get a good artificial leg, learn how to use it, and then just walk in on her some fine day like I was good as ever.

"Well, Doolittle called her in California and told her all about what had happened to me, without telling me. He also arranged for her to fly to Washington so we could be together, without telling me.

"So one day I'm sitting in my wheelchair in the room at the hospital and, all of a sudden, there she is at the door. I jumped up from the chair and started for her, forgetting about the leg. I skidded flat on my face right at her feet."

Ted laughed again. I couldn't join in.

I incorporated the scene in the book. When Dalton Trumbo wrote the script for Metro-Goldwyn-Mayer he chose this afterthought of Ted's as the ending of the motion picture. To this day, the sight of Van Johnson (Lawson) taking his header in front of Phyllis Thaxter (Ellen) jolts sleepy viewers of the Late Late Show wide awake with its naked impact.

Eleanor Roosevelt, who often visited Ted and Ellen during and after Ted's siege at Walter Reed, did not like that ending of the motion picture, she firmly informed me after the picture had been run for the President at the White House projection room.

"You should never have had the actress stoop down and try to pick him up off the floor," she scolded in her unusual voice.

"But that's what actually happened," I said, surprised.

"That doesn't matter," Mrs. Roosevelt continued, firmly. "A lot of our boys are going to come home without legs and arms. Their families must be taught that they prefer to do things by themselves, no matter how difficult. They won't want to be pampered. It would have been much better if you had ended the picture with the actress just standing there while he tried to get himself off the floor."

I couldn't think of anything to say except, "Mrs. Roosevelt, they'd throw rocks at the screen."

The six *Collier's* articles and the longer book manuscript were held in the deep freeze of censorship for months after they were completed. One entire episode, about the low-level flight of *The Ruptured Duck* across the country from Eglin Field, Florida, to Alameda, California, to be put aboard the carrier *Hornet* (Ted flew the bomber *under* the Golden Gate Bridge as he came in for a landing) was deleted because, as the censor explained, "We must not reveal to the Japanese that we have a landing field at Alameda."

"How about changing 'Alameda' to 'a West Coast field,' " I proposed.

"Oh, that's different," the nut said, and restored the whole exciting scene to the script.

The Pentagon was less amenable in the debate over the original title of the book. My wife had suggested, and all hands had accepted, *For Thirty Seconds Over Tokyo*. It was a title that explicitly expressed and delineated the high cost of waging war against a far-off enemy. The months of preparation and training, the daring investment of a full task force deep in Asian waters, the loss of all the planes, the capture of two crews, the execution of three of the fliers, and Ted's amputation, were the price paid for a thirty-second bomb run.

But a title like that smacked of defeatist thinking, the censor ruled. He struck the *For* and would never relent.

Publication was held up for a year after the mission because F.D.R. had said, in his arch manner, that the B-25's had flown to their several Japanese targets "from Shangri-la." Also, the first Pentagon communiqué insisted that no planes had been lost on the mission. The Shangri-la ploy persisted even after the Japanese torpedoed and sank the *Hornet* many months after the raid and announced to the world that this was the carrier from which the Doolittle fliers had taken off.

Weeks after the Japanese announcement, I was called to the Pentagon and sternly reprimanded. It had learned that someone at Random House had made copies of the script which was supposed to be under lock and key and had distributed them to selected friends of the publishing house. A Colonel Fitzgerald spoke darkly of the prospect of a year in prison and a ten-thousand-dollar fine if this sort of proliferation ever occurred again.

But at long last, *Thirty Seconds* was liberated. It was the longest series *Collier's* ever ran. The Book-of-the-Month chose it. It appeared in British, Spanish, Swedish, Norwegian and other editions, including two rival Chinese editions. The latter was puzzling until one afternoon at a cocktail party I attended in Chungking in 1945. An attractive Chinese girl said to me proudly, above the standard din, "I was the first to publish your Lawson book. I beat my competitor by several months."

I congratulated her warmly and asked her how she managed it.

"Easy," she said. "I stole it from the *Collier's* articles as they came out. He waited to steal it from the Random House book."

The Chinese publishers gave their looted properties the same title, *I Bombed and Destroyed by Fire the Great Eastern Capital.* Through 1945 it was topped on the Chinese Best Seller list only by *Within Four Seas All Are Neighbors,* by Wendell Willkie, a tome known elsewhere in the world by the much more prosaic title *One World.*

Babe Ruth's story, "as told to Bob Considine," presented no such foreign and domestic complications. Babe cut out only one scene. Speaking of his wastrel years, before Christy Walsh put a damper on his reckless spending, Babe recalled that on an excursion to a Havana race track he was approached by a pack of Cuban operators who assured him that they'd be happy to fix the next race for him as a gesture of inter-American amity.

Babe was delighted to join the conspiracy. The sharpies had a heart-to-heart talk with the jockeys, then returned and gave Babe the name of the next winner. Babe said fine, he'd bet thirty thousand dollars. To win. The startling size of the bet so impressed the hoods that they re-fixed the race, and all got away with parts of Babe's money.

"No good for the kids," Babe said, scratching the item out of the script.

Ruth was dying of cancer during the time we put his book together. I was assured by his attorney, Melvyn Gordon Lowenstein, and his good friend J. Paul Carey, that he did not know. I was instructed not to bring it up in any way during the interviews. If I did, I was assured, Babe might "go out the window." The disease had eaten his once basso voice into a rasping whisper. His stomach hung like a deflated basketball from what had been the chest of a grizzly.

"Goddamned teeth," he'd say, shaking his head. Babe had made his own eccentric diagnosis of his massive trouble, ". . . a couple of infected teeth." To humor him, his doctors (at one time he had eight) ordered the teeth extracted. It had no more or less effect on his condition than the major surgery which revealed the depressingly malignant tumor at the back base of his brain.

The surgery was performed by Dr. Hippolyte Wertheim, an internationally known specialist, and watched with fixed fascination by several doctors who shared a secret that Dr. Wertheim was not privy to. They knew that Dr. Wertheim's "ulcer," about which he had been complaining, was cancer of the stomach. Thus a doomed man worked fruitlessly to save another doomed man. The doctor died shortly after Babe's death on August 14, 1948.

Babe's book should have written itself, but it became so difficult I had to call on Fred Lieb, the veteran baseball historian who had covered Babe's capers on and off the field since 1914, to fill in the salient facts of his colorful life. Even in his prime there were two things Babe couldn't remember about people: their names and faces. The cancer compounded that failing. Babe was always too busy making history to bother with remembering it.

Working with what was left of Babe Ruth stirred dusty memories within me. I remembered particularly a hot day in 1918 in the Swamppoodle section of Washington, D.C. A tipsy sailor rolled into our street, noticed a bunch of us sitting on the curb in front of our plumbingless house, and said, "How would you kids like to go to the ball game with me?" We yelled happily and soon were on a streetcar with our benefactor, headed for Seventh and Georgia Avenue, home of the Washington Senators. The sailor bought tickets for the twenty-five-cent benches in right field. We were properly awed. It was the first big league game any of us had seen.

We rooted shrilly for the Senators but they lost to the Boston Red Sox 1 to 0. Jim Shaw, who grunted on nearly every pitch, was our pitcher. Young Babe Ruth pitched for Boston. Everybody knew that pitchers were not supposed to know how to hit, but late in the game Ruth hit a home run over the right-field wall and won his own game.

Now here we sat in the trophy room of his Riverside Drive apartment thirty years—or was it centuries?—later. The withered titan found it difficult not to immerse himself now and then in waves of self-pity. All the real or imagined slights he had suffered during his last years with the Yankees and his brief and aborted stretch with the Boston Braves bugged him as he neared his death.

"How do you like this dumb bastard!" he husked angrily one day, jabbing a bony finger at a sports page feature about him. I had read the article and found it highly flattering.

"What's wrong with it?"

"What's wrong with it? I'll tell you what's wrong with it. It calls me 'the former home run king,' that's what's wrong with it. Where's he get that 'former'? Answer me, who ever beat sixty?"

The apartment fairly bristled with mementos of the fifty-four records Babe broke or equalled during his twenty playing years. But his favorite was not a trophy. It was the framed original of a cartoon by Burris Jenkins, Jr., which appeared in the New York *Journal* in 1933, Babe's last year with the Yankees. It showed Babe as a mighty giant striding majestically past Yankee Stadium, "The House that Ruth Built," while at his heels snapped viscious-looking animals representing fans who had been booing him and owners who hesitated to appoint him manager.

"The best thing ever done on me," Babe would say, gazing at the picture.

There was never anyone quite like Babe. Nobody ever looked like Babe or was shaped like Babe, except his saloon-keeping father. Certainly nobody could ever play more positions more superbly than Babe. A new generation forgets that he was one of the greatest defensive outfielders the game ever knew, could relay a ball to the infield or home plate like a rifle shot, and was never known to throw to the wrong base. He was the finest left-handed pitcher in baseball when Ed Barrow began easing him into the Red Sox outfield on days when he was not scheduled to pitch and the club was opposed by a right-handed pitcher. His World Series pitching record of 29⅔ scoreless innings survived all assaults from 1918 until Whitey Ford surpassed it in 1963. His fifteen World Series home-run mark endured from 1932, his last series, until Mickey Mantle edged past him in 1964. His record of sixty home runs, set in 1927, stood up until 1961 when Roger Maris of the Yankees hit sixty-one in the course of a season that had been expanded from 154 to 162 games. Babe's 714 lifetime home-runs record appears inviolable. Willie Mays would have to live as long as Methuselah to top it.

It was difficult to relate these Ruthian feats with the shell I worked with near his end. He would not give up, however. Occasionally he'd get bored with the labor of remembering something that had happened to him years before, get up from his comfortable chair and say, "Let's get the hell out of here and hit a few." We'd go down to his Lincoln Continental and head for the golf course.

The first stop would be at an Italian butcher shop on crowded Ninth Avenue, where his appearance always evoked shouts of delight. Babe had a bizarre routine at this place. He'd pick up a meat cleaver and give mock chase to the proprietor, calling out, "Hey, you crazy dago bastard, give me some decent meat for a change." It made everybody happy, including the Babe. Then we'd drive to Bayside, a flat and busy little public course in Brooklyn, and change into golf gear while the club's cook prepared the meat, always a hamburger.

More often than not, Babe could not swallow the meat. He would settle for a couple of eggs boiled so briefly that he could drink them. His friend Toots Shor sometimes supplemented that egg diet by having his chef prepare Babe a puree of mashed lobster meat.

The frustration of an egg meal at Bayside was generally alleviated by the arrival of several cold bottles of National Premium beer, a Baltimore brew Babe preferred. He'd down them, belch sonorously, and approach the first tee—always the cynosure.

Babe had taken up golf comparatively late in his baseball career, but his inherent sense of timing, magnificent wrists, and coordination had quickly shrunken his scores down into the high seventies. He could, of course, hit a wood shot a country mile. But now you did not want to watch him. He'd breeze the clubhead through a few easy practice swings to loosen up, settle down, plant his feet, regard the ball intently, and swing away at it with all his might.

There wasn't enough might. The ball would lob lazily down the fairway and stop about 150 yards away. Or less, sometimes. Babe could never believe his eyes. He would stand there for a terrible moment at the end of his follow through. One day he simply dropped his club and blubbered helpless curses through the ashes of his throat.

It was stifling, even inside the deep shade of St. Patrick's Cathedral. Babe's flower-draped coffin was borne in slow cadence toward the great doors and the hearse that waited at the curb. Handkerchiefs showed everywhere in the crowded pews, some used for perspiration, some for tears.

Old teammates Joe Dugan and Waite Hoyt, who had shared a thou-

sand and one days and even more nights with Ruth in the Golden
Days, walked side by side in the line of honorary pallbearers.

"I could use a cold beer right about now," Dugan whispered to
Hoyt.

They walked a few more measured steps before Hoyt replied.

"So could the Babe," he said with simple reverence.

Stanislaw Mikolajczyk, the last free premier of Poland, wanted his
story written for him twice: a series for King Features Syndicate's
newspaper clients here and abroad, and a book. He felt there was a
difference between journalese and literature. He had just escaped
from what would have been certain imprisonment and probable death
at the hands of a government which had been taken over by his Communist countrymen, Wladyslaw Gomulka, Jakob Berman, and Bole-
slaw Bierut. He wished to sound an alarm that would ring from every
front page, shake the complacent West, warn it that it could expect
only trouble from the Soviet Union and her new Eastern European
satellites.

As for the book, Mikolajczyk wanted it to be his enduring report
on his life and times, his interpretation of the events which transformed the largest Catholic nation in Europe into a Marxist state.

He had a peasant's patience, this former leader of the Peasant
Party. He'd spend an hour explaining to me some tricky nuance of,
say, the Polish Referendum of June 30, 1946, which might then take
up hardly a full sentence in his story. All our work was done in the
dim parlor-office of his suite in a seedy West Side hotel in the Eighties.
The door to the suite was kept bolted, guarded by a young Pole
prominently armed with a .38 poked tentatively in his chest holster.
Now and then arrived callers: Poles in stiff black suits reminiscent of
old newsreels of international conferences, or of some lesser Hitch-
cockian charade. I'd be asked to leave the room. Polish tongues would
be flying back and forth like shrapnel as I departed.

Mikolajczyk's grasp of English was tenuous, but he preferred to
work in that language rather than filter his revelations through an
interpreter. Problems arose. There were times when he would lead me
down a path of increasingly flabbergasting contradiction, and I would
have to call for a halt and retrace our steps back to the fork in the
narrative road where we embarked on that particular tack. There
I'd find that the trouble was a simple semantic breakdown. He'd

smile in his engaging way, shrug, and say, for example, "I meant to say that Stalin was *not* a good man. So I forgot the not. I must be more careful, yes?"

But at long last my job ended. The articles had gotten much attention around the world, and the matter of the book had been cleared up. There had been a political disagreement with the editors of Vanguard, the first choice of Gertrude Algase, who had become Mikolajczyk's agent at the request of another of her clients, Francis Cardinal Spellman. Vanguard recoiled at Mikolajczyk's strong anti-Communism. The ideological climate was much more comfortable for Mikolajczyk at Whittlesey House, a wing of McGraw-Hill.

On the night my long chore ended I asked the premier if he would kindly step to the desk and look over my shoulder.

"I want you to read the two most beautiful words in the English language," I said. The rubicund little exile peered down solemnly as I put my fingers on the typewriter keys and wrote at the bottom of the final paragraph, "THE END."

He was confused for a bit. Then, wreathed in smiles, he exclaimed, "Ah! Now we go drunk!"

And that we did.

One of the more lethal banes of a ghost's life is the hero's lawyer, that is, if he tends to search through a completed manuscript and throw out everything that may conceivably harm his man's image. A chilling example of this kind of renovation came after Bill Slocum and I put the finishing touches on *Dempsey—By the Man Himself* (Simon and Schuster). Slocum is a second-generation ghost; his father spooked for Ruth.

Working with Dempsey was akin to being given box seats at the unfolding of one of the greatest, rawest, wildest stories in the history of sports. Jack spared nothing: the grinding poverty of his early days, his saloon fights to stay alive, the brutish beatings he took as a boy (one so savage that he was carted away from the fight unconscious in a wheelbarrow), his slacker trial after World War I, his wives, wrangles with Jack Kearns . . . the works. He told his story in the only way it could be told, in basic English that was always closer to the Anglo-Saxon than to Mayfair. And so we faithfully recorded it.

Jack's lawyer blanched when he read the manuscript. He shredded it of most of its vitality, to the distress of the publishers and of *Look,* which had the magazine rights. Dan Mich, *Look's* editor, sent an urgent plea to Dempsey to permit *Look* to print the story as it was first written.

But the lawyer was adamant. Not only that, he had swung Dempsey to his prim point of view.

"Hell," Jack said to *Look's* man, "those two bastards Considine and Slocum had me cussing on every ——— page!"

It was engrossing working with Specs O'Keefe, too. Specs is one of the poorest insurance risks in the nation. His testimony after he turned state's evidence sent eight of his fellow Brink's robbers to prison with life sentences, plus eighty years "beyond life." One of his associates in the $1,218,211.29 cash heist, Joseph F. McInniss, was given *nine* life sentences, plus three additional stretches of eight to ten years, two and a half to three years, and, to crown the anticlimax, a two-year bit "to take effect from and after the (other) sentences imposed upon you," intoned Judge Felix Forte.

O'Keefe had been criminally bent long enough to share the underworld's contempt for a man who would "sing" on his friends. But he had been provoked beyond endurance. The Brink's robber with whom he trusted his $100,000 share of the booty, to hold while he served a term in a Pennsylvania brig for a relatively minor robbery that backfired, lost Specs's nest egg on the races. Free at last, Specs demanded of the mob that it live up to a quasi gentlemen's agreement it had voted for several years before: a share-the-loot plan designed to take care of just such emergencies. The mob gave him a quick answer. It hired Trigger Burke, one of the nation's foremost assassins, to get rid of him.

Trigger missed Specs twice at close range. On the first try, made with a machine gun that sped past Specs's car on a dark Boston street, Specs instinctively threw himself sideways across the front seat a split second before the burst of shells streaked past the point where his head had been and blew out the windshield. Burke nearly got him the second time, when he caught Specs fleeing into a parking lot. Specs made strategic use of several parked cars as shields. But his wristwatch was shot away by one bullet that left a bloody crease where the timepiece had been. Another bullet struck a breast-pocket notebook that deflected it oddly. It entered Specs's chest and emerged

a few inches away, and all he lost was blood. He picked himself off
the ground and blazed away at the departing car with his .45.

"They flew," Specs remembered in his meticulous way.

His neatness, his impeccable manners, quiet voice, and keen humor
were somewhat unnerving to encounter. But that was Specs. He
thoroughly captivated Bennett Cerf when (having been made a sort
of present of him by the FBI) I took him to meet the publisher.
Bennett, a master of the concise, gave the resultant book the longest
title in the history of Random House: *The Men Who Robbed Brink's
—The Inside Story of One of the Most Famous Holdups in the History
of Crime as told by Specs O'Keefe one of the Ringleaders to Bob
Considine in cooperation with the FBI.*

Gazing admiringly at Specs as if he had just identified the Mystery
Guest on "What's My Line?" Bennett asked, "If you fellows had
gotten away with the Brink's robbery, what would you have done for
an encore?"

Specs shrugged. "Fort Knox, I suppose," he said.

Cerf was delighted to press a five-thousand-dollar advance on
Specs. It represented, Specs told me, the first legitimate money he had
ever made in his life. He liked being legit, liked the hotel where I had
stashed him (the stately Plaza), liked the long sessions over a recording machine in my cluttered office, like being able to step up to the
men's bar at the Bull and Bear in the Waldorf at day's end and buy
a drink in the open. He no longer felt "hot," and soon I, too, lost that
vaguely uneasy feeling that it was risky to consort with him.

He charmed everyone I introduced him to, including Louella
Parsons and the dowager Mrs. William Randolph Hearst, whom he
met at a gay party at Luchow's. They hadn't the remotest idea who
he was. As the wine flowed, a suggestion was made that Joe, as we
were calling him, elope with Mrs. Hearst ". . . and unite your two
great fortunes." The beautiful lady laughed happily. The man who
led the tip-toe parade of hooded hoods into the Brink's counting
house on a clammy night in Boston, bowed gallantly.

The book was finished now, and it was time for Specs to leave New
York and return to the less secure preserves of Boston. I called from
the lobby of the Plaza on get-away-day and Specs said he was all
packed and would be right down. I told him I would meet him at the
cashier's cage. I had paid his modest bill by the time he arrived
bearing his suitcase and somewhat out of breath.

"I'm sorry I'm a bit late," he said in his gentlemanly way. "I had to spend a little time . . . unpacking."

"Unpacking?"

Specs shook his head bemusedly. "I packed my clothes, shoes, toilet articles, and so forth," he explained, "and then their towels, soap, light bulbs, ashtrays . . . you know. I was closing the suitcase when I guess a wonderful thought hit me. I said to myself, 'What the hell am I doing this for? I don't *have* to do it any more.' It took me a little time to put the stuff back."

He was distressed that I paid the bill. He looked thoughtfully through the cashier's grille at the matronly employees and beyond them to an old safe.

"You probably won't understand this," he said quietly. "But all of my life I, and most of the people I ran with, would have found it impossible to do what you just did—pay a bill—without figuring, inside, 'Now, how do I take it back from them so I won't be a sucker?' " Specs took another wistful look through the grille.

"It would be so easy," he sighed.

At least one review of *The Men Who Robbed Brink's* etc., the one printed by the Boston *Record American,* set a record as book reviews go. It did not appear in the book-review section. It covered almost the entire front page of the newspaper through all editions and spilled over to two more pages. It wasn't that the book was worthy; it was just that it was newsworthy. In an offhand way it solved three Boston stick-ups which had stumped the police for ten years past, and which had deprived Boston organizations of $182,000.

A special puzzler for the police had been the $43,000 holdup of the accounting office of Boston's big busy Hotel Statler on the day before the titanic Brink's robbery. The statute had long since run its limit in the Statler case, but not the humiliation of the police who could never locate a clue until Specs's book came along with his casual solution:

> Gus and I had watched this one for a long time, and we probably would have waited still longer if we hadn't been so edgy over all those delays on the Brink's thing.
>
> It was a big day for the Statler. Lots of people in the lobby, lots of activity. We went up the steps to the office on the mezzanine, steps that aren't used much. Near the top we took off our hats and put them on a step. Then we pulled a couple of

brown paper bags—with eye-slits in them—over our heads, took out our guns and walked in.

Well, they froze. We must have looked pretty terrible at that. There were some poor people at their desks, on one side of the room. They sat there like statues. There was a poor old fellow in uniform there, too, a guard of some kind. Gus stuck his gun at him, made him lie down, and tied him up. A nice-looking kid, a messenger, I guess, suddenly made a break for the door we had come through. I got in front of him and showed him what I had.

"Don't do that, son," I said to him, quiet. "You wouldn't want to get hurt now, would you? You just go over there and lie down next to the guard and nothing will happen to you."

We scooped up the cash, told them all to stay put, backed out, took off the bags, put our hats on and quickly joined the crowds in the lobby.

People were all excited. Some were clapping. Former Secretary of State General George C. Marshall was coming in a door. The manager was there, bowing and showing him in.

We went out another door with the forty-three. . . .

There were others I helped: war photographer Sammy Schulman, FDR's favorite lensman, Harold Stassen, Robert E. Stripling, chief investigator of the House Un-American Activities Committee, and a forgotten number of inarticulate ballplayers, fighters, and war heroes for whom I did magazine pieces. The least-rewarding were the ballplayers. They have a genuine horror of controversy. Years ago a Philadelphia baseball writer assigned to spook a daily article signed: "By Jimmy Foxx," during the World Series conscientiously called on the slugger and asked him if he had thoughts about the tone of the upcoming articles.

"Yeah," Jimmy said, "don't hurt nobody's feelings."

It's a philosophy that runs as steadfastly as the Amazon through this realm of legitimate fraud.

10 *You Meet Such Interesting People*

I MET Toots Shor the day I went to work for the New York *American*. He had come a considerable distance since his own arrival in New York in the late twenties, a big, cheerful, apple-cheeked fellow out of Philadelphia. He had been a doorman and a bouncer at rough-and-tumble places like the Napoleon and Leon and Eddie's and had worked for a spell for Sherman Billingsley at a time when Billingsley owned a fleet of drugstores. Billingsley's interests were hardly pharmaceutical. Owning a drugstore during Prohibition was tantamount to being a legalized bootleggcr.

From a lowly and sometimes bruising beginning, Bernard Shor had risen in stature to the post of manager of Billy LaHiff's Tavern, one of the classic restaurant-hangouts in the annals of pre-war New York. He was soon to split with LaHiff's son over who had first dibs on the cash register.

Now in 1937 he was on the verge of hustling a bankroll with which to build a place of his own. He spoke of it as his "store."

"Follow him and you'll learn about New York," Bill Corum promised, turning me over to him.

The first place he showed me on the day we began making the rounds was Jimmy Johnston's office in Madison Square Garden. That testy little terrier of a man, a master raconteur, was nearing the end of his reign as boxing's leading matchmaker. He was slowly but surely being muscled out of the picture by Mike Jacobs, the veteran ticket speculator, and Jacobs' slightly undercover partners, Damon Runyon, Bill Farnsworth, and Ed Frayne. Their Twentieth Century Sporting Club had Joe Louis. The Garden monopoly, and thus Johnston, was stuck with heavyweight champion Jim Braddock, a much less glamorous soul than Louis.

But if the clouds were gathering around Johnston, neither he nor Toots gave any indication. Toots's respect for the man over whom he towered was infectious. I swiftly felt the same reverence and maintained it through a subsequent period when Johnston sued me for two million dollars for writing in a *Saturday Evening Post* article about the coups and double crosses that led to Johnston's downfall and resulted in his becoming financially dependent on his conqueror, Jacobs.

On that first day we spent together Toots took me directly from Johnston's office to Tony Canzoneri's bar.

Looking back, the wonder is that we didn't go there first.

We had many things in common from the start of our friendship: sports, growing families, our separate religions, financial problems, politics. But primarily I think he was attracted to me because I shared his enormous and wholesome respect for booze.

Toots is the greatest drinker I ever saw. When he holds up one of his short drinks of Hennessy and soda and says, "Booze . . . beautiful booze," it is not unlike Harry Winston's admiringly candling an egg-sized emerald. People who do not know Shor well are inclined to think his main occupation is drinking. They see him drinking with his customers at lunch, with friends who drop into the store after lunching elsewhere, with the early evening diners, the middle evening crowd, the late diners, and the after-theater people. Sometimes after the last customer has stumbled into the night and the chairs have been stacked on the tables to prepare for the clean-up, Toots goes to the bar and drinks with his bartenders.

If the above appalls, let it hastily be added that Toots never lets his drinking interfere with his business. As for those who presume that drinking *is* Shor's business, have a care. He is sternly pragmatic about this. He may have lived through a night that would have killed a Guardsman (and his horse), but Toots will be at work at 9 A.M. No matter what the morning and afternoon bring in the way of fueling and refueling, Toots always makes the family dining table promptly at six, to have dinner with the children and the smallest member of the household—Mrs. Shor.

Toots has strong feelings about friends who complain of hangovers or who miss a day's work after trying to keep up with him. He tells them they shouldn't drink, that they give drinking a bad name. He is easily offended also by the inevitable challenges he receives. Most of these confrontations subside before the first bottle is opened. Toots has a disarming trick that tends to deflate a challenger at what amounts to the weigh-in. He will regard the would-be champion with a look of withering pity and say, "You're amachoor night. Tell you what: I'll drink a bottle of brandy for a warm-up, and then we'll start." Even the dumbest of Toots's challengers somehow comprehend that he means what he is saying.

Jackie Gleason, a good minor-league drinker with commendable staying powers, fine bladder, and a liver which many feel is up there in the class of Toots's, insulted the champion with a loud challenge one midafternoon after Toots had polished off a few Madison Avenue friends and sent them dazedly back to work. He ordered two fifths of cognac brought to the table, and the "bottle of the century," as it came to be known, was on. Like the Dempsey-Firpo fight, it didn't go the distance. Or, more specifically, Gleason didn't go the distance. He had hardly finished his bottle (Toots had already lapped him by ordering his own second bottle) when he faltered in a most humiliating way. He had to go to the bathroom. He got as far as the archway that divided the restaurant from the bar and collapsed. Joe Harrison, the captain, and several waiters rushed to him.

"Leave him there!" Toots bellowed.

And there Gleason lay, stretched out stiff, while Toots enjoyed a few more drinks at the nearby table. Pretty soon, the first of the early diners began arriving. These are almost always out-of-towners who read about the place or hear references to it—or Toots—on the air. The early diners of that particular evening found themselves forced to detour around one of the most familiar stomachs on the American scene as they were led to their tables by an impassive captain.

Toots almost always drinks cognac, but discourages such steadfastness in others. He is particularly wary of martinis; calls them "bombs." Corum once spent a day in Toots's, which is not an unusual incident in the life of the pub. Bill had a few martinis before lunch, a couple during lunch, and a few more during the afternoon and evening. Naturally, as dinner time approached, he ordered a martini or two. After dinner Toots asked him what he'd like to drink.

"I'll have a martini," Bill said to the hovering waiter.

"Jiminy crickets, Bill, you shouldn't drink the same drink all the

time." Toots said, supping his brandy and soda. "You should mix 'em
up, change over to something else after you've eaten."

"Okay," Bill said. "Bring me a Gibson."

Toots feels it is his duty to drink.

"I owe it to my friends," he told me early in the great game of
knowing him. "Suppose you're stuck in some joint like Hollywood,
let's say, and you haven't been to New York for a long time, and you
keep thinking about having a drink with me when you get here—what
kind of bum would I be if I said, 'Sorry, Sam, I'm not drinking today.'
I've got to fade guys like that."

Toots is a firm believer in the proposition that once a person steps
outside the confines of Manhattan, he's in Bridgeport. One night in
the store he listened to his friend Tom Coleman, the Wisconsin Republican national committeeman, extolling the wonders of Wisconsin
steaks.

"I'll grant that this is a pretty good steak you serve here," Tom
said as he knifed one of Toots's sirloins. "But the kind of steaks I get
in Madison, Wisconsin, are something else again. Toots, you can cut
them with a butter knife, and when you go to bed that night you go
to sleep with the satisfaction of knowing that you've had the best steak
in the world."

Toots looked at him.

"And when you wake up in the morning you're still in Madison,
Wisconsin," he muttered.

Toots is a concise commentator on any passing scene.

He attended a War Bond sales luncheon at the Waldorf on a day
when ballplayers from the New York Giants were "auctioned" off to
various corporations which had taken tables for the patriotic affair.
In a burst of chauvinism beyond the call of duty, a corporation head
"bid" three million dollars for Lou Chiozza, a .200 hitter.

"That's an insult to money," Toots said grimly.

On another occasion while drinking with a table of sportswriters
Toots began a sentence, "That was a good piece Jimmy Cannon
had. . . ."

"Who read it to you?" one of the writers brayed.

Toots dropped his head and appeared to blush.

"You hurt his feelings," another writer said to Toots's heckler.

"No, he didn't," Toots said, looking up. "I was just trying to think
who *did*."

When Corum became President of Churchill Downs and entrepreneur of the Kentucky Derby, Toots accepted the appointment as a call to arms. He ordered a full turnout of all available friends of Bill, from Bob Hope down to busted sportswriters whose fare and keep Toots quietly paid.

"Friendship," Toots said piously. Many feel that Toots is best known for saying "Crumb-bum," or "Creepy crumb-bum." His word is "friendship." On the rather frequent occasions when he is called upon to make a talk he implores all friends who have the faintest command of the language to "write a little something for me." At times by actual count he has had a dozen ghosts banging out bon mots and lyrical panegyrics. But when the time comes for him to get to his feet and give forth with the amalgam of all their skills, he dismisses the script, kicks an imaginary pebble or two, and in the manner of a whale, beached, he wheezes into his "Friendship" speech. It's all about friendship; what friendship has meant to him.

One had better not tamper with friendship, if he wishes to remain in Toots's somewhat harried and shaky circle. He is the only Puritan Jew I know, a man of almost tyrannical morality. With one or two exceptions, he will not permit any married man to bring a woman other than his wife into his restaurant. His long-term friendship with Ted Husing was terminated abruptly one night when Ted said a bad word at a table within earshot of a family at another table. That violated friendship, Toots decided. If Ted wanted to curse, let him curse at the Stork—owned by Toots's eternal foe, Billingsley.

Flying to the first Derby which Corum ran, Toots surprised me by ordering a bourbon when the stewardess asked what we'd like to drink.

"Bourbon?" I said, hoisting an eyebrow.

"I'm only going to drink bourbon on this trip," Toots said solemnly. "I owe that much to Bill, now that he's operating in Kentucky."

It made him sick, but he stuck with the stuff.

What made him sickest at that Derby, however, was to have a friend foully double-cross him. It had been a long day and a costly one. But now the ninth and final race was under way, and Toots's box rang with the exhortations and shouts of his guests: Baby, his wife, Frank and Liz Conniff, and John Daly. They all had the same horse and had bet all they had (and some they borrowed) on it.

The field swept into the backstretch with their horse running a steady sixth. But he looked good to everybody, and everybody was saying so at the top of his lungs. Everybody except the only guest who knew the first thing about racehorses, Don Ameche. Ameche had his glasses trained on the horse.

"We're dead," he quietly announced.

As the cheering subsided in sighs, Toots's party became aware that great excitement began to boil in the next box which held Luro, the famous Argentine trainer and a group of friends.

Their screams reached a shrill ecstasy when a rank outsider, trained by Luro, passed under the wire a winner. It paid forty-four dollars.

"How about Luro, that filthy, slimy bum?" Toots grumbled as he led his depleted troops back to the hotel. "Friendship! He don't know the meaning of friendship. Imagine having a good thing like that running and not even telling us. Some friendship!"

Conniff was surprised.

"I didn't know you two were friends, Toots," he said, "When did you meet?"

"Last night," Toots said, stricken by the treachery.

Toots is very religious, in a somewhat informal and often unnerving way. When his good friend Joe Noonan was faced with a palpably political prison sentence (some said Joe took the term to escape drinking with Toots), Toots each day prayed at Temple Emanu-El, St. Thomas' (Episcopal), and St. Patrick's (Roman Catholic). I asked him why.

"I'm touching all bases," Toots said piously.

One hot day in Jersey, where he takes a place for the summer, Toots took his Catholic children to Mass at St. Mary's in Deal. They were gone for more than an hour. When the car drove up to the house the children bounded out buoyantly and went their separate ways. Toots got out wearily, sweating profusely and looking spent.

"We caught a double-header by mistake," he explained. He meant he had stumbled into a high Mass.

When Baby's mother died, and a wonderful old Irish lady she was, relatives Toots had never heard about swarmed to Campbell's funeral home on upper Madison Avenue. Some of them were marvelous stereotypes of the professional keeners best described in O'Connor's *The Last Hurrah*. More than one of them appeared to keep one eye on the late lamented and the other on Toots—to be sure to accompany him whenever he returned to his bar. The dear people didn't want him to be alone at a time like that, particularly drinking alone. All of them, with all their laments and endearing reminiscences, kept the fragile Baby Shor in a constant state of tears.

One night during the wake I looked in on the room where the bier rested. The place was empty, except for torrents of floral pieces. A fresh batch of relatives had come in from Jersey, had found Baby in an adjoining room, and had started her crying again.

Toots spotted me as I advanced toward the bier, Rosary in hand.

"Thank Christ you're here," he said, stepping through a Gates Ajar arrangement. "These goddam Catholics are driving me nuts."

Toots has positive opinions on just about every person he ever met, and many he never will. He reserves for his large and enthusiastic list of enemies a singular phrase of damnation. "He's a piece of raisin cake," he'll say of some foe. It somehow makes him feel better, as if he had stuck a pin in a small effigy of the person involved.

When Toots heard a rumor that a New York mob planned to kidnap Billy Rose, he scoffed derisively. He and Rose were not friendly.

"What's wrong with it?" his informant said. "Billy is rich and small enough to pick up and run with if the cops try to break up the snatch."

Toots shook his head.

"It won't happen," Toots said. "Who could they contact?"

Toots took a remote dislike to Rev. Billy Graham during the preacher's first New York crusade.

"How about that Billy Graham?" he demanded one night at a table where he was having a drink with Baby and a few friends. Toots always introduces vituperation by asking a "how about" question. Those of us at the table had known him long enough to know that the question didn't require an answer; he was simply cueing himself.

"Two hundred and fifty dollars for a suit, that's what he pays," Toots said, scandalized. "I read it right in the paper: two hundred and fifty bucks for a suit!"

Baby cupped her pretty chin in her hand, sighed, and silently heard him out. It was quite a monologue, a ringing call for the return of the simple ecclesiastical life, a condemnation of the frills and showmanship of the Graham crusade, a dour suggestion that New York's resident Men of God needed no outside psalming.

Baby is a patient woman, but when she reaches the limit of that patience, she has an amazing knack of silencing her outsized mate with one rapier thrust. She waited until Toots had made a particularly righteous point. Then she garroted him with one line.

"Get a load of Bishop Sheeny," she said to the rest of the table.

Toots takes a lot of abuse from his friends; not as much as he dishes out, to be sure, but a lot.

"You've got the head of a pig," he remarked one day to Gleason as they exchanged thoughts.

"And you've got the body of one," Jackie responded.

Before great fame came to Gleason he had a spell of hard luck, and Toots gave him signing privileges. It was a secret only the two shared. Few out-of-work comedians had ever eaten better. As the weeks lengthened, Jackie put on weight and, alas, importance. He began signing ten-dollar tips onto the bill, which the waiters immediately collected from the till.

It hurt Toots to say it to his friend, but it had to be said.

"Jackie, please don't sign such tips on those checks of yours I'm picking up," Toots said.

Jackie was thunderstruck.

"And have your waiters call you a cheap bastard?" he demanded.

Gleason more than evened matters when he struck it rich. He stayed with Toots's place.

"Every creep I help moves right over to Twenty One soon as he makes good," Toots likes to moan. He is sensitive about lost customers, though he is first to admit that he has driven more people away from his place perhaps than any other publican in history.

"I'll never come in this place again," a tough guy who felt he and his girl had been kept waiting too long for a table shouted at Toots one night. He pushed the girl into the revolving door, then paused for one last shot at Toots, who was regarding him blandly.

"What's more, I'm going to tell all my friends to stay out of here," he blazed, stepping into the door.

"Tell him," Toots said, yawning.

Movie mogul Louis B. Mayer never came back to Toots's after the night he complained about bad service.

"I've seen some of your pictures," Toots said in answer to the complaint.

Toots gets a lot of mail, some of it distressing. He was very proud of being invited with Baby to dine with the Trumans at the White House until Bob Hope, who read about it in Hollywood, wrote:

"They put a hog in Tiffany's window."

A complete stranger wrote:

> Dear Mr. Shor: My wife and I dined at your restaurant during our recent trip to New York. We found the food delicious, the drinks very nice, the atmosphere and service fine. But if you expect to make a success in your business, you'd better get rid of that fat slob of a headwaiter who spent most of his time insulting patrons who seemed to be old friends.

Toots thinks anybody who orders wine with his dinner is a show-off. The legend has spread that his wine cellar consists of a five-gallon jug of Gallo. That's not true. He has been seen drinking Dom Perignon on the premises, but only because Don Ameche or Frank Conniff, two professional winos, ordered it. It was once believed that Shor's restaurant did not possess a wine bucket. But that was a lie spread by some piece of raisin cake. It did own one.

Toots won't have anything on his menu that he can't pronounce. This imposes certain hardships—and risk of scurvy—on his regulars. But it is all elementary to Toots. His friend Mel Ott invited him to New Orleans years ago to feast on the delicacies of Antoine's, La Louisianne, and Galatoire's. Toots returned unimpressed.

"Sauces," he said, dismissing the whole area with a word. "If you got good meat who needs sauces?"

Toots's is a meat and potatoes joint. He's intensely proud of his cuisine and demands respect for it, to which his waistline and those of many of his more persistent and loyal customers attest. Strangers in the place sometimes marvel at the enthusiasm of Toots's eaters; even tend to grow huffy about it. They don't understand that it is difficult to order anything in small portions in Toots's.

"No wonder you're getting fat," former baseball commissioner Ford Frick said to me one day as the waiter brought my simple late breakfast which the menu swore was Roast Beef Hash with Egg. There was a blob of roast beef bigger than home plate, and some sort of chain reaction had taken place with respect to that egg. It had become an imposing mound of scrambled eggs.

Frick, commendably trim, was having his customary lunch: a sweet Manhattan and a peanut butter sandwich. Toots has a built-in reverence for rank and prestige, particularly if those holding it prefer his place. If anybody named Gus Fink ever ordered a sweet Manhattan and a peanut butter sandwich within Toots's hearing range, the proprietor would order him thrown out and barred for life.

Frick's comment was not the first, or last, of its kind heard in Shor's. One afternoon a good regular eater named John Begley ordered and easily consumed four of Toots's Bloody Marys, a bowl of oxtail vegetable soup, a large slab of roast beef, baked potato, salad, several bottles of beer, a wedge of graham cracker pie, coffee, and a couple of post-luncheon stingers.

A guy at the next table tapped him on the shoulder.

"What time are you being electrocuted?" he asked John.

Toots maintains a box at Yankee Stadium, at Shea also, always has a block of tickets in the second ringside row at Madison Square Garden on fight nights, and serves as a philanthropic dispenser of tickets to Broadway shows that are complete sellouts for months to come. He pays silently through his impressive nose for such seats, but nothing is too good where real palship is involved.

Sports are his forte, but Toots doesn't exclude the other arts, even though uncomfortable things happen to him when he strays afield. Mike Todd, when the two were speaking, once persuaded Toots and Baby to attend the opening of Maurice Evans' *Hamlet*. Toots joined in the small talk during the first intermission; when the bell summoned the Shakespearean buffs back into the theater, Toots boomed, "I bet I'm the only bum in the joint that's going back just to see how it turns out." He liked *Faust* well enough, he told a friend after he had been liberated from the Met and was safely back at his store, "But there's too much music in it." The movie version of one of the master works of Feodor Mikhailovich Dostoyevsky left him unmoved. "I just took in a movie about a bunch of crazy Russian actors running around and yelling," he told me one night as he came into the store. "It's called 'The Brothers Kalamazoo.' "

Leopold Stokowski hurt Toots's feelings the night a friend managed to get him to Carnegie Hall. Toots looked on with astonishment and rising gorge as Stokowski took a dozen bows after the first number. "Look at that creep," Toots said to his friend. "I saw Hubbell pitch a no-hitter and he didn't take no bows. Let's leave at the half."

It was his second and last ordeal at Carnegie. Previously, he had gone there to see his friend Paul Draper dance. When he weathered that exposure to elfin grace, Toots lumbered to the curb and dissolved into a taxi. "Toots Shor's," he commanded. The driver's head wheeled in wonder.

"Mister, I've been working this stand for ten years," the hacker said, "and this is the first time I ever took anybody from here to there."

Toots has an overriding contempt for thrift. He can't understand, during those times when he is raising money to expand his store, move into a new one, or double-deck the martinis, why the banks do not readily come forth and offer him unlimited credit. When William Zeckendorf paid him $1,500,000 for his Fifty-first Street place to make way for what is now a routine Sixth Avenue skyscraper with much less character, Toots took a terrible revenge on his bank. It had previously given him a hard time. So he carried the check in his pocket for an unnervingly long time, thus depriving the bank of making money on it by lending it out at fancier rates to other stiffs in need. It cost Toots a lot of money in the interest he would have received in a regular savings account, but he feels it was worth it.

A real estate dealer in Deal, New Jersey, who had been renting Toots and his family a furnished summer place for several seasons at four thousand dollars, said to him in a burst of conscience, "Toots, I can get you this place, for keeps, for twenty thousand dollars, lock, stock, and barrel." Toots didn't like to be hustled in that manner.

"Lissen," he said, "why should I buy it for twenty grand when I can rent it for the next twenty years at four grand a summer?" The man went away, somewhat confused. So did Shor's auditor who some years ago suggested to him that if he closed his place on Sunday during the summer time—when business was slack—he could save five hundred dollars a week. Toots made a fast count on his fingers.

"Jiminy Crickets," Toots swore mightily, "at that rate I could close seven days a week and save $3,500."

Though no fool, Shor and his money were soon parted. He was out of action for two years because his original benefactor, Zeckendorf, could not help him to return—as promised. Toots had to make the same weary rounds that he had made nearly a quarter of a century before, when a few grand here and a few grand there built his original place. This time, because of rising costs and a dream of bigger and better things, a lot more money was involved. Several millions . . . a lot of money for a fellow who, with Baby and sportswriter Jimmy

Cannon, had approached the door of his first place on opening night with forty cents in his pocket. He paused on that occasion and threw the quarter and the dime and the nickel in the gutter and said, "I might as well walk in flat-pocket."

But he made it. He had a Friend at Chase Manhattan. The friend was the Teamsters Union Pension Fund, which invests in other profit-making organizations. Toots got his money and built his dream place. Everything was new, including new needlers. . . .

"Why don't you call the new joint 'Toots Shor's Hoffabrau'?"

"Oh, you're so funny, y'creep."

"By the way, Toots, I just came from Twenty One and one of the Kriendler boys said they're very grateful that you built your place next door to them; it's a place for their chauffeurs to eat."

"Oh, you're killing me, y'piece of raisin cake."

One midafternoon in the new place the lights suddenly dimmed ominously.

"Thank God they've electrocuted the chef!" Cannon said to Toots.

Toots had nothing to say.

That doesn't happen very often. . . .

Toots broke the only good leg he had, on the lamentable evening of March 13, 1966. He had attended the Gridiron Dinner the night before as a guest of Warren Rogers, then the chief Washington correspondent of the Hearst Headline Service and now in that same position with *Look.* Warren had just previously been admitted to the Gridiron, one of the choicest clans in the land, and been given the privilege of inviting two guests to the princely dinner whereat the only guest who did not appear in white tie and tails turned out—unpredictably—to be the President of the United States. Warren sent the first invitation to Toots, who was massively touched.

Warren had met Toots through Paul Garvey, former White House correspondent for the Voice of America and U.S. Information Service, and that was the best kind of credential to present to Shor. To Toots, Garvey's stamp of approval had no peer save perhaps the purple splendor of the Choice U.S. Prime Beef stamp. Garvey had become, in Toots's mind, a much more authentic wit than most of the big name stars that frequent his place. It was Garvey who observed, while serving in Seoul during the war, "There's nothing wrong with Korea that couldn't be helped by a seventy-five-story Airwick." And while on duty in Southeast Asia, Paul wrote two enduring song titles: "The

Rain in Laos Falls Mainly in the Ha-ouse," and "Every Little Breeze Seems to Whisper Disease."

But, as of 5:30 P.M., March 13, 1966, Toots wished that Garvey had never met Rogers, or had kept him a secret. He lay on the floor of his bedroom in the Statler Hilton, where he had been packing to fly back to New York. His right leg was twisted under his bulk, broken at the femur. Frank Conniff and I rushed in from neighboring rooms. Our friend was in intense pain. Frank and I pondered the difficult matter of whether to try to lift him onto the bed or obey the dictum of First Aid and leave him be—for fear of adding to his trouble by moving him. Toots made up our minds.

"Lift me up on the bed," he commanded through gritted teeth.

We did, and still plan to lay joint claim to the A.A.U. weightlifting record.

I went with Toots in the ambulance to Georgetown University Hospital, where during ensuing and highly expensive weeks he held a court that made Perle Mesta wince with envy. But on the night of the Great Fall, my friend was a pitiable sight as he lay racked with pain on an ambulance bed about as wide as a ruler. His moans were heartrending.

"Toots, it's Sunday, and this town's dry, but I'll get you a drink somehow," I said. "What do you want?"

My friend's face twisted with agony.

"A Coke," he said.

A thing like that could be remembered with "What hath God wrought?"

Arthur Baer was born in Philadelphia, the seventh of fourteen children, and was packed off to work at fourteen as a lace designer. He made twelve dollars a week drawing scrolls and flowers and was considered one of the most promising young southpaws in the lace dodge. At twenty, still promising and still at twelve dollars, he took a ten-dollar-a-week paycut to work as a copyboy on the Philadelphia *Ledger.* The paper was owned by Adolph Ochs. After that, Baer worked only for Pulitzer, Munsey, and Hearst, a parlay of titans deserving of his talent.

The *Ledger* gave him his chance to cartoon—sports cartoons which he signed with a whimsical-looking little bug in the corner. The bug got off some comment on the larger figure, usually derisive. Hence, Arthur Baer became Bugs Baer. One day in 1912, taken by too many tankards, he joined his friend Wally Wallgreen, later a fixture on World War I's *Stars and Stripes,* and roamed to Washington.

It was an eventful first day and night in town. Bugs coaxed a bartender at the old Ebbet House into drawing beer for him in exchange for a sketch. The sketch took longer than usual. When it was finished Bugs showed it to him. The bartender took a punch at him. Before the end of that momentous day, Bugs voted illegally for a Democratic candidate for the District of Columbia delegation to the Convention that in time nominated Woodrow Wilson, spent some time with the belles at Mahogany Hall (a bordello which Mrs. Wilson eventually caused to be shut down, to the dismay of many members of Congress), and slept in the White House on a couch in the press room.

Bugs became a writer by something akin to osmosis. He was sent by the Washington *Times* to the Charlottesville, Virginia, spring-training camp of the Washington Senators to draw cartoons of the ball club —then consisting mainly of Walter Johnson. It was a difficult assignment at the beginning, but it got considerably worse. The *Times*'s baseball writer took drunk for a week. Bugs protected him, writing reams of copy about the ball club and wiring it back to Washington under the writer's name. The man was unable even to open telegraphic assignments and suggestions he received. Bugs would open his wires and take care of the sports editor's requests, and somehow find time to do his own work. On the seventh day of double duty, Bugs opened a message addressed to the souse which read: "YOUR STUFF HAS BEEN GREAT LATELY. TELL BAER THAT IF HIS CARTOONS DON'T IMPROVE WE'LL HAVE TO LET HIM GO."

That is how the world lost a so-so sports cartoonist and gained one of the most remarkably trenchant craftsmen ever to hone the language.

"I don't care who runs the country as long as someone runs Bugs Baer twice a day," Ring Lardner once wrote. Matter of fact, somebody *did* run Bugs twice a day. In 1931, by which time Bugs was writing out of New York for the Hearst Newspapers, W. R. Hearst became attracted to the work of another humorist in the rival *Evening World.* The byline was "Graham Wire," the stock head was "Wiregrams by Graham Wire." The *World* thought so much of its man that it sometimes ran him on the front page. He wrote a great deal like Bugs, but frequently was even more hilarious.

Hearst ordered Bradford Merrill, his general manager, to hire Wire. Merrill assigned Damon Runyon to attend to the preliminary negotiations, Runyon being at heart a fixer and proselytizer. It was a difficult assignment for Runyon because he was only one of three men who knew that "Wire" was Bugs . . . Bugs in search of broader fields for his torrents of thoughts . . . Bugs in quest of a moonlit buck. The third man was Jack Wheeler, general manager of the North American Newspaper Alliance, who had talked Bugs into the ruse in the first place.

Runyon had become privy to the secret by his innate habit of prying. He could not approach any person's desk or typewriter without reading the man's correspondence or peering over a shoulder to see what was coming out of a typewriter. Because of his early years in the composing rooms of the papers to which his father had wandered, Runyon could read from any angle. Thus it was no great problem for him to discover one day at the New York *American* that Bugs was composing under the Graham Wire signature.

Runyon could not have been more pleased with the discovery. Now he "had" something on Baer.

Bugs looked at him steadily.

"You give me away and I'll break your arm," he said. Which he could have done without great effort, for Bugs was always in good shape.

That threat must have remained in the back of Runyon's mind during the days that followed the assignment from Merrill. He reached an interesting solution. He showed up at Merrill's office one day to report solemnly that he had talked at great length with Mr. Wire and Mr. Wire said he would not think of ever working for William Randolph Hearst.

Bugs's split personality as a writer soon after melded into the one that has since been uniquely identifiable. Henceforth he operated with only one spigot. Out of it gushed, in lively spurts, refreshment for his cult—and I am one of his true believers.

Bugs wrote the history of Europe in one sentence: "Europe's a place where they name a street for you one day and chase you down it the next."

That's what Toynbee was trying to say in five million words.

Nothing escaped the flash floods of his concise and explosive wit and wisdom.

He asked the same question that had perplexed world diplomacy as Khrushchev, possessor of appalling thermonuclear might, alarmingly thumped away at his desk in the UN Assembly. But a bit differently.

"Diplomats are wondering what kind of international omeleting is going on in Nikita's egghead when he sets the tempo with a half-soled Moscow metronome?" Bugs asked. "Will he use the same technique on the President, or will he pour it out of a boot?"

Bugs wrote sketches for Lillian Russell and Lew Dockstader, but was still fresh half a century after those two were wisps lost in space and time. Nothing he regarded, as he peered down from his tower of genuine walrus ivory near Stamford, Connecticut, failed to kindle his eye:

Paying alimony is like buying oats for a dead horse. . . .

There's no such thing as a little garlic. . . .

He's so dumb they had to tear down the schoolhouse to get him out of the second grade. . . .

What would you charge to haunt a house? (Bugs wrote that line for a comedian who wanted a devastating boffo with which to silence any heckler. The first time he used it, against a lady souse, the rest of the audience cheered. But when the cheer died down, the lady asked "Hic, how many rooms?")

Chiang Kai-shek's troops have been on that island so long their stomachs have high and low tides. . . .

Getting Toots Shor to Campbell's funeral parlor the night of Jimmy Walker's wake was like towing a sick whale without any hope of ambergris. . . .

In 1918 I heard my Country's call. It had been calling since 1917. . . .

Ping Bodie was out, trying to steal second. His head was full of larceny, but his feet were honest. . . .

Pratt slid home on his surname. . . .

DiMaggio [who popped to the catcher his first four times at bat in the 1950 World Series] could have done all of his hitting in a chimney. . . .

[Of the Versailles Treaty] All it will do is fatten the wolf again. . . .

Trying to get those Yankees out was like trying to throw a porkchop past a hungry dog. . . .

[To the UN] Do something soon, or put back the brewery. . . .

[Of the UN] The world's first veto was a growl from the back of a cave. . . .

Success hasn't changed Toots a bit. He's still a bum. . . .

Shor gave Bugs a big black-tie dinner on his seventieth birthday. Bugs wasn't for the idea at all. He laid down harsh reservations: no politicians (except Jim Farley), and drinks at the bar would be served only to gentlemen wearing caps. Even after Toots agreed, Bugs was difficult. Bugs wired him:

TOOTS SHOR'S ROACH RANCH
51 WEST 51
NEW YORK CITY

YOURS OF THE 13TH INSTANT RECEIVED AND DULLY NOTED. HOLD EVERYTHING FOR 30 YEARS AND MAKE IT A CENTENNIAL.

It was as close to an Elizabethan revelry as the twentieth century has produced. Shor made the mistake of seating Bugs next to the lectern at the head table. At the most solemn moment of every eulogy to him, Bugs goosed the speaker. He had written during Prohibition that "the fellow who named it Near Beer is just a bad judge of distance." He demonstrated something along those lines at his banquet. After a while he could no longer lift his Burgundy glass as high as his waiting lips, but he retained the ability to tip the glass at the top of its rise, or perigee. The wine would cascade down what began as a spotless dress shirt. By the time the evening ended—if it did—Bugs looked like the sole survivor of the St. Valentine's Day slaughter.

It reminded him of a line he had written about an artful check-dodger: "He suffers from an impediment in his reach."

Just before Christmas 1963, Bugs faced a serious operation. It would be touch-and-go, and he knew it. As somberly as he was capable of putting it, he wrote:

"What kind of Christmas story do you write when you are not sure how much string is left in your ball of twine? What do you write just before they clap the cone over your schnozzola and you are in one of those rare rooms where Emily Post says it's okay to put your feet on the table?"

Bugs pulled through neatly and dropped a note to a friend at the Lambs Club: "I've got so many tubes in me I don't need a doctor. I need a switchboard operator."

But it took something out of him, as he felt he should explain when invited by Bob McCorkindale of King Features Syndicate to participate in the fun and games scheduled for the syndicate's next outing. He wrote:

> Owing to my advanced seniority, I no longer take part in capering on the greensward. The last time I competed in the father-and-son Olympics was in 1930 at the Friars outing. The contestants in the hundred-yard dash were Jim Corbett, Joe McGurk, Saturday Night O'Brien, Willie Collier, Steve Riordan, Rube Goldberg, and George M. Cohan. I was winning footily, but at seventy-five yards I had to go behind a bush and adjust my truss.
>
> But will come. Will be driven out there by my nurse, Thelma Orner, who permits me to eat very little. I rarely wrap up any food to take home, as you have nothing that matches my pet chameleon. Pardon my delay in answering your invitation but I soak all letters in a tub for two weeks.
>
> Yours until you hear different. . . .

Bugs sent Miss Orner to his dentist not long after that bearing two items, (1) a letter, and (2) his upper plate.

"Dear Docster," the letter read:

> It will surprise you to learn I am sending in my upper appetite by carrier pigeon, parcel post, and registered nurse. While taking my usual two cautious bites of a cherry, I stubbed my porcelain cuspidor on the second bite. Thereby losing one of the little whites of my artificial smile. Miss Orner has volunteered to carry the message to Garcia and has the ghastly dentifacts in her purse.
>
> A man is really rich when he has a spare upper maxillary in his vanity case. I looked up my spare and it fitted exactly, except for being a little on the Mortimer Snerd side. However, I will be glad to get the original back and popped into place. There's no use of your holding my bridgework for ransom as it is not worth 500 tractors, and also because I have that second set.
>
> I never take my plates out except to brush them. Some people keep theirs in a glass of water overnight. I tried it once and in the morning they looked much happier than I felt.
>
> Now, dickery old doc, you go ahead and vulcanize that old vacuum and give the finished gems to the nurse. I enclose the tooth that jumped the reservation. If it hasn't got a trade-in value you can donate it to the American Museum of Natural Curiosity.
>
> Yours till the last notch in your Adler Elevator Chair.

Once at a benefit where many Broadway people did quick turns, vaudevillian Al Trahan, caught without his writer, pleaded to Bugs, "Give me a couple of lines, I'm next on." Bugs said, "Just go out there, shoot a gun, and fall on your ass." Trahan did that, and only that, and broke up the audience.

"Humor is tragedy, standing on its head and with a rip in its pants," Bugs once said. His rule has been to make it sting, but never draw blood. He has been sued for libel only once over the long and saucy span. "I won the case," Bugs recalls. "The dame claimed I called her ugly, and I didn't at all. All I wrote was that she could safely cook naked in a lumber camp."

Irving S. Cobb said it best: "The Bugs Baers do not come in bunches like grapes. They appear but once in a millennium." Or longer, I've always felt. . . .

Bob Ripley, like many of his cartoons, was a bit hard to believe. After all, how many people have you known who owned a Chinese junk powered with a diesel robust enough to outrun most of the powered boats on Long Island Sound? He was the only American I ever knew who had a harem and made no bones about it. The talk of the neighborhood around Mamaroneck was that he took a daily steam bath with his beauties and often ran across them barefooted. To male neighbors stuck with monogamous natures, this seemed like the very last word in happy motoring.

It wasn't Nirvana, apparently. There was one party at his weird estate that did not come off too well. There were only four guests at B I O N that night. Rip had invited Bugs Baer, who wisely declined on the ground that Christmas was a day which should be celebrated in the bosom of one's family. Rip didn't agree. After all, he felt quite festive in the traditional Yuletide array of bright mandarin kimono, hat, and brocaded slippers.

Just before the chef brought the turkey, alas, the phone rang and one of Bob's oldest flames—long since relegated to limbo—was calling from the evil Mamaroneck station. With his Old World courtliness, he invited her over instantly to share the feast which even nonbelievers insist was built around the birth of Christ. She brought along her son, a child of fourteen who stood well over six feet and had dressed that day, dementedly enough, in a tight-fitting Boy Scout suit.

Regrettably, Rip's real guests were not getting along too well. One was a French actress, the other a Russian actress. Both were plastered. One was being moved out of a treasured bedroom at the spooky place and didn't like it one little bit. It was hardly the proper Dickensian setting. Matters were not helped when the Boy Scout announced that he had had so many milkshakes during the afternoon he no longer looked with joy on the traditional delights of a Christmas dinner. Worse, his mother, who had taken a seat of honor near Ripley, suddenly reached into a voluminous purse, brought out a picture of her late husband, and propped it up against an array of wine glasses. Every now and then she would look at the picture and burst into loud tears.

The Boy Scout, who was seated in the darkness of a corner in the wild dining room, would occasionally bray, "But Mama, where *is* Dad-dy?"

Meanwhile, the two whores who were Rip's prime guests were regarding each other with increasingly malevolent glares. Ultimately, one reached into the carefully stitched rear end of the turkey and seized, therein, a ball of dressing. She extracted it, at some expense to her wrist, cranked up, and hurled it across the table—smack-dab into the kisser of her foe for Rip's attentions.

"But Mama, where *is* Dad-dy?" the boy wailed.

"It wasn't a happy Christmas," Rip later told Mrs. Baer. It may have been that year's record understatement.

Things had to be right around Rip's place. My wife and I took a place just across Lake B I O N from him in 1942, shortly after the birth of our son Barry. An almost daily visitor, particularly at times when Millie was nursing the baby, was one of the more entrancing flowers in Rip's harem. She was an exquisite creature of Chinese-Japanese mixture, given to the more colorful gowns of both cultures. She invariably paddled across the little body of water in a small boat, and she made a delightful picture in a setting of quiet waters and great weeping willows. Just as invariably, she always brought the baby a little flower, and would tuck it daintily behind his ear as he nursed. Then she would sit through the procedure, her lovely face sometimes fathoms deep in thought. We often wondered about the dear girl's story.

One Sunday Rip invited us to one of his great parties. The girl was in the process of being chastised by being sent to her room. She had offended the laird and master, who was in full ceremonial robe, by playing gin rummy with Nick Kenny, who was to the Hearst organization at that time what John Masefield was to the British Crown and Edgar Guest to Henry Ford I. Nick had contributed some enduring gems to poesy. One piece about the death of his dog had sent countless readers of the *Mirror* into paroxyms of woe, particularly that line which said: "And don't forget what *d-o-g* spells backward!"

Another flight of fancy that involved the Almighty with certain unnervingly mundane matters ran:

> "Snow fell from Heaven
> Like dandruff from God's shoulders. . . ."

Then there was a touching refrain from what Nick called a Patty Poem, struck in honor of his daughter of the same name. She was a sentimental child, Patty, as the poems in her honor so winningly evidenced. Take, for example, Nick's threatened sale of "My Old One-Tube Set." Patty, naturally, objected to any such transaction. Nick asked why, in a kind of rollicking verse where even the rhyming of "orange" seemed faintly possible:

> "She pointed to its dusty face,
> Two baby lips were there.
> 'I kissed it last night, Daddy Dear,
> When you were on the air.' "

There was every reason why a dear girl who had little claim to fame chauvinistically save the attack on Pearl Harbor would have been pleased and proud to be playing gin rummy with the poet laureate of the Burma Shave Company, but then Ripley hove into ominous view.

"How many times must I tell you not to mingle socially with my guests," Rip stormed. "Get off to your room!"

The girl ran, whimpering. It seemed an excessive punishment to Millie. My wife went off to search for her and found her in a darkened little bedroom which featured cohabiting Buddhas. The light fixture was made from a Japanese parasol. The girl lay on the bed, sobbing.

In an effort to make her forget the ugliness of the scene, Millie picked up a beautiful lacquered box from the dresser. "What exquisite work this is!" she said. She is one of the rare persons who pronounce "exquisite" properly.

The girl lifted her face from her pillow and looked around. "Oh," she said, and then, after a bit: "I keep my baby's ashes in there."

Millie put the box down swiftly, but sympathetically.

"Don't feel badly," the girl said. "The ashes are not there now. When Bob gets mad at me he hides them."

Years later, there was another brush with the rule of an American maharajah.

That would be my friend Bob Ruark, dead at forty-nine and stretched out inside a yellow pine box in the study of his hauntingly unfinished home in Palamos on the Costa Brava. He had died of his bad plumbing a week before in London after chartering a flight from Barcelona with a view to refueling his lost blood. It was a calculated risk, and Bob lost. There wasn't enough blood in all Middlesex to keep this robust soul going, so now what was left of him was back in the place he had on the water at Palamos, and all around him were people who knew nothing about him except his books and his bragging. Bob was a good writer, a marvelous illustrator, an excellent broadcaster, a pretty good speaker, a tireless companion, and a magnificent braggart. I don't speak of braggadocio meanly. It takes a certain amount of courage to be a braggart, for one must always be prepared to defend his position, substantiate his claims.

Bob Ruark could, more often than most.

His celebrated grandfather, endless source of wisdom for articles and, in time, for a book he and many fancied, was more a figment of yearning than one of fact. The Old Man was a concoction of personal need, born in great age and wisdom from his need for a forbear. Bob had no relatives he felt deserved him, and maybe he was right. He was prouder of knowing Bernard Baruch and shooting birds on Hobcaw Barony with that older braggart than he was of his own father and mother. It is doubtful if he ever introduced them to the self-confessed adviser to Presidents.

Bob would have liked some of the touches at his funeral, just as Winston Churchill would have reveled in seeing Queen Elizabeth II *and* Charles de Gaulle *and* Clement Attlee singing "The Battle Hymn of the Republic" in St. Paul's on the day he was consigned to peace eternal in ceremonies he personally had arranged. Bob would have liked for example, the thoughtfulness of the girl who stopped the Spanish newsreel cameraman from taking a shot of a great tiger Bob had killed in India years before. The tiger's skin and hideously fanged head were hung from a wall in such a manner that the beast seemed to be springing into the room.

"Stop!" the girl ordered, and the cameraman's light man snapped off the bulb in wonder. Then the girl raced about the place in search of a missing ingredient, as if under tacit orders from the dead man stretched out in his yellow box. Shortly she returned with the keys to Ruark's Rolls Royce, which dangled from a little case made of a leopard he had killed. The exposed key ring fitted neatly over one of the ominous teeth of the tiger on the wall.

"Bob used to sit where you're sitting now and look at his Rolls's keys in the leopard case hanging from the tiger's tooth and say, 'How rich can you get?' " the girl said.

I took another drink of Ruark's White Label Scotch.

The spoils of his safaris pressed around the coffin like creatures tremulously met at a water hole. The bier stretched across a rug made of hides of zebras his guns had felled. Like rigid acolytes, two enormous elephant tusks showed at the head of the casket. From the white walls of the library the glazed eyes and heads and flaring horns of an impala, a crant, a Robert's Eye, a great koodoo, lesser koodoo, sable, nyala, and two fierce black buffalo regarded the somber scene.

Not one relative had come to say farewell. But this man was not unmourned. Christian, the noble cook, sat in soundless grief in the dimly lighted room with Pascual, the gardener, Pascual's wife, and Pascualito, whose education my friend was underwriting when all his hot blood left him. There were, in addition, Gafarot the grocer, Reixac the butcher, and Samso the baker, all in stiff black and genuinely touched.

"Fourth head I've lost in a fortnight," the Polish sculptor Nicky Tregor said, as he drank the dead man's Scotch. "Nina Dyer commits suicide. George Litman just dies. Rubirosa hits a tree. Now Bob."

Four sad Spaniards in black carried Ruark out of the house and set his bright yellow box down in the emerald garden. The sun was intolerable. Father José Fonosas, a young priest given to gestures, stepped forward when the mourners stopped moving about. He fished notes out of his cassock, settled his glasses on his nose, and launched into a religious ceremony unlike any he had ever celebrated or witnessed in Catholic Spain. His bishop had not gone into any great detail about this assignment. He had simply said go ahead, it would be all right: Ruark's rich friend, Ricardo Sicré, had made a nice contribution to an orphanage.

The priest droned on in Spanish, pointing now and then to the box that embraced this spent skyrocket of a man. He had never known Bob. Bob was not one to take formal religion seriously and tended to laugh aloud at its emissaries. Once at our place in New Jersey he watched me lead my brood home from Sunday Mass at St. Mary's, Deal, all of us feeling outrageously pious. Looking me over as he lolled on our porch in his shorts, he said, "Okay, now take off your deacon's suit and mix us up a mess of martinis."

The beach life at the edge of Bob's garden went on uninterrupted for the most part. But some bathers who had noticed the little Spanish hearse and two cars into which erupting volcanoes of vivid flowers were being arranged came to the hedge and peered into the garden, straining to hear what the priest was saying.

What he was saying, and he summed it up at the end in painful English, was "Let God be mindful of his servant, Roberto Ruark, and grant him peace."

U.S. Consul General to Barcelona John Ford did not know Bob either, but he had done his homework.

"In twelve years the roots of a tree reach ever deeper," he said in Spanish. "They cling to the earth. It is difficult for them to be pulled out without leaving a deep scar. The people who have known Bob Ruark for the past twelve years in this region will remember how much affection and recognition he showered on Palamos. He will leave an empty space in this corner of Spain and a heaviness in the hearts of them who shared this part of his life.

"I recall a passage from his book *The Old Man and the Boy,* where the old man who was his grandfather is dying and he says to the boy who was Ruark, 'I gave you the best things I could give, and now you are the Old Man because I am tired and I am going to leave.'

"Ruark wrote that his eyes filled with tears, but the Old Man said to him, 'Let it alone. Like I've always told you, if there existed a way to mock death I would have already learned how. Your time will come, too, although it now looks impossible.'

"Ruark wrote, 'But How, When and Why?' because he couldn't find anything better to say.

"We have here the answer to his questions, really. Here in Palamos will sleep forever one who came to this land and planted here his roots."

My friend's casket looked too small for a fellow who had once flattened Bobo Newsom in a player-versus-writer fight, and during the war had decked a big union goon aboard a Merchant Marine war transport on which he commanded a Navy gun crew. When the four sad Spaniards slid it into the hearse a good foot of it protruded out the rear.

The funeral party emerged from the bottom of the garden and walked into town behind the hearse, behind the flower cars and Bob's Rolls Royce, which followed in empty elegance save for the chauffeur, like the riderless horse of a dead leader. I wondered if his boots were in the car, turned backwards.

And so we marched slowly between ranks of people who had come up from the beach, some in Bikinis, to look upon a cortege moving through a travel-poster town. One could hear my friend in the box saying, with his fierce black and white smile, "What a way to go!"

Ruark wanted to be Hemingway. But *Hemingway* wanted to be Hemingway, too. He would never move over, never give a tumble to the younger man who reflected so many of his facets. Bob never gave up the chase while Hemingway lived—hunting, guzzling, wenching, boasting, mimicking, trying on his mantle for size after his suicide.

Hemingway had too much of a lead.

I had only the flimsiest relationship with Hemingway and don't believe I could have called him Papa if I had known him well. The first knowledge I had that my hero was aware of my existence came in a letter from him which the *Mirror* forwarded to me one spring while I was covering the baseball training camps in Florida. I was deeply impressed and thrilled to turn the Havana-mailed letter over and read on its rear flap:

> Ernest Hemingway
> Finca la Vigia
> San Francisco de Paula
> Cuba

I assumed it was a response to a column I had written a week before, an interview with Quentin Reynolds in which Quent described the thrill and rigors of spending a weekend as Hemingway's guest. There was a particularly glowing reference to Hemingway's knockdown of Tom Heeney, the former heavyweight contender best remembered as the man Gene Tunney defended his title against before abdicating it. Reynolds told me Heeney was working for Hemingway as a sparring mate.

I assumed correctly. It was a response to the column. A retort.

"If I ever meet you I'm going to flatten you on sight," Hemingway's letter began. He denied that he had ever decked Heeney. Heeney, Hemingway wrote, was his friend, not his employee.

He seemed to have forgotten the whole thing by the time we met. He was in New York to see his publishers and do a little drinking at Shor's. We talked sports for hours and I dropped him off at his hotel. I asked him what his plans were for the next day, and he said he was going to work the whiskey out of himself at George Brown's gym in the morning—would I like to come along?

Puffed and puffing from the night before, Hemingway came out of his corner of the gym ring weaving and bobbing and glaring at his friend Brown, an accomplished and gentlemanly muscleman who catered physical fitness to select New York tycoons and blades. He got in close to Brown and tried to knee him in the groin. Brown stepped back and jabbed him sharply in the nose. Hemingway lunged at him like a bear, tried to stomp on his feet, and rubbed the lacings of a glove roughly up and down Brown's ear. Brown broke away, feinted him, and busted him a good right in the face. And so it went for three two-minute rounds. When it was over, Hemingway came over to where I stood and leaned his heavy hairy arms on the top rope. The blood from his nose had saturated his mustache. He smiled triumphantly and gasped, "Wasn't that a wonderful workout!"

A licensed referee would have stopped the fight and disqualified him at any point during the three rounds.

I saw him a few times after that at Shor's place where he liked to sit around and drink and talk sports. He had a good sports background in boxing lore and was fair on baseball. There's something about those dudes. Thomas Wolfe dreamed more about going home to Ebbets Field than to North Carolina. It becomes a big thing for them to be known as rooters for this or that team, or fighter, and the worse the team or fighter, the greater the reverence paid.

When Castro took over, Hemingway had a good word to say for him. When Simon Bolivar's skin peeled off of Castro and he was himself again, I tried and failed to reach Hemingway by cable, phone, and his agent to ask his comment.

When I next saw him at Shor's, he was bearded, subdued, and much thinner. He was standing alone at the bar; he beckoned to me and asked me to have a drink. We had several.

"You've blown some weight. How did you do it?"

He took a sip and thought.

"I stopped drinking with creeps," he said seriously. "As long as I can remember, I drank with creeps. I'd go into a bar anywhere in the world, somebody would spot me, make a big thing about buying me a drink, and finally I'd say sure, thanks, and now have one on me. So I'd wind up drinking with this creep I had never seen before and didn't want to be with and never wanted to see again. I took on a lot of booze that way over the years. One day I decided to stop drinking with creeps. I decided to drink only with friends. I've lost thirty pounds as a result."

Everybody at places like Shor's was sorry when the word came that Ernie was dead. To us, who didn't know him as well as the biographers lurking in the wings, there didn't seem to be any reason for putting the gun in his mouth and pressing the trigger. We held out some hope that, as had happened before, there would be a later bulletin canceling the obituaries. He had survived a couple of world wars, brushes with beasts, and a splintering plane crash on safari. On that occasion, after all the requiems, he emerged from the bush brandishing a bunch of bananas and a bottle of gin. His friend Shor, relieved to the extent of tears, sent him an insulting one-word cablegram. It read: "SHOW-BOAT."

There was a lot of showboat in Ernie and some of its residue is still perpetuated at the place in Cuba where he spent, off and on, twenty-five of his best and most productive years. Castro has made it a museum of sorts which can be visited by appointment only. He has observed his promise to Mary Hemingway not to propagandize the place as the shrine of a renowned American who applauded his revolution.

I made the pilgrimage in 1964 when Castro invited a couple of dozen reporters to Havana and Santiago de Cuba to take a well-programmed look at how he was making out. Hemingway's place, twelve miles out of Havana, is as he left it on July 24, 1960, to go to Pamplona to see the bulls run and to explain *Bloody Summer,* his disappointing account of the *mano-a-manos* tour of Antonio Ordoñez and Luis Miguel Dominguin.

There are fresh flowers everywhere in the house, and the airy place is spotless. His favorite chair is still there in what must be called the living room. It is done in a chintzy pink print that is at odds with the heads of menacing beasts glaring down from the walls. The bar table still nudges at an arm of the deep chair, offering a variety of lived-with half-empties: White Horse, Gordon's, Noilly Prat, Martell. A large metal ice bucket snuggles at the foot of the bar. I had an uneasy feeling that it might be filled. There is a footstool near the chair on which Hemingway left a number of items he was reading or planned to read. On top of the pile is Allan Villers' *Give Me a Ship to Sail.* Luncheon for three is always about to be served at Finca la Vigia, but never is. The table is set each noon by Rene Villaralo, a now middle-aged Cuban brought into the ménage as a child to be a companion to Hemingway's sons. The china, silver, and glassware glitter from careful attention. The table flowers are sparkling fresh. There will be two wines. Papa will sit in the big chair facing Miss Mary and the guest beside her. . . .

It was something of a relief to get the hell out of the dining room.

Villaralo led us into Hemingway's combination bedroom-workroom. Directing our attention to the freshly made double bed on which there were a number of books and magazines and a Helen Wills white sun visor, he said that the master often fell asleep late at night amid such debris. This was what he had rolled in during his last night in that bed, the good and faithful servant said with his emotions gathering like a storm.

Ruark's *Poor No More* lay near one of the pillows of the uncommonly short bed. How much that would have meant to Bob!

Hemingway wrote standing up, his man recalled. He showed us the plain white bookcase that rose about as high as the author's once-barreled chest. He used its top layer as a desk. Hemingway would confront it every morning, write down his thoughts in longhand with a pencil, and then transcribe them on a beat-up portable he had carried through at least one war. That was atop another bookcase,

where he also breakfasted: juice, tea, Rye-Krisp. He always\
in his bare feet, Villaralo told us, because he said he could not\
with his shoes on. In the wintertime he would protect his feet f\
the cold tiles with a thin rug made from the skin of some sm...
animal he had shot. He kept a bookkeeper's account of how many
words he wrote each day and marked the total on a writing board
which would not be out of place in a drugstore inventory. Sometimes
he wrote as many as seventeen hundred words a day ("if he was going
fishing the next day," Villaralo explained). Sometimes he wrote only
three hundred. Sometimes he just stared. He never used his regular
desk except as a kind of display table. The day I was there it held a
collection of bullets of different caliber, lined up like smart troops, his
war correspondent brassard, a snapshot of Mary, and one of Marlene
Dietrich singing to gaping GI's. Under the glass top of the desk was
an illuminated religious card, a prayer of Ignatius Loyola: "Soul of
Christ, sanctify me. . . . Soul of Christ, save me."

The Duchess of Windsor's 1957 Cadillac nuzzled to the curb on
the Vendôme side of the Ritz in Paris. The chauffeur put my bag and
beat-up portable in its yawning trunk as the Duchess reached a fash-
ionably gloved hand out from the rear door of the car. She was
brittlely hospitable under her thick car blanket. And off we went
through a cold and clammy Paris to share a weekend that meant much
to them, for it would be the twenty-fifth anniversary of the Duke's
abdication because of her.

"He's actually playing golf in this weather," she said when I inquired about him. "He's playing with a couple of boys who are hardly
thirty or thirty-five. It seems so foolhardy to me. But, then, I don't
play golf." The Duke was sixty-seven, she sixty-three. It had not been
a good year for them, she said. He had lost the young British accountant who was so adept at helping them keep their financial affairs
straight, and the Duchess' long-time secretary had abruptly quit.

It was something less than Bourse-shaking news, but I was glad she
was talking at all. I had come to hear them talk, not to confront them
with tedious questions.

"He had a wife and four small children in London," she was explaining, wielding her fine diction. "The wife couldn't see his spending

three weeks out of every month with us. As for my secretary, she simply quit."

I tried to murmur sympathetically, but nothing came out. It would be a very long weekend. We watched the gray-green countryside slide by for a time.

"I am so sorry you won't see our place with the flowers out," the Duchess said in time. "We call it The Mill. It was built in the sixteen hundreds and remodeled in seventeen thirty. The agent did not want to show it to me. Got me halfway out here and tried to turn around and drive me back to town. I would not hear of it.

"Well it was almost as grim as he made it sound—no bathrooms and otherwise in terrible state. But the Duke loved it on first sight. He liked the space—it's twenty acres—and the water running through it. He works better, thinks clearer, out here, and we can make it in twenty minutes from the place we bought from the government in the Bois de Boulogne.

"We fixed it up nicely, I think you'll agree. You'll be sleeping in what was the cow barn."

It seemed appropriate, I said, and the Duchess nodded agreeably. We turned off the main road and into a twisting little lane that led past a well-stocked French farm.

"Sells all his milk to Maxim's," the Duchess noted.

The car slowed to a stop in time in front of a rustic and somewhat battered wooden gate.

"Well, this is it," she said. "The Duke lived in palaces all his life, but he loves this best of all. I lived in something less than palaces, a lot less, come to think of it. But, never mind, here we are. If the Duke likes it here, I like it here."

The gate was opened by a raw-jawed farmer's wife, and the widened view revealed a pleasant cobbled court surrounded by low-slung buildings constructed to mill grain in Elizabeth's age. A Mercury station wagon was being unloaded before the main lodge.

"The Duke's back from his golf," she exclaimed as we drove up to the door. She led me inside past a polished bell from the racing cutter *Britannia,* sailed by Edward VII and George V.

"Darling, where are you?" she trilled as she ascended a staircase with a balustrade made of the thick red plush roping one associates with the prize ring. There was no response.

"He must be walking the dogs," the Duchess said as we came into the large living room. She dropped her coat absently and began thumbing through her mail with the avidity of a school girl. It gave me time to look around: a room where grain once was stored now was miraculously transformed. The centuries-old beams, scrupulously whitewashed, looked down on a handsome decor: a huge red-and-white patterned rug, comfortable divans and chairs, fireplace, beautiful late fall flower-and-leaves arrangements, a large painting of the Duchess in blue taffeta by Étienne Drian and a larger one of the Duke, as Prince of Wales, astride his favorite chestnut hunter and wearing his nattiest pink coat.

The mail held no great attraction for the Duchess. She dropped it back on the table, crossed the room, and opened the French doors that led to a flat-stoned terrace marked by a sundial placed there in 1730. As we walked toward the mill race that once had turned the long-gone mill wheel, the Duke came up the lower path with the four pugs. He was hatless and wearing a red woolen shirt and red-and-white polka-dotted silk muffler.

He was kind enough to remember a meeting of twenty years before when, as Governor of the Bahamas, he invited a group of New York sportswriters to Nassau to cover a British Red Cross charity golf match involving Bobby Jones, Walter Hagen, Gene Sarazen, and Tommy Armour. He had served as scorekeeper and pin-holder.

We strolled inside. Tea was ready: intricately arranged shrimp in their shells, hot little squares of melted cheese and bacon on toast, cornbread, petits fours, jam, marmalade.

"It's China," the Duchess said of the tea, pouring her husband a second large cup, with milk.

"We much prefer it to India's," the Duke said, seriously. "We get it in New York. It's the same tea your J. Pierpont Morgan used to bring over for his grouse shooting. I carry it on all my trips, even to golf. Had a spot of it after today's round. The other chaps did a most unusual thing. They brought out splits of champagne and actually drank them. Imagine anyone having a *split* of champagne. . . ."

When tea was done, the Duchess retired across the room to a partly completed jigsaw which apparently had stumped but bemused her for some time past, and the Duke and I began a meandering dialogue that was to last the remainder of the weekend. First off, he produced an advance copy of the London *TV Times* in which, surprisingly, he had a signed article of a most intimate nature. He suggested I read it, and in the silence of the room I read:

> This I can say: in these past 25 years I have never, for one moment, regretted the decision I took then.
> That weekend party at Melton Mowbray in 1931, when I first met Wallis Warfield, changed the course of English history. It certainly changed the course of my life—but how empty my life would have been if I had never gone to that weekend house party.
> A man can come to a point in his life when there are two clearly defined paths ahead. He has to take one or the other and it is then when he is most alone. Only he can decide—no one can do it for him.
> As Shakespeare put it:

> > "There is a tide in the affairs of men,
> > Which, taken at the flood leads on to fortune;
> > Omitted, all the voyage of their life
> > Is bound in shallows and in miseries."

> My path led on to great good fortune, the fortune which comes from the knowledge that time has long since sanctified a true and faithful union.

The Duchess had read the article. Still puzzling over her jigsaw, she spoke up as I handed the magazine back to the Duke. She spoke without emotion.

"I was against the abdication," she said of the event that rocked Britain and the world. "Mrs. Simpson was more against the abdication than anybody. I'm not at all sure it would be different if it happened today. It is out of the question, I think, for anyone with the title of Defender of the Faith to marry a divorced woman. Perhaps if I had been a British girl it might have been more acceptable. The British didn't like Americans very much twenty-five years ago."

The Duke stuffed a small prepared barrel of tobacco in the bowl of his slender pipe and lighted it as he listened to the Duchess.

"If I had it to do over again the same thing would have happened," he said seriously. "There would be nothing different. We've had a fascinating life together. I had a great life before the abdication, certainly. But this life of ours for the past twenty-five years together has been simply flawless."

From the other side of the room the Duchess, still engrossed in her puzzle, asked, "Who said, 'Old men forget, young men don't know'?"

They had both been in London not long before, for business and Christmas shopping. I asked him if he had seen his niece, the Queen. He seemed surprised.

"Oh, no," he said. "I don't see my family any more, really, except of course at coronations and tragedies. I don't see them because they won't see the Duchess. Simple as that."

He cocked his ruddy, sandy-haired head quizzically. "Would you see your family if they wouldn't see your wife?" he asked.

I asked him if he would comment on an article, printed in France just previously, stating that he still enjoyed a handsome income from the British Crown.

"I never got a nickel," he said. "I've heard for years that great story that I inherited my grandmother Queen Alexandra's jewelry. I inherited absolutely nothing. I put in seventeen hard years of work for my country and the Commonwealth. I went straight from Oxford into four years of war, then came out in 1919 and worked until 1936. I'm not even assigned a secretary."

His show of polite indignation waned when I wondered aloud how things would be this day, had he taken the Duchess' advice and given her up.

"If I were king?" he asked, raising an eyebrow. "I don't think I could have done anything differently, really. I would have been bound, as my brother was bound, by the limitations of a constitutional monarchy. A king has no influence in government. My government was all against anything belligerent in its outlook toward Germany and Italy, though I must say that Anthony Eden quarreled with Hitler and Mussolini personally.

"It takes a king a long time even to partly influence his government. As you get older, you can point out to the politicians where they are wrong, wrong from your point of view, that is. But you have no power to disapprove of their acts. My father exerted a certain amount of influence at times near the end of his life, but surely not the power to disapprove."

Would there always be a British royal family?

The Duke of Windsor thought about that for some time.

"Always is a very big word," he said with a smile. "But the way things are going in the world, ours may be the last, one of these years.

I remember before the first World War that my family was constantly receiving and returning visits of what we called the foreign relations —Queen Victoria's host of descendants.

"I saw Kaiser Wilhelm II, my father's first cousin, at a shooting party at Sandringham. He could make himself very pleasant when he wanted to, though a real Prussian. I remember him mostly because that was the day I had my first automobile ride.

"Czar Nicholas, another first cousin, visited us eight years before he and his family were murdered. Alphonso XIII of Spain married one of my father's first cousins and used to come to us for shooting and polo. I was called to Windsor Castle from Oxford when my father entertained Archduke Franz Ferdinand, soon enough killed at Sarajevo. Very elegant sort of fellow. I remember Carlos of Portugal, too, fat and jolly little fellow. Assassinated, you know. And so on.

"Anyway, there were twenty monarchies in Europe when I was young. Now there are seven: Great Britain, Norway, Sweden, Denmark, Belgium, Holland, and Greece. Wars play hell with monarchies."

How had the years altered the Crown he wore?

"The colonies, chiefly," he said. "We had the lot when I was King."

"You were actually King-Emperor, weren't you?" the Duchess asked idly from her jigsaw.

"Yes, I was," the Duke said as if speaking of some remote relative. "But I wasn't the last. My brother was until 1947. That's when India went."

"This puzzle is just too much," the Duchess said. "The worst part of it is they say on the box how many hours it should be done in. It takes us days! It's disgraceful."

The Duke nodded, then continued, "Actually, there was always pressure about India from the Socialists. I never met Gandhi or Nehru. When I went out there as Prince of Wales they were both in jail. Later, I watched Gandhi when he came to London to see my father. Wore that extreme outfit.

"Now they've given Kenya independence. Mark my words, there'll be Mau Mau troubles there. But I suppose things will settle in time, even though some of those African nations aren't as yet fitted for self-rule. I'll say this for the British—they've always let their colonial peoples into the civil-service class. Would you have a drink?"

As we walked toward a small bar in the next room, I asked him about his golf.

"Oh, that," he shrugged. "I remember the old one about the golfer who was asked what his handicap was and he replied, 'me.' That's pretty much my own story. I must be an eighteen handicap right now. But I remember that once I had a seventy-five, holing all putts."

We were not out of range of the Duchess.

"You have pleasant memories," she observed cheerfully.

He poured me a Scotch and himself a bourbon. I asked for ice.

"Did you specify ice because of your experience with British hospitality?" he asked with a twinkle. "We always have ice here. This is an Anglo-American home."

"It's better for you without ice," the Duchess remarked, from fathoms deep in her puzzle.

Did they anticipate being interviewed on TV on the occasion of this anniversary?

"Not a chance," said the Duke, who once appeared with the Duchess on "Person to Person," on which program the Duchess had plainly startled Edward R. Murrow with how she could play jacks and balls.

"Everybody who gets off a plane after an eight-hour trip seems to get interviewed on television now," the Duchess said, giving up on her puzzle. "They're either motion picture people who want to advertise themselves or politicians."

"We're too old-fashioned for that sort of thing, really," the Duke said. "And handicapped, too. We cannot discuss politics, or express much of an opinion on anything."

"We don't have anything to say on TV," the Duchess agreed. "The Duke is right, we're old-fashioned. Why, I don't even fly. I flew from Miami to Nassau in 1940 and haven't been in the air since."

I asked her why she didn't fly.

"It's very simple," said the beautiful woman who rocked an empire. "I'm afraid.

"Now, shall we freshen up for dinner?"

The Duchess, in something black, with green shoes, emerald bracelet, and five strands of pearls, was standing before a dancing fire in the cozy reception room of the "big house" when I arrived from my plush cow shed for dinner. The fire was flattering, but hardly needed. She was stunning.

The Duke clumped down the sharp-turning staircase, with two pugs plopping behind him. The Duchess had said offhandedly earlier in the day that the Duke usually dressed for dinner, guests or not. It was an understatement. His dinner jacket was in one of his family's plaids. His shirt was fluffy and lacy. His "black tie" was as thick and broad as the mustache of a red-headed RAF ace. His socks were Argyle. We had a drink and, rather wildly, the talk turned to television again.

"I got interested in your television because I like baseball very much," the Duke said, looking into his little bowl of iced Polish vodka. "I was having a manicure at our place in the Waldorf, actually, and on came the Series. Fascinating! In time, I became so interested in your television that I began watching the late shows. That's shameful, of course. Worse, I even picked up some of your commercials."

I was about to ask a question when it became apparent he was not finished with the thought. He cleared his throat and then in the most jovial manner recited:

"Double your pleasure, double your fun, Doublemint, Doublemint, Doublemint gum!"

The Duchess smiled wanly.

"I learned another one during the TV golf matches," the Duke continued, and forthwith sang the Miller's High Life theme.

"French television is so sad," the Duchess said. "The news is excellent, but before you get it, and sometimes after you get it, there's a play or a sad song. French television women stars usually throw themselves into the Seine at the end of each show. Shall we dine?"

The candle-lit dining room nearby was in fine taste, a taste which included the food.

"The French oysters are much better," the Duchess, a renowned authority on haute cuisine, said during that course. "They have a coppery taste. I can't bear American oysters. They're so mushy. Now, Dungeness crab, that's different. There's nothing better than the Dungeness at Twenty One in New York."

The Duke interrupted to say that the main course would be grouse sent to him by the Duke of Buccleuch.

"It's spelled almost like Bookloosh and pronounced Baklush," he said. "Very odd, and I might say a very rich family."

The Duchess placed an immaculately manicured index finger on the button of a metal turtle near her plate and a bell-buzzer rang inside the iron reptile with startling clarity. I jumped.

"Whenever the Duke remembers a name at dinner I always ring the buzzer," the Duchess said merrily. "That's his reward. Women are so much better at names than men, haven't you noticed? Time and time again a husband fumbles around at a party and finally, in desperation, whispers to his wife, 'What's his name?' The wife always remembers. Women also make very good executives." She seemed to be daring one or both of us to challenge that. I waited for the Duke, but his concentration was on his grouse.

"Name ten," I said, after a bit. She plunged immediately into a list that included Mrs. Michael Paul, who headed the brokerage firm of A. M. Kidder; Mary Roebling, president of a bank in Trenton, New Jersey; Mary Lasker, Peggy Joyce, Marion Davies, Mrs. Mortimer Davis, Margaret Biddle, Dorothy Shaver, ". . . and I don't even know the people in the Middle West and the Coast, but I'm sure there are dozens of fine business women there.

"Oh, and what about Marjorie Post?" she continued, quietly triumphant. "Marjorie keeps tabs on everybody who eats a Post Toastie. She tests new products at General Foods. She's terrific at meetings. If I had a fortune like Marjorie's, I'd taste the products, too."

The phone had been ringing through the last half of the Duchess' tribute to the she-wolves of Wall Street, and now Robert, their all-around man, came in to whisper to the Duke, "Lord Dudley is calling from London, sir."

The Duke put down his utensils with a sigh. He had skipped lunch to play golf and had recently described himself as famished.

"Why do they always call at this time?" he asked. He got up and trooped off to a neighboring room and its uncertain French phone. "Hello, Dudley?" we heard him shout. Then, "Yes? . . . No! . . . Yes? . . . oh, no!"

"Something's wrong with Dudley," the Duchess divined. "He's the Duke's most faithful friend. A wonderful friend to us."

As the Duke continued his thunderous affirmative-negative responses over the thin, trembling line to London, the Duchess discoursed on grouse.

"There are three kinds of grouse," she said, "white, gray and black —or is it pink? Anyway, one type never leaves England. . . ."

The Duke returned to his place at that point, passing, as he did, a fine framed sketch of himself as he looked in his buoyant twenties.

"Poor old Bruce Ogleby," he said.

"Why, he was your aide-de-camp," the Duchess said, concerned.

"It's Primrose," the Duke said with simple eloquence. There was a decent period of silence, broken finally by the Duchess.

"What's the grouse that never flies away from England?" she asked.

The Duke looked up from his grouse, interested.

"I don't know," he said, ready to be told.

"But you did know when I asked you the other night," the Duchess pursued.

"Well, I don't know now," said England's foremost expatriate.

We moved on from the late lamented Primrose and home-based grouse to travel. Inevitably, I mentioned Switzerland.

"A terrifically well-ordered hospital, Switzerland," the Duchess said. "The Swiss have no show of wealth. They have developed the art of being inconspicuous. We know a couple of Swiss bankers who must be among the richest men in the world, but they always stay at small, cheap places."

The Duchess rose and moved serenely alone into the bar-TV room, and soon she called out that the news was on. The Duke and I went through the low-slung door, stooping. Chancellor Adenauer was on screen, arriving in Paris for his talks with President de Gaulle.

"Adenauer's a fine man," the Duke said, settling into his chair. He started into an anecdote about the Chancellor.

"Shhh!" the Duchess said without taking her eyes off the TV set. "I want to hear the news." Then she half-turned to me and said, "He always talks during the news."

The Duke chuckled amiably, lighting his pipe. "I do at that," he said.

As de Gaulle and Adenauer went through their paces and the commentator babbled in French, I looked about the pleasant room and was struck by an embroidered cushion in one of the chairs. On it was sewn, "Don't look now, somebody may be gaining on you." In my room in the cow shed there was a cushion emblazoned with, "Smile at the poorest tramp as you would at the highest king."

Scenes from the action in the Congo were on when I looked back

at the TV set. The Duke had picked up Disraeli, one of the pugs, and
was thoughtfully stroking him.

"We're living in terrible times," he said. He was about to go on
but the scene changed to a discussion of French labor-management
problems. The Duke, whose French was uncertain, shook his
head. "Terrible," he said. "Now if they had social security in The
States. . . ."

"They certainly do have social security in The States," the Duchess
said, without turning away from the set. Then, "Wait a minute. This
is marvelous!" The on-screen discussion enraptured her.

"The Duchess knows French so much better than I," the Duke said
regretfully. But his mood soon brightened.

"That's football!" he said delightedly, as the picture turned to a
Rugby match. "The French have become very sportsminded since
the German occupation. I think our football is much more interesting
than your brand in America. Your football, I must say, is quite boring.
I don't speak ill of your baseball, however. That's enchanting. Who's
playing, dear?"

"I think it's two French teams," the Duchess said, scanning the
action.

"That's too French for me," the Duke boomed, and we all laughed
heartily, and called it a night—another night—at Moulin de la
Tuilerie.

The next morning, Sunday, the Duke gingerly picked his way across
the cobbled courtyard from the main house to my cowshed guest
quarters. A dismal rain, gray as slate, fell on the tableau: The Duke
was hatless but his trim body was encased in a long woolen bathrobe
of bright red. The four pugs were underfoot. White doves fanned
about him.

"Halloooo!" he called through the opened upper half of the split
door. "Anybody home?"

"Only us cows," I said.

"You must see my barn," he said. The dogs, doves and I followed
him across the yard to a low-slung stone building, ancient before my
country was born. The Duke, dogs, and I entered. The birds had other
plans.

"I call it my museum," he said of the large room. It was at least
that. There was enough memorabilia to stock a wing of the British

Museum, and only then did I understand the concern the Duchess had expressed the night before about the security of the estate. "A lot of what might have been is here," she had put it.

"This table might interest you," the Duke said, falling easily into the role of guide. The beautifully carved piece held a small forest of silver-framed photographs of certain illustrious forebears, a great green tongue of jade combed from some forgotten voyage, and a neat little gold plaque on which was engraved:

On this table King Edward VIII
signed the Instrument of Abdication at 10:30 A.M. December 11, 1936.

If the Duke attached any emotional importance to the object, his cheerful face masked it. He touched a long match to the kindling and crushed paper beneath the fireplace logs, and after a gay shower of sparks the chilled place was aglow with light and warmth. The Duke peeled off his robe and sat down in a deep chair near his hooded break-fast tray. He wore a turtleneck baby-blue sweater, fawn slacks with thin blue stripes forming large squares, and buff and green woolen socks.

I asked him about the abdication speech of a quarter of a century before, that superbly phrased and so touchingly delivered declaration of the heart. Was it true, as often hinted at in America, that Sir Winston Churchill had had a hand in its styling?

"I wrote it myself," the Duke said quickly, as if denying a Baconite claim. He uncovered his toast, buttered a bit, and relaxed.

"I did call him that day and told him I planned to go on the radio that night with a statement I had prepared," he said, his blue eyes re-weighing those crowded hours. "Old Winston said, 'I'd like to see what you have to say.' Naturally, I invited him to come to Fort Belve-dere and I showed it to him. Wouldn't you? I think that if anybody was about to make a speech of that moment, that importance, and had Old Winston in his house, and didn't ask him to look it over, well, that person should have his head examined. Certainly, he made a few suggestions."

He shook his head, affectionately.

"He was always dramatic, Old Winston."

I asked the Duke which member of his family he felt he would most miss that early morning of December 12, 1936, when he sailed away from Portsmouth in H.M.S. *Fury*.

"I don't think anyone's ever asked me that," he said, cocking his head as if to recollect better.

"I really don't think I missed anybody, longed for anybody in my family," he said after a while. "I would miss Fort Belvedere. I made Fort Belvedere. As for persons, the only one in my mind was in France, getting her divorce. I hoped she would marry me."

I had read that the parting from his mother, Queen Mary, was a tearful one.

"Really?" the Duke asked with surprise. "The only nice thing, human thing, my mother said to me during that time when I was fighting a very lonely battle was, 'Isn't it a pity it'll be so long before you see her again?' "

The reference was to the then-prevalent six-month period of cloister during divorce proceedings.

"It was a strange age," he mused, lighting up his first pipe for the day. "My lawyer told me that if I even stayed in the same country with Wallis during that period, he would retire as my counsel."

We browsed the room after breakfast. There, under glass, rested the coronet he wore at the coronation of his father half a century before. About the place were arranged four yellow-skinned drums, one of which had shared his World War I service with the Grenadier Guards. Up and down the beams that framed the door were tacked the slender racing plates of hunters and jumpers he had ridden in a day when his hair-raising croppers were regarded as royal slapstick.

He took me for a climb through the large rock garden that rose from the boarded and winterized swimming pool. "Charlie Cushing —you knew him around New York—used to call this Cardiac Hill," the Duke called back as he negotiated the slippery stepping stones without drawing a deep breath. "Fine man, Charlie was. As friendly to caddie as to the president of the club." At the summit of the garden he turned and viewed the little walled complex of the old mill, and he could not have been more pleased by what he saw than if he were beholding Buckingham as Edward VIII.

It was time to join the Duchess and a newly arrived luncheon guest, their good friend Margery Wilson, an attractive American widow who lived in New York and Paris. As we walked toward the main house along the rushing mill race, the Duke chatted about a variety of things.

Christmas cards: "I wish I could stop sending them, as my cousin Mountbatten did, but the Duchess thinks it might offend old friends. . . ."

The Hoovers, Herbert and J. Edgar: "Great fellows!"

New York traffic: "Abominable! It's your Fifth Avenue busses, bumper to bumper for miles."

The then-delicate Berlin situation: "Your Roosevelt had a lot to do with that, I must say."

Suicidist Robert R. Young: "A great friend . . . poor Bob."

Clothing: "I'm not a full-fledged client of your man H. Harris, in New York. He does your President, you know. I met Kennedy when he was a boy living with his parents at the American Embassy in London. But that's neither here nor there. I just get my pants from H. Harris. They don't make good pants in England, for some reason, just as they don't make good coats in America. So I have the coats done on this side and the trousers in New York. The Duchess calls it 'pants-across-the-sea.' "

We rubbed mossy shoes on the mat outside the living-room French doors and came in out of the damp gray day, followed by four damp gray pugs who marched immediately to the fireplace and faced it like pleased figurines. Mrs. Wilson curtsied ever so briefly and affectionately as she accepted the Duke's outstretched hand.

"Here's the news," the Duchess called from among her treasury of British Sunday newspapers. She gave the Duke an astonishingly complete rundown of current happenings. It would have done justice to their favorite American newscaster, Bob Trout of CBS. Drinks came along as she finished, while the Duke leafed through the pages of the *Express*.

"Ah," he exclaimed, as he spotted a picture of the Duchess, taken the previous week at the opening of the new show at the Lido in Paris. She and the Duke had simply been part of a large party held there. But only the Duchess' picture appeared. The caption cruelly noted that the photograph of her was taken at a "strip" place.

"It's a jolly good picture of you, dear," the Duke said warmly.

A pleasant luncheon followed, with talk as varied as those opposite poles of subject matter, psychiatry and the Peppermint Lounge, then New York's busiest Twist parlor. The Duchess announced that she was determined to avoid the former like a scourge but look in on the latter when she and the Duke were next in New York.

"You have to be rich to go in for psychiatry," she observed, studying the neatly written menu near her plate, the better to describe the oncoming dish.

"Or lonely," Mrs. Wilson suggested.

"A good friend to talk to is the best thing," the Duchess said quietly. "There is nothing better than that."

The Duke nodded, and the little room was suddenly hushed, and I a witless intruder.

The sober mood was still about as the Duke walked me to the car that would take me back to Paris. I had one more question. The Duchess had said the night before, "He should've given me up. It would have been so much easier on him." I asked him if he wanted to say anything about that.

"She lost out in that argument," the Duke of Windsor said with steady pride. "I won."

Westbrook Pegler was the writer most of us chose to ape when I was coming along. Any young sportswriter who tried to write in Damon Runyon's patented present tense ("I am sitting in Mindy's . . .") was laughed at and thereafter suspect. But to write a good hard sentence like Peg was to be admired; not many could. Peg could keep a forty-word sentence under iron control, like Clyde Beatty in a cage of wild beasts, once he took command. Taking command was something else. At a fight, ballgame, or trial he would rip more unfinished leads out of his typewriter than the rest of us combined, crush them into balls, and drop them at his feet. It was sometimes difficult to resist stooping to appropriate something he had discarded as unworthy of his by-line, because it was probably better than the product on which I was about to settle.

Peg was a considerate man with his peers and inferiors. He would make a point of dropping a note to a newcomer in the business, if something the newcomer had written attracted him, compliment him, and wish him well. He gave me one of my first national notices. In an Esquire piece about New York sportswriters, he wrote that there were four others who worked on out-of-town papers who could hold their own if they ever chose to come to New York. He mentioned Bill Cunningham, then writing the sports column for the Boston *Post*, Ed Danforth of the Atlanta *Journal*, Warren Brown of the

Chicago *Examiner,* and me. It was a breathtaking experience to see my name in the body of an absorbing article about men ostensibly beyond me in prestige and skills.

After I reached New York, Peg and his wife, Julie Harpman, a former reporter who was as gentle in her estimate of mankind as Peg was barbed, were fine to Millie and to me. We discovered what so many before us had: that Pegler, the shatterer of images and piercer of stuffed shirts, was not the same Pegler one might run into at dinner or later. The latter Peg was filled with laughter, good stories, unswerving devotion to Julie—who had a heart condition—and his gallantry charmed all within sight and sound. It was another Pegler who pulled up a chair to a typewriter each day, lighted a cigarette as if it were a fuse, and exploded.

"Something snaps in his brain just before he hits the first key," became an awed cliché among his envious contemporaries.

One day at the *American* our sports department was filled with the noise of heavy hammering on the floor above, where construction work of some sort was under way.

"What's that?" Ed Frayne asked, as sledgehammer blows shook the place.

"That's Pegler, writing his column," Sid Mercer said without looking up from his typewriter.

Peg wrote several tender columns, as if to confound those who swore he was constitutionally incapable of sentiment. He enjoyed Walt Disney's *Snow White* and said so with considerable warmth. When Bill Corum was pinked by a bullet fired by the brother of an attractive lady Bill was, alas, in the very act of romancing, the cover-up story given to the newspapers was that Bill was struck by a stray shot while strolling along Park Avenue. Like everybody else, Peg liked Bill, even though Corum had once raked him sharply for predicting that the chief result of the Joe Louis-Max Baer fight at the Yankee Stadium would be a race riot in Harlem. Now, Peg sprang to his wounded friend's defense. He wrote a column soundly denouncing Park Avenue and all its people for hurting Bill.

He once wrote a kind piece about President Truman, too, but a closer scanning suggested that the tribute was not as inspired by Truman as by Peg's demoniacal hatred of Roosevelt. Two other Pegler columns that were honestly intended to be filled with sweetness and light (he once considered naming his column "Sweetness and Light") backfired. He had been rapping Knute Rockne for several years when Arch Ward, sports editor of the Chicago *Tribune,* arranged the first meeting between the two. They hit it off famously. Peg sat down to write what he considered an apologetic column. It was the only one Rockne sued on. In the other instance, Peg's good friend E. Phocion Howard, who ran a racing paper named the New York *Press* and often made a point of inviting prominent sportswriters to spend some time with him at his big rented house during the Saratoga meeting, died while Peg and Julie were his house guests. Peg's obituary-column was a moving tribute to his old friend "Phoce." For several paragraphs, that is. Then Peg launched into an attack on touting, on papers like the *Press,* and finally got around to the late-lamented.

"I guess he was just a bum," Peg's obit ended.

Peg and Julie, Runyon and his wife Patrice, and Millie and I spent a night at Tom Taggart's landmark spa at French Lick, Indiana, before moving on to Louisville for the running of a Kentucky Derby. It was a pleasant evening. Taggart sent a bottle of champagne to our table during dinner. The next day, Peg and I went to the cashier's cage to check out. He was the first in line. The girl in the cage smiled sweetly at him and said Mr. Taggart had instructed her that there would be no check for the Peglers. Peg protested at some length, stopping only when the girl said plaintively that she would lose her job if she disobeyed Mr. Taggart. I got the same treatment when I asked for our bill.

"Wasn't that nice of Tom?" Peg asked as we moved toward his car, following our baggage. He was going to drive us to Louisville.

"Sure was."

He was silent for a time, and I supposed he was reflecting on how nice Taggart had been. I was wrong.

"I can't wait to knock his brains out," Peg mused.

After Peg parted company with Scripps-Howard and joined Hearst's King Features Syndicate at more money, KFS attempted to capture his turbulent talents in a short biographical blurb to be distributed to prospective clients. It was a losing effort, of course. Finally, KFS's able public-relations man, Joe Willicombe, Jr., asked him to write the sketch himself. Peg snorted. But one day a sketch, unsigned, arrived.

It remains a treasured item in the syndicate's files:

Westbrook James Pegler was born in Minneapolis August 2, 1894, the son of Arthur James Pegler, an Englishman who had been a farm hand in Le Mars and other towns in an area of Iowa where there were a colony of English second sons whose fathers paid the Iowa farmers to teach them farming. For the most part they rode broad farm plugs over hill and dale yelling "Yoicks!" an Elizabethan term meaning, "I say, what ho!" and "tantivy," whose meaning is obvious to all right-thinking Americans. His mother was Frances Nicholson Pegler. The Nicholsons came from Conemara, Ireland, and are descendants of the Irish kings.

Arthur James was a third son, however, and had to work as a plow-jockey until he could escape to Council Bluffs where he painted front porches with a technique which was the basis of the school which employs the fried egg and a violin to depict the death of Aristotle.

After a while he went to Minneapolis where he became a reporter, sometimes working for three papers at once and earning up to $45 a week. There was no income tax in those days so thus, like E. H. Harriman, he was able to found a fortune. He later worked in Chicago where he became a tradition and in New York where he became a septuagenarian. Then he retired to live on a ranch near Tucson, Arizona, where now at 90 he writes letters of great vigor and beauty about his feet, which hurt from arthritis. He does this on a double-deck Smith-Premier, model of 1894 which burns soft coal.

Westbrook Pegler went to Horace Greeley grammar school and Lane Technical High School in Chicago and quit in disgust because he could not learn long division. He went to work for the United Press as cub in 1910 and, being a thoughtful little fellow, used to hang around police stations musing on the mysteries of long division, a series of reveries which gave the world the Westbrook Pegler Method, which is worked with salted peanuts. In 1912 he went to Loyola Academy, a Jesuit high school and, in the Spring of 1913 he went back to the U.P., his education completed. That Fall he got a job as cub on the Des Moines *News*. In 1914 he became bureau manager for the U.P. in St. Louis and in the Spring of 1916 he was sent to London. He was assigned to Queenstown with the destroyer *Flotilla* in the Spring of 1917, and after a spat with Admiral Sims he was sent to France with the AEF where, in due course, he had a spat with Pershing and was relieved and sent back to London, where he had a spat with Maj. Gen. Sir Frederick F. B. Maurice, the British chief of staff, because the boss told Pegler to ask Maurice who had supremacy in the air in France and Maurice gave him an oblique answer to which Pegler retorted, "Why don't you answer the question?"

After the war Pegler became markets editor of the United News in New York. He also held down the positions of sports editor, cable editor, fashion editor, society editor, and editor until he was hired by the Chicago Tribune Syndicate in 1925 to do sports. This phase ended in 1933 when he went cosmic for Roy Howard, spending a good deal of this time in Washington.

In 1944 he went to King Features and a lot of people wanted to know what he and Howard had scrapped about. Nobody would believe there had been no scrap and finally Pegler said "go to hell" and refused to discuss it any more. For God's sake has a man no privacy?

In 1942 Pegler received the Pulitzer Prize for distinguished reporting. He has an honorary degree as Doctor of Laws from Knox College and has twice won the National Headliners Club annual award, which don't mean a thing. He has also received the American Legion Award for Americanism.

In 1954 he received the "Silver Lady" Award for being "the outstanding reporter and columnist of the year" from the Banshees, a New York luncheon club composed of editors, writers, artists, and others in the creative trades. But it was awarded by King Features because King Features Syndicate wanted to make him feel good at the age of 60. It made him feel real good, too. At the same luncheon a remarkable and unique tribute was paid him by 25 winners of the Congressional Medal of Honor, who presented him with a special citation for Americanism.

He quit smoking in the year 1947, but not drinking. He likes to drink. Don't you? His hobbies are golf and thinking. Not very good at either but always in there swinging.

Peg's epic clash with Quentin Reynolds, which resulted in Reynolds' successful libel action, and his running wars with Walter Winchell and Drew Pearson, organized labor in general, and Eleanor Roosevelt in particular, the New York *Post,* Henry Luce, and the detractors of Sen. Joe McCarthy left him little time for laughter in his later years with King Features. Julie's untimely death in 1954, after she had enjoyed herself so much being with him in Geneva at the Eisenhower-Bulganin-Khrushchev-Eden-Faure summit meeting, knocked the remaining levity out of him. Fearless to the end of his stay with Hearst, he took on Hearst. Bill's Task Force, Peg wrote, reminded him of the Rover Boys.

I saw him at the office in New York just before he was about to leave, or be asked to leave, King Features. Peg said he hoped to take things easy for a bit, then start writing magazine pieces.

"Maybe even some fiction," he said.

"You'll be great, Peg," I said, and meant it. "You'll murder that kind of pitching."

It was a shock to learn later that he had decided to write for the John Birch Society's magazine. He left there soon enough, and the story spread that he had quit because he found the John Birchers too liberal for his blood. Whatever his reason for leaving, Peg dropped a notch in the profession he had graced so long and often so superbly. He found ventilation in *The Councilor,* a four-page sheet published twice monthly in Shreveport, Louisiana, as the official journal of the Citizens' Council of Louisiana. In its issue of February 20, 1966, the man who once was moved deeply by *Snow White* wrote:

> I have known Mike Quill for a hundred years as a cheap, flannel-mouthed shanty-Irish bum. The people of New York should have killed him cold stone dead on the sidewalk during his insurrection against the biggest and worst city in the world. This louse never was any good and should have been dumped for the benefit of our country 'way back in Roosevelt's time. And that big melodious pansy should have been run out of our capital because he was crazy from the effects of that disease which started in the marrows of his legs. The decay went to the brain about the time that he began to meddle with the world in an obsession that he was ordained by God or Fate or his own lantern-jawed, money-loving old lady to slaughter millions of human beings and deliver his own trusting country into ghastly carnage. Now Lyndon Johnson inherits tumult and is afraid to bring it to a halt.
>
> If Johnson had the trace of honor and the courage which his office calls for he should have moved right in and taken the initiative away from that long limpid faker named Lindsay who won the election to the City Hall in a clowning match with Bill Buckley. Johnson then should have clamped down some kind of material law to bring the idiot citizens out of their daze. This

Quill donkey is a mush-mouth faker who has been getting by on his Irish brogue for God knows how long. There is an old fable that Quill walks with a limp in his r-r-rump, assisted by a blackthorn shillaleh because the Black and Tans or the Irish Republican Army kicked him out of some stinking cobbeen around Cork back in the days of the Thrubble over the Republic. Well, he does put on the limp but again, let us not forget that Roosevelt used that act, too.

. . . When the State and the City of New York and Lyndon Johnson with his stinking Democratic Party can't run the buses in spite of such filthy apes as mush-mouth Quill, this country is shot to hell for sure.

They still laugh at Calvin Coolidge, but you remember what he did when the Boston cops abandoned the people in a Police strike when he was mayor. He fired the whole rotten Irish mob and made them take it and like it. And not one of them ever got his job back. Not one. And every last one of those apes was a flannel-mouth mick from Dublin or Cork like mush-mouth Mike Quill.

An editorial note preceded Pegler's piece in *The Councilor*. It noted, "The late Mike Quill had fifty-five Communist and Communist-front citations in a 1944 Congressional report, now hidden from the public by Rep. Edwin Willis. Most of those listed were of Russian Khazar ancestry, but Quill said he was an Irishman. This Pegler column was written prior to his strange death, but it contains so many important references of historical value that it is being printed as written."

I miss Peg . . . the Peg one might run into at dinner, or later.

11. *Bigger Game*

Thanks chiefly to the Hearsts, father and son, my past thirty years have been crowded with the kind of opportunities and breaks all reporters dream about. They bought me a box seat near a world stage whose boards resound to the trod of a cast of characters unmatched in this century.

The dramatis personae include the glorious, inglorious, thrilling, boring, noble, despicable, kind, wicked, just, sadistic, immortal, transient. It holds every President since Hoover, every responsible hoodlum since Capone, three Popes, every renowned ballplayer since Walter Johnson, every football Hall of Famer since Jim Thorpe, every top fighter since Dempsey ruled, yes, and Churchill, Khrushchev, Nehru, Diem, Sukarno, de Gaulle, Franco, Castro, Ulbricht, kings and ex-kings, astronauts, atomic scientists, assassins, actors, actresses.

I have long since lost track of how many miles I've traveled in search of stories. It would be an impressive figure, for I've traveled in Afghanistan and Australia, Brazil and Burma, Chile and China, Denmark and the Dominican Republic, Eire and Eniwetok, France and Finland, Communism's Germany, Greece, Hungary and Helvetia, Iceland and India, Japan and Jordan, Korea and Kuwait, Libya and Liechtenstein, Malta and Monaco, Netherlands and Norway, the Philippines and Poland, Rumania and Rhodesia, Spain and Sweden, Thailand and Turkey, United Arab Republic and the Union of Soviet Socialist Republics, Vatican City State and Vietnam, West Germany and Westminster Abbey, Xochimilco and Xenia, have at least flown over Yap and Ypsilanti, but never once have set foot on Zambia.

Still, it's not too bad for a bloke who never ventured the 230 miles from his native Washington, D.C. to New York until he was twenty-three.

It is not easy or perhaps even sensible to attempt to choose one figure out of that fabled cast, or one scene or act that transcended all others. But near the top of those who played their historic roles would be Douglas MacArthur.

MacArthur would have risen to eminence—a comet trailing a tail of idolizers and critics—at any period in American history. His bearing (some thought it overbearing), his looks, voice, military skills, and sure sense of being one with history moved him with natural buoyancy to the top.

He was born with a silver sword in his mouth. His father, Arthur MacArthur, joined the Union forces in 1862 at the age of seventeen. He won the Congressional Medal of Honor at eighteen, at Missionary Ridge. He and his men were raiding a strong Confederate earthworks when the soldier who carried the regimental flag pitched forward with a bullet in his head. With a bravery that was later to be rendered hackneyed by a generation of lurid lithographers, MacArthur seized the flag and led the charge through a withering fire. He was the first man to mount the works, and there he planted the flag, changing the tide of battle.

His son Douglas won just about every honor West Point could bestow: highest scholastic marks since a cadet of twenty-five years before, John J. Pershing. He was First Captain of Cadets, first West Point ball-player to score a run against Navy . . . and first to have his mother, a militant matriarch who adored him, live on the campus.

After graduation, MacArthur was attached to his father's group of officers assigned by President Theodore Roosevelt to serve as observers of the Russo-Japanese War. The group was the guest of the Japanese, whose young officers young MacArthur came to know and admire. In fact, he participated in the Battle of Mukden with them, a classic carnage in which the Russians lost 97,000 dead and the Japanese between 40,000 and 50,000. At the height of the battle the elder MacArthur received an urgent message asking him to order his son back to the safety of General Nogi's headquarters. General MacArthur assumed that his son had left the safety of headquarters to find a position that gave him a better view of the gigantic battle. As a matter of fact, Douglas had done just that. But the sight of a Japanese company striving unsuccessfully five times to win a Russian position near his vantage place had been too much for his soldierly instincts. Whereupon, 1st Lt. Douglas MacArthur, U.S. Army Engineers, raced to the ranks of the deflated Japanese company, roused its spirit, and led it up the hill by a new route to capture the Russian battery.

In the Mexican border troubles he infiltrated the insurgent General Huerta's territory disguised, he liked to say later, as a "Mexican bum." (It was a description which later drew a snort of derision from his West Point classmate Gen. Hugh Johnson: "I'll say this much, Doug must have been the damned tallest Mexican bum that ever lived.") His most extravagant act in that disorder was the capture, single-handedly, of the crews of three locomotives. The entourage of flat-wheeled junk clanked into American-held territory in shabby grandeur —under the muzzle of Capt. MacArthur's revolver.

In World War I he was gassed, twice wounded, decorated thirteen times for bravery under fire, cited seven additional times for valor, led trench raids, became the youngest (thirty-eight) general in the AEF, returned home to become the youngest (thirty-nine) superintendent of West Point, married wealthy Louise Cromwell Brooks, who took her brother Jimmy (who was to marry Doris Duke, among others) along on the honeymoon.

The morning after the wedding night, the bride (who was later to marry actor Lionel Atwill) swept into the room where Jimmy was having his coffee and said blissfully, "He may be a general in the Army, but he's a buck private in the boudoir." Jimmy always classed it as one of the greatest tributes ever paid to the man, any man.

World War II seemed almost to be a staggering manuscript written especially for Douglas MacArthur: Bataan, Corregidor, The Escape, "I Shall Return," the island-hopping, Leyte, Manila . . . the stern but just terms of the surrender on the deck of the U.S.S. *Missouri*.

But there were frustrations that were never fully ventilated. He deeply resented the continued autonomy of the U.S. Navy though it gave lip service to his position as Supreme Commander of Allied Forces in the Pacific. He told me years later that he considered it the height of folly that FDR and his advisers in Washington had seen fit to favor Eisenhower and the Russians, ". . . while I was forced to operate against a far-flung enemy with scarcely 11 percent of the total output of the American war production."

Most of all, MacArthur was offended by being bypassed in the evolution of what turned out to be the deciding move of the war. In the latter part of July, 1945, he received a request from the Pentagon.

A Brig. Gen. Thomas Farrell was en route with a special message. Would MacArthur please see him?

It was a bother. The Pentagon had a distressing habit of inflicting its couriers on him. MacArthur had bigger things to contend with. He was drawing up plans for the invasion of Japan, scheduled for October. It would be the most mammoth military thrust of all time, and the accepted U.S. casualty estimate was that 600,000 men would be killed before the expected fanatical defense of the islands was crushed.

Tom Farrell, a fine engineer and great gentleman, cooled his heels in MacArthur's outer office for some time—upon his arrival at the Supreme Commander's Philippine headquarters—before being told that MacArthur would see him. For fifteen minutes.

"For thirteen minutes he walked up and down his office telling me about his invasion plans," Farrell told me later. "He was a magnificent figure to behold, and the plans were wonderful, but I was worried about delivering my message. Then, with two minutes left, he looked at his wristwatch and asked me what I had come to see him about.

"I took a breath and told him that we had developed the atomic bomb; that we had tested it at Alamogordo, New Mexico, the previous July sixteenth; that the experts figured the bomb was the equivalent of twenty thousand tons of TNT; that we had two of them ready to be dropped and crews ready to carry out the mission from Tinian."

MacArthur was asked then to issue a directive which would keep the skies clear of routine U.S. air raids over certain Japanese cities during the first clear daytime weather that might accrue around the first week of August.

He agreed, dismissed Farrell, and went back to his invasion plans. Only after Hiroshima and Nagasaki did he learn, to his quiet indignation, that he had been cut out of the tiny top group who knew about The Bomb. It particularly irritated him that his one-time aide on the other side of the world, General Eisenhower, had been kept abreast of the years-long development and proving of the weapon that abruptly ended the costliest war in history.

I wrote the first MacArthur biography, *MacArthur the Magnificent,* published in 1942 by David McKay in this country and Hutchinson in England. It did not have his imprimatur nor his disapproval. It was not until 1950 that I met him, and then under somewhat strained circumstances.

Several days before my scheduled luncheon with the general I wangled a seat aboard his C-54 *Bataan,* bound from Tokyo's Haneda airport to the tin strip at Taegu, Korea. The passenger list was impressive: W. Averell Harriman, on orders from President Truman to review the continuing American retreat and discourage MacArthur from doing anything desperate to reverse the trend, Lt. Gen. Matt Ridgway, destined to replace MacArthur as Supreme Commander of UN forces, Lt. Gen. Lauris Norstad, who became head of NATO's forces, Maj. Gen. Roger Ramey USAF, and perhaps a dozen more generals.

The plane was commanded and piloted by MacArthur's aide and personal pilot, the intrepid Col. Tony Story. As it approached its destination, two events occurred: (1) U.S. fighter planes took up positions on all sides to protect the *Bataan* and its prized passenger list from enemy air attack, and (2) Story strolled down the aisle handing out .45's. He explained placidly that in order to land on the short emergency strip at Taegu it would be necessary for the *Bataan* to pass over positions occupied by North Korean troops and batteries spread along the Naktong River. We could be forced down and, if so, would need the guns.

Tony offered guns to Harriman and to me, in the order named, of course. Harriman waved his aside and I, the only other civilian on the plane, said "Thanks but no thanks," too. Curiously, General Norstad also disdained the offer. Tony went back to the cockpit and landed without further incident on the cramped runway. In a zillion miles of air travel, Story is the finest pilot I've known.

The visiting brass was warmly welcomed by Gen. Walton Walker, soon to meet his death in a jeep accident, and by other field officers. Immediately after a skimpy lunch, which he hardly touched, Harriman asked to see the war. Jeeps rolled up, and our party was taken first to division headquarters for a briefing that seemed to some of the group quite thorough.

"Now let's go to regimental headquarters," Harriman said. And off we went, in the direction of the enemy. There we had a splendid briefing that satisfied almost everyone in the group. But not Harriman. "I'd like to see a battalion headquarters," he said. To reach it we had to ride through ghost villages bereft of even the dogs. At one point the driver of the lead jeep lost his way and for a half hour the string of jeeps followed him down a wrong road.

"I'll take that gun now," General Norstad said quietly. "I'd look pretty silly if we were jumped and I didn't have one."

At battalion headquarters I noticed a single file line of Koreans approaching the group.

"Ours or theirs?" I asked General Gay, commander of the First Cavalry. The lean old pro who had fought under George Patton in World War II shrugged. "We'll know when they reach us. If they shoot, they're theirs."

The sun was getting low, but Harriman had not seen enough.

"Shall we go to a company headquarters?" he asked. Nobody answered. So the string of jeeps moved to the shoreline of the parched and pebbly Naktong. Our artillery was hitting their tree-shrouded encampments across the river with phosphorescent shells. The only adjacent company headquarters lay a half mile down a narrow dirt road that ran along the Naktong's edge and was exposed to the enemy throughout its length. Our group huddled like a football team awaiting the next play.

"Just as well we're not fighting Germans," General Gay said to me. "They'd have hit us with a round of their eighty-eights while we stood here trying to make up our minds."

It was eventually decided that the jeeps would make a dash for it, one at a time, at one minute intervals. Harriman's jeep would go first, carrying Walker and Ridgway with him. The driver gave it the gas, and it pounded down the dirt road, kicking up a plume of dust. We watched it with keen interest.

"Golly, I hope I don't get Averell Harriman killed here today," Gay sighed. Then he turned to me and said, "We're next, let's go."

The company HQ was a dismal hole filled with soiled and exhausted men. The lieutenant's voice was flat and tired. He had been retreating since the war began and now, in what was called the Pusan Perimeter, there wasn't much more room in which to retreat. A sergeant put it more bluntly to Harriman.

"They'll overrun us tonight," he said.

It turned out to be an accurate appraisal, but when it happened we were en route back to Tokyo after a hair-raising take-off by Colonel Story. In order to get up sufficient speed on the inadequate stretch of tin strip, Tony did not put his flaps down until within a few yards of the deep mud at the end of the runway. We leaped into the air in a manner most unbecoming to a matronly C-54.

It was a depressing ride back to Toyko. Harriman became air sick while trying to eat a bite of the cold dinner. The generals were morose or lost in their own appraisals of what they had that day witnessed: proud Americans being pushed toward the sea by Asiatic rabble.

I couldn't wait for the meeting with MacArthur and the golden chance to shower him with all the questions and misgivings that welled in me. But wait I did, and until the scheduled moment, the precise moment. The lieutenant colonel in charge of me appeared in the lobby of the Imperial exactly when he phoned that he would. As the driver of the car with the VIP license plate prepared to drive into the roadway that led to the handsome U.S. Embassy Residence, where Mac-Arthur reigned, the lieutenant colonel let loose a nervous command.

"Take a turn around the block!" he half shouted at the driver. He rechecked his watch and explained. "We're not due until two," he said, "and it's only two minutes till two now."

I must have looked bewildered as the car sped around the block, sending chickens, old women, and children scampering.

"It's hard to explain," the lieutenant colonel said. "But when you're invited to lunch with the General and he says two o'clock, he means two o'clock. It's as bad to be two minutes early as two minutes late."

I began to shake, wondering what calamity would befall all of us if the car had a blowout. But we made it to the doorway so punctiliously that just as it was opened by a Japanese servant the grandfather's clock in the foyer chimed twice.

The chimes seemed to turn everything on. Gracious, vivacious Mrs. MacArthur, standing by herself on the far side of the living room, daintily skipped toward me, extending her hand. Simultaneously, there was a gruffly masculine command of " 'ten-shun!" just outside. The general had arrived and was passing through his towering guard of honor and entering his palace.

Eyes alight with excitement, Mrs. MacArthur dropped my hand and rushed to the general as if they were being reunited after a twenty-five-year separation, instead of a four-hour cleavage. MacArthur lifted her off the floor with his left arm around her slender waist and kept her airborne while her feet made little fluttering motions several inches above rug level, while he acknowledged her introduction of me with his right hand.

It was a frustrating luncheon. He never gave me the slightest opening to blurt the first of all the questions I had in mind. Nor would

Mrs. MacArthur or Col. Sid Huff, one of his aides, who completed the group at the table. MacArthur preferred to talk sports. His range of knowledge was flabbergasting. Though he had not been in the United States for fifteen years, he rattled off facts and figures about then-current athletes as if he were a daily companion. He knew the roster and even the physical condition of the West Point football players Coach Red Blaik would have on hand for the 1950 season (indeed, Blaik had sought and gained his approval before installing the two-platoon system).

Luncheon courses came and went, generally ignored by MacArthur despite Jean's pretty-please pleas that he eat more. My senses reeled. To be so close to a big story and yet so far was intolerable. Now he had embarked on a dissertation—I had missed the beginning of the story—having to do with the troubles he had had with West Point authorities when he, exercising his rights as manager of the football team, had scheduled a game against Bucknell.

"They didn't want to accept Christy as an amateur," MacArthur said, his eyes reliving a crisis of his youth. "Small wonder, Christy was the most superlative punter in the sport."

"Christy who?" I asked numbly. The general dropped his dessert spoon in pained surprise.

"Christy Mathewson, who else?" he boomed.

It was akin to hearing George Washington praised for his surveying or Lincoln for his rail-splitting.

To my dismay, the general dabbed his lips with his napkin, rose from the table, and steered a slow but steady course toward the front door, I at his side. Mrs. MacArthur bade me good-bye. Huff shook hands and disappeared with her into another room. The Japanese servant had opened the door by now, and I could see my car sitting at the end of a double line of spit-and-polish honor guards, all looking eleven feet tall.

It was too much.

"For God's sake, General," I said. "We're getting our brains knocked out in Korea. What are you going to do about it?"

He paused for a bit, turned and put his hand on my shoulder.

"Considine," he said very quietly, "I'll have my headquarters in North Korea in a month's time. Good day."

I left, troubled and empty-handed. I had reached for a momentous story affecting millions and finished with a forgotten footnote to the sports career of Christy Mathewson of John McGraw's New York Giants. I decided that MacArthur was becoming senile.

One month later he effected the Inchon landing, an astounding achievement in a bay the enemy had left poorly defended because next to the Bay of Fundy it has the greatest variance of tides. In another month MacArthur's forces took Pyongyang, capital of North Korea, and still another month later his Seventh Division reached the Yalu, the Manchurian border.

Military historians and buffs for generations to come will weigh and debate the debacle that ensued after some 200,000 Chinese "volunteers" streamed out of Manchuria. They used roads, a slender rail line, marshaling yards and depots, airfields, and maintenance sites which MacArthur had been forbidden to bomb. MacArthur, who had scoffed at fears in Washington and London that the Chinese would intervene, now effected a Dunkirk. About 105,000 UN troops and 91,000 Korean civilians were evacuated from Hungnam by Christmas, 1950, and regrouped below the thirty-eighth parallel. The Chinese and reheartened North Korean forces spread down the peninsula like spilled ink, recaptured Pyongyang, then Seoul, capital of South Korea. MacArthur's multilingual forces stiffened and stopped the counterattack along a jagged line that averaged seventy miles into South Korea.

On February 1, 1951, the UN General Assembly, aloof from Russia's Security Council veto, named China the aggressor in Korea. Seven weeks later, as he prepared to go back on the offense against Chinese forces now numbered at 600,000, MacArthur threatened the Peking government with air and naval attack.

He neglected to clear his threat with President Truman or the United Nations.

On April 11, 1951, with Seoul recaptured and UN forces headed northward again, the MacArthurs had luncheon guests at the Embassy Residence in Tokyo, among them Sen. Warren Magnuson. In the course of the meal, Jean looked over the general's shoulder and saw Colonel Huff beckoning to her. He looked stricken. She excused herself quietly, without disturbing the story the general was telling. The story was still unwinding, in the familiar purple, pear-shaped tones, when she returned and took her seat. She waited until the punch line, gave the laughter time to subside, then touched him gently on the shoulder, leaned close to his ear, and whispered the news that he had been fired.

His guests directed their attention elsewhere, fiddled nervously with their food, unaware that the world knew what their host had just been told. They did not hear what Mrs. MacArthur had whispered. Their first knowledge came when MacArthur's face relaxed. He looked fondly at his wife and said, "Jeannie, we're going home at last."

Huff then entered, tears running down his cheeks. He handed the general a Signal Corps envelope marked "Action for MacArthur." It might just as well have been stamped "Inaction for MacArthur." It was the message from President Truman:

> I deeply regret that it becomes my duty as President and Commander-in-Chief of the United States military forces to replace you as Supreme Commander, Allied powers; commander-in-chief, United Nations command; commander-in-chief, Far East; commanding general, U.S. Army Far East.
>
> You will turn over your command, effective at once, to Lt. Gen. Matthew B. Ridgway. You are authorized to issue such orders as are necessary to complete desired travel to such place as you select.

The rest of his life was bathed in lights and shadows.

The emotions he stirred by his homecoming and superb speech to the Congress were followed by the puzzle of his quasi-political tour. It began with a speech to the shirt-sleeved Mississippi Legislature at Jackson. He could have sprayed them with a Gatling Gun and never hit a Republican. The flight from New York to Jackson, made in a DC-4 chartered by H. L. Hunt, the shy, horse-playing Texas multimillionaire whose politics were well to the right of Louis XIV, was pure shambles. Tremendous headwinds at proper altitude caused the pilot to drop as low as five hundred feet in order to arrive in Jackson at the scheduled hour. For four hours and more the plane bounced and bucked in heavy turbulence. MacArthur, who was never much for flying, became airsick. So did Mrs. MacArthur, son Arthur, all four aides the general had with him, Hunt, and all but three or four of the remaining forty-odd passengers. Young Arthur was the first to make it to the toilet in the rear of the aircraft. He was in there a long time.

Thinking I'd cheer the general up a bit, I scribbled a note and had it passed up to MacArthur, who was in the aisle seat, first row, starboard. It read:

> Dear General: I am very happy to observe that in keeping with his distinguished military background Arthur got to the can fustest with the mostest.

It didn't do much for him. He tilted his seat back as far as it would go, interrupting the retching of one of his aides behind him, and leaned against the headrest. Mrs. MacArthur, feeling better now, got him a cold towel and put it over the face of the sick man who only a short time before had won acclaim that ranged from a courtly bow from Emperor Hirohito to an ear-splitting welcome to New York by a crowd of five million.

At last the plane put down at Jackson and taxied to the area where the band was playing, the honor guard was braced, and the cornpone officialdom awaited. MacArthur muttered something from beneath his towel. Mrs. MacArthur translated for the others. The general wished to be the last to deplane and would all others please get off now.

I stayed behind to see how he'd make it. He straightened the seat and wiped his face with the towel. His face was the color of liverwurst, or, commensurate with the man himself, pâté de foi gras. He put on his tailored trenchcoat and pulled his belt sharply around his waist. Then he moistened the palm of his right hand, spread his thinning hair sidewise over his bald spot and reached up to the hat rack. His unique, slightly crumpled campaign hat, crowned with seasoned gold braid, had made the trip on a small white airline pillow. He snapped it on at the rakish angle which only he could achieve and headed down the aisle for the door. I was sitting next to the door.

"Now may I have the Air Medal?" I asked him.

His eyes glinted a smile.

"No," he said, "but you rate the Purple Heart."

He stepped through the door and paused on the top step while the band thumped and flags fluttered. He put his slightly shaking right hand to the peak of his cap, as only he saluted.

He was a poster, as challenging as James Montgomery Flagg's Uncle Sam, pointing and saying, "I Want *You*."

MacArthur was pitilessly exploited by the Old Guard of the GOP at the 1952 Convention. He made a rasping and not well-informed

Keynote Address in which some political reporters detected a subtle command to the Convention to choose Sen. Robert A. Taft over Dwight D. Eisenhower. At one of the Address' several nadirs, the old soldier who looked a foot shorter in civilian clothes complained querulously about the rising cost of a dozen eggs. He never bought an egg in his life. His generations of quartermasters had bought billions of them.

The general's keen disappointment over Taft's loss on the first ballot was comparatively mild compared to his reaction to his meeting, in mid-December of 1952, with the aide who once sat outside his office —President-elect Eisenhower.

I may have forced that rare confrontation.

While the President-elect was making his promised tour of the Korean battlefront, hopeful of finding an honorable way out of the frozen and costly stalemate, MacArthur told a National Association of Manufacturers convention at the Waldorf Astoria that he had an easy and efficient plan for just that. In Washington President Truman told reporters that if MacArthur had a plan he should send it to the Pentagon because he was "still on the payroll." MacArthur ignored that.

En route from Guam to Pearl Harbor aboard the cruiser *Helena,* which Ike and his party had taken somewhat against his will, I said to one of his designated Cabinet officers that I thought it would be a good idea if Eisenhower and MacArthur got together and exchanged thoughts on the best ways and means of bringing the war to a close.

He said he thought so too.

I probably would never have filed a story about the possibility of their meeting if I had not still been steaming over one of those communications foul-ups which only the Navy can contrive. Minutes after boarding the *Helena* at Guam, an Eisenhower aide took me aside and confided that the cruiser would slow down as it passed Wake Island and bring aboard by helicopter several Cabinet officers-designate, including John Foster Dulles. I whipped below to my quarters, knocked out the story, marked it "Urgent," and gave it to the ship's communications officer.

It was a nice feeling to return to the deck of the still docked ship and see my competitors, Don Whitehead of the Associated Press and Merriman Smith of the United Press, chatting idly at the rail—blissfully unaware that I had clobbered them.

Three days later I received a garbled message from INS-New

York. It was not too difficult to decipher. Barry Faris wished to know how in hell I was scooped by AP and UP on the big story each had about Dulles and others to be flown to the deck of Ike's cruiser. I had beaten Don and Smitty by forty-eight hours with the story. My scoop had been sent from the ship to the main communications center on Guam, and someone there simply forgot to relay it.

I deliberated a long time over whether to try a comeback with as flimsy a story as "Ike-Mac Meeting Favored." The more I thought about it the more I was convinced that it was the only course left to the two men if they were remotely interested in (1) ending a war that had already cost the United States nearly 30,000 dead, and (2) repairing the GOP's yawning gap between the Taft Republicans and the Eisenhower Republicans.

So I wrote it as if they had every intention of meeting. Papers on the INS circuit played it big. Don and Smitty received "rockets," churlish messages from their home offices suggesting they had gone off fishing while INS worked and won the day. Automatically, it became their duty to confirm the story or, better still, knock it down. The Eisenhower people were not talking; nor were they speaking to me. Two rather terrible days passed, and then Jim Hagerty called the three of us in the wardroom and handed us mimeographed handouts. The message was short and, to me, sweet. It said that President-elect Eisenhower and General MacArthur would meet in New York, shortly after Eisenhower's arrival back in the United States, to discuss the war.

They did, at the town house of John Foster Dulles. They had not seen or spoken to each other since shortly after World War II when Ike passed through Tokyo as Army Chief of Staff. After the meeting, they went their separate ways—Eisenhower back to Columbia University's presidential home, MacArthur to his huge and memento-laden suite in the Waldorf Towers. Neither would speak to waiting reporters. Instead, aides issued a barren handout which said simply that the two had met and discussed possible measures to end the war. MacArthur was not invited to the Inauguration of his one-time aide.

In the months that followed, the aging general sought and found the anonymity which had escaped him for half a century. Public appearances were rare. As chairman of the board of Remington Rand, an ornamental rank bestowed upon him by tycoon Jim Rand, the general would journey in his chauffeured car to Rowayton, New York, each weekday to attend luncheon at Rockledge, the posh lair where Rand's executives would gather each noon. It was somehow fitting and proper that MacArthur's workdays' travel was unique. Headed north out of the city each day his car traveled a practically empty highway, on the other side of which the cars of inbound workers nuzzled bumper to bumper. Returning home to his redoubt in the Waldorf the general's car also had clear sailing while Westchester-bound traffic on the other side of the road inched toward eventide's martini.

Obtaining an interview with him became roughly akin to scaling Everest. All calls to the Waldorf were answered with a firm request that the caller contact the office at 90 Church Street which the Army had provided for him for life as a five-star general. Those who found a shortcut and got through the Waldorf switchboard struck an even more imposing buffer: Maj. Gen. Courtney Whitney. General Whitney's devotion to MacArthur knew no horizon. It ran over into utter possessiveness. MacArthur became his prisoner as well as his idol. He had full veto power, or at least exercised it, over MacArthur's appointments list. He was willing to accept the bitterest protests from old friends of MacArthur he turned away.

As a protector, Whitney passed his severest test in a pitched telephone confrontation with MacArthur's landlord, Conrad Hilton. Hilton told me the story.

"It's my duty to my stockholders to return them as much as I can on their investment," he complained. "Well, as you know, I gave General MacArthur a ridiculously low rate when I knocked down walls and made that apartment for him, when he came back from Japan.

"I could get five hundred dollars a day for that suite today. But I can't get MacArthur on the phone . . . and I own the phone! I can't get through to him to tell him I want the suite. All I get is that goddam Whitney."

Connie could have gone through Mrs. MacArthur but he was too much of a gentleman. Jean was the one unblocked path to her man, the only member of the retinue Whitney could not dominate. It was through her good offices that I was permitted to see the general on January 27, 1954, the day after his seventy-fourth birthday. When the first opportunity offered itself, I asked him if he would tell me what had happened when he had met with Eisenhower at Dulles' place. Not a word beyond the skimpy communiqué had ever been forthcoming.

"I'd be happy to," he said surprisingly. "There were just the three of us in the study. I opened the meeting. I spoke for an hour and fifteen minutes. At the end of that time Eisenhower jumped up from his chair and paced the floor. His face was flushed. 'It's magnificent!' he said. 'It's . . .' What I had urged was that he become the world's peacemaker, in short, put an end to the Cold War.

"But Dulles interrupted.

" 'General,' Dulles said, meaning Ike, 'You will recall that on the ship returning from Korea we agreed we would undertake nothing of this nature for one full year. We agreed that we'd devote the first year to consolidating our position.' He spoke for perhaps fifteen minutes.

"I watched Ike. I could see his enthusiasm dying bit by bit. When Dulles finished, we were back where I had started. I stood up and almost took Ike into my embrace. I put my hands on his shoulders and I said to him, 'Ike, this is the last time I'll ever address you that way. You are about to assume a position that is the loftiest in this world. I'm proud that a man who has been as close to me as you have been has achieved this tremendous prominence.

" 'Your victory in Europe, your honesty, your integrity, your radiant and wonderful personality have combined to make you unique. You are loved and respected by every nation in the world. Even in Soviet Russia you are deeply respected. You have the greatest opportunity for good since the birth of Jesus Christ. You have in your hands today the power to make the greatest impression made on civilization since the crucifixion of Christ. If, when you go in the White House, you act instantly and dynamically on this program you cannot fail to be remembered in history as a Messiah.

" 'But you don't have much time. Through our blunders in Asia we have given the enemy a hold—ever strengthening—on half of the population of the earth and 60 percent of its natural resources when properly exploited. We have presented to him on a platter the warm ports which will increase his strength. We are letting him come toward Africa. By rejecting our ancient tradition that victory is the only reason to enter into battle, we have encouraged him everywhere.

" 'There is still time to turn the tide!' I said to my old comrade in arms. 'That tide can be turned only by you, the most beloved and respected man on earth today. You and I have soldiered together for a long, long time. We've had our ups and downs. I've made my share of mistakes, and you've made yours. [MacArthur smiled and nodded at this point.] I have from the start felt toward you the affection of an older brother for his junior. Don't hesitate to take command! Yours is a Messianic mission. Believe me, your name will be called Blessed!

" 'But if you wait a year, I predict, on my life, that for every day of your first three months in the White House your popularity will diminish. For every day of the next three months your influence will wane. And for every day of the following six months you will lose standing geographically. At the end of a year you will no longer be what you are today—a transcendent figure. You will be, by that time, chiefly titular head of the Republican Party and busy with the mean little tasks of holding your Congressional majority in the next year's elections.' "

MacArthur sighed.

"I could not have seen more clearly if I had been staring into a crystal ball," he said and then added, not without emotion in his voice, "There were tears in Eisenhower's eyes and in mine as we looked silently at each other. Then the silence of the room was broken by the cool, calculating voice of the lawyer. Dulles had taken the floor again. His mood was a bit patronizing, if good-natured.

" 'Very interesting, very interesting,' Dulles said. And turning to Eisenhower he added, 'You know, General MacArthur could be just as wrong in this as he was when he backed Bob Taft against you.'

"I could feel Eisenhower freeze. After a bit, I took my hands off his shoulders and said, 'I guess that's all there is to say.' We prepared to leave. But before we parted I said to him, 'You won't have to worry about me, once you're in the White House. I want nothing. I don't propose to take any part in public debates or attempt to push legislation or politics. Good-bye. God bless you.' "

It was too much for one interview, but nevertheless I asked him if he would spell out the never-before detailed "easy and effective" way in which he would have ended the war in Korea (where the uneasy armistice had been signed the previous July 27, 1953).

His hands shook.

"Of all the campaigns of my life—twenty major ones to be exact—the one I felt most sure of was the one I was deprived of waging," he said with an underlay of bitterness. "I could have won the war in Korea in a maximum of ten days, with considerably fewer casualties than were suffered during the so-called truce-period, and it could have altered the course of history.

"The enemy's air would first have been taken out. I would have dropped between thirty and fifty tactical atomic bombs on his air bases and other depots in that neck of Manchuria from just across the Yalu from Antung [northwestern tip of Korea] to the neighborhood of Hunchun [just north of the northeastern tip of Korea near the border of the U.S.S.R.]

"Between thirty and fifty bombs would have more than done the job. Dropped under cover of darkness, they would have destroyed the enemy's air force on the ground, wiped out his maintenance and his airmen. His only means of rebuilding would have been over the single-tracked trans-Siberian railroad. It is an excellently run railroad, but it could never have handled the matériel needed to rebuild the enemy's air force in a sufficient space of time.

"With the destruction of the enemy's air power I would then have called upon five hundred thousand of Chiang Kai-shek's troops, sweetened by two U.S. Marine divisions. These would have been formed into two amphibious forces. One, totaling four fifths of my strength and led by one of the Marine divisions, would have landed at Antung and proceeded eastward along the road that parallels the Yalu. The other force, led by the other Marine division, would have landed simultaneously at Unggi or Najin, hit the same river road, and charged very quickly westward. Forces could have joined in two days, forming a wall of manpower and firepower across the northern border of Korea. I had nearly all the shipping I needed, in Japan, and could have procured the rest from Pearl Harbor. That was no problem.

"Now, the Eighth Army, spread along the thirty-eighth parallel, would then have put pressure on the enemy from the south. The joined amphibious forces would press down from the north. Nothing in the way of supplies or reinforcements could have moved across the Yalu. North Korea, holding not less than one million to one million and a half of the enemy, could not have sustained him. It had been picked clean.

"The enemy commander would have been starved out within ten days after the landings. I suggest now he would have sued for peace immediately after learning not only that his air had been taken out, but that we had spread across his supply routes.

"You may ask what would have prevented the enemy's reinforcements massing and crossing the Yalu in great strength. It was my plan as our amphibious forces moved south to spread behind us—from the

Sea of Japan to the Yellow Sea—a belt of radioactive cobalt. It could have been spread from wagons, carts, trucks, and planes. It is not an expensive material. It has an active life of between sixty and one hundred and twenty years. For at least sixty years there could have been no land invasion of Korea from the north. The enemy could not have marched across that radiated belt.

"Russia? It makes me laugh when I recall the fears of the Truman-Acheson-Marshall-Bradley-General Staff group that Russia would commit its armies to a war in China's behalf at the end of an endless one-track railroad to a peninsular battleground that led only to the sea. Russia could not have engaged us. She would not have fought for China. She is already unhappy and uncertain over the colossus she has encouraged.

"The truce we entered into—that stupendous blunder of refusing to win when we could have won—has given China the breathing time she needed. Primitive airfields in Manchuria have been transformed into modern installations with ten-thousand-foot runways. China had only one concentrated arms-producing area before Truman relieved me. Now she has built or is in the process of building four more. In fifty years, if she can develop her plane-building facilities, China will be one of the world's top military powers.

"It was in our power to destroy the Red Chinese army and Chinese military power. And probably for all time. My plan was a cinch. I was refused the right to carry it out by a group of isolationists and the politically-minded Joint Chiefs. You may be surprised to hear Truman, Acheson, Marshall, and the others called isolationists. They were the true isolationists! They made only one revision in what we came to know as isolationism in this country. They expanded their walls to include Western Europe. They never comprehended the world as a whole. They never understood the enormous forces of Asia.

"Under Eisenhower—a naive and honest man who does not want to offend anyone—we have maintained that isolationism. In time, we will scuttle our holdings and interests in the Pacific."

And so it came time to put his house in order. If there was any doubt about the wisdom of taking inventory, it was removed by a somber—but traditional—inquiry from the Army. It asked him what kind of a funeral he preferred. It asked the same question of the two other retired five-star generals, Eisenhower and Omar Bradley.

Bradley, youngest of the three at seventy, said he preferred something simple. Eisenhower's answer was not revealed. MacArthur replied that he wanted a state funeral.

However grim the inquiry, which came to MacArthur after a grueling prostate operation, it is necessary. A state funeral involves planning in advance. The accouterments of ceremonial burials are not easily whistled up, even in Washington—which is itself a kind of national memorial ground, what with its monuments, sarcophagi, and statuary recalling Washington, Jefferson, Lincoln, Lee, the Unknown Soldiers, and John F. Kennedy.

The Army's purpose in questioning its rarest old soldiers was also to learn where in Arlington National Cemetery they wished to lie. MacArthur surprised the Army by stating that after his state funeral he had completed plans to be buried in Norfolk, Virginia. His mother was born there, and the city had discreetly offered him one of its architectural antiquities as his final resting place.

MacArthur chose to lie in state first in New York, then Washington under the Capitol Rotunda. He listed the type and number of military units he would prefer and accepted suggestions as to the routes of the funeral parade. The television networks were kept informed, so as to draw up plans for camera positions, lighting, direction, production.

That much out of the way, MacArthur began dedicating much of his days and nights to writing what he called his reminiscences rather than autobiography. He kept the early portion of this labor so secret than not even his almost constant shadow, General Whitney, knew about it.

"What are you doing, General?" Whitney asked him one day as MacArthur handwrote page after page on a yellow foolscap pad, discarding one dulled pencil point for a sharp one.

"After he told me, I had a new job," Whitney said later. "My job was to keep his pencils sharpened. It kept me busy, believe me."

When he had completed nine hundred pages of manuscript (some of it written on both sides), he handed the mound to Whitney and told him to find a purchaser. He said he thought of it as his legacy to Jean and Arthur.

Whitney called Henry Luce. It is problematical whether Whitney knew that in 1945 Bill Hearst, then a war correspondent, flew to Tokyo with a certified check for $500,000, signed by W. R. Hearst, Sr., to offer it to MacArthur for his memoirs. To Hearst's astonishment, MacArthur said he had no intention of ever writing a book about his life and his wars. As the years rolled on, and an assortment of approved and frowned-upon biographies appeared, it seemed he was carrying out his intention not to tell his own story.

Then this deluge. Whitney delivered it in a Japanese lacquer chest which exactly fit the manuscript. After the contracts were signed— amounting to about one million dollars divided between Time, Inc. and McGraw-Hill—Luce held a party for MacArthur in the Time-Life Building and professed to reporters that when Whitney first dumped the manuscript on his desk he nearly fainted, because it was the only copy in existence.

MacArthur was photographed holding the boxed pads, surrounded by Time, Inc. brass.

"How about letting me have a pad or two of it for the night?" I asked him. Time-Lifemen blanched, but recovered when MacArthur shook his head and smiled.

"Can't do that, I guess," he said. "But I'd like you to know one thing: not one word of this was written by a ghost."

Memories of West Point grew clearer and dearer to him near the end. One day he rang for Whitney and suggested they take a ride up to the Point, just to look around. It turned out to be something short of the Prodigal's Return. He was browsing through one of its hallowed halls, explaining things to Whitney—who was also in mufti—when a young duty officer stopped him.

"Sorry," the stiff young man said, "this is a restricted area. No visitors are permitted."

MacArthur's reply could have set a new A.A.U. record for understatement.

"I used to go to school here," he said quietly. "My name's Mac-Arthur."

But that was not what it was like the lovely May day in 1962 when he was presented with the highest honor West Point bestows, the Sylvanus Thayer Award. He was eighty-two.

The military is traditionally unimaginative, blunt, hard, concise. But when it comes around to saying farewell to one of its beloved, it can do things that brings tears and make the tenderest of Broadway's plays seem like a peep show.

MacArthur seemed submerged in his funereal black suit and unfashionably wide-brimmed black homburg when he stepped to the side of the sun-washed parade ground. The Cadet Corps in all its starchy gray glory was lined up on the far ground. A jeep with a handrail behind the driver's seat pulled up and MacArthur climbed aboard, along with Academy Superintendent Maj. Gen. William C. Westmoreland, and they stood in the rear of the jeep, holding onto the rail, as it pulled across the field for the review.

Softly, so movingly, the band began playing the haunting songs he knew when he was the handsomest knight in all the AEF . . . "Tipperary" . . . "There's A Long, Long Trail Awinding" . . . "K-K-K-Katie" . . . "My Buddy."

It was hard to bear.

So was the valedictory later in the V-shaped dining hall which he had built as Superintendent.

"Duty-Honor-Country. Those three hallowed words reverently dictate what you ought to be, what you can be, what you will be," he said to the Corps. "They are your rallying points: to build courage when courage seems to fail; to regain faith when there seems to be little cause for faith; to create hope when hope becomes forlorn. Unhappily, I possess neither that eloquence of diction, that poetry of imagination, nor that brilliance of metaphor to tell you all that they mean."

For the next forty-five minutes he disproved that assertion in a way that cast the most melancholy spell over the assemblage. There were tears in the eyes of big strapping Cadets who wouldn't have shed one before a firing squad as MacArthur concluded:

"You are the leaven which binds together the entire fabric of our national system of defense. From your ranks come the great captains who hold the nation's destiny in their hands the moment the war tocsin sounds. The Long Gray Line has never failed us. Were you to do so, a million ghosts in olive drab, in brown khaki, in blue and gray, would rise from their white crosses thundering those magic words: Duty—Honor—Country.

"This does not mean that you are warmongers. On the contrary, the soldier, above all other people, prays for peace, for he must suffer and bear the deepest wounds and scars of war. But always in our ears ring the ominous words of Plato, the wisest of all philosophers, 'Only the dead have seen the end of war.' "

He took a step away from the microphone and rested a hand on the side of the lectern. Even those closest to him had difficulty hearing his finish, delivered without recourse to his notes:

"The shadows are lengthening for me. The twilight is here. My days of old have vanished, tone and tint; they have gone glimmering through the dream of things that were. Their memory is one of wondrous beauty, watered by tears, and coaxed and caressed by the smiles of yesterday. I listen vainly for the witching melody of faint bugles blowing reveille, of far drums beating the long roll. In my dreams I hear again the crash of guns, the rattle of musketry, the strange, mournful mutter of the battlefield.

"But in the evening of my memory, always I come back to West Point. Always there echoes and re-echoes: Duty—Honor—Country.

"Today marks my final roll call with you, but I want you to know that when I cross the river my last conscious thoughts will be of The Corps, and The Corps, and The Corps . . . I bid you farewell."

Dwight D. Eisenhower considered the Presidency a kind of sixth star to wear. He accepted it as a natural and inevitable promotion, as he had accepted all previous jumps in rank and extensions of duties. It was not something he campaigned for, or even secretly yearned for. It was simply a case of his number coming up at the right time and place. He had turned it down, earlier, when President Truman made his extraordinary offer to step aside in 1948 and present him with the Democratic nomination. The timing, the rhythm, wasn't right or perhaps seniority—sacredest of sacreds—was subtly involved. So he grinned and said no—to the utter consternation of the consummate politician who made the offer.

He was a bit more approachable four years later, but only a bit. Various emissaries to his court at SHAPE, notably Sen. Henry Cabot Lodge, perennial hopeful Harold Stassen, and old friend and President-fancier George E. Allen, returned to the United States without the vestige of his promissory note. All they seemed sure of was that if he ran, which was still questionable in view of his known antagonism toward politicking military men—MacArthur, let's say—he'd run as a Republican. That was considered a substantial straw. Like most career officers of his generation, Ike had never cast a vote in a national election.

But the wave continued to build, and it crashed loudly one night at Madison Square Garden, early in '52.

In subsequent months and years, many rose to take a bow for overcoming the inertia of Dwight David Eisenhower (who, incidentally,

was originally named David Dwight Eisenhower). The woods were
filled with kingmakers. But an authentic one was never mentioned, nor
did she want to be. She was Jacqueline Cochran, intrepid wife of
financier Floyd Odlum.

John Hay Whitney, destined to become Eisenhower's Ambassador
to the Court of St. James's, and a foremost contributor to his campaign in word and deed, was chairman of the ear-splitting "We Like
Ike" rally at the Garden. He asked Jacqueline to co-chair. She declined but offered to serve its best interests. She flew her plane to
various places in Texas and Oklahoma and stimulated various groups
to move en masse on New York for the big occasion at the Garden.
Several chartered trains, even brought along their own horses.

It was a night to remember, even for the Garden. The place was
jammed beyond the fire department limits and shook with "We Want
Ike" chants led by radio-TV personality and former Eighth Air Force
colonel Tex McCrary. There were about fifteen thousand outside the
place, including a fine I'm-for-Ike worker who nearly got clubbed by
a cop, Mrs. Jimmy Doolittle.

Jacqueline stayed with the film taken of the event while it was
developed. Then, still sleepless, she carried the can to Idlewild, caught
a TWA plane to Paris, and headed for Eisenhower's headquarters in
the Astoria Hotel. She was told by a functionary in the outer office that
the general would give her thirty minutes.

Eisenhower talked for twenty minutes before he gave her an opening. She has quick reflexes.

"General, you've been talking exactly twenty minutes and you
haven't heard a word of my message," she snapped. "I think it's only
fair that you let me talk the rest of the allotted time."

Eisenhower burst out laughing, and gave her the floor.

She talked (she recalled later) for eight minutes and thirty seconds.
It was a report on the enthusiasm that had exploded at the rally. She
turned over the can of film to him and, her work done, prepared to
leave. But Eisenhower, the reluctant dragon, held her with a gesture.
He punched a button and instructed an officer to take care of the
luncheon date he had scheduled with an oil man. The general and
the lady aviator lunched.

At five o'clock that afternoon the uncut film was shown to Eisenhower, Gen. Alfred Gruenther, his chief of staff, and other intimates.
As it ended, and before the lights in the room were turned on, Eisen-

hower and his party got up and left the room. Jacqueline Cochran found herself the only patron for a time. When Ike and his group came back she launched into another pitch. Was not the film a symbol of his country's call? Could he any longer avoid the inevitable?

Suddenly, tears came into Eisenhower's eyes. "I wish my mother could've seen this," he said.

Then he dictated the letter—to be carried back to New York by Jacqueline, and to be seen by only a few. The letter said Yes.

Miss Cochran raised some of the basic rent money for the New Hampshire primary, where Eisenhower's victory illuminated "the clear-cut call." Gov. Sherman Adams called her just before the primary and told her he needed $25,000.

"When?" she asked.

"Yesterday," Adams said.

"You've got five from me and five from Floyd right now," she said, "and I'll get you the rest." She called John Hertz in Chicago. Hertz promised $10,000 but asked that his name not be mentioned. Jacqueline was indignant, though she was fonder of the Hertzes than of any other persons she knew.

"Then keep your ten thousand," she said over the phone. "I'm looking for people who are willing to stand up and be counted, people who believe in something and have the courage to let everybody know it." Hertz came through swiftly. Another $5,000 was found somewhere else—and Ike was on his way.

The preliminary scratchings of the historians have not been overly kind in their assessment of Dwight Eisenhower, the President. The decades may temper their judgment, swing them more to Herbert Hoover's conviction: "Ike is the most intellectually honest man we've ever had in the White House."

There was a human side to him that wasn't always too evident. In Korea in December, 1952, on his trip to "do something about the war in Korea" and in response to his declaration that if elected he would go to Korea, he visited, near the end of that trip, the area along the front where his son, Maj. John Eisenhower, was serving, I believe, as executive officer of a front-line group. There was an obvious warmth between the two, though John to outsiders was as cool and correct as the weather itself, and the weather was abominably cold.

As we were prepared to leave that section, having had lunch with the so-called troops, and witnessed an embarrassingly planned napalm attack by Navy fighters on Chinese and North Korean positions scarcely two or three miles away from where we camped in the snow, the President-elect took his son John aside. None of us in the party could hear what transpired between them, but I'll never forget the sight. Eisenhower stood quite close to his son, facing him, and I could see his words, inaudible to me. I could see them because they were condensed into steam by the extreme cold. They came in short decisive puffs, faintly reminiscent of the Camel cigarette sign on Broadway, and broke against the son's receptive face. Occasionally John would say something and his smaller and less intense puff of breath would come back at his father. At the end of the ectoplasmic dialogue, the President-elected tapped his son on the arm, turned, and went back to his little plane.

Many days later we arrived at Kaneohe Marine Base in Hawaii on the island of Oahu. We were there several days, during which time we saw little or nothing of General Eisenhower. Merriman Smith, Don Whitehead, and I had filed a great deal of copy from the Cruiser *Helena* enroute from Guam to Pearl Harbor, much of it having to do with a major staff meeting that Eisenhower would hold once he reached Hawaii with Chief-of-Staff General Omar Bradley and other Pentagon figures. We were surprised, however, to find that Eisenhower's chief interest after arriving in Hawaii was golf. Scarcely half an hour after arrival at his cottage at Kaneohe, he emerged, not to confer with Bradley and the others, but in golfing gear. He moved quickly and decisively to the first tee where the other members of his foursome awaited him. They apparently had been alerted hours in advance because they were dressed ready to go. One was a Marine colonel who was champion of the base. I asked him, while waiting for Eisenhower to appear, what sort of game he shot. The colonel looked steadily at me and without cracking a smile said, "One shot worse than the General's game." I daresay he's a much higher ranking Marine officer today.

General Bradley made himself available on the first tee but, like the rest of us, was discouraged from following Eisenhower around the nine-hole course. So Bradley, some of the handful of reporters, and our photographer wandered in time to the ninth green to await the conclusion of the round. Bradley was very eager to get back to Washington. Indeed, his plane, he told us, was gassed and ready to leave. But as Eisenhower putted out, a deep frown furrowing his brow, it became apparent that the long-awaited conference was not going to take place then and there. The President-elect walked off the green immersed in a deep study and strolled within ten feet of where his five-star colleague and old friend, Bradley, stood.

"That old eight-iron sure let me down," Ike muttered. He continued walking to the practice tee, followed by his caddy, scattered a handful of golf balls about the tee, and proceeded to practice his eight-iron shots. Bradley left for Washington.

The next morning Merriman Smith decided to accompany John Foster Dulles on a tour of the islands by light plane. When Smitty leaves a story, that story can be diagnosed as dead, or nearly as close to death as news can become. Whitehead and I remained behind in our barracks not far from Eisenhower's cottage. We had breakfast together and in the course of discussing how remote we were from Eisenhower, although we had accompanied him thousands of miles and were sitting there within fifty yards of the man, I said to Don, "This is ridiculous. Let's go over and talk to him."

Don did not appear to think much of the idea, but being an alert reporter he thought less of letting me go alone. There was always an outside chance that I would get in, and if INS got in, AP would look pretty stupid not being there. A Marine guard blocked our way before we could put foot on the concrete pathway leading up to the step of the cottage. We explained that we had accompanied the President-elect from the time he left New York, but that of course meant nothing to the guard. He had his orders not to admit anyone.

I said to him, "At least send this message in to General Eisenhower. Tell him that Bob Considine is outside with Don Whitehead and that I would like to have a cup of coffee."

With great misgivings the guard turned, went to the door, and delivered the message. Out came an Army lieutenant who was serving as Eisenhower's secretary on the trip. If anything, he was as hostile as the Marine guard. But I insisted, more sternly than I can usually insist, that the message be delivered. I probably said that if it were not, I would see that the General heard about this lieutenant's refusal to do so. Well, that must have conjured up in his tormented mind the whole rigmarole of promotion and reprimand, because he went inside and after about ten minutes emerged again in the bright sunlight and said, "The General will see you with the understanding that it is only for coffee and that no questions will be asked."

That was better than nothing, barely better once we tasted the coffee. Ike seemed in a relaxed mood despite the restrictions that we were working under. He talked in general terms about the trip and then, unable to resist a question that I had wanted to ask him since I had seen him that day at the front with his son, I said to him, "General, it's none of my business, but what were you telling Major John that day we went up to his front?"

Eisenhower seemed almost pleased that someone had finally asked him.

"I'll tell you what I said to John," he said. "I said to John, 'John, if you get killed in this war, it'll be a terrible thing for your mother and for me, but that's a soldier's life. We take that risk when we put on the uniform. Somehow your mother and I could live through a thing like that. But for Godsake don't get captured. Don't let them capture you. If you should be captured and they held you over my head, I would not be able to serve as President of the United States!"

The silence that followed was broken by the hurried arrival of Jim Hagerty, somewhat the worse for wear from the night before, as was I. We had been at the same place together. He had been tipped off that we had gained admission to the sacrosanct confines of the cottage, probably by the nervous young lieutenant. Jim was red-eyed and unshaved, indicating he had hurriedly thrown on his clothes to perform his customary duty of buffer between Eisenhower and the press, which was his job, of course. Jim sat in on the rest of the small talk, and the longer it went, the smaller it got.

I don't recall what was said after Eisenhower's extraordinarily blunt revelation of what he had told his son. My mind was filled with an earlier scene, one that suddenly dovetailed with the present and made grim sense. I recalled a smoky autumn night at the home of a mutual friend, Howard Young, at Ridgefield, Connecticut. Eisenhower, then President of Columbia University, was a weekend guest and Mr. Young was kind enough to invite Frank Farrell of the New York *World-Telegram* and me to share the weekend with him.

Late on Saturday night of that weekend as we sat around over a drink of Scotch, I asked the General if he had ever known of any attempt to take him as a prisoner of war during World War II. He said with some show of heat that there was never any chance that he could ever be taken prisoner. But I reminded him that the Germans had been very adept at plucking high-ranking officers and even Mussolini out from under protective or hostile surroundings. They had captured several British generals, I recalled, in the desert warfare and had snatched Il Duce off what amounted to a mountainous crag as Italy went down the drain. *Reader's Digest* had carried a story that the Germans had made an elaborate plot to ambush and seize Eisenhower after D-Day and had failed chiefly because Eisenhower's driver had taken a wrong turn on a routine trip near the front.

Eisenhower repeated, "No, there was never any chance that I could be captured. It's completely out of the question."

And I further insisted, "But why?"

The future President of the United States looked at me steadily and then said very quietly, "I always had a gun."

What he had been telling his son, obviously, there in the snow in Korea, was to use his gun on himself rather than be captured.

An almost childish spark of jealousy sputtered back and forth between Eisenhower and MacArthur. They made no particular effort to conceal it. It must have baffled and even annoyed MacArthur to watch Eisenhower's swift rise from the rank of lieutenant colonel to Supreme Commander of Allied Forces in Europe.

Their differences began in the Philippines, or perhaps earlier. During and after the time when the Bonus Marchers were run out of Washington, the genial Maj. Eisenhower proved to be an ideal buffer between four-starred Douglas MacArthur and a sometimes critical press. But he resented other aspects of the job, as he sat outside MacArthur's splendid office. Years later, in the White House, he told an old friend, Maj. Gen. Melvin Maas (USMC, retired), a former Congressman from Minnesota:

"Mel, now you stop worrying about taking up too much of my time. I enjoy seeing you. You know, when I had a desk outside the office of the old general [MacArthur] quite a few of you Congressmen treated me like I was his batman. They'd toss me their coats and hats on the way in to see him and expect me to hang them up.

"I never forgot them. And I'll never forget how you used to hang your own hat and coat up, and say a friendly word."

Eisenhower's transfer from Washington to the Philippines was made at the request of MacArthur after he left his post as Chief of Staff and became military adviser to the Commonwealth in 1935. There is evidence that MacArthur received and accepted credit for much that Eisenhower did to beef up the lackluster Filipino military. Eisenhower did not approve when MacArthur took the baton and rank of field marshal of the Commonwealth's military forces in 1936. When Germany and the Soviet Union invaded Poland in 1939, Eisenhower requested transfer back to the United States.

"People think we're not friendly," Eisenhower volunteered in an interview he granted me in the summer of 1951 at Supreme Headquarters at NATO. "Why, when Mamie and I left the Philippines in 1939 he and Mrs. MacArthur came down to the ship to see us off."

On the occasion of the 1951 interview, Eisenhower was curious about details of the speaking- and personal-appearance tour MacArthur had engaged in during the weeks that followed his emotional pledge to the Congress and the nation to "fade away."

"I understand you've been on the road with the old general," Ike said, settling in his office chair. "What sort of reception did he get?"

I said he had received great welcomes everywhere.

"That's odd," Ike said. "I understood he had a bad turnout in Houston."

"No, sir. The police estimated about a million showed up for that one."

Ike frowned slightly. "They told me he had a bad turnout," he said. The room was silent, save for the sound of my swallowing. I was stoking a question that every reporter in the business wanted to ask him. Ike had successfully avoided involvement in the still raging debate over MacArthur's dismissal by President Truman and the conduct of the war in Korea. The President (who had appointed Eisenhower to head up NATO's military arm, and who had once virtually offered him the Presidency in 1948) stood firmly opposed to any escalation of the Korean War. He was particularly determined—as were most other UN allies—that the war did not spread beyond the Yalu.

"General," I asked, "what would you have done if you had been in the old general's shoes when the Red Chinese came over the mountain?"

He sat up quickly in his chair and his eyes turned a brittle blue.

"I'll tell you what I would have done," he said. "I would have put every plane I had in the air and bombed the hell out of their supply depots in Manchuria. What's more, I would not have asked Washington's permission, nor the UN's permission. And if either raised hell I would have simply told them that I had done what was necessary to save the lives of thousands of men from a dozen allied nations."

I changed the subject immediately and let his words sink deeply into my memory while we talked of lighter things—including a spur on Joe DiMaggio's heel. Twenty minutes later, we walked toward the door, the interview completed. I pondered over whether to speed to INS headquarters in Rue Caumartin by cab or phone my glorious scoop from the nearest booth. I had a story that would hit every front page in the world.

"Come back and see us soon," Ike said at the doorway. Then he reached out his hand, smiled his million-dollar smile, and said, "Of course, Bob, everything I've said today is in the room."

A scoop gives off a muted scream when it dies.

Ike resisted the blandishments and appeals of those who wanted him to run for the GOP nomination until the following May. Then the combined exhortations of Lucius Clay, George Allen, Henry Cabot Lodge, Harold Stassen, Sherman Adams, Tom Dewey, Herbert Brownell, and the others became too flattering to resist. He returned to America and early in June flew to his boyhood town of Abilene, Kansas, to make the formal announcement. It was an informal formal announcement, as things turned out. Wind and rain and bad acoustics ruined his painfully worded address, which he read as if for the first time. The next day at his first press conference—held in a movie house—he met some of the people he would have to put up with for most of the next decade.

For a good many years the general had found himself surrounded by a servile press. It wished to ask him nothing much more difficult to answer than, "How are you feeling, sir?" and "How are the Allies working together, sir?" But now he was in politics. The questions were no longer obsequious. Right off the bat, there in the little movie theater, some fellow he had never seen before threw him a curve.

"Give us your feeling about socialized medicine," the fellow asked from the floor. As an Army man since 1911, when he entered West Point (after the bitter disappointment of being turned down by Annapolis) Ike had been the beneficiary of the service's type of socialized medicine. He paused a moment and delivered the first of what turned out to be a treasury of circumlocutionary answers.

"I don't like the sound of socialized medicine," Ike said. "Socialism leads down the path to anarchism. Anarchism leads down the path to communism." Pencils flew across notebook pages. But Ike had not finished. He continued, "On the other hand, every man, woman, and child in this country who needs it should have free medical care."

Pencils stopped flitting.

Then there was the distressing business about Edward R. Murrow. Murrow had made an almost preposterous request of James C. Hagerty, the excellent public relations man who had joined the Eisenhower camp as a kind of campaign gift from Tom Dewey. Murrow wanted to bring CBS's television cameras into the movie house and televise the press conference live.

Impossible, Jim ruled. Ike felt the same way. And so did a majority of the assembled "written word" reporters, a number of whom have long since left their newspapers and wire service jobs for greater fame and fortune in TV.

The protests failed to impress Murrow. Just after the press conference began, he personally led his crew and their cameras into the theater and turned on the tubes. The other networks followed suit. There were distressed mutterings from the candidate and from Hagerty. But Murrow knew he was on safe ground. It was hardly likely that a man who had just announced that he wanted to be President of the United States would then (on camera) deny to television what he was readily giving to the assembled paper and pencil reporters.

After becoming President, Eisenhower permitted his off-the-cuff news conferences to be filmed and selected excerpts used on TV later the same day. Live telecasts of these sometimes informative, ofttimes exasperating, affairs did not begin until John Fitzgerald Kennedy took over.

Ike's introduction to the rough and tumble political arena did not jar his basic simplicity or homely speech. Visiting the plain little house where he and his six brothers grew up under the eye and counsel of his pietistic Mennonite parents, Ike looked around and said, nostalgia in his voice, "By golly, I didn't know until years later that we were poor."

He maintained that uncomplicated wonderment throughout his White House tenure. After one of the last of his long string of stag dinners, the President led his guests into the Red Room for the traditional demitasse, after-dinner drink, and talk. What turned out to be the last question we asked was that of Pat Weaver, then with NBC.

"Sir, you've had more in life than any other man who comes to mind," Weaver said. "Fine parents, happy boyhood, West Point, marriage to a wonderful girl, fine son, Supreme Commander of the greatest armed force in history, liberator of Western Europe, president of Columbia University, leader of a defense force reaching from Norway to Turkey, and President of the United States. Is there anything else you'd like to be?"

Ike gazed thoughtfully into his Chivas Regal.

"Yes," he said, looking up. "I'd like to be my grandson David."

Even if the Presidency should come eventually to Richard Milhous Nixon it is doubtful if that supreme achievement would bring him completely out from the state of shock into which he was plunged by the events of 1960. He lost to John Fitzgerald Kennedy by 118,550 votes out of 68,335,642 cast. The 34,108,546 votes he attracted, losing, was 172,294 more than Eisenhower drew, winning, in 1952. As long as he lives, Nixon and many of his followers will contend he was gypped by a fast count in Illinois's Cook County (Kennedy 1,378,343, Nixon 1,059,607) and elsewhere in tightly knit Democrat-bossed strongholds.

Commonly accepted reasons for the defeat were Nixon's agreement in the first place to debate J.F.K. on television, his poor showing and poorer appearance in the first of those confrontations, and "slanted" newswriting and reporting.

Any person assigned to cover that unique and arresting period in American politics knows that other reasons contributed heavily to Nixon's loss. His chosen running mate, Henry Cabot Lodge, was a colossal deadweight who confined himself to one speech a day during the campaign and seldom missed his long afternoon nap. Lyndon Johnson, working chiefly through old and powerful cronies in the Senate (who knew he would return to the Senate to help or haunt them if the Democratic ticket lost) was of enormous help to the Kennedy cause in those parts of the South steeped in misgivings about the candidate's Catholic background.

A clear majority of U.S. publishers supported Nixon. Their editorial pages reflected their choice. This, of course, did not inhibit contributing columnists. A notable example was the New York *Herald Tribune*. Its publisher, John Hay Whitney, President Eisenhower's Ambassador to the Court of St. James's and as determined a patron of the Republican Party in New York as, say, Tom Yawkey was of American League baseball in Boston, regularly featured the columns of Walter Lippmann and Joseph Alsop, who went all out for Kennedy.

The straight reporting on the campaign—the who, when, where, what, why—was down the middle, as it should be and almost always is. Editors alternated newsmen assigned to the candidates, a guard against either nominee's influencing or alienating. I made whistle-stop swings with both men. Traveling with Kennedy was more pleasant than with Nixon, and more rewarding from a news sense. Between stops, Kennedy would stroll down the aisle of the plane to pass the time of day or comment on what he considered the state of the union. Nixon, particularly near the crucial end of the campaign, retreated into his shell—his green-curtained enclosure in the forward section of his plane—leaving his man Herb Klein and his dear, brave Pat, smiling with everything except her eyes, to fend for him.

There were extenuating circumstances beyond these: Nixon's campaign was filled with the expected, the most likely to happen. There seemed to be some unwritten code that ruled laughter out of trips with him. Kennedy's voyages were marked by the antic, the unexpected: a kid in West Virginia who had obtained his autograph and now was turning the slip of paper this way and that in a bewildered effort to to decipher his appalling handwriting; a feverish Negro in a car equipped with an ear-splitting loudspeaker system driving recklessly in the candidate's parade while he shouted into his mobile microphone, "Jack Kennedy is the greatest man ever walked the streets of Jersey City since Jesus Christ."

Nixon settled into a lucrative law practice after his defeat and appeared to have resigned himself, as Tom Dewey had before him, to the bitter realization he would never sleep in Lincoln's bed. On the morning after his stunning defeat by President Truman, Dewey announced he would never again run for public office. He kept his word. Nixon made no such promise. He yielded to pressures, some of them applied by General Eisenhower, to run for governor of California against Pat Brown, the incumbent. Most signs indicated that it was a good move. It would give him a platform from which he might launch a subsequent and perhaps even successful Presidential drive. He had beaten Kennedy in California (3,259,722 to 3,224,099) in face of a 3 to 2 Democratic registration in that politically eccentric state. But he lost badly to Brown, who had only a pale fraction of Kennedy's appeal. The day following that debacle Nixon made an embarrassing and poignant spectacle of himself at a news conference he attended against the best available advice. He didn't seem himself.

I had experienced a preview of that aberration. On July 4, 1962, I took my daughter Deborah to Rebild Park near Aalborg, Denmark, to make a film short and write a piece about that remarkable annual salute to the United States. It was the fiftieth anniversary of what long has been the best-attended Independence Day celebration anywhere in the world, including America. Eisenhower had been the scheduled speaker, but he canceled his laid-on trip to Scandinavia that summer after the Swedish press criticized him for a reference he had made about Sweden's suicide rate. He asked Nixon to substitute. Several Danish newspapers and politicians carped on the ground that Nixon was prepared to run for governor of California and the occasion traditionally called for a fully nonpartisan American speaker.

But all was serene as the crowd of about fifty thousand gathered on the benches and grassy slopes of the natural amphitheater. Luncheon was served to several hundred guests of honor under a big, cool tent. I was leading Deborah to a table reserved for reporters when Nixon spotted us and called us over to the table where he sat with the top officials of the event. I demurred but he insisted most generously. We sat down, and for the next few courses of the pleasant smorgasbord he could not have been a kinder host. We agreed that this entire affair gave a fellow patriotic goose bumps.

"And how about that amazing coincidence about the man who started this whole thing—what's-his-name Henius?" I asked, making minuscule talk.

Dick seemed to stiffen a bit.

"What about him?" he asked.

I pointed to a package of publicity handouts we had all been given. "He came back here from Wisconsin or some place on the thirty-fifth anniversary—fifteen years ago—and was killed right here on the grounds," I said. "Car hit him. Eerie, isn't it?"

Nixon turned to the chairman of the festival seated next to him.

"That's a typical American newspaperman for you," he said. "Notice that? He knows something about this occasion that I don't, and I'm the speaker." I thought for a moment he was joking and then realized with a start that he was terribly serious. "They always know more about everything than *you* do. And if they don't know, they make it up."

He turned back, looked at me blankly for a second or two, and then the anger dropped from him like a cloak. He grinned engagingly.

"Present company excepted, of course," he said, and the luncheon resumed.

He made a good hands-across-the-sea speech which was roundly applauded by King Frederik IX, Queen Ingrid, and their attentive subjects. I saw Nixon later at the hotel in Aalborg. All of us had been shaken by an even more unnerving coincidence than the one of thirty-five years before which had so annoyed him, when I brought it up. Nixon had been followed to the speaker's platform by Henry Henius, gray-haired son of the founder of the celebration. He had flown from Los Angeles for the occasion. He spoke warmly of his father's dreams for staunch U.S.-Danish relations, got a nice hand from the crowd, returned to his seat next to Nixon, sat down, pitched forward, and died of a heart attack.

It was a long time after the 1960 election before I had an opportunity to talk shop with Nixon. We met in his office in the Wall Street district. He sent out for sandwiches and coffee rather than take time out for a more formal meal, because he was quite busy. He was due to fly to San Francisco soon after for the Convention that nominated Barry Goldwater on the first ballot. Four years earlier, every mention of Nixon's name caused ovations through the Republican Party. Now, on this hot day in 1964, he had only two delegates who had announced they would vote for him—and even they dissolved in the strong solvent of Goldwater's gospel.

I asked him how he accounted for the Arizonan's enormous appeal.

"Barry makes a good appearance," Nixon said. "I like him very much, personally. He's intelligent, talks well, and he believes what he says. But the thing that draws people to him most is that just about everybody who is against something, who dislikes somebody or some group, or hates this or that, feels he has a friend in Barry. People like that feel he's on their side."

It seemed as good a time as any to ask him how he now assessed the 1960 election.

"What would you say was the one thing that beat you, the one incident or bad break that made the difference?"

He did not hesitate.

"When President Eisenhower was asked at one of his last news conferences at the White House to name a case or two where I had contributed to the shaping of his Administration's policy he said, in effect, 'Give me a week to think about that,' " Nixon answered, as if he had reflected on it many times. "He could have said something like, 'Well, we sent that fellow on a lot of trips around the world in the past eight years and he always came back with reports on what he had seen and people he had talked to. Naturally, some of his thinking filtered down into our policies.' But he didn't say that. He just said 'Give me a week to think about that. . . .' That beat me, more than the debates or anything else."

Nixon stood up, strode part of the way across his office, turned to me and added something.

"He's a great American," he said with ringing warmth.

Joseph P. Kennedy, Sr., approved of the series I proposed to write for INS entitled "The Amazing Kennedys." Millie and I were invited to lunch at his handsome home on the water at Palm Beach. It was early 1957. There were five of us: the Ambassador, as he liked to be called, in tan shorts and sunglasses; Mrs. Kennedy, dressed as if for a garden party and as fresh and young as any of her children; old family friend Bill Cunningham, the former sportswriter who often reflected in his writings and broadcasts Kennedy's ironclad conservatism; and Millie and I.

The sun on the patio was dazzling, the lunch delicious, the Ambassador's monologue relaxed. At seventy, the keen-eyed veteran of many a political and business war had the air of a man calling it a day. It had been quite a "day." His competitive fires had raged for more than half a century, reaching back to the decision to fight his way into Harvard instead of going submissively to the Jesuits at Boston College. He vowed that he'd show the Brahmins that the son of a saloonkeeper and parochial Catholic Democrat politician could be just as rich and just as intellectual and just as social as they. He did just that, made a mint, and turned to public service under Roosevelt. He was chairman of the Securities Exchange Commission and chief architect of most of the rules that regulate it today; Ambassador to the court of St. James's during the critical 1937–40 period. He brought his family home, campaigned so bitterly against the entrance of the United States in World War II that he was called pro-Hitler and anti-Semitic, and fell silent as three sons and a daughter went proudly off to war. But he was not a man to stay clammed for long.

"Preservation of our way of life is not assured by winning the war," he said in a speech at Colby College, Maine, a month after V-E Day. "We must defend it against cynics who would destroy our ideals and paralyze our aspirations, utopians who advocate plans to wreck our economic system; those who promote racial discrimination, industrial strife, corruption in public office, and those who would have us shun our responsibilities in a world order." With a glittering eye on the Truman Administration, then barely three months old, fellow Democrat Kennedy cried, "Men without training in economics, education in political science, perspective or balance, direct the future of this country because they are the only kind who take the trouble to participate in public affairs. Don't criticize these. Oppose them and all they stand for, by voice and by vote."

He was nominating John Fitzgerald Kennedy for Congress, but only he and his son knew that. And both knew he was nominating a substitute.

The elder Kennedy sounded off so vehemently on high taxes after the war that JFK was later to say of him, with the faintly amused reverence he held for him, "My father is a Democrat, a Taft Democrat."

The Korean War enraged Old Joe. World War II had claimed his oldest son and pride and joy, Joe, Jr., and his first son-in-law, Capt. John Robert Cavendish, Marquess of Hartington, eldest son and heir of the Duke of Devonshire. That death widowed Kathleen, eldest daughter of the Kennedys, and she in turn was killed in a plane crash in Europe several years later. The big war had so nearly taken Jack, too; indeed, a memorial mass had been said for him and other members of his PT-boat crew during the period when they were missing in action.

"Suicidal," Old Joe said of President Truman's Korean War policy in a speech at the University of Virginia Law School, as General MacArthur's forces retreated from the Yalu in the face of multitudes of Red Chinese. He urged that the United States withdraw from Korea "and any other place in Asia where we cannot hope to hold our defenses." He further urged that the United States get out of Berlin and thereafter devote a considerable portion of the defense budget to fortifying Canada and Latin America.

"We have no reason to believe that cooperation on their part will not be forthcoming," he told an audience that included his law student son Robert. "We can, and should, insist on it."

It was against a background as controversial as the above that we lunched and the master of the household sketched his new role in life.

"I'm just a has-been," he said, comfortably. " 'The doctor of sick empires,' as somebody once called me, is sidelined. The only one left to mind the store. I've cut all strings with public service. When I learned that Jack had support for the vice-presidential nomination at Chicago, and his name might be brought up, I resigned from President Eisenhower's commission studying our foreign intelligence. My day is done. Now it is my sons' day."

When the ripple of polite deprecations died down, I asked him for his capsule assessment of each of the Kennedys.

"Good idea," the Ambassador said in his steely and decisive way, but with a note of pride and affection in his voice. "Now you take Jack. Nobody's more courageous than Jack. He's a real intellectual, that boy, and a first-class historian, too. Don't let anybody tell you he had help when he was writing *Profiles in Courage*. I can see him now, lying on that couch out there on the lawn, working on that book by the hour. His back was killing him, but never a word out of him."

He ticked off the others, male heirs first:

"Now you take Bobby. Bobby's a tough one; he'll keep the Kennedys together, you can bet. He's a lot like me; he never forgets an enemy. And keep your eye on Teddy, too. That boy shows a lot of promise. He's just a kid now, but his class shows right through."

The Kennedy girls were dealt with swiftly, concisely. His voice saddened twice, once when he spoke of Kathleen, who served overseas with the Red Cross during the war, and when he mentioned Rosemary. "She's what we call our quiet one," the Ambassador said. The retarded eldest daughter was then at St. Coletta's, a Jefferson, Wisconsin, school for the handicapped—one of several beneficiaries of the Joseph P. Kennedy, Jr., Foundation.

He had left one out. Young Joe. I asked discreetly if he would say something about him.

The man who was one of the top financiers of the age, cool beyond calculation under fire, suddenly and terribly burst into tears at the luncheon table and for five aching minutes was racked with grief that cannot be described. Tears did not run, they literally cascaded down his bronzed, freckled face. He tried to speak, but nothing coherent issued. Mrs. Kennedy sat silent and composed. Cunningham stared at the ocean. Millie kicked me under the table.

"No," the Ambassador finally said, wiping his now reddened face. "No. I can't talk about Joe." He pointed at his wife. *"She* can. But I'll never be able to."

"Joe was a wonderful boy," Mrs. Kennedy said calmly. "A good boy. He had so much to live for. . . ."

My question had ruined the pleasant afternoon.

Young Joe's death seemed to have set a pattern for dramatic disasters that lay ahead for this vibrant, vital clan. He had completed his twenty-five bombing missions and his required number of dangerous reconnaissance trips as a Navy pilot by early August, 1944. He was scheduled to be returned to the States and spend the remainder of the war as a trainer of younger pilots. With the coming of peace, he would take up his life's work: politics. He had fully inherited his father's devouring curiosity about all things political, and the father's appetite to get in the thick of a fight and there take a stand. He had studied for a year under Harold Laski at the London School of Economics "the better to see both sides of the street." At Harvard Law he had raised his strong voice to support his father's stand against any weakening of U.S. neutrality toward the burgeoning war in Europe. He was a staunch isolationist, went to the isolationist-minded 1940 Democratic Convention as a delegate from Massachusetts, voted for James A. Farley (who, ironically, loathed Kennedy, Senior), and refused to make F.D.R.'s nomination for a third time unanimous.

But on August 13, 1944, when he could have come home, Young Joe volunteered for one of the more secret and dangerous missions of the war. The Nazis were hitting London and the invasion ports with the V-2 rocket, which flew so high and descended so swiftly that none was ever intercepted and few were even picked up on radar. The only defense Allied strategists could conceive was the destruction of the launching sites.

There were no bombs powerful enough to demolish these heavily built positions. Winston Churchill was later credited with the plan that proved to be the answer: cram as much TNT into a surplus bomber as it would hold, have a two-man crew take off with it, bail out over some Allied-held portion of France, and permit a "mother" plane to guide the unmanned bomber to the V-2 site and cause it to dive upon it.

Kennedy's co-pilot on the perilous mission was Sgt. Wilford Willy, USN, Fort Worth, Texas. Their four-engined B-24 lumbered into the sky with 24,000 pounds of high explosives, made its contact with the shepherding planes, and Kennedy and Willy prepared to parachute.

The B-24 suddenly blew up so violently that nothing was ever found of either man.

A year later Jack Kennedy put together a tender little book, privately printed, which he called *As We Remember Joe.* Joe's brothers and sisters, his grandparents, war buddies, and friends each contributed. It was illustrated by a reproduction of the Navy Cross, awarded posthumously, and by a handwritten and poignant letter Secretary of the Navy James Forrestal wrote to the father. The touching book's tributes ranged warmly from the material to the spiritual.

Ensign James Simpson wrote, "I was in the plane testing and double checking three minutes before takeoff. I shook hands with Joe and said, 'So long and good luck, Joe. I only wish I were going with you.' He answered. "Thanks, Jim. Don't forget, you're going to make the next one with me. And, say, by the way, if I don't come back, you fellows can have the rest of my eggs.' We never saw him again."

Jack wrote, concluding his own chapter, "Through it all, he had a deep and abiding faith—he was never far from God—and so, I cannot help but feel that on that August day, high in the summer skies, 'death to him was less a setting forth than a returning.' "

A few days after the incident at Palm Beach I had a drink with the junior senator from Massachusetts at the Park Lane in New York and mentioned the Ambassador's emotional outburst.

"He always does that when Joe's name comes up," JFK said fondly. Then, after a pause, he said, "I'll tell you something about Joe. Joe was our star. He was the oldest, the smartest, and the strongest of the whole bunch. He was taller, could run faster, jump higher, hit harder. He got the best marks in school. And the prettiest girl. Joe would have been the Congressman from our district. Joe would have beaten Cabot Lodge for his Senate seat in fifty-two by a bigger majority than I did. Joe would have gotten the bid last Summer to run on the ticket with Adlai Stevenson, whereas I lost out by about twenty votes."

J.F.K. suddenly smiled.

"And Eisenhower would have run over him like a truck," he said of his brother, "and right now he'd still be picking up the tattered threads of his political career and trying to put it back together again."

He chuckled a bit.

"You know what I wanted to do," he said. "I wanted to be in *your* business, to write, to travel. But the moment I heard that Joe was dead, I knew I didn't have a chance. I was next in line. My father raised all of us to find our place or take an active interest in public affairs. When Joe died, I became *it*. If I had been killed, Bobby would have had to pick it up, because he was next in line. And if anything had happened to Bobby, it would be Teddy's duty."

The Ambassador sent me a flattering wire from Palm Beach when "The Amazing Kennedys" appeared in print. He expressed astonishment that on such short acquaintance I had caught "the true flavor of how things really are" with the family. A mutual friend later told me the elder Kennedy had liked the start of the first article especially. It read:

> In Sen. John Fitzgerald Kennedy, Roman Catholic Massachusetts Democrat, one of America's best-known families may have produced the man who will bring the dreams of three active generations of politicians to full flower.
> Possessed of a passion for public service, bright, handsome, decorated, young (39) Jack Kennedy has become a major spokesman for his party, a trusted figure on Capitol Hill in bipartisan work, and a man most prominently mentioned for a Democratic Presidential nomination—perhaps as early as 1960.

I saw the Ambassador at the Park Avenue offices of his empire shortly after his son was elected. He had taken the cliff-hanger in stride. He was most affable. Yes, Jack would make a fine President. Nobody ever had better training for the job. Sure, he would have troubles: Eisenhower had dumped a lot of difficult, unfinished problems in his lap. No (he laughed), there would be no fatherly advice given on how best to run the White House.

"I doubt if I'll ever go there," the Ambassador said with a laugh.

The *Journal American* photographer who had been taking shots as the Ambassador talked attracted his attention. He touched the knot of his own necktie.

"Mr. Kennedy, would you mind straightening your tie?" he asked.

The Ambassador raised his hand to the knot of his tie and wiggled it back and forth. As he did so, the photographer let go with another flash.

The father of the President of the United States sprang from his chair like an old but agile tiger, and for a split second it appeared, startlingly, that he would lunge for the cameraman's throat. Then he caught himself and, livid, said in the quietest but most menacing voice, "Goddam you, you tricked me into that picture. If you want a picture of me adjusting my tie, say to me 'I want a picture of you adjusting your tie,' and you'll get it. But goddam you, if you ever try to trick me again. . . ."

The thoroughly frightened photographer started to apologize, but was cut off by a glare that packed the glint of a scimitar. Then the Ambassador sat down again and continued talking to me about his son in the most matter-of-fact tones.

"How many states would Jack have taken if he had not been a Catholic?" I asked him, a trustee of Notre Dame, Knight of Malta, Knight of the Equestrian Order of the Holy Scpulchre, and Grand Knight of the Order of Pius IX.

"All of them!" he said instantly and emphatically.

At the Inauguration, the Ambassador was the picture of the re-strained, quietly proud father who was watching the culmination of a mighty dream, the climax of a struggling saga that reached back to the Potato Famine of the 1840's and the awesome decision of young Patrick Kennedy to leave his thatch-roofed home in New Ross and join the ragged, starveling migration to a strange New World.

He seemed to listen more attentively and respectfully than many others to the long benediction offered by Richard Cardinal Cushing, a trying twenty minutes for the young President and countless more present in the subfreezing cold. Midway in the Cardinal's pious but unnervingly nasal peroration, a short circuit in the platform's heating apparatus sent whiffs of smoke ascending past his face.

"Fumes from Purgatory," someone whispered in the deep-frozen press rows.

The Cardinal persevered through the smoke, on and on and then on some more. Near the limit of endurance in the press section, whose flooring had not been cleared of the previous night's blizzard, another

voice was heard. It was that of Bob Hartman, Washington correspondent of the Los Angeles *Times*.

"Well," Bob muttered grimly, "we *warned* you Protestant sons of
bitches."

Herbert Hoover was an even eighty. He had had a busy day in
West Branch, Iowa, at the little whitewashed house where he was
born, also at the dedication of still another school bearing his name,
and at a picnic in a public park arranged by the adoring committee so
that young and old could mingle with the thirty-first President of the
United States. Now he was en route back to New York and his more
familiar digs at the Waldorf Towers. The conveyance was a United
Air Lines Convair, Mainliner O'Connor, the executive plane set aside
for him that day by UAL's president, Pat Patterson. Miss O'Connor,
duenna of the company's stewardesses, was in charge of things aloft.
She tucked a blue blanket around Mr. Hoover's shoulders and, at his
request, brought him a martini.

His devoted little secretary, Miss Barney, had fetched the telegrams,
cablegrams, and letters sent to West Branch for the occasion. All were
affectionate. He listened attentively, with the help of his hearing aid,
as she read a sampling, signed by the great and the humble of the
world.

When the time seemed right, I asked him a rather personal question.
I asked him if, at eighty, he harbored any bitterness toward old political foes who pilloried him in the past as chief architect of the Depression and who had coined or countenanced the use of Hooverville as
a synonym for Shanty-town; indeed, had accused him of personally
running the hungry Bonus Marchers out of Washington and Anacostia
Flats.

"No, I bear no hard feelings," Mr. Hoover said, after taking a
reflective puff on his pipe and a sip of his drink. Then a look of merri-
ment in his clear blue eyes. "But what you ask reminds me of the
story of the prayer meeting. The preacher's sermon was on brotherly
love. When he finished, he addressed a question to the congregation.
He asked if there was anybody in the house who could say in all
honesty that he didn't have an enemy in the world.

"Well, there was a big silence, and then an old fellow about my time in life got up and said he personally didn't have an enemy. So the preacher praised him and urged the others in the house to lead the same kind of exemplary life. Then he asked the old fellow to tell the folks just how he happened to have no enemies.

"The old fellow said, 'I outlived the bastards!' "

The popularity polls listed Lyndon Baines Johnson as a casualty of the war in Vietnam. It hurt him deeply, aged him faster than a Chief Executive with the greatest string of legislative successes on record should have aged. As with Woodrow Wilson, and one supposes all the others, aging went forth without the comforting arm of mellowness.

He would see us—Frank Conniff, Marianne Means, who had been our girl at the White House and was now writing a national column, and me.

We entered the White House like burglars through the inconspicuous staff door. Mustn't be seen by the regular White House correspondents. They would be understandably angry and their relations with the President, already edgy, would worsen. And vice versa, in spades.

The guard at the desk gave us a friendly frisk with his eyes, breathed something into a phone, and pointed to a little elevator. There was a pause in what once was called the Fish Room, then a little march across one of the outer offices, and there in the doorway of the last redoubt of the Free World stood its loneliest man.

He looked deep into us as he offered his big, tough hand, a probing steel-blue look that was some kind of final assessment of the course he would take with us. Almost without words he motioned us to our places on the two facing divans, separated by a coffee table, that reach out from the fireplace in the wall opposite his desk. He lowered his well-tailored bulk into the rocking chair that faced us . . . just as John F. Kennedy used to marshal his guests. It was not the same rocker. Kennedy's was slender, darkly wooded, and with trim, squared beige cushions. L.B.J.'s was a rocker built for a man like L.B.J. He swung it heavily until he faced Conniff more squarely, leaned forward with a look as challenging as a sequence from *High Noon,* and said in a voice that was low-pitched but oddly menacing, "All right, now. Are you going to bomb Hanoi and Haiphong, bomb 'em off the map, or are you going to pull out? Let's have the answer right now."

Conniff said he never considered those extremes as the only alternatives.

The President hunched back comfortably in his rocker and some of the lines in his face seemed to ease. It was the answer he wanted to hear, and that had not been happening enough of late. He took off his glasses and rubbed his eyes and then his whole face. It was 6:30 in the evening and dark as pitch beyond the French doors that led into the garden. He would keep us pinned there—sometimes riveted there —until 9:30.

"I didn't start this," he said of the war in a voice that grew stronger and a shade angrier as the night wore on. "I inherited it. It was getting more difficult not long before the full responsibility fell on me. Right in this room, when Kennedy called on Ike after the election [1960] Ike told him that the big problem he was going to have as the new President would be in Southeast Asia.

"Just before Dallas, Kennedy told me that we were going to have to fight in South Vietnam, not just *advise*." He swung his eyes at us and there was again challenge in them. "Now, is it going to be said of me that I let Kennedy down? Am I going to be remembered as the fellow who pulled out, who became as scared as a rabbit in the field?"

He did not need an answer.

"I sent ambassadors to thirty countries, tried everything," he said, frustration as well as anger welling in him. "They just don't want peace, don't want to negotiate—now." He lingered on *now* before going on.

"We keep the pressure on them all the time," he said. "Not too much, not too little. I read here and there that they still think they're winning, but every day we show them that they aren't winning, and eventually even they will realize it. We're killing them on the ground, day in and day out. The figures we released aren't estimates. We count every body we find. That isn't hard: they leave most of their dead and wounded. We're killing or wounding them at something like the rate of seventeen to one. How long can they last at that rate?"

He ordered a drink for us and a Dr. Pepper for himself when one of us suggested that it must be time for him to go on to dinner. And for the next hour he spoke almost without the prompting of questions, covering a score of troublesome national, international, and personal problems. It was plain he deeply resented what he felt were the more unjust accusations against and interpretations of his policy in Vietnam. Twice he picked up a phone and asked the girl in the outer office to bring in charts, graphs, and polls. His foes among the Washington columnists had that week abundantly noticed that his popularity quotient had subsided to fifty-four. That happened to be the same figure President Eisenhower ascended to in the heady wake of his first victory over Adlai Stevenson, one of the polls deduced.

"Yet they say I'm in a hell of a fix because I used to have a sixty," he said, genuinely perplexed.

He was more disturbed by several then-current stories that implied he had rebuffed certain overtures from the enemy to negotiate a peace. The most discussed of these stories was Eric Sevareid's article in *Look* detailing Ambassador Stevenson's last days, made sadder, it was charged, because his transmission of peace feelers had been short circuited at the White House.

"Do you think Adlai or anybody else could get a peace offer and I, the President, wouldn't hear about it?" he asked incredulously. "They try to give the public the idea that I'm purposely wrong in my handling of Vietnam. No President does what he thinks is wrong." He looked around the room, solemnly, and said, "Only thirty-five men have reached this office in history. I don't think any of them ever willfully set out to do something wrong." His eyes fastened on the soundproofed AP and UPI teletypes faintly chattering near his desk.

"But go over there to those tickers and you can find at least six mean statements about me on the wires," he invited.

We thanked him for giving us all this time. It was 8:30 and each of us had visions of his dinner being kept warm upstairs, and of Lady Bird trying to keep a soufflé inflated against catastrophe. L.B.J. ignored the murmurs of gratitude, ordered another drink for us and another Dr. Pepper for himself, and turned to a subject that had bugged every one of his predecessors: the failure of the press and/or public to get the real essence, the thrust, of a speech. He phoned the girl to fetch him his still-echoing Chicago speech of May 17, 1966. He marked several passages with one of the green-ink "seventeen-cent-souvenir pens" he had bestowed on us earlier.

"All that seems to have been stressed in my Chicago speech was the line about 'some Nervous Nellies and some who will become frustrated and bothered and break ranks under the strain and turn on their leaders, their own country, and their own fighting men.' But I don't see much about *these* passages," he said, pointing them out and handing me the marked text. These were his neglected words:

> As Commander in Chief, I am neither a Democrat nor a Republican. The men fighting in Vietnam are simply Americans. Our policy in Vietnam is a national policy. It springs from every lesson we have learned in this century. We fought in the First World War and then failed to build the system of collective security which could have prevented the Second World War.
>
> Standing in Chicago, October 5, 1937, Franklin Roosevelt said: "When an epidemic of physical disease starts to spread, the community approves and joins in a quarantine of the patients in order to protect the health of the community against the spread of disease."
>
> The country failed to back him. And then we saw what happened when aggressors felt confident that they could win all the way. That was what President Truman remembered in 1947 in Greece and Turkey. That is what he remembered during the blockade of Berlin and when the attack came in Korea.
>
> This is what President Eisenhower remembered in 1954 when he laid before the Senate the SEATO Treaty, and during the crisis over Quemoy and Matsu. That is what President Kennedy remembered when, in the face of Communist aggression in Laos and Vietnam, he began to send our forces there in 1962.
>
> We have learned over the past half century that failure to meet aggression means war, not peace. In carrying out that policy we have taken casualties in Berlin, in Korea, and now in Vietnam. Every morning I look at those casualty figures. I measure them not as statistics, but man by man.
>
> But I tell you that if we fail in frustrating this aggression the war that would surely come to Asia would produce casualties in the hundreds of thousands—perhaps in the millions. Your government is determined to resist this aggression at the minimum cost to our own people, to our allies, and to the world.

At 9:15, after another fruitless effort to thank him and go our way, I asked him what kind of a work day he put in. The details of it were more than fresh in his mind, he said, because he had spent some time earlier in the day with Jim Bishop, who was doing an in-depth article on him.

"I wake up at six, six-thirty as a rule," he said, relieved to be talking about something beyond Vietnam. "I get up, go to the bathroom, wash my teeth, and shave. I use an electric razor. Then I get back into bed and start working. The tea comes in. Might have four, five cups. Then the boys start coming with the overnight reports. I give them their instructions. At seven-thirty, McNamara calls. Then Rusk. Then I might talk on the phone about the budget. I might talk three, four times to McNamara before I get out of bed. He's not a fellow who talks very long.

"Then, of course, I read the casualty list.

"I get here to this office at ten-thirty or eleven and from then on it's one thing after another: a prime minister, a delegation from some-place, who knows?

"I'm not much for lunch. I never have any of those formal lunch-eons. Today I had a bowl of soup, a sandwich of some kind, and some tapioca. Then I keep going until maybe three-thirty, four. After that I used to take a swim with friends, friends I'd invite. But I've had to give that up. It's a terrible thing, but if a President starts out with, say, a hundred friends, well, he's lucky if he winds up with one.

"So now, mostly, I go from here back to my room and go back to bed. I mean really to bed: into pajamas, like you're going to bed at night. There aren't any telephone calls, unless it's important, of course. The room is as dark as night. I go sound to sleep. The rule is that I sleep until I wake up. That's usually about five o'clock or so. I take a cold shower, brush my teeth . . . like starting a new day.

"Matter of fact, I do have two days every day—one that lasts from the early morning until, say, four and the other day that lasts from six to ten or so. I always come back here about six and work. I go over and eat dinner about ten, not much, have a massage and watch the eleven o'clock news on TV. Frank Stanton put in three sets, side by side, just as I've got here in this office. I can put the picture on all three by this remote control gadget," he said, demonstrating. "Then I push this button and the sound comes on inside whichever set is showing a picture that interests me.

"I'm back in bed about midnight, reading the bulldog edition of the Washington *Post*. From then on, usually till two-thirty, sometimes three-thirty, I go over the memos and papers I've taken to bed . . . the ideas, speech outlines, things like that. I mark them 'Approved,' 'Dis-approved,' or 'See me.' Then sleep."

Now he accepted our thanks, took a look at the AP and UPI, and showed us out. Marianne, two hours late for dinner at the Bill Whites, whistled up a cab. Conniff and I walked over to Duke Ziebert's place near the Mayflower, mostly in silence—not an ordinary condition for either of us.

All I could think to say was, "What a hell of a lousy job that poor man's got."

Endit

THE Future of Journalism is a hardy topic that has begun to mesmerize discussion groups and pundits in increasing numbers. Endlessly soaring production costs, sometimes senseless strikes, and inroads made on the public mind and the advertiser's dollar by electronic news make some wonder if the Great American Newspaper is long for this world. Depression symptoms of decline are easily available. There are now only three cities in the nation—New York, Washington, and Boston—where the reading public has a choice of more than two shades of editorial opinion. New York once had a dozen thriving papers. Mergers have blended many hallowed (and money-losing) mastheads into one, and united the shades of ruggedly individualistic titans who fought memorable newspaper wars in the long ago. New York City's *World Journal Tribune* alone stitched together the graves of Hearst, Pulitzer, Scripps, Howard, and Bennett when its ten unions permitted it to publish.

The Cassandras are perpetually puzzled to learn that the newspaper business as a whole continues not only to survive but prosper in this land where it found its finest freedoms. As of September 30, 1965, there were 1,751 U.S. dailies and 9,392 weeklies. There has been little variation from the figures of ten years before, except in circulation. The 1955 total circulation reached 56,147,359; in 1965 it was 60,357,563.

Newspapers follow population movements as swiftly as do gas stations, shopping centers, and the PTA. Consequently, the suburban press is booming all around the great population centers. The off-beat and scruffy Bohemian press, springing up impudently in the land's Greenwich Villages, is growing like weeds. Some purists believe that portions of it should be weeded and burned, after a thorough examination of the First Article of the Constitution, of course. But who knows what splendid truffle this grubbing press might uproot?

There will always be room for and need of newspapers. The technology is bound to change. It has been relatively static for the better part of the century. Soon, the superb teamwork of tree chopper, newsprint maker, reporter, editor, compositor, and pressman will not be prey at the moment of fruition to a flat tire on a delivery truck. Or frustrated by a newspaperboy's toothache, or his bad aim. The family's morning newspaper may well emerge from the household's TV set or facsimile machine, which will silently "print" it while the family sleeps at night and drop it on the living room floor at dawn. The afternoon paper will be ready for the breadwinner as he returns at dusk to home and hearth, created in this same manner.

But however exotic the technology, reporters always will have to gather in the wheat and the chaff of every blessed day's news, editors will have the eternal task of separating that harvest, and those who live the charmed life of commentators will rise and fall on their interpretation of what the news means. There is perhaps only one achievement the computers will never be capable of, and that is the simple job of witnessing a happening and describing it swiftly, clearly, and honestly. How difficult that triple play can sometimes be! How warmly rewarding when it is realized!

I'll croak in this business, given the opportunity. Where else can a man hope to build a bridge between himself and others every day, whether it be as rickety as the one that snapped in half at Tacoma or as durable as the Golden Gate? On what other field of endeavor is a competitor called upon to come up each day with words and thoughts not used the day before? Every time a reporter picks up a phone to call in a story or spins a fresh sheet of copy paper into his typewriter, he shoots his roll—like a craps player going for broke.

Call it vanity, call it arrogant presumption, call it what you wish, but I would grope for the nearest open grave if I had no newspaper to work for, no need to search for and sometimes find the winged word that just fits, no keen wonder over what each unfolding day may bring.

Besides, it's better than working for a living.

Index